D1533156

Beginning SQL Server 2008 for Developers

From Novice to Professional

Robin Dewson

apress®

Beginning SQL Server 2008 for Developers: From Novice to Professional

Copyright © 2008 by Robin Dewson

ISBN-13 (pbk): 978-1-59059-958-7

ISBN-10 (pbk): 1-59059-958-6

ISBN-13 (electronic): 978-1-4302-0584-5

ISBN-10 (electronic): 1-4302-0584-9

Printed and bound in the United States of America 9 8 7 6 5 4 3 2 1

Lead Editor: Jonathan Gennick
Technical Reviewer: Jasper Smith
Editorial Board: Clay Andres, Steve Anglin, Ewan Buckingham, Tony Campbell, Gary Cornell,
    Jonathan Gennick, Matthew Moodie, Joseph Ottinger, Jeffrey Pepper, Frank Pohlmann,
    Ben Renow-Clarke, Dominic Shakeshaft, Matt Wade, Tom Welsh
Project Manager: Kylie Johnston
Copy Editor: Nicole Abramowitz
Associate Production Director: Kari Brooks-Copony
Production Editor: Ellie Fountain
Compositor: Susan Glinert
Proofreader: Nancy Sixsmith, ConText Editorial Services, Inc.
Indexer: Broccoli Information Management
Artist: Kinetic Publishing Services, LLC
Cover Designer: Kurt Krames
Manufacturing Director: Tom Debolski

Distributed to the book trade worldwide by Springer-Verlag New York, Inc., 233 Spring Street, 6th Floor, New York, NY 10013. Phone 1-800-SPRINGER, fax 201-348-4505, e-mail orders-ny@springer-sbm.com, or visit http://www.springeronline.com.

For information on translations, please contact Apress directly at 2855 Telegraph Avenue, Suite 600, Berkeley, CA 94705. Phone 510-549-5930, fax 510-549-5939, e-mail info@apress.com, or visit http://www.apress.com.

Apress and friends of ED books may be purchased in bulk for academic, corporate, or promotional use. eBook versions and licenses are also available for most titles. For more information, reference our Special Bulk Sales–eBook Licensing web page at http://www.apress.com/info/bulksales.

The source code for this book is available to readers at http://www.apress.com.

This book, as many of my books are, is dedicated to my family. First, to my mum and dad whom I love very much and who made me what I am today. Without their help, understanding, and patience when it came to my use of the television for the Sinclair ZX80 and the Sinclair ZX81, and without helping me find and organize my further education, I probably would have wasted a great opportunity. To my three kids—Ellen, Cameron, and Scott—who have been brilliant and wonderful and whom I am very, very proud of in many ways. And they are such great kids because they have who can only be termed the best mother kids can have, right there helping, loving, and, yes, screaming at them when needed. Julie, I love you more than I love my Irn-Bru, rugby, and lemon meringue pie . . . and you know how much those mean to me!

Contents at a Glance

Contents

About the Author

ROBIN DEWSON has been hooked on programming ever since he bought his first computer, a Sinclair ZX80, in 1980. His first major application was a Visual FoxPro program that could be used to run a fantasy league system. It was at this point that he met someone who would become a great help in the development of his PC life, Jon Silver at Step One Technologies. In return for training, Robin helped Jon with some other Visual FoxPro applications. From there, realizing that the marketplace for Visual FoxPro was limited, Robin decided to learn Visual Basic and SQL Server.

Starting out with SQL Server 6.5, Robin soon moved to SQL Server 7, accessing the database via Visual Basic 5. He became involved in developing several applications for clients both in the UK and in the United States. From there, he moved through SQL Server 2000 and 2005 and through Visual Basic 6 and C#. Robin now specializes in using Visual Studio .NET to write C# applications against SQL Server 2008.

Robin has several Apress books on SQL Server available. You can contact him at robin@fat-belly.com or at http://www.fat-belly.com.

About the Technical Reviewer

JASPER SMITH is an independent SQL Server consultant specializing in scalability, availability, and manageability, and he has worked with SQL Server for the past eight years. He is a Microsoft SQL Server Most Valued Professional (MVP) and is a frequent speaker at Professional Association for SQL Server (PASS) conferences. He runs and authors content for his web site, http://www.sqldbatips.com, which specializes in free SQL Server tools such as Reporting Services Scripter, ExpressMaint, and SQL 2005 Service Manager.

Acknowledgments

Once again, there are so many people to thank, from the great Damian Fisher, for teaching me how to play the drums, to Andrew and everyone at host-it Internet Solutions, my ISP, for putting up with my incessant hassling over SQL Server and DotNetNuke. Thanks to my bosses Bill Cotton and Aubrey Lomas and coworker Andrew O'Donnell at Lehman Brothers, as well as Andrew Harding, a great DBA; and thanks to Robert McMillan (Toad), a great mate from college with whom I got back in touch after many years. Cheers also to Simon Collier for whipping me at table tennis week in and week out. Thanks to all at Bedford Blues Rugby Club who make my Saturdays, well, exciting.

There are several people at Red Gate Software whom I have to thank for many reasons, including Tony Davis, who has been brilliant for many years with my SQL Server work, and Richard Collins, who organized the Apress and Red Gate collaborations. Also, thanks to Salar Golestanian at SalarO for producing excellent skins that I use on my web site creations.

Thanks also to my mother-in-law, Jean, for being so brilliant when things needed doing and keeping my wife sane. And to my late father-in-law, David, who was a brilliant person with all in my family.

Thanks, of course, to all at Apress, especially Kylie Johnston and Jonathan Gennick for help with this book, as well as Paul Carlstroem and Gary Cornell.

And finally, I have to acknowledge Mr. and Mrs. Barr for making Scotland's other national drink.

Introduction

*B*eginning SQL Server 2008 for Developers is for those who see themselves as becoming developers, database administrators, or a mixture of both but have yet to tread that path with SQL Server 2008. Whether you have no knowledge of databases, have knowledge of desktop databases such as Microsoft Access, or even come from a server-based background such as Oracle, this book will provide you with the insight to get up and running with SQL Server 2008.

Right from the start, this book will expand your basic knowledge, and you will soon find yourself moving from a beginner toward a competent and professional developer. This book aims to cater to a wide range of developers, from those who prefer to use a graphical interface for as much work as possible, to those who want to become more adept at using SQL Server 2008's programming language, Transact SQL (T-SQL). Where practical, this book demonstrates, explains, and expands upon each method of using SQL Server 2008 so that you can evaluate which works best in your situation.

This book contains plenty of examples that let you see how areas of SQL Server work and how you can apply the technology in your own work. You will learn the best way to complete a task, and you'll even learn how to make the correct decision when presented with two or more choices. Once you reach the end of this book, you will be able to design and create solid and reliable database solutions competently and proficiently.

Who This Book Is For

This book is ideal for developers starting out with SQL Server 2008 or for those looking at becoming database administrators. The book is laid out so that it works well with both of these camps.

How This Book Is Structured

The book helps you decide which version of SQL Server 2008 to buy, shows you how to install and configure SQL Server 2008, and explains how to use the graphical user interface (GUI) tool, SQL Server Management Studio. You will use this tool to work through a fully functional database example that is built from a design covered within the book, using graphical and code-based try-it-out exercises. You'll then learn about the security of your database and how to enforce a secure and reliable database setup. Once you back up your database, you'll learn how to work with the data. You'll start with simple coding techniques and move on to more complex ones. Your final task will allow you to build and produce reports on your database. Throughout the book, I explain each item, informing you of what is happening and ensuring that as you progress through the book, you're building on knowledge gained from previous chapters. You'll be building your expertise in a clear and structured manner.

Prerequisites

You will need to have either an evaluation or full version of SQL Server 2008 Developer Edition. In addition, it's ideal, but not compulsory, to have either the Windows Vista Ultimate or Business version if you want to alter security settings for specific Windows logins.

Downloading the Code

Example code from this book is available via the Apress web site (http://www.apress.com). Navigate to the book's home page, then look in the left sidebar for the section called "Book Extras." You'll find the link to the code examples there.

Contacting the Author

You can contact Robin Dewson via e-mail at robin@fat-belly.com or via his web site at http://www.fat-belly.com.

CHAPTER 1

▪ ▪ ▪

SQL Server 2008 Overview and Installation

Welcome to *Beginning SQL Server 2008 for Developers*. This book has been written for those who are interested in learning how to create solutions with Microsoft SQL Server 2008, but have no prior knowledge of SQL Server 2008. You may well have had exposure to other databases, such as MySQL, Oracle, or Microsoft Access, but SQL Server uses different interfaces and has a different way of working compared to much of the competition. The aim of this book is to bring you quickly up to a level at which you are developing competently with SQL Server 2008. This book is specifically dedicated to beginners and to those who at this stage wish to use only SQL Server 2008. It is also for those developers who have SQL Server 2005 experience and want a quick method to get up to speed on SQL Server 2008. You may find this book useful for understanding the basics of other databases in the marketplace, especially when working with T-SQL. Many databases use an ANSI-standard SQL, so moving from SQL Server to Oracle, Sybase, etc., after reading this book will be a great deal easier.

This chapter covers the following topics:

- Why SQL Server 2008?
- How do I know if my hardware meets the requirements?
- Can I just confirm that I have the right operating system?
- What can I do with SQL Server 2008?

We will also then look at installing our chosen edition and cover the following:

- Installing SQL Server 2008 on a Windows XP platform
- Options not installed by default
- Where to install SQL Server physically
- Multiple installations on one computer
- How SQL Server runs on a machine
- How security is implemented
- Logon IDs for SQL Server, especially the sa (system administrator) logon

Why SQL Server 2008?

The following discussion is my point of view, and although it no doubt differs from that of others, the basis of the discussion holds true. SQL Server faces competition from other databases, not only from other Microsoft products such as Microsoft Access and Microsoft Visual FoxPro, but also from competitors such as Oracle, Sybase, DB2, and Informix, to name a few.

Microsoft Access is found on a large number of PCs. The fact that it is packaged with some editions of Office and has been around for a number of years in different versions of Office has helped make this database ubiquitous; in fact, a great number of people actually do use the software. Unfortunately, it does have its limitations when it comes to scalability, speed, and flexibility, but for many small, in-house systems, these areas of concern are not an issue, as such systems do not require major database functionality.

Now we come to the serious competition: Oracle and Sybase. Oracle is seen as perhaps the market leader in the database community, and it has an extremely large user base. There is no denying it is a great product to work with, if somewhat more complex to install and administer than SQL Server; it fits well with large companies that require large solutions. There are many parts to Oracle, which make it a powerful tool, including scalability and performance. It also provides flexibility in that you can add on tools as you need them, making Oracle more accommodating in that area than SQL Server. For example, SQL Server 2008 forces you to install the .NET Framework on your server whether you use the new .NET functionality or not. However, Oracle isn't as user friendly from a developer's point of view in areas like its ad hoc SQL Query tool and its XML and web technology tools, as well as in how you build up a complete database solution; other drawbacks include its cost and the complexity involved in installing and running it effectively. However, you will find that it is used extensively by web search engines, although SQL Server could work just as effectively. With the new functionality in SQL Server 2008, Oracle will be under pressure to expand its existing functionality to meet this challenge. SQL Server has always been a one-purchase solution, such that (providing you buy the correct version) tools that allow you to analyze your data or copy data from one data source such as Excel into SQL Server will all be "in the box." With Oracle, on the other hand, for every additional feature you want, you have to purchase more options.

Then there is Sybase. Yes, it is very much like SQL Server with one major exception: it has no GUI front end. Sybase iAnywhere, which is mainly used for small installations, does have a front end, but the top-of-the-range Sybase does not. To purists, there is no need for one, as GUI front ends are for those who don't know how to code in the first place—well, that's their argument, of course, but why use 60+ keystrokes when a point, click, and drag is all that is required?

Sybase is also mainly found on Unix, although there is a Windows version around. You can get to Sybase on a Unix machine via a Windows machine using tools to connect to it, but you still need to use code purely to build your database solution. It is very fast and very robust, and it is only rebooted about once, maybe twice, a year. Another thing about Sybase is that it isn't as command- and feature-rich as SQL Server. SQL Server has a more powerful programming language and functionality that is more powerful than Sybase.

Each database has its own SQL syntax, although they all will have the same basic SQL syntax, known as the ANSI-92 standard. This means that the syntax for retrieving data, and so on, is the same from one database to another. However, each database has its own special syntax to maintain it, and trying to use a feature from this SQL syntax in one database may not work, or may work differently, in another.

So SQL Server seems to be the best choice in the database marketplace, and in many scenarios it is. It can be small enough for a handful of users, or large enough for the largest corporations. It doesn't need to cost as much as Oracle or Sybase, but it does have the ability to scale up and deal with terabytes of data without many concerns. As you will see, it is easy to install, as it comes as one complete package for most of its functionality, with a simple install to be performed for the remaining areas if required.

Now that you know the reasons behind choosing SQL Server, you need to know which versions of SQL Server are out there to purchase, what market each version is aimed at, and which version will be best for you, including which version can run on your machine.

Evolution of SQL Server

SQL Server has evolved over the years into the product it is today. Table 1-1 gives a summary of this process.

Table 1-1. *The Stages in the Evolution of SQL Server*

Year	Version	Description
1988	SQL Server	Joint application built with Sybase for use on OS/2.
1993	SQL Server 4.2, a desktop database	A low-functionality, **desktop** database, capable of meeting the data storage and handling needs of a small department. The concept of a database that was integrated with Windows and had an easy-to-use interface proved popular.
1994		Microsoft splits from Sybase.
1995	SQL Server 6.05, a small business database	Major rewrite of the core database engine. First "significant" release. Improved performance and significant feature enhancements. Still a long way behind in terms of the performance and feature set of later versions, but with this version, SQL Server became capable of handling **small e-commerce and intranet** applications, and was a fraction of the cost of its competitors.
1996	SQL Server 6.5	SQL Server was gaining prominence such that Oracle brought out version 7.1 on the NT platform as direct competition.
1998	SQL Server 7.0, a web database	Another significant rewrite to the core database engine. A defining release, providing a reasonably powerful and feature-rich database that was a truly viable (and still cheap) alternative for **small-to-medium businesses**, between a true desktop database such as MS Access and the high-end enterprise capabilities (and price) of Oracle and DB2. Gained a good reputation for ease of use and for providing crucial business tools (e.g., analysis services, data transformation services) out of the box, which were expensive add-ons with competing databases.
2000	SQL Server 2000, an enterprise database	Vastly improved performance scalability and reliability sees SQL Server become a major player in the **enterprise database** market (now supporting the online operations of businesses such as NASDAQ, Dell, and Barnes & Noble). A big increase in price (although still reckoned to be about half the cost of Oracle) slowed initial uptake, but the excellent range of management, development, and analysis tools won new customers. In 2001, Oracle (with 34% of the market) finally ceded its No. 1 position in the Windows database market (worth $2.55 billion in 2001) to SQL Server (with 40% of the market). In 2002, the gap had grown, with SQL Server at 45% and Oracle slipping to 27%.[a]

Table 1-1. *The Stages in the Evolution of SQL Server (Continued)*

Year	Version	Description
2005	SQL Server 2005	Many areas of SQL Server have been rewritten, such as the ability to load data via a utility called Integration Services, but the greatest leap forward was the introduction of the .NET Framework. This allowed .NET SQL Server–specific objects to be built, giving SQL Server the flexible functionality that Oracle had with its inclusion of Java.
2008	SQL Server 2008	The aim of SQL Server 2008 is to deal with the many different forms that data can now take. It builds on the infrastructure of SQL Server 2005 by offering new data types and the use of Language Integrated Query (LINQ). It also deals with data, such as XML, compact devices, and massive database installations, that reside in many different places. Also, it offers the ability to set rules within a framework to ensure databases and objects meet defined criteria, and it offers the ability to report when these objects do not meet this criteria.

[a] *Gartner Report, May 21, 2003*

Hardware Requirements

Now that you know a bit about SQL Server, the next big question on your list may well be, "Do I have a powerful enough computer to run my chosen SQL Server edition on? Will this help me refine my decision?"

Judging by today's standards of minimum-specification hardware that can be bought—even the low-cost solutions—the answer will in most cases be "Yes" to most editions. However, you may have older hardware (things move so fast that even hardware bought a couple of months ago can quickly be deemed below minimum specification), so let's take a look at what the minimum recommendations are and how you can check your own computer to ensure that you have sufficient resources.

CPU

The minimum recommended CPU that SQL Server will run on is a 1GHz processor for the 32-bit edition and a 1.6GHz for the 64-bit version, or a compatible processor, or similar processing power; however, 2GHz is recommended. However, as with most minimums listed here, Microsoft wholly recommends a faster processor. The faster the processor, the better your SQL Server will perform, and from this the fewer bottlenecks that could surface. Many of today's computers start at 2GHz or above, but the faster the processer the better. You will find your development time reduced for it.

However, it is not processor alone that speeds up SQL Server. A large part is the amount of memory that your computer has.

Memory

Now that you know you have a fast enough processor, it is time to check whether you have enough memory in the system. SQL Server requires a minimum of 512MB of RAM onboard your computer, although you shouldn't have too many more applications open and running, as they could easily not leave enough memory for SQL Server to run fast enough. Microsoft recommends 1GB or above, and really double that at least for when you start using your SQL Server in earnest.

If you wanted to run the Enterprise Edition, then a minimum, and I mean a bare minimum, of 1GB really should be installed, especially if you want to use any of the more advanced features.

The more memory the better: I really would recommend a minimum of 1GB on any computer that a developer is using, with 2GB ideal and sufficient to give good all-around performance. If a process can be held in memory, rather than swapped out to hard drive or another area while you are running another process, then you are not waiting on SQL Server being loaded back into memory to start off where it left off. This is called **swapping**, and the more memory, the less swapping could, and should, take place.

Taking CPU speed and memory together as a whole, it is these two items that are crucial to the speed that the computer will run, and having sufficient speed will let you develop as fast as possible.

When it comes to installing SQL Server, insufficient memory won't stop the install, but you will be warned that you need more.

Hard Disk Space

You will need lots! But name a major application these days that doesn't need lots! For SQL Server alone, ignoring any data files that you are then going to add on top, you will need over 1GB of space. Certainly, the installation options that will be used later in the chapter will mean you need this amount of space. You can reduce this by opting not to install certain options—for example, Books Online; however, even most notebooks these days come with a minimum 40GB, and 80GB is not uncommon either. Hard disk space is cheap as well, and it is better to buy one disk too large for your needs than have one hard drive that suits now, and then have to buy another later, with all the attendant problems of moving information to clear up space on the original drive.

Again, you will need spare space on the drive for the expansion of SQL Server and the databases, as well as room for temporary files that you will also need in your development process. So think big—big is beautiful!

Operating System Requirements

You will find that SQL Server 2008 will run on Windows Vista Home Basic Edition and above, as well as Windows XP. From the server side, it will work on Windows Server 2003 with Service Pack 2 and Windows Server 2008. It will also work on the 64-bit operating systems for Windows XP Professional, as well as the 64-bit editions of Windows Server 2003 and 2008. So there is plenty of scope for running SQL Server on many operating systems.

The Example

In order to demonstrate SQL Server 2008 fully, together we will develop a system for a financial company that will have features such as banking, share purchase, and regular buying, including a unit trust savings plan and so on. This is an application that could fit into a large organization, or with very minor modifications could be used by a single person to record banking transactions.

The book builds on this idea and develops the example, demonstrating how to take an idea and formulate it into a design with the correct architecture. It should be said, though, that the example will be the bare minimum to make it run, as I don't want to detract from SQL Server. The book will give you the power and the knowledge to take this example, expand it to suit your financial application needs, and give it the specifics and intricacies that are required to make it fully useful for yourself.

But before we can get to this point, we need to install SQL Server.

Installation

The remainder of this chapter will guide you through the installation process of the Developer Edition, although virtually all that you see will be in every edition. Some of the differences will be due to the functionality of each edition. Microsoft offers a 120-day trial version at http://www.microsoft.com/ sql/evaluation/trial/, which you can use to follow along with the examples in this book if you don't already have SQL Server 2008.

This book will cover many of the options and combinations of features that can be included within an installation. A number of different tools are supplied with SQL Server to be included with the installation. We will look at these tools so that a basic understanding of what they are will allow us to decide which to install.

Installation covers a great many different areas:

- Security issues
- Different types of installation—whether this is the first installation and instance of SQL Server or a subsequent instance, for development, test, or production
- Custom installations
- Installing only some of the products available

Most of these areas will be covered so that by the end of the chapter, you can feel confident and knowledgeable to complete any subsequent installations that suit your needs.

This book uses the Developer Edition because it is most suited to our needs, as developers, for it doesn't have all the operating system requirements of the Enterprise Edition. Insert the CD for the Microsoft SQL Server 2008 edition of your choice in your CD-ROM drive and start the installation. What the upcoming text covers is a standard installation.

Beginning the Install

First of all, ensure that you have logged on to your machine with administrative rights so that you are allowed to create files and folders on your machine, which is obviously required for installation to be successful.

If you are using a CD-ROM and the installation process does not automatically start, open up Windows Explorer and double-click autorun.exe, found at the root level of the CD-ROM. If you are not using a CD-ROM, double-click the installer executable that you downloaded.

You may now be presented with the installation screen for Microsoft .NET 3.5 Framework if it is not already installed. .NET is a framework that Microsoft created that allows programs written in VB .NET, C#, and other programming languages to have a common compile set for computers. SQL Server 2008 uses .NET for some of its own internal work, but also, as a developer, you can write .NET code in any of Microsoft's .NET languages and include this within SQL Server. With SQL Server 2008, there is also the ability to query the database using .NET and LINQ rather than T-SQL.

■**Note** Including .NET code is an advanced topic and outside the scope of this book. For more information, try *Pro SQL Server 2005 Assemblies* by Robin Dewson and Julian Skinner (Apress, 2005).

Once this is installed, you are presented with the SQL Server Installation Center. This screen, shown in Figure 1-1, deals with planning an installation, setup processes, including new installations, upgrades from previous versions of SQL Server, and many other options for maintaining SQL Server installations.

When you click on the Installation item on the left of the Installation Center, you can then select from the first item of the list of Installation options, New SQL Server stand-alone installation or add features to an existing installation, and the SQL Server 2008 installation starts.

A quick system check is performed before you enter your product key and accept the license terms of SQL Server. There are a number of support files that SQL Server uses as part of the installation process, as well as to ensure that a clean and valid installation occurs. In Figure 1-2, you will see that there is one warning in the process, but it is still possible to proceed. Provided no errors are listed in your process, click Next.

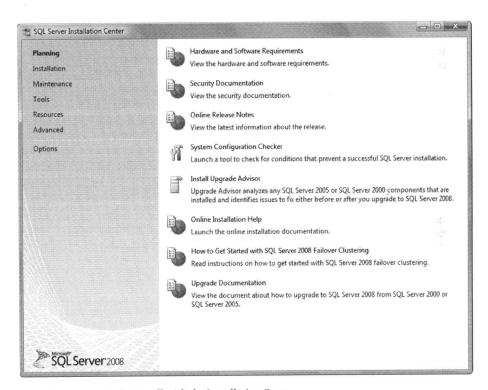

Figure 1-1. *Beginning the install with the Installation Center*

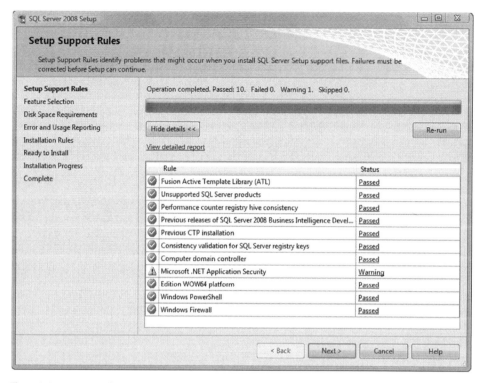

Figure 1-2. *System configuration checks*

Choosing the Features to Install

We now come to the Feature Selection screen, where we have to make some decisions. As you see in Figure 1-3, this installation will have everything installed, because this will be your development instance where you'll be testing every aspect of SQL Server away from any development of projects taking place. This is therefore going to be more of a training environment. However, you can be selective regarding what parts of the components you want to install. For this book, you will need Database Engine Services, Reporting Services, Client Tools, and Business Intelligence Development Studio for building reports, so ensure at least that these are checked.

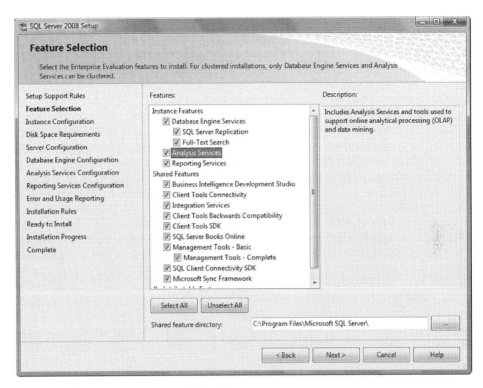

Figure 1-3. *Selecting every component to install*

Let's briefly take a look at most of these components:

- *Database Engine Services*: This is the main core for SQL Server 2008 and installs the main engine, data files, etc., to make SQL Server run.

  - *SQL Server Replication:* When you want to send data changes not only on the database it is being executed on, but also on a similar database that has been built to duplicate those changes, then you can use this option to replicate the changes to that database.

  - *Full text search:* This option lets you allow searching of the text within your database.

- *Analysis Services*: Using this tool, you can take a set of data and dice and slice and analyze the information contained.

- *Reporting Services*: This allows reports to be produced from SQL Server instead of using third-party tools such as Crystal Reports. We look at this component in more detail in Chapter 14.

- *Client Tools:* Some of these tools sit on the client machine and provide the graphical interface to SQL Server, while others sit on the client and work with SQL Server. This is the option you would package up for rollout to developers to sit on their machines.

- *Microsoft Sync Framework:* When working with offline applications such as those on mobile devices, there has to be some sort of synchronization mechanism in place. This option allows these interactions to occur.

- *SQL Server Books online:* This is the help system. If you need more information, clarification, or extra detail on any area of SQL Server, then this is the area to turn to.

- *Business Intelligence Development Studio:* When you want to analyze data using analysis-based services, then you can use this GUI to interact with your database. This book doesn't cover this option.

- *Integration Services:* This final option allows you to build processes to complete actions, such as importing data from other data sources and manipulating the data. You will see Integration Services in action in Chapter 7 when we look at building a backup maintenance plan.

Of these components, Analysis Services and Business Intelligence Development Studio fall outside the scope of this book, and we only touch upon Integration Services as mentioned.

Note At this point, SQL Server no longer has the option to install the sample databases. Microsoft is also altering the way sample databases and samples are delivered, so you may find newer versions on the SQL Server web site, http://www.microsoft.com/sql, or at http://www.codeplex.com/SqlServerSamples.

Naming the Instance

As you know, SQL Server is installed on a computer. It is possible to install SQL Server more than once on one computer. This could happen when you have a powerful server and it has enough resources such as memory and processor to cope with two or three different applications running. These different applications want to have their own SQL Server databases. Each install is called an **instance**. We are now at the stage that we can name the instance of the install. Each instance must have a unique name attached to it, although "no name," known as a **default instance**, is also classified as a unique name.

Naming instances is important as the first step to organizing your environments. For example, you may have an instance for development, another instance for system testing, and finally one for user testing. It is bad practice to share production server hardware with anything but production databases. If you don't, and if you have a rogue development action that occurs and crashes the server, you will stop production from running. Although you would have to make this decision at the start of the install process you are currently going through, it is a useful second reminder here when naming the instance.

The default instance is available, which is what is selected when you are not giving the install a specific name; once you install SQL Server outside of a learning environment, you should avoid this, as it gives you an installation with no name and therefore no hint as to its use. As you are still learning, the easiest option to understand is to use the default instance, so select Default Instance as shown in Figure 1-4 and then click Next.Once you have instances installed on the server, they will be listed here. You can also see the path detailed for each of the directories for the three services selected in the previous step.

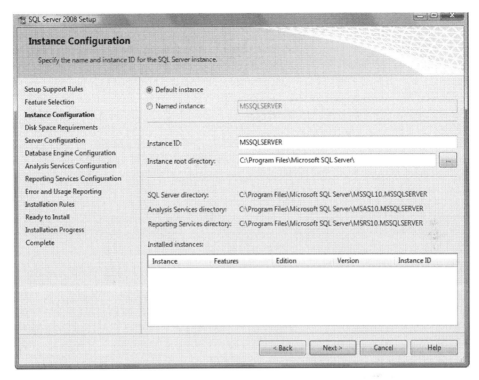

Figure 1-4. *Naming the install instance*

Choosing Service Accounts

SQL Server and other services, as defined in the Feature Selection screen (shown earlier in Figure 1-3), require you to log on to Windows before starting, just as you need to log on to Windows before using the system. SQL Server, Reporting Services, and so on can run without you or anyone being logged in to the computer that the install took place on. They can run just so long as the computer has fired up successfully. This is normal when SQL Server is installed on a server that is held in a remote location like a server room.

We will look at these options in more detail toward the end of the chapter. The options you see in Figure 1-5 will install SQL Server with a low-level set of privileges.

You can always change these later via the Services icon within the Control Panel. However, it would be much better to use the SQL Server Configuration Manager, found in Configuration Tools. By using the Configuration Manager, the account will be added to the correct group and be given the right permissions. Click Next.

If you look at the SQL Server Browser, which is another name for SQL Server Management Studio, it will be disabled by default. Many SQL Server installations will be on servers, quite often on remote servers; therefore, there should be no need to have the SQL Server Browser running. Normally, you will connect to SQL Server from a client machine. However, I am making the assumption that this installation is not on a server and is on a local computer, so change this option to start automatically.

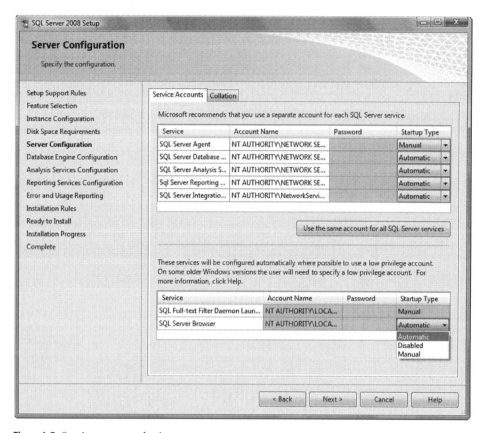

Figure 1-5. *Service account selection*

Selecting an Authentication Mode

We now come to how we want to enforce security on your SQL Server installation. As Figure 1-6 shows, there are two choices: Windows authentication mode and mixed mode. You will learn more about modes later in the chapter but very, very simply, Windows authentication mode denotes that you are going to use Windows security to maintain your SQL Server logins, whereas mixed mode uses either Windows security or a SQL Server defined login ID and password. We also need to define a password for a special login ID, called sa, if you are working with mixed mode. Again, you will learn more about this in a moment, but for now you must enter a valid password. Use a meaningful and impossible-to-guess password, but not one that you will forget.

It is also necessary to define a SQL Server Administrator account. This is a special account that you can use to log on in dire emergencies, such as when SQL Server refuses connections. This special account allows you to log on, debug the situation, and get SQL Server back up and running. Normally, this Administrator account would be a server account ID, but for now, use the account you have used to log on to your computer.

You will also see a similar screen for Analysis Services, and the settings are the same.

Figure 1-6. *Authentication choices including the SQL Server administrator account*

Defining the Data Directories

The Data Directories tab, as shown in Figure 1-7, is where you define where SQL Server stores its data, backup directories, and temporary database by default. For each instance, you define where the relevant folders should reside. As stated earlier, you can have several installations on one physical server, and it is not uncommon for a physical server to hold more than one production installation of SQL Server. For example, there could be an installation for accounts, another for product control, and so on. Each instance would have its data held in a different data directory. This includes any temporary databases that are created and any log files that are generated, so although the physical server is shared, the installation is isolated. As we are only dealing with one instance within this book, leave these settings as they are.

The FILESTREAM tab is another type of data directory, but ignore this for now. We'll discuss this more later in the book. However, to give you a small insight, FILESTREAM is used when dealing with large amounts of unstructured data. In the past, this data was held totally separate from SQL Server, but now FILESTREAM allows the data to be managed by SQL Server, and this tab informs SQL Server of where it resides on the physical server.

You will see these same tabs in the next step if you selected Analysis Services.

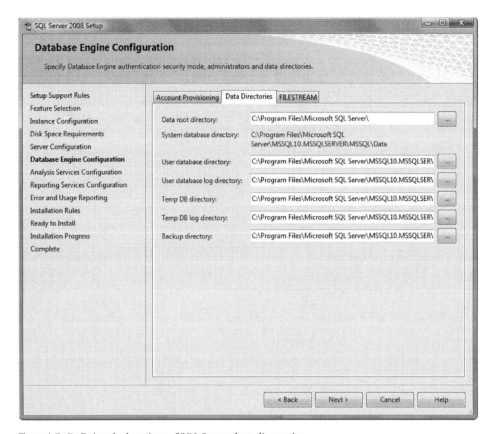

Figure 1-7. *Defining the locations of SQL Server data directories*

Creating the Reporting Services Database

As we selected Reporting Services to be installed, we need to create a database for the reporting server to use. There are three different possible installation options for Reporting Services: Native, SharePoint, and installed but not configured. If you select the last option, SQL Server Reporting Services will be installed on the server but will not be configured. This is ideal if you're setting up a specific server just for the reporting options. Once installed, you would then have to create a reporting database.

The Native mode configuration, as shown in Figure 1-8, is the simplest and the one we will be using. It installs Reporting Services and also creates the necessary databases within our SQL Server. It will only be available if you are installing on a local instance rather than a remote instance and if Reporting Services is also on that local instance. Default values are used for the service account, the report server URL on the local instance—which will be localhost—the report manager URL, and the name of the Reporting Services database.

If you have a SharePoint installation and you want Reporting Services to use this architecture, then select this option, which allows you to use SharePoint's functionality. This is outside the scope of this book.

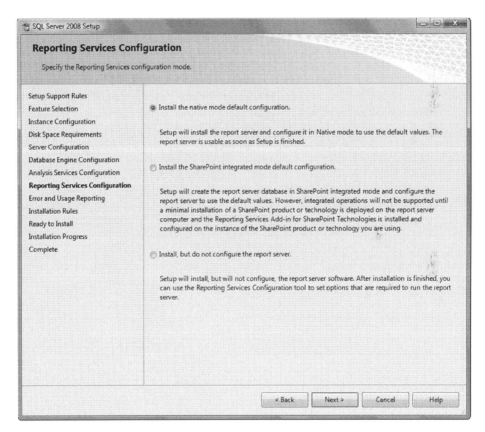

Figure 1-8. *Installing native mode configuration for Reporting Services*

Configuring Error and Usage Reports

Within SQL Server, it is possible for any errors to be automatically reported and sent to Microsoft. These include fatal errors where SQL Server shuts down unexpectedly. It is recommended that you keep the error settings shown in Figure 1-9 enabled. No organizational information will be sent, so your data will still be secure. This is similar to sending reports when Excel crashes, for example. It is better to have this switched to active. Sending the errors to Microsoft will hopefully produce faster patch fixes and better releases in the future. It is also possible for SQL Server to take information about how you are using SQL Server. This is also a useful setting to have switched on, so that Microsoft can receive information that might help it improve the product. However, it would be useful to have this switched on in a production environment where it is more relevant.

When you click Next, you will be met with a screen detailing the installation rules. There is nothing to do; just click Next, where the final screen (see Figure 1-10) is displayed. The setup collection is complete, and you are ready to install.

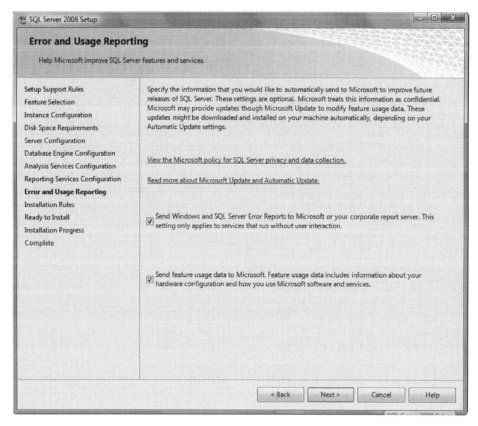

Figure 1-9. *Error and Usage Reporting settings*

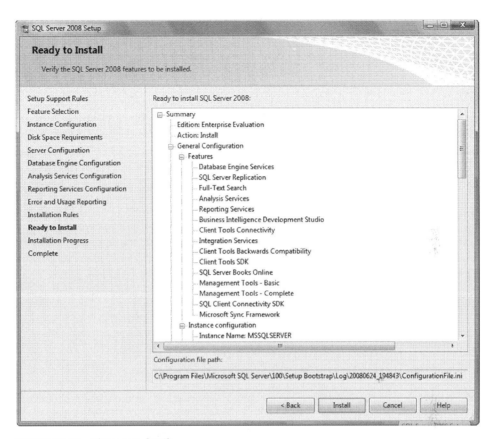

Figure 1-10. *Complete setup details*

Security

To discuss the Service Account dialog box that we came across in the installation properly, we need to delve into the area of Windows security.

In this section, we will first examine the concept of Windows services as opposed to programs, and then move on to discussing different types of authentication we can choose when installing SQL Server.

Services Accounts

SQL Server runs as a Windows service. So what is a service? A good example of a service is any anti-virus software that runs continuously from when the user restarts a computer to the point that the computer shuts down. A program, on the other hand, is either loaded in memory and running, or not started. So what is the advantage of running a service? When you have a unit of work that can run as a service, Windows can control a great deal more concerning that process. A service can be set to start automatically before any user has even logged on; all other programs require a user to be logged in to Windows in order for the services to start.

A service also has absolutely no user interface. There will be no form to display and no user input to deal with at run time. The only interaction with the process runs either through a separate user interface, which then links in to the service but is a totally separate unit of work (for example, SQL Server Management Studio), or from Windows management of that service itself. Any output that comes from the service must go to the Event Log, which is a Windows area that stores any notification from the services that Windows runs.

Having no interface means that the whole process can be controlled without human intervention. Providing the service is designed well, Windows can take care of every eventuality itself, and can also run the service before anyone has even logged in to the computer.

In most production environments, SQL Server will be running on a remote server, one probably locked away in a secure and controlled area, possibly where the only people allowed in are hardware engineers. There probably isn't even a remote access program installed, as this could give unauthorized access to these computers. SQL Server will run quite happily and, with any luck, never give an error. But what if one day there is an error? If SQL Server is running as a program, you'll have to make some sort of decision. Even if SQL Server crashes, there at least has to be some sort of mechanism to restart it. This means another process needs to be run—a monitoring process, which in itself could result in a whole ream of problems. However, as a service, SQL Server is under Windows control. If a problem occurs, whether with SQL Server, Windows, or any outside influence, Windows is smart enough to deal with it through the services process.

If you do log in to the computer, as you likely will while working through this book, because SQL Server will be running on a home or local system, then you can use this Windows user ID for SQL Server to also log in and start its service. This is known as a **local system account**.

On the other hand, you can create a Windows login that exists purely for SQL Server. This could exist for several reasons. For example, your Windows account should be set up so that the password expires after so many days after being set, or locks out after a number of incorrect password attempts. This is to protect your computer and the network, among many other things. However, SQL Server should use a separate account that also has an expiring password and the ability to lock the account after a number of successful attempts. This kind of non–user-specific, "generic" account removes the link between SQL Server and a person within an organization. If you are looking at the domain account option as shown earlier in Figure 1-5, this account is likely to be in a network environment or a production environment. There is an option to define a different account for each service. This is quite a crucial option when moving to a corporate environment due to the security implications that you must deal with.

SQL Server has several different processes that exist for different work. SQL Server is used to run SQL Server itself, and SQL Server Agent runs processes such as batch jobs. SQL Server should only really need to access itself. Therefore, it should only require a domain login with very restricted privileges.

SQL Server Agent, which runs batch processes and complex tasks including working with other servers, needs a more powerful domain account. Your network administrator may have created these accounts and will know which account is best to use or best to create for these tasks.

It's time to move on to the options we are given during installation regarding authentication mode.

Looking at the Authentication Mode

Probably the most crucial information in the whole setup process, and also the biggest decision that you have to make, concerns the authentication mode you wish to apply to your server. As we saw earlier in the setup process, there are two choices: **Windows authentication mode** and **mixed mode**.

Windows Authentication Mode

To log on to a Windows 2003/XP/Vista machine, a username must be supplied. There is no way around this (unlike in Windows 9x/ME where a username was optional). So, to log on to Windows, the username and password have to be validated within Windows before the user can successfully log in. When this is done, Windows is actually verifying the user against username credentials held within the domain controller, or, if you are running Windows/SQL Server on a standalone machine at home, the credentials held locally. These credentials check the access group the user belongs to (the user rights). The user could be an administrator, who has the ability to alter anything within the computer, all the way down to a basic user who has very restricted rights. This then gives us a trusted connection; in other words, applications that are started up after logging in to Windows can trust that Windows has verified that the account has passed the necessary security checks.

Once we have logged in to Windows, SQL Server uses a trusted connection when working with Windows Authentication mode. This means that SQL Server is trusting that the username and password have been validated as we just mentioned. If, however, the username does not exist, then based on the user ID alone, you won't be able to log on to that machine. If the login isn't valid, SQL Server will check the Windows group that the user belongs to and check its security to see if that group is set up to access SQL Server. If that user has administration rights to your computer, then the user may well be able to at least connect to SQL Server.

Someone else can also log on to your machine with his or her user ID and password, providing they have access to it. Although he or she might be able to get to SQL Server by finding the executable on the C drive, SQL Server will first of all check to see whether that user has a valid login within SQL Server.

We are in a bit of a Catch-22 situation here. You need to know about security for your install process, but to demonstrate it fully means working with SQL Server Management Studio, which the next chapter covers. We will keep that area simple, so let's look at an example involving security now.

Try It Out: Windows Authentication Mode

1. Ensure that you are logged on to your machine as an administrator. If you are on a local computer, chances are that your login is in fact an administrator ID. If this computer is on a network and you are unsure about your access rights, ask your PC support desk to help you out with the ID and password. On Windows Vista, you may need to change your user control access to avoid many dialog boxes confirming that you wish to continue with each step.

2. From Start /Control Panel, select User Accounts.

3. When the Users and Passwords dialog box comes up, click Create a New Account on XP or Manage Another Account on Vista, followed by Create New Account.

4. Once the Name the Account and Choose an Account Type dialog box comes up, enter the username JThakur, as shown in Figure 1-11.

5. Ensure that the account type specified is Limited on XP or Standard on Vista. This means that it will not have administrator privileges. Once ready, click Create Account.

Figure 1-11. *Creating a new user account*

6. Stay in the Name the Account and Choose an Account Type dialog box, as you want to add a second username. Repeat the preceding process using the following details:

   Username: VMcGlynn

   Account type: (Computer) Administrator

7. Log off from Windows and then log on using the first ID that you created: JThakur.

8. Once logged in, start up SQL Server Management Studio by selecting Start ➤ All Programs ➤ Microsoft SQL Server 2008 ➤ SQL Server Management Studio. You will need to populate the dialog with the server name of the install. Click on Browse For More, then select Database Engine and select the install. We go through this in more detail in Chapter 2. The dialog should look like Figure 1-12.

9. Examine the error message that appears, which should resemble what you see in Figure 1-13. JThakur as a login has not been defined within SQL Server specifically and does not belong to a group that allows access. The only group at the minute is a user who is in the Administrators Windows group. Recall that JThakur is a Limited user.

10. We will now try out the other user we created. Close down SQL Server, log off Windows, and log on using the second ID we created—VMcGlynn. Once logged in, start up SQL Server Management Studio and connect to your server. This time the login will work.

We have created two usernames: one that has restricted access (JThakur) and one that has administration rights (VMcGlynn). However, neither of these specific usernames exists within SQL Server itself: after all, we haven't entered them and they haven't appeared as if by magic. So why did one succeed and one fail?

The Windows security model has ensured that both IDs are valid. If the ID or password were incorrect, there would be no way that you could be logged in to Windows. Therefore, when you try to connect to SQL Server, the only check that is performed is whether the user has access to SQL Server either via membership of an operating system group or through the specific logged-in user account. As you can see in Figure 1-14, neither JThakur nor VMcGlynn exist.

Figure 1-12. *Attempting to connect to SQL Server*

Figure 1-13. *Failed login to server*

Figure 1-14. *Object Explorer for SQL Server*

However, you can see that there is a Windows group called BUILTIN\Administrators. This means that any username that is part of the Administrators group will have the capacity to log on to this SQL Server. Hence, avoid if possible setting up users as administrators of their own PCs.

In a production environment, it may be advisable to remove this group from the system if you do allow users to be administrators. As VMcGlynn is a member of the Administrators group, then this username will also be a member of the BUILTIN\Administrators group.

Mixed Mode

If we installed SQL Server with mixed mode, this means we could use either Windows authentication, as has just been covered, or SQL Server authentication.

How does mixed mode differ from Windows authentication mode? To start with, you need to supply a user ID and password to connect rather than SQL Server taking the Windows ID, or the group the user belongs to, of the logged-in account. There is no assumption that the username supplied is a valid ID. Using mixed mode is also appropriate in many cases when working with ISPs. To clarify this, if you are working on your remote data at a local client machine, the remote machine would need to know the credentials of your login, and the easiest method is to use SQL Server authentication. Do not get confused here, though. If you want to work with your data at your ISP, the ISP may provide some sort of tool, or you may use SQL Server Management Studio to connect to your data. You would then be able to do what you want. The web site code, if written in ASP.NET, will use a Windows account to log in, so although you may lock out your SQL Server mixed mode account, it should not stop your web site from working.

You will learn how to add usernames to SQL Server (as opposed to adding Windows users) when I talk about security in Chapter 4.

This leaves one area of security left that needs to be discussed here: the sa login.

The sa Login

The sa login is a default login that has full administration rights for SQL Server. If you had selected mixed mode authentication during the installation process, you would have seen that you would be forced to include a password for this account. This is because the sa user ID is such a powerful login. It also exists in every SQL Server installation; therefore, any hacker knows that this user ID exists and so will try to connect to the server using it. Prior to SQL Server 2005 when creating a password became compulsory, many installations had the password blank, therefore allowing hackers instant access. If you logged in to SQL Server as sa, you will have full control over any aspect of SQL Server. SQL Server inserts this ID no matter which authentication mode you install. If you have a Windows account defined as sa—for example, for Steve Austin—then this user will be able to log in to the server if you have set up the server as implementing Windows authentication mode without any further intervention on his part. Try to avoid login IDs of sa.

In a mixed mode installation, sa will be a valid username and validated as such. As you can guess, if any user gets ahold of this username and the password, it would be possible for that user to have full access to view and amend or delete any item of data. At worst, the user could corrupt any database, as well as corrupt SQL Server itself. He or she could even set up tasks that e-mail data to a remote location as it is being processed.

It is essential to set up a strong password on the sa account in the Authentication Mode screen if you choose mixed mode. It is a major improvement in SQL Server 2008 that you are now forced to enter a password, although it is possible to set up a very easily guessed password. Do not use passwords such as password or adminpwd, for example. Always keep the password safe, but also make a note of it in a safe place. If you forget the sa password and this is the only administration ID that exists, you will need to reinstall SQL Server to get out of this problem. A good password is one that mixes numbers and letters, but doesn't include letters than can be made into numbers and numbers into letters. For example, pa55word is just as easy to guess as password. Or 4pr355 for Apress.

There is also another reason not to log on to SQL Server with the sa username. At times it will be essential to know who is running a particular query on a SQL Server database. In a production database, someone may be running an update of the data, which is filling up the disk space or filling up the transaction log. We will need to contact that person to check whether he or she can stop the process. If that person logs in as sa, we will have no idea who he or she is. However, if that person logged on with an identifiable name, he or she would have an ID in SQL Server, which we could track.

By restricting the sa login so that people have to use their own accounts, we can ensure a much higher degree of system monitoring and integrity.

There will be times when we'll want mixed mode authentication; it is perfectly acceptable to wish this. Internet providers use mixed mode, as many applications may be on one web server. If this ISP is a reseller (in other words, many people around the globe use the one computer), you will not want these people to have the ability to see your data. We have also decided not to have sa as an administration logon at this point. So what do we do? Well, we create a logon ID that will have the access privileges we wish; in other words, the ability to just see the data and work with the data that we need, and no more. The ISP may require you to supply a user ID and password that it uses to create an account on its SQL Server instance. You will encounter more about this in Chapter 4.

■**Note** Regardless of the authentication mode, it is important that you always supply a strong password.

Summary

By this point, you should understand the small differences between each version of SQL Server. You should also know how to check your computer to see if it is suitable for a SQL Server installation.

By following the steps given earlier, you should have a successful installation of SQL Server 2008 on your computer. You may even have completed the installation twice so that you have a development server installation as well as a test server installation. This is a good idea, and something to consider if you have only one installation so far. Whether you are working in a large corporation or are a "one-man band," keeping your production and development code separate leads to greatly reduced complications if, when developing, you need to make a production fix.

This chapter introduced you to security in SQL Server so that you can feel comfortable knowing which way you want to implement this and how to deal with different usernames. You may not have any data yet, but you want to ensure that when you do, only the right people get to look at it!

You are now ready to explore SQL Server 2008. One of the best ways of managing SQL Server is by using SQL Server Management Studio, which will be discussed next.

SQL Server Management Studio

Now that SQL Server 2008 is successfully installed on your machine, it is time to start exploring the various areas that make this an easy and effective product to use. This chapter concentrates on SQL Server Management Studio (SSMS), which you will use to develop and maintain your databases and the objects SSMS contains.

SSMS is the graphical user interface (GUI) you will use to build your database solutions. This is an easy-to-use and intuitive tool, and before long, you will feel confident in using it to work with SQL Server quickly and efficiently. I will be discussing several aspects of SSMS in this chapter. You can then use this knowledge throughout the book. I'll discuss some aspects in more detail throughout the book.

SSMS is crucial to your success as a developer. Learning about it and working with actual samples throughout the book will make your life easier. Therefore, by the end of this chapter, you will have gained experience with it and be proficient in the following areas:

- The components of SSMS
- How to configure SSMS

Let's start right away by having a look at SSMS and how it is used to work with SQL Server 2008.

A Quick Overview of SSMS

As I touched on in Chapter 1, SQL Server runs as a separate Windows process on a suitable Windows-based computer, be it on a standalone desktop machine, or on a server or network. If you open Task Manager and move to the Processes tab, you will see, among other processes, sqlservr.exe. This process or service runs in its own process space and is isolated from other processes on the machine. This means that SQL Server should not be affected by any other piece of software that does not talk to any SQL Server component. If you have to kill any other component's process, the SQL Server engine should continue to run.

SQL Server runs as a service that is controlled and monitored by Windows itself. SQL Server ensures that it is given the right amount of memory, processing power, and time from the operating system by instructing Windows what it needs. However, pressures on the server mean that SQL Server modifies what it requests based on what is available. Because SQL Server runs as a service, it has no interface attached to it for a user to interact with. As a result, there needs to be at least one separate utility that can pass commands and functions from a user through to the SQL Server service, which then passes them through to the underlying database. The GUI tool that accomplishes this is SSMS. There are other tools that you can use, and you could even create your own GUI, but I'll only be concentrating on SSMS within this book.

SSMS can be used to develop and work with several installations of SQL Server in one application. These installations can be on one computer or on many computers connected through a local area network (LAN), a wide area network (WAN), or even the Internet. Therefore, it is possible to deal with your development, system testing, user testing, and production instances of SQL Server from one instance of SSMS. SSMS helps you in the development of database solutions, including creating and modifying components of a database, amending the database itself, and dealing with security issues. Getting to know this tool well is crucial to becoming a successful professional SQL Server developer, as well as a database administrator.

One of the tools within SSMS that we will use for completing tasks is Query Editor. This tool allows program code to be written and executed, from objects, to commands that manipulate data, and even complete tasks such as backing up the data. This program code is called **Transact SQL** (T-SQL). T-SQL is a Microsoft proprietary language, although it is strongly linked with a standard set by the American National Standards Institute (ANSI). The current specification Microsoft bases its code on is ANSI-92.

Query Editor is a tool within SSMS that allows you to programmatically build the same actions as dragging and dropping or using wizards. However, using T-SQL within Query Editor can give you more control over certain aspects of certain commands. Note that the name "Query Editor" comes from the fact that it sends **queries** to the database using T-SQL. Don't worry if you don't quite grasp this—all will become clear very soon.

Let's spend some time taking a look at SSMS in more detail.

Try It Out: Touring SQL Server Management Studio

1. Start up SSMS as you saw in Chapter 1, and select Start ➤ Programs ➤ Microsoft SQL Server 2008 ➤ SQL Server Management Studio.

2. Click the Options button to bring up a Connect to Server dialog box similar to the one in Figure 2-1. Note the following items in this dialog box:

   - *Server Type*: For the purposes of the examples in this book, leave the server type as Database Engine. The other options are other types of servers that are available for connection.

   - *Server Name*: The second combo box contains a list of SQL Server installations that the Connect to Server dialog box can find, or knows about. In the dialog box in Figure 2-1, you will see the name of the computer that the local install is on. If you open the Server Name combo box, you can search for more servers locally or over a network connection using `<Browse for more...>`.

   - *Authentication*: The final combo box specifies which type of connection you wish to use. We installed SQL Server with Windows authentication in Chapter 1; therefore, this is the option to use. If you had installed SQL Server with Mixed mode, then you could change this option to SQL Server authentication, which would enable the next two text boxes and allow you to enter a username and password.

Figure 2-1. *SQL Server Management Studio Connect to Server dialog box without expanded options*

3. Click Options, which switches you to the Connection Properties tab. Here you will see specific properties for this connection, as shown in Figure 2-2:

   - *Connect to Database*: This combo box provides a list of databases based on the server and login details in the Login tab. Clicking the down button for this combo box allows you to browse for and select a database on the server to which you wish to connect. Only the databases that the Windows account or SQL Server login can connect to will populate this list. Also, any error in the login details will cause an error message to be displayed here instead of listing databases.

   - *Network*: This area details how we want this connection to be made with SQL Server. At the moment, there is no need to change the current settings.

   - *Connection*: This area deals with connection timeouts. The first item, Connection Time-out, defines how long the connection should wait before returning an error. For local installs and even most network installs, a setting of 15 seconds should be more than enough. The only situation that may require you to increase this setting is if you were connecting over a WAN or to a SQL Server installation at an ISP. The second option, Execution Time-out, details the timeout value for any T-SQL code that you execute. A setting of 0 means that there is no timeout; there should be few, if any, occasions when you would want to change this setting.

   - The final option is a check box for whether you want to encrypt your connection to SQL Server. This is useful for those times when the connection is going outside your organization.

Figure 2-2. *SQL Server Management Studio connection properties*

4. Once you are happy with all of the items in the Connection Properties tab, click Connect. This brings you to SSMS itself. If you have ever used Visual Studio .NET (VS .NET), you will notice that SSMS has a reasonably similar layout. This is deliberate on Microsoft's part, as the company is making SQL Server more integrated with .NET. Your layout should look like the one in Figure 2-3, with only minor name changes based on the server you have connected to and the connection you have used. This figure shows I have connected to FAT-BELLY SQL Server using the Windows account FAT-BELLY\rdewson. Figure 2-3 also shows the Object Explorer details window, which may not be displayed initially but can be displayed from the menu option view. Finally, the version number will probably differ depending on any patch releases to SQL Server since the book was written.

5. The first area of SSMS we will look at is the Registered Servers explorer. Access this explorer, shown in Figure 2-4, by selecting View ➤ Registered Servers or by pressing Ctrl+Alt+G. This area details all SQL Server servers that have been registered by you on this SSMS installation. At present, there will only be the server just registered, but as time progresses, you will see more. This explorer will also show registered services for other services such as Reporting Services (which is covered in detail in Chapter 14). By clicking the buttons, it will only show the servers registered for that service.

6. If you need to register another server, right-click the Local Server Groups node and select New ➤ Server Registration to bring up a dialog box very similar to the Connect to Server dialog box shown earlier. Go ahead and do this now to familiarize yourself with the New Server Registration dialog box, shown in Figure 2-5. You don't need to register servers to connect to them, but it will make it easier to find any regular servers.

7. As you can see, the only real difference from the Connect to Server dialog box is that the Server Name combo box is empty and there is a new section called Registered Server. In this area, you can give a registration a different name, such as Development Server or User Testing Region, and on top of this give the registration a description. You don't have a server to register, so just click Cancel now. When bringing up the New Server Registration dialog box, you may have noticed an option to create a new server group. Along with using a different name, I suggest you also group your registrations so that you can instantly tell where a server resides.

Figure 2-3. *SQL Server Management Studio graphical interface for SQL Server*

Figure 2-4. *A list of registered servers*

Figure 2-5. *The New Server Registration dialog box*

8. Moving back to SSMS's explorer window below the registered servers, take a look at Object Explorer, which should have been present when you first brought up SSMS. If it isn't there or if it disappears, you can redisplay it by selecting View ➤ Object Explorer or by pressing F8. You will likely use this explorer the most, as it details every object, every security item, and many other areas concerning SQL Server. You can see that SSMS uses nodes (which you expand by clicking the + signs) to keep much of the layout of the Object Explorer (the hierarchy) compact and hidden until needed. Let's go through each of the nodes you see in Figure 2-6 now:

- *Databases*: Holds the system and user databases within the SQL Server you are connected to.

- *Security*: Details the list of SQL Server logins that can connect to SQL Server. You will see more on this in Chapter 4.

- *Server Objects*: Details objects such as backup devices and provides a list of linked servers, where one server is connected to another remote server.

- *Replication*: Shows the details involving data replication from a database on this server to another database (on this or another server) or vice versa.

- *Management*: Details maintenance plans, policy management, data collection, and Database Mail setup, which you will learn more about in Chapter 7, and provides a log of informational and error messages that can be very useful when troubleshooting SQL Server.

- *SQL Server Agent*: Builds and runs tasks within SQL Server at certain times, with details of successes or failures that can be sent to pagers, e-mail, or operators defined within SQL Server. The running of these jobs and the notifications of these failures or successes are dealt with by SQL Server Agent, and the details are found in this node. We will look at this more in Chapter 7, where you will schedule backup jobs.

Figure 2-6. *Object Explorer nodes*

9. Select the topmost node, the server node, in the Object Explorer to see a summary page similar to the one in Figure 2-7, if you opened up the Object Browser summary screen as mentioned previously. This area is known as the documents area. You don't have to be on the top node for this page to be of use, as it will provide a summary of any node within this explorer. This works a bit like folders within Windows Explorer, where you can navigate through each item to get a summary of details of objects within the node. The left column matches the groupings below the node you have selected in Object Explorer, and the right column details how compliant your database is compared to a set of policies defined. You will see policies detailed in Chapter 4.

Figure 2-7. *Summary page*

10. Moving to the menu bar of SSMS, the first item of interest is the View menu option. Three of the first four options on the View menu, shown in Figure 2-8, bring up the two explorer windows, Object Explorer and Registered Servers Explorer, and the summary page we encountered previously. Therefore, if you ever need to close these items to give yourself more screen space, you can reopen them from the menu or with the shortcut keys you see defined. The other remaining option alters the servers displayed in the Registered Servers explorer, where you can switch between Database Engines and Compact Engine databases. The other options on the View menu are as follows:

▨**Note** A Compact Edition database is one that resides on hardware such as PDAs.

- *Template Explorer*: Provides access to code templates. In the examples in this book, we will be building objects using T-SQL. Rather than starting from scratch, we can use code templates that contain the basic code to create these objects.

- *Solution Explorer*: Displays **solutions**, which are convenient groupings of objects, T-SQL, or special programs called stored procedures, among other items.

- *Properties Window*: Displays the set of properties for each object.

- *Bookmark Window*: Allows you to create **bookmarks**, which you place into various locations in your code to allow you to jump quickly to those locations.

- *Toolbox*: Holds a list of objects that are database maintenance tasks, and details where these tasks can be altered.

- *Error List*: Shows errors found in the code you have entered in the editor.

- *Web Browser*: Brings up a web browser within SQL Server, ideal for searching the Web for answers to SQL Server problems for which you may require information.

- *Other Windows*: Allows you to access other windows generated when running T-SQL from Query Editor, which may hold error messages or results from queries.

- *Toolbars*: Brings up toolbars for Query Editor, diagramming the database, and integration with Visual SourceSafe for source control, if they are not opened by default.

- *Full Screen*: Removes title bars and explorer windows, and then maximizes SSMS to show as much of the main pages as possible.

Figure 2-8. *The View menu options*

11. SQL Server has two built-in tools as well as the capability to include other tools when they are launched. These can be accessed through the Tools menu, shown in Figure 2-9, along with the means to customize keyboard commands, show or hide toolbar buttons, and so on, as is the case with other Microsoft products such as Word. The first two options are available outside of SSMS from the Performance Tools sub programs list from the Start menu. These programs are separate from SSMS. In particular, note the following options:

    • *SQL Server Profiler*: There will come a time when you'll wish to monitor SQL Server's performance. This tool will monitor and log events, running code, and so on that you have informed it to check when they happen within SQL Server.

    • *Database Engine Tuning Advisor*: It is possible to take a workload of data and process it through your solution. This advisor can suggest ways to improve the performance of this process.

    • *Options*: This option lets you access different options you can use to set up your SSMS as you like. We will take a look at each of these options in the next section.

Figure 2-9. *The Tools menu options*

12. The final part of SSMS that we will take a look at is the main SSMS toolbar, as you can see in Figure 2-10. Some of the icons, such as the Save icon, will be instantly recognizable, but we will go through each button so that it is clear what they all do.

Figure 2-10. *Main toolbar*

13. In the next section, you will see how you can write code to add objects, work with data, and so on. Clicking the New Query button opens up a new query window, which allows you to do this using the connection already made with SQL Server.

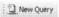

14. Similar to the New Query button, the New Database Engine Query button also creates a new query window. However, it gives you the option of having a different connection to SQL Server through which to run your code. This is a good way of testing code with a different connection to ensure that you cannot see data that should be secure, such as wages, via that connection.

15. Data within a specialized database known as an analysis database allows you to interrogate the data and analyze the information contained within. The three New Analysis Service Query buttons allow you to build different types of analysis queries. I include this information here only for your reference, as analysis databases fall outside the scope of this book.

16. SQL Server editions also include an edition called SQL Server Compact Edition. This allows SQL Server to run on devices such as PDAs. If you have this installed, then clicking the SQL Server Compact Query button will allow a SQL Server Compact query to be run. Again, this book does not cover this particular function further.

17. As with every other Windows-based product, it is possible to open and save files. The Open button (the first one shown in the following image) allows you to search for a T-SQL file. The next two buttons change their function depending on what you are doing, but in the main, the Single Save button gives you the option to save the details of the window that is active in the main documents area of SSMS. The Multiple Save button gives you the option to save all the open tabs in the documents window.

18. The last set of buttons open up explorers and document tabs that we have covered already. From left to right in the following image, these buttons access the Registered Servers Explorer, summary page, Object Explorer, Template Explorer, and Properties window.

Now that we've covered the main areas of SSMS, we'll next take a closer look at the Options area off the Tools menu, as it warrants a more detailed discussion.

Examining SSMS's Options

As you saw earlier, the Tools menu has an Options menu choice. This allows you to choose what options you would like to set as part of the setup for SSMS. We will go through each node and option in this area one at a time, except for the options dealing with Analysis Services, which are not of interest to us just now.

Environment Node

The first node we'll look at is the Environment node, which covers the SSMS environment and how you would like it to look and feel. This contains the General, Fonts and Colors, Keyboard, and Help nodes, which you'll see next.

General Node

The General node, shown in Figure 2-11, contains the following options:

- *At Startup*: This option controls how SSMS behaves when it is started. You have a choice of four options here. It is possible to open Object Explorer after prompting for a connection, open a new query window after prompting for a connection, open both of these after a connection, or open with an empty SSMS and no connection.

- *Hide System Objects in Object Explorer*: In SQL Server, system objects are hidden. This is a good option to have enabled unless you are a database administrator. For example, if you're creating a desktop package that will be rolled out onto developers' desktops, then set this. It won't stop developers from using the system objects, but it will declutter their view.

- *Environment Layout*: The layout can either be defined as tabbed documents (a bit like Excel) or as MDI (a bit like Word).

- *Docked Tool Window Behavior—Close button*: If checked, when you click the close button, only the active document is closed. Unchecked means that all windows will be closed.

- *Docked Tool Window Behavior—Auto Hide button*: You can pin toolboxes or unpin explorers to hide them. Unpinning windows affects only the currently active document.

- *Display NN Files in Recently Used List*: This indicates the number of recently opened files to place under the File menu option.

Figure 2-11. *Environment area, General options*

Fonts and Colors Node

As you might guess, the Fonts and Colors node options, shown in Figure 2-12, affect the fonts and colors for different areas of SSMS. The Display Items list box contains a list of all the different areas that can be set. By selecting one of these items, you can define the color of the foreground and background as well the font type and size.

Figure 2-12. *Environment area, Fonts and Colors options*

Keyboard Node

The Keyboard node section, shown in Figure 2-13, allows you to define fast keys for commands you run often. Any T-SQL stored procedure can be defined. The examples in this book assume you are using the standard keyboard scheme.

Note A **stored procedure** is a set of code that is stored within SQL Server, a bit like a program.

Figure 2-13. *Environment area, Keyboard options*

Help Node

The help system for SQL Server as a whole has been altered: you now have the ability to use not only the help installed on the computer, but also the online help; thus, you have access to the most up-to-date information. Configure the help system through the Help node options shown in Figure 2-14.

Figure 2-14. *Environment area, Help options*

Source Control Node

When creating code or objects, you can integrate a source control system with SQL Server so that changes are immediately stored for safety. For each source control system, it is possible to define a plug-in that will then populate the combo box, as shown in Figure 2-15. You can then use this source control along with source control buttons and menu options.

Figure 2-15. *Source Control options*

Text Editor Node

The Text Editor node contains options that affect how you work with text.

File Extension

Files specific to a particular Microsoft product have their own unique file extension so that they are instantly recognizable to users and can then be linked to the relevant product. These products have different filtering when accessing them through Open from the File menu so that you will only see files with the relevant extension. This also holds true for SQL Server, but it is possible to alter these extensions within the File Extension option, as you see in Figure 2-16, although I strongly recommend that you don't. You'll come across a few of these extensions throughout the book, although the majority are for more advanced work.

Figure 2-16. *Text Editor ➤ File Extension defaults*

All Languages ➤ General

Taking a look at the second option within the Text Editor node, you can see how different text editors' options can be set. The All Languages node sets the options from both the Plain Text and XML nodes below, as shown in Figure 2-17. Of the general options discussed here, the first three are for the XML editor:

- *Auto List Members*: Lists the members, properties, and values available to you when typing.

- *Hide Advanced Members*: Shows more commonly used items.

- *Parameter Information*: Displays the parameters for the current procedure.

- *Enable Virtual Space*: Adds spaces so that comments are placed at a consistent location when using a text editor.

- *Word Wrap*: Specifies text to be wrapped to the next line once you type past the end of the viewing area.

- *Show Visual Glyphs for Word Wrap*: Enabled when word wrap is checked. Shows text glyphs when a line has been word wrapped. This is a logical character that doesn't physically exist, and therefore will not appear on any printouts.

- *Apply Cut or Copy Commands to Blank Lines When There Is No Selection*: Pastes a blank line if this is checked and you "copy" a blank line. If this is unchecked, nothing is inserted.

- *Line Numbers*: Displays line numbers only against the code. This helps when an error occurs and is reported back, because the error message will mention the line number.

- *Enable Single-Click URL Navigation*: When working with data and a URL is displayed, then as the cursor moves over it, the cursor will change to a hand to indicate a URL, and clicking it will open up a browser.

- *Navigation Bar*: Displays a navigation bar at the top of the code editor.

Figure 2-17. *Text Editor ➤ All Languages ➤ General options*

All Languages ➤ Tabs

The Tabs node deals with tabs within editors. As you can see in Figure 2-18, there are only two sections:

- *Indenting*: The first two options are for plain text and XML. When you press Enter, these set whether the new line starts at the leftmost point (None) or at the same point as the preceding line (Block). The Smart option is for XML only and determines whether the new line is tabbed, depending on the context of the XML element.

- *Tab*: This sets the number of characters for a physical tab (via Tab Size) and the number of characters in an intelligent tab, or an indent (via Indent Size). If you want spaces in the tabbing or indentation, then click the Insert Spaces option; otherwise, tabbing will use tabulation characters.

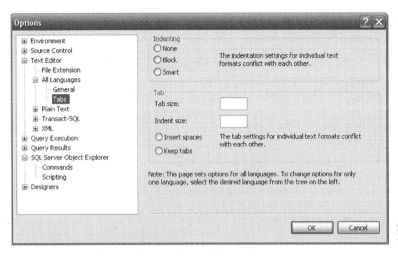

Figure 2-18. *Text Editor ➤ All Languages ➤ Tabs options*

Query Execution Node

The Query Execution node contains options that affect your T-SQL code. You can change the environment in which you write T-SQL and how SSMS interacts with SQL Server when running T-SQL.

SQL Server ➤ General

When we come to running T-SQL code within Query Editor, a number of options affect how it will run, and these are shown in Figure 2-19. The settings are only for SSMS and don't apply to other connections such as a .NET program connecting to the data.

- *SET ROWCOUNT*: Defines the maximum number of rows to return before stopping. A setting of 0 means that every row should be returned. This option is more often defined at the top of your T-SQL code to reduce the number of rows for that query—for example, if you have a large table and you want to see only a few rows as examples.

- *SET TEXTSIZE*: Sets the maximum size of text data that will be seen in the results pane within SSMS.

- *Execution Time-out*: Specifies how long you are prepared for the query to run before forcing it to stop. This can be useful especially in a production environment, when you don't wish a query to take up a large amount of processing time.

- *Batch Separator*: Separates batches of code by a word or character. At present, this is set to GO. Although you could change this, it is best not to, because GO is known universally as a batch separator.

- *By Default, Open New Queries in SQLCMD Mode*: Allows you to use SQLCMD-based keywords and extensions in your queries. We don't look at SQLCMD within this book, but if you want to run code as a batch file, then Books Online can show you how.

Figure 2-19. *Query Execution ➤ SQL Server ➤ General options*

SQL Server ➤ Advanced

This area deals with how SQL Server executes T-SQL code within SSMS, and the options available here are shown in Figure 2-20. In Chapter 3, we go through those options relevant to someone learning SQL Server when creating a database. The only two options not covered in that chapter that you should know are the following:

- *Suppress Provider Message Headers*: Status messages about the query that is running will not show the data provider. Therefore, by selecting this option, you suppress the data provider for SQL Server from being displayed (.NET SqlClient Data Provider).

- *Disconnect After the Query Executes*: After your query has completed, disconnect the connection. This is ideal for situations where you have a limited number of connections or you want to keep the connection count down.

Figure 2-20. *Query Execution ➤ SQL Server ➤ Advanced options*

SQL Server ➤ ANSI

Like the options for the previous area, the options for the ANSI area are discussed in Chapter 3. For now, note the default settings shown in Figure 2-21.

Figure 2-21. *Query Execution ➤ SQL Server ➤ ANSI standard options*

Query Results Node

When you run T-SQL code, the database returns the results to SSMS. The Query Results node is where you can modify how these results will look.

SQL Server ➤ General

These options in the SQL Server area, shown in Figure 2-22, detail how results will be displayed and where they will be saved:

- *Default Destination for Results*: This option defines how you would like to see the results of a query that returns some data.

- *Default Location for Saving Query Results*: This option specifies the default directory for saved results.

- *Play the Windows Default Beep When a Query Batch Completes*: If you wish SQL Server to beep you at the end of a query, check this option, and if you run a lot of queries, be prepared to lose a lot of friends. I would leave this unchecked **unless** you are going to be running a long-term query, which will allow for notification when the query finishes so you don't have to sit and watch it.

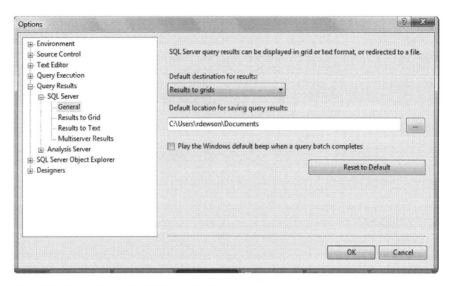

Figure 2-22. *Query Results ➤ SQL Server ➤ General options*

SQL Server ➤ Results to Grid

When we run T-SQL to retrieve data, SSMS can place it within a grid, a bit like in Excel (although it will be read-only), or represent it as text, like in Notepad (also read-only). You can also save the data to a file, which is based on Results to Text options. The Results to Grid options, shown in Figure 2-23, cover how the results will look if we are outputting to a grid:

- *Include the Query in the Result Set*: The T-SQL used to run the query is placed prior to the results.

- *Include Column Headers When Copying or Saving the Results*: If you want to copy information from the results—for example, to place it within an e-mail—then selecting this option will include the column headers as well as the results.

- *Quote strings containing list separators when saving .csv results*: When you return results to a grid and then right-click and select Save Results As, the resulting .csv file will place quotation marks around text columns that contain commas.

- *Discard Results After Execution*: Once the query executes, any results displayed will be immediately discarded at the end, therefore leaving nothing to display.

- *Display Results in a Separate Tab*: Instead of the results appearing below the query, they can instead be in their own tab, giving more space for a larger set of results to be displayed.

- *Maximum Characters Retrieved*: This option defines the maximum amount of data to be displayed in a single cell for results.

Figure 2-23. *Query Results ➤ SQL Server ➤ Results to Grid options*

SQL Server ➤ Results to Text

These other results options, shown in Figure 2-24, affect how results are displayed when they are in text format:

- *Output Format*: This combo box presents you with five different formatting options: Column Aligned, Comma Delimited, Tab Delimited, Space Delimited, and Custom Delimiter. These different options allow you to set your output delimiter so that you can import your data into other systems.

- *Include Column Headers in the Result Set*: Uncheck this if you just wish the results. Again, this is ideal for when you are passing data on to other systems.

- *Include the Query in the Result Set*: The T-SQL used to run the query is placed prior to the results.

- *Scroll As Results Are Received*: As rows are returned, if they extend past the end of the page, then the results are scrolled so that the last row of data is displayed.

- *Right Align Numeric Values*: Any numeric values are aligned to the right instead of the left.

- *Discard Results After Query Executes*: Once the query executes, any results displayed will be immediately discarded at the end, therefore leaving nothing to display.

- *Display Results in a Separate Tab*: Instead of the results appearing below the query, they can instead be in their own tab, giving more space for a larger set of results to be displayed.

- *Maximum Number of Characters Displayed in Each Column*: This option defines the maximum amount of data to be displayed in a single cell for results.

Figure 2-24. *Query Results ➤ SQL Server ➤ Results to Text options*

SQL Server ➤ Multiserver Results

I don't cover how to deal with multiserver connections, but the Multiserver Results option allows you to define how you want the results to look.

SQL Server Object Explorer ➤ Commands

The first option defines the number of rows to return when viewing the Audit logs. Once you've defined your tables or views, you can right-click to open a pop-up window, then either edit or display a predefined number of rows. This is an ideal option, as it means that SQL Server doesn't return either the full set of data or a set of data to cache defined by its own logic. You are in control of the volume of data. I would keep the options set to the default. Figure 2-25 shows the default settings.

Figure 2-25. *The number of rows to return as default when using SSMS*

SQL Server Object Explorer ➤ Scripting

As you progress through the book, there will be several times when you will be asked to, or have the option to, script what you are doing. This means that if you are creating a database or a table or are dealing with one of many other areas, you can output what you have been completing graphically to T-SQL code in a script. These options, shown in Figure 2-26, detail how you want the script to be generated:

- *Delimit Individual Statements*: Each T-SQL statement is superseded with the batch separator, so that each statement runs in its own batch.

- *Include Descriptive Headers*: This option places a short descriptive header at the top of the script. This normally contains details such as the date and time that the generation took place and the name of the object, among other details.

- *IncludeVarDecimal*: This feature will be removed in a future version of SQL Server. However, this option will allow decimal datatypes to be defined as variable in length.

- *Script Change Tracking*: Change tracking is new to SQL Server 2008 and is used to track what changes have been made to rows of data. By setting this option on, you define the script to be built so that any table with change tracking on will have the T-SQL code to do the same.

- *Script for Server Version*: This option defines which version of SQL Server the script should be aimed at.

- *Script full-text catalogs*: We don't go into detail on full-texting your tables in this book, but if you wish the generated script to include the catalogs that hold the full-texting details, this option will do that when set to True.

- *Script USE <database>*: If you need to prefix every action with a USE statement that defines which database the script should run against, set this to True.

- *Generate Script for Dependent Objects*: It is possible when generating a script to only script some of the objects. Use this option if you wish to ensure that the objects you choose and any other objects that use these are also scripted.

- *Include IF NOT EXISTS Clause*: At times, you will be creating scripts that are for creating objects. The IF NOT EXISTS clause tests if the database object exists, and if it does, it removes it before creating the object.

- *Schema Qualify Object Names*: Every object belongs to a schema, as you'll learn in Chapter 4. This option allows this grouping of objects to exist.

- *Script Data Compression option*s: It is possible to compress your data, which will reduce the space used on hard drives. You may think that in today's times, with huge hard drives, that compressing data is not required, but with vast volumes of data, and many server rooms at capacity, this can be a very useful option. Setting this to True will include any compression options within your script.

- *Script Extended Properties*: It is possible to place extended properties—in other words, properties over and above the standard—on objects. Set this option to True to place these properties in the script.

- *Script Permissions*: This option places the permissions against each object in the script. It then defines who can access which object.

- *Convert User-Defined Data Types*: It is possible to create your own data types. We look at data types in Chapter 5. User-defined data types are built from the base data types. Setting this option to True converts any user-defined data type for a table to be put back to the SQL Server base type.

- *Generate SET ANSI PADDING Commands*: When scripting a CREATE TABLE statement, surround the command with the ANSI padding commands. ANSI padding details how data is held when it doesn't fill the size defined for the data type.

- *Include Collation*: You saw collation when creating an instance of SQL Server. This option allows you to say whether you wish to include collation in your script.

- *Include IDENTITY Property*: This is an option for columns in a table. You can autogenerate a number each time a row is added. You will see this in action in Chapter 7. Setting this option to True will include definitions for the IDENTITY property within your script.

- *Schema Qualify Foreign Key References*: In Chapter 4, you will see what schemas are. This option places the schema qualifier as a prefix for table references for foreign keys.

- *Script Bound Defaults and Rules*: This is not covered in this book. Leave it set to False.

- *Script CHECK Constraints*: You can use a check constraint to define a valid set or range of values for a column in a table. Set this to True for this to be scripted.

- *Script Defaults (and Onwards)*: You will see all these objects discussed throughout the book. Setting these to True ensures that they are scripted.

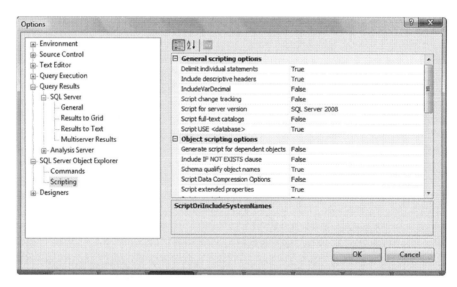

Figure 2-26. *Scripting options*

Designers ➤ Table and Database Designers

As you will see in Chapter 6 when we diagram the database we will be creating, it is possible for certain actions to occur automatically. These options, shown in Figure 2-27, determine what will happen:

- *Override Connection String Time-Out Value for Table Designer*: You have a certain amount of time to apply table designer updates. It is possible to override this by selecting this option.

- *Auto Generate Change Scripts*: In the designer, when you change a table or a relationship, for example, it is possible for the designer to generate a script of the changes made. This is ideal for when you create changes and need to ability to replicate what you have performed in another environment.

- *Warn on Null Primary Keys*: In a designer, if you have defined a primary key that can have NULL values, this option will produce a warning. This is covered in Chapter 6, when you will be looking at keys and indexes.

- *Warn About Difference Detection*: This option produces a warning when a difference has been found on the work you have been completing.

- *Warn About Tables Affected*: This option produces a warning for any tables affected by a change. Changing something in a diagram may affect other tables. This option allows you to see those effects.

- *Diagram Options*: *Default Table View*: This option determines how a table is shown in the designer. By default, it shows the column names only.

- *Diagram Options*: *Launch Add Table Dialog on New Diagram*: When you create a new diagram, selecting this option prompts you to select which tables you want to add to the diagram.

Figure 2-27. *Table and Database Designers options*

Designers ➤ Maintenance Plans

In Chapter 7, we will be taking a look backing up and restoring the database. It is possible to build a maintenance plan graphically to do this sort of task and other maintenance tasks, such as reindexing and so on, as you can see in Figure 2-28. When building a graphical maintenance plan, it is possible to create actions automatically when you double-click them in the designer toolbox. When you double-click a shape, it is possible to make a connection to the new shape from the shape you have selected in your designer. You will see this demonstrated when we create a maintenance plan.

That completes our look at the options that are relevant to us. The next section discusses the Query Editor within the documents area of SSMS.

Figure 2-28. *Maintenance Plans options*

Query Editor

As we progress through the book, the creation of objects, the manipulation of data, and the execution of code will be shown either by using the graphical interface and options that Object Explorer provides or by writing code using T-SQL. To write code, we need a free-form text editor so that we can type anything we need. Luckily, SSMS provides just such an editor as a tabbed screen within the document view on the right-hand side. This is known as a Query Editor, and it can be found when you click New Query of the main toolbar or by selecting File ➤ New ➤ Database Engine Query.

We discussed some of the options that affect the Query Editor, such as how text is entered and how results from running the T-SQL code are displayed, in the preceding section. There is not a great deal to say about the editor itself, as it really is a free-form method of entering commands and statements for SQL Server to execute. However, the Query Editor has a toolbar that is worth covering at this point in time. Figure 2-29 shows this Query Editor toolbar.

Figure 2-29. *Query Editor toolbar*

The first three buttons, as shown in the following image, work with connections to the server. The first button requests a connection to the server if one doesn't currently exist, the second disconnects the current server connection, and the third allows you to change the connection you are using.

The next item is a combo box that lists all the databases in the server you are currently connected to. If you wish a query to run against a different database, you can select it here. The database the code will execute against, providing you have permissions, is the database that is displayed.

The next buttons are concerned with executing the code entered in the Query Editor. The red exclamation mark and the Execute button execute the code. The blue tick parses the code but doesn't actually run it. Parsing the code doesn't find every error that could occur, but it ensures that the syntax is correct. The last option is a grayed-out button that turns red when code is executing. If you would like to send a cancel command to SQL Server, then press this button. This may not always cancel the query instantly, depending on what is executing and whether your server is local or remote. There will be a delay in sending the command while SQL Server "pauses" to receive the command.

The next two buttons help you analyze the T-SQL query for optimization. We won't cover optimization within this book.

Rather than typing T-SQL code by hand, we can use a type of wizard that allows a query to be built up by selecting tables and columns via check boxes and so on. Pressing the button shown in the following image brings up this wizard, known as the Query Design Editor, which you will see in action in Chapter 9.

The following button allows you to work with code templates. Templates feature the basics of commands or actions. They have options that act as default values. Pressing this button brings up a dialog box to change the values in each of a template's parameters.

The next set of buttons deals with the query. The first two place details on how your code was executed and statistics about the code within the output. The third button runs your code as if it were run by SQLCMD, which is a command-line utility for executing SQL batches. These options are not covered within this book.

The first two buttons shown in the following image affect how the results from the query are displayed, either as text or as a grid, respectively. The third button sends results to a file.

Finally, we can comment out lines of code by clicking the first button shown in the next image, or we can uncomment code by clicking the second button. The third and fourth buttons will place or remove indentations of code. All of these buttons work only on currently selected lines of code.

Summary

SSMS is a tool for working with SQL Server that you will see in action throughout this book, whether we're working with the graphical interface or using Query Editor to write T-SQL code. As you learned in this chapter, the main areas of the tool are the Registered Servers Explorer, the Object Explorer, and the main documents window that will contain graphical representations of objects in the database.

Database Design and Creation

Now that you've installed SQL Server and examined the main tools you'll use as a SQL Server developer or administrator, it's almost time to start building the ApressFinancial database solution. However, you can't do this yet because you still don't know what the database will hold. At this point in time, all the information you have so far is that you'll be building a database to hold some financial transactions for a personal or corporate financial tool. You'll gear this database toward a financial tool that a corporation might use, because SQL Server can be scaled from one user to thousands of users very easily. The next step is to gather more information about the requirements of the solution and about what information is required to be stored in the database. Once the information gathering stage is complete, you'll then be able to create the database within SQL Server 2008. Don't get too hung up on the example throughout the book. Its main intent is to demonstrate to you how to build a database solution from the ground up.

The design of a database solution is not a simple task; it requires a great deal of work. This chapter will provide you with insight into the vast area that is database design. Armed with this information, you'll proceed through arranging the data so that retrieval is as efficient as possible (this is referred to as normalizing the data) and ensuring that data duplication is minimal or, ideally, that no data duplication exists. You'll also need to know how the system and the data within it will be used on a day-to-day basis. Finally, you'll need to know what type of system is being built—for instance, whether it will receive instant data updates or just be used to analyze already defined data. Once the design is complete, building a database solution will be a much smoother process. A good design will ensure you've gathered all the information you need to build the correct tables with the correct information without duplication.

Although the methods and processes involved with the design may not meet the needs of every organization and its methods, this chapter will present an overview of the processes involved, and it will show you how to build up information and ensure that the design is well-thought-out. This chapter will cover the following topics:

- What a database is, what it consists of, and where it is stored

- How to define the type of system: transactional or analytical

- How to collect data about the current system and seek out information about the new system

- How to create a database through SQL Server Management Studio, a wizard, or a Query Editor window, and how to set database options in a Query Editor window

- How to review the database details

- How to remove a database using SQL Server Management Studio and a Query Editor window

---

▨Note No specific formal design techniques will be used in this chapter's exercise, as this is not a book specifically on database design. However, the processes—both physical and logical—to get to the final design of the database will be the same.

Defining a Database

A **database** is a container for objects that not only store data, but also enable data storage and retrieval to operate in a secure and safe manner. A SQL Server 2008 database can hold the following (although when a database is first created, some of this information has not yet been built):

- **Table** definitions
- **Columns** within those **tables**, which make up **rows** of data
- **Programs** (either **stored procedures** written using *T-SQL* or **assemblies**) used to access or manipulate the data
- **Indexes**, which are used to speed up the retrieval of data
- **Views**, which are specialized ways of looking at the actual data
- **Functions**, which are repetitive tasks that can be applied to rows of data

The preceding list contains a fair number of technical terms, so let's take a few moments to look at their definitions:

- *Tables*: These are where data is kept within the database. A database must contain at least one table to be of use, although you can have a database with no user tables and only system tables. **System tables** are special tables that SQL Server uses to help it work with the database. These tables contain information within rows and columns, much like in Excel, but they have a great deal more power than cells within Excel. **Temporary tables**—another type of database table—can take several different forms.

- *Columns*: These provide a definition of each single item of information that builds up to a table definition. A column is made up of cells that all hold data, much like a column in Excel. Unlike in Excel, though, where each cell can hold a different type of data, a column within a SQL Server table is restricted to what the data within it relates to, the type of data it will hold, and how much information can be stored in it. Each table must have at least one column, although the column doesn't need to contain any information.

- *Rows*: A row is made up of one cell from every column defined for the table. There can be any number of rows in a table; you are limited only by your disk space, the amount of disk space that you defined as the maximum in your database creation definition, or the amount of disk space on your server. A row will define a single unit of information, such as a user's bank account details or a product on an e-commerce site. Rows are also called **records**.

- *Stored procedures*: When it comes to requiring a program to manipulate or work with data, or perform the same data-intensive task repeatedly, it's often better to store this code in a stored procedure. Stored procedures contain one or more T-SQL statements, which are compiled and ready to be executed when required. Stored procedures are permanently stored in the database, ready for use at any time.

- *T-SQL statements*: A T-SQL statement is a program statement that SQL Server can use to work with your data.

- *Assemblies*: These arrived with SQL Server 2005. Assemblies are similar to stored procedures, in that they can be used to manipulate or work with data, but they are used more for procedural logic, as you might find in a .NET program. An assembly can be more than a replacement for a stored procedure and can take on many different guises—for example, you can also build data types using an assembly.

- *Indexes*: These can be regarded as predefined lists of information that can inform the database how the data is physically sorted and stored, or they can be used by SQL Server to find rows of data quickly using information supplied by a T-SQL query and matching this information to data within columns. An index consists of one or more columns from the table it is defined for, but it is not possible for an index to cover more than one table. An index in SQL Server is very much like the index of a book, which is used to locate a piece of information faster than looking through the book page by page.

- *Views*: These can be thought of as virtual tables. Views can contain information combined from several tables and can present a more user-friendly interface to the data. Views can also add a great deal of security to an application, but they do give reduced functionality over the use of stored procedures or direct access to the tables. Views can also be indexed to speed processing of data within.

- *Functions*: A function is similar to a stored procedure, but it takes information one row at a time or produces information one row at a time as you work through the rows of data you are processing. For example, you would use a stored procedure to produce output to create a statement, but you would use a function to go through each transaction one at a time to calculate interest on a daily basis.

Also within every database is a set of system tables that SQL Server uses to maintain that database. These tables hold information about every column, information about every user, and many other pieces of information (i.e., metadata). System-table security in SQL Server 2008 is such that you cannot access these tables directly—only through views. There is no need to investigate system tables at this point, as their data can't be modified and the information they produce is useful only for working with advanced functionality.

Prebuilt Databases Within SQL Server

Several databases are installed and displayed when SQL Server is first installed. This section explores each of these databases, so that you'll know what each does and feel comfortable when you come across them outside of this book.

Let's first look at the most important database in SQL Server: the master database. We'll then cover the tempdb, model, msdb, and AdventureWorks/AdventureWorksDW databases.

master

master is the most important database in SQL Server, so I must start off with a warning:

Directly alter this database at your own peril!

There should be no reason to go into any of the system views within this database and alter the records or column information directly. There are system functions that allow a constructive alteration of any of the data in an orderly fashion, and these are the only approaches you should use to alter the master database.

The master database is at the heart of SQL Server, and if it should become corrupted, there is a very good chance that SQL Server will not work correctly. The master database contains the following crucial information:

- All logins, or roles, that the user IDs belong to
- Every system configuration setting (e.g., data sorting information, security implementation, default language)
- The names of and information about the databases within the server
- The location of databases
- How SQL Server is initialized
- Specific system tables holding the following information (this list is not exhaustive):

  - How the cache is used
  - Which character sets are available
  - A list of the available languages
  - System error and warning messages
  - Special SQL Server objects called **assemblies** (tables within every database that deal with SQL Server objects and therefore are not specific to the master database)

The master database is the security guard of SQL Server, and it uses the preceding information to ensure that everything is kept in check.

▧**Note**   It is crucial that you take a regular backup of the master database. Ensure that doing so is part of your backup strategy. Backups are covered in more detail in Chapter 7.

---

tempdb

The tempdb database is—as its name suggests—a temporary database whose lifetime is the duration of a SQL Server session; once SQL Server stops, the tempdb database is lost. When SQL Server starts up again, the tempdb database is re-created, fresh and new, and ready for use. There is more to this process, but before we delve into that, you first need to know what the tempdb database is used for.

A database can hold data, and that data can be held in many tables. You use commands and functions to retrieve and manipulate that data. However, there may be times when you wish to temporarily store a certain set of data for processing at a later time—for example, when you pass data from one stored procedure to another that is going to run right after the first one. One option is to store that data within a table within the tempdb database. Such a table could be thought of as a "permanent" temporary table, as it will exist until it is specifically deleted or until tempdb is re-created on a SQL Server restart. Another type of temporary table that can exist is a temporary table created within a stored procedure or query. This type of table will also be placed within the tempdb database, although its lifetime will only last until all users of the table finish. We'll look at both of these types of tables in Chapter 11 when we examine advanced T-SQL. Both of these scenarios are fine, as long as the tempdb database is not refreshed. If it is, then your data will be gone, and you will need to rebuild it.

You may be thinking that this is not an ideal solution. After all, wouldn't it be wonderful if temporary information could be stored somewhere outside of the database? Well, that's not really where tempdb would be used. It really should be thought of only as transitional storage space.

Another reason tempdb is refreshed is that not only is it available for a developer to use, but also SQL Server itself uses tempdb. Actually, SQL Server uses tempdb all the time, and when you reinitialize SQL Server, it will want to know that any temporary work it was dealing with is cleaned out. After all, there could have been a problem with this temporary work that caused you to restart the service in the first place.

Being just like any other database, tempdb has size restrictions, and you must ensure that it is big enough to cope with your applications and any temporary information stored within it. As you read through the next sections, you will see that a database has a minimum and a maximum size. tempdb is no exception to this, and you should ensure that its settings provide for expansion so it can grow as required.

■**Caution** Because tempdb has a limited size, you must take care when you use it that it doesn't get filled with records in tables from rogue procedures that indefinitely create tables with too many records. If this were to happen, not only would your process stop working, but also the whole server could stop functioning and therefore impact everyone on that server!

As indicated in the first paragraph of this section, there's more to say about tempdb's refresh process, which we'll examine in the next section.

model

Whenever you create a database, as you'll do shortly in this chapter, it has to be modeled on a predefined set of criteria. For example, if you want all your databases to have a specific initial size or to have a specific set of information, you would place this information into the model database, which acts as a template database for further databases. If you want all databases to have a specific table within them, for example, then you would put this table in the model database.

The model database is used as the basis of the tempdb database. Thus, you need to think ahead and take some care if you decide to alter the model database, as any changes will be mirrored within the tempdb database.

msdb

msdb is another crucial database within SQL Server, as it provides the necessary information to run jobs to SQL Server Agent.

SQL Server Agent is a Windows service in SQL Server that runs any scheduled jobs that you set up (e.g., jobs that contain backup processing). A **job** is a process defined in SQL Server that runs automatically without any manual intervention to start it.

As with tempdb and model, you should not directly amend this database, and there is no real need to do so. Many other processes use msdb. For example, when you create a backup or perform a restore, msdb is used to store information about these tasks.

AdventureWorks/AdventureWorksDW

AdventureWorks and AdventureWorksDW are the example databases found in SQL Server if you selected to install them during setup. These databases are based on a manufacturing company that produces bicycles. They exemplify the new features in SQL Server 2008 as well as demonstrate the features that arrived in SQL Server 2005, such as Reporting Services, CLR functionality, and many others, in a simple, easy-to-follow way.

The following excerpt from the Microsoft documentation provides a concise overview of what the AdventureWorks databases are about:

> *Adventure Works Cycles, the fictitious company on which the AdventureWorks sample databases are based, is a large, multinational manufacturing company. The company manufactures and sells metal and composite bicycles to North American, European, and Asian commercial markets. While its base operation is located in Bothell, Washington with 290 employees, several regional sales teams are located throughout their market base.*

The example databases are not meant for novice SQL Server developers, although you'll have no problems with them after you learn the basics of SQL Server.

Now that you know what databases are in SQL Server, let's start building one! We'll start by deciding what type of database to create, depending on what we'll use it for.

Choosing the Database System Type

Before we can design a database, we have to decide whether the system will be an **Online Transaction Processing** (OLTP) system or an **Online Analytical Processing** (OLAP) system. We could find this out prior to our first meeting with the users, or even during the first meeting, but the choice of OLTP or OLAP will probably be indicated in the initial proposal.

Before we make the decision, we need to understand these two key types of systems.

OLTP

An OLTP system provides instant updates of data. There is a good chance that an OLTP database system has a separate user front end written in a .NET language such as Visual Basic .NET (VB .NET), C#, or ASP.NET. This user front end calls through to the database and instantly updates any changes a user has made to the underlying data.

OLTP systems require many considerations to ensure they're fast, reliable, and can keep the data integrity intact. When you design an OLTP system, it's crucial that you get not only the database structure right, but also where the data physically resides. It's common to find that OLTP systems are normalized to third normal form (more on what this term means later in the chapter), although this may not happen in every case. By normalizing your data, you will aid the achievement of one of the main goals of an OLTP system: keeping data updates as short as possible. When you normalize your data by removing redundant or duplicate columns, you should ensure that the data to be written is as compact as possible. In many OLTP systems, normalization is king.

Backups

Many OLTP systems are in use 24 hours a day, 7 days a week. The high frequency of changes in such a system's data means that backing up the database is a necessary and mandatory task.

It is possible to back up a database while SQL Server is in use, although it is best to perform a backup when SQL Server is either not in use or when there will be a small amount of activity updating the data taking place. The ideal time frame might be in the middle of the night or even during a break period.

Whenever you decide to perform a backup, it's crucial that you constantly monitor and check it within an OLTP system to see that the system is still performing as desired. You would not be the first person to find that what you thought was a valid backup that could be restored in a disaster situation was in fact corrupt, incomplete, or just not happening. Therefore, periodically take a backup from production and reload it in to a secure development area just to confirm that it works.

Indexes

Speed is essential to a successful OLTP system. You should see a higher number of indexes within an OLTP system as compared to an OLAP system, with these indexes used not only to help relate data from one table to another, but also to allow fast access to rows within tables themselves.

■**Note** Chapter 6 covers how to build indexes, how indexes work, and how to manage indexes within your solutions.

OLAP

When considering an OLTP system, you must keep in mind that an update to the database could happen at any moment in time, and that update must be reflected within the database instantly. It is also crucial that the system performs many updates simultaneously, and that it does not corrupt any data when it does so.

An OLAP system is designed with the premise that the data remains fairly static with infrequent updates. These updates could be every night, weekly, monthly, or any other time variant as long as updates aren't happening on a frequent basis, like in an OLTP system. As the name "Online Analytical Processing" suggests, in this system a large amount of the processing involves analysis of existing data. There should be little or no updating of that data—ostensibly only when the data within the analysis is found to be incorrect or, as mentioned previously, when more data is being applied for analysis. Backing up the data will probably take place only as a "final action," after the database has had changes applied to it. There is no need to make it a regular occurrence.

Systems designed for OLAP sometimes do not follow any design standards or normalization techniques, and most certainly have fewer indexes than an OLTP system. You tend to see no normalization in an OLAP system, as it is easier to take data and to slice and dice it without having to bring in data from a normalized table. There will be few or no updates taking place in an OLAP system, so performing transactions and keeping them compact aren't concerns. Most OLAP systems will contain no normalization. Quite often, you'll find one or two large flat tables—rather than several tables related together—and therefore as there are fewer relationships, there will be fewer indexes.

■**Note** OLAP systems are also known as **data warehouses**, although data warehousing is only one part of the overall OLAP system design. Put simply, a data warehouse is the database that holds the information used within the OLAP system.

Example System Choice

So, when you take into consideration all of the information presented in the preceding sections, it is fairly obvious that although the data updates will be relatively infrequent in our example system (in other words, only when a financial transaction occurs or a statement is generated), there will be updates occurring online with instant results expected. Therefore, our system will be an OLTP system.

Gathering the Data

One of the first things you should do before building a database is find out what information the database system has to hold and also how that information should be stored (e.g., numerical or text, length, etc.). To achieve this goal, you'll perform a data-gathering exercise, which could involve talking with those people who are the owners of the system and those who will be using the system.

For larger systems, you would hold several meetings, each of which would pinpoint one area of the system to discuss and research. Even then, several meetings may be spent going back and discussing each area. You could also conduct interviews, distribute questionnaires, or even just observe any existing processes in action, all in an effort to gather as much information as possible about the database and how it will be used.

The key indicator of whether or not a database solution is successful is not found so much in the building of the system, but rather in the information-gathering process before the first line of code is actually written. If you're working off of an incorrect piece of information, or you're missing an element that might be crucial to the final solution, then already the system is flawed. Involving the users as much as possible at the earliest stage and then including them as the design progresses should result in a significant reduction of errors and missing parts in the final product.

For our example financial program, the first people we want to talk to are the owners of the data that will be displayed. These are the people in the banking department who handle checks, cash withdrawals, credit card transactions, and so forth, and also those people who handle the purchase and sale of stock shares, unit trusts, life insurance policies, and so on. These people will know what documentation or statements are sent to which customers, as well as the information those statements contain. In addition, these people will likely have a good idea about how customers may want to reconcile these statements, and also what data will be allowed to be downloaded and inserted into your SQL Server database.

At the first meeting, we examine all the documentation to see what information is stored in the current system. We find out at the meeting that the current system sends out different statements—one statement for the customer's current account and a separate statement for each financial product the customer owns. When we examine the statements, we focus on the information each contains that we need to capture to produce a similar statement. This could be not only customer-related information, but also regulatory statements.

With the information from all the documentation in hand, we can start discussions about what is required from the system we are to build. Obviously, a great deal of information is discussed in these meetings, some of which is useful and some not. Make sure that the discussions are recorded in the order in which the people present make points and not in "logical" order. This simulates meetings where people "remember" items that have to be catered for, where one point raised may make someone remember a point elsewhere.

Out of our initial discussions, we note the following points:

1. The software must be able to handle working with more than one product. The main product is a current checking account that a bank or a single user might use to hold banking details. The system also must be able to manage by-products such as loans, life insurance policies, and car insurance policies, and it should be able to record any trading of shares on the stock market.

2. Statements are produced on a monthly basis or at any time the customer requests them from the system. If a customer requests a statement within the month, there will still be a statement produced for that month.

3. Interest accrues daily on accounts that are in credit and is subtracted daily from overdrawn accounts.

4. Annual, monthly, or single-premium products can be held for a customer or held by a customer in a standalone version of the system. We need to know when to start and stop collecting payments, and we also need to determine which products we send out a reminder for (e.g., a notice to let a customer know her car insurance policy is up for renewal).

5. If a collection for a product fails, the system needs to recognize this so the amount can be collected the next time a collection is due.

6. Each product will have its own statement, but only banking statements will be produced on request.

7. Trading of stock shares is allowed, so the system needs to record and display the current value for a customer's specific share at any time.

Notice how the information in this list is in no set order, as this is how information tends to come out. Also notice that there is also a little bit of duplication of information in points 2 and 6; if this is not realized and understood, it could cause problems.

Note This is the only data-gathering exercise performed for our example database. The information gathered here should be cross-checked later in the design phase with the users, although this is beyond the scope of this book.

Determining the Information to Store in the Database

Using the notes we took in the previous section, we'll now try to find every area each point has an interest in. Looking at the list of areas that require information to be recorded and stored within our database, it's clear we need to arrange them in some sort of order. We're still looking at our solution from a logical viewpoint, and we're not ready to start building anything in SQL Server yet.

First off, let's scan through the points listed and try to group the information into specific related areas. The list items are numbered, so we'll be able to easily demonstrate the groupings. The following list shows some initial groupings and reasons for them:

- Financial products
  - 1: We are dealing with more than one product. We need to record each product.
  - 2: Statements will be produced for each product, and specific product information for those statements will be recorded here, such as the name of the product.
  - 4: We need to record what type of premium is associated with this product.
  - 5: This point deals with a financial product's premium collection.
  - 6: This point deals again with statement production.
- Customers
  - 2: Customers can request statements.
  - 3: We need to record the amount of interest for a customer.
  - 4: A list of the different products associated with each customer is required.
  - 7: For each share, we need to keep a current value.
- Customer addresses
  - 2: We need each customer's address in order to send a statement.
  - 6: As with point 2, we need the customer's address to send a statement.
- Shares
  - 1: We trade shares on the stock market; therefore, we need to record share information.
  - 7: We need to keep a given share's value.

- Transactions

  - 2: A list of transactions is required for statement production.

  - 4: Regular and ad hoc premiums have to be recorded.

  - 5: We need to record failed transaction collection.

  - 6: Statements will be produced for each product.

These five distinct groups could translate into five distinct tables within our proposed database. At this point in the logical design process, we would base our design on these five tables. From here, it is then possible to start examining the information that should go into these logical tables. There might be duplication of data with columns in the "wrong" table, and the potential for multiple columns to hold "similar" information or the same column in more than one table.

Let's look at the list points in turn in the following sections and examine what information should be stored in each "table." The information listed in the sections that follow is taken from the discussion with the users, and a list of the columns is supplied that may initially form the basis of the tables. Each column has a description, so when we go back to the users, they'll understand the purpose of the columns. Also at this stage, we'll add columns to hold any identifiers for finding the records; in the following sections, these are denoted with (**K**). These are potentially our keys, which we'll cover in more detail later in the "Building Relationships" section of this chapter.

Financial Products

The aim of this table is to hold the different products the company sells. From bank accounts to life insurance, all products will be held here. This table will be used when producing statements and creating transactions when the user's balance changes—for example, when buying further shares:

- *Financial Product ID (K)*: This is a unique identifier.

- *Financial Product Name*: This is the name of the product, such as checking account, share, loan, and so forth.

- *Frequency of Payment*: For each product, this indicates how often payments are collected for those products that require it, such as a loan, a regular savings account, and so on.

Customers

This table will hold customer details, such as the customer's products and balances. To clarify and reiterate, there will be items currently within this table that will no longer reside within it once we normalize the data. For example, you will see an attribute for "Account Numbers for Each Product." When we proceed through normalization, you will see how attributes such as this are "moved:"

- *Customer ID (K)*: This is a unique ID for each customer.

- *Financial Product Balance*: This is the current balance of each product.

- *Title*: This is the customer's title (Mr., Ms., etc.).

- *First Name*: This is the customer's first name.

- *Last Name*: This is the customer's last name.

- *Address*: This is the customer's address.

- *Account Numbers for Each Product*: This is the account number of each product the customer owns.

- *Financial Products Details*: This contains details of each financial product the customer owns.

Customer Addresses

This table will not exist, as we will get this information from a third-party address database.

Shares

This table will hold the details of each stock share, such as its current price and its price history:

- *Share Price ID (K)*: This is a unique ID for each share.
- *Share Name*: This is the name of the share.
- *Current Price*: This is the current price of the share.
- *Previous Price*: This contains previous prices of the share.
- *Price Date*: This is the date the price was set at this level.
- *Stock Market Ticker ID*: This is the ID for this share on the stock market.

Transactions

This table will hold the details of each financial transaction that takes place for each product.

- *Financial Transaction ID (K)*: This is a unique ID for each financial transaction.
- *Customer ID*: This is the customer's unique identifier, as defined in the "Customers" section earlier.
- *Date of the Transaction*: This is the date the transaction took place.
- *Financial Product*: This is a link to the financial products table.
- *Amount*: This is the amount the transaction is for.
- *Debit/Credit*: This flag denotes whether the transaction is a debit or a credit.

External and Ignored Information

At this point, we have a first draft of the logical tables and attributes, but there are still no relationships between these tables. There is one more piece of information that we need to know, which concerns information not recorded, as it won't be included within this database.

The example database will not hold every item of information that is required to make the system complete. This is to keep the example simple and to avoid having extra tables that will not be used within the book's exercises. However, there may be other times when you may wish to implement only some of the tables—for example, when performing a viability study (in other words, when you're building part of a system to prove the viability of an idea). Or perhaps there are third-party tools available that can fill in the gaps.

For example, a system might use an external addressing system, and instead of holding all customer addresses within the system, it may use a cross-reference ID. A table could also exist to hold all of the financial transactions for products not covered where specialized tables are required, such as for company pension plans.

Next, let's move on to consider relationships between the tables in the database.

Building Relationships

Much like people, databases can be temperamental creatures and need a bit of TLC. Good relationships can provide this kind of care and attention.

At the moment, the tables in our example database are essentially single, unrelated items. Of course, they have columns with the same name in different tables, but there is nothing tying them together. This is where defining relationships between the tables comes in. Binding the tables together in this way ensures that changes in one table do not cause data in another table to become invalid.

Using Keys

A **key** is a way of identifying a record in a database table. We can use keys to build relationships between tables because a key refers to a whole record—a property we can exploit when working with columns that, for example, have the same name in different tables. Using a key as a shortcut, we can make the link between the two very easily. Keys can also uniquely identify a record in a table when that is an important part of the database's design.

A key can be defined on a single column if that's enough to identify the record, or it can be defined on more than one column if not. The sections that follow introduce the three kinds of keys you can use in a database: primary, foreign/referencing, and candidate/alternate. We'll also look at using a SQL Server method called a constraint instead of a primary key.

Primary Key

The **primary key** is probably the most important key type. First and foremost, the column (or columns) on which the primary key is defined must only contain unique values. A primary key cannot be defined on a column, or a sequence of columns, that does not return a single row. To this end, it is not possible to define a primary key for any columns that allow NULL values. A further restraint is that a table may have only one primary key.

A primary key can be used to link data from one table to data from another. For instance, in our example database, we have two tables: one holding customers and another holding customer banking transactions. We define a primary key on the customers table on the customer ID that is generated uniquely each time a new customer record is inserted. This is then used to link to the many records within the banking transactions table, to return all the transactions for that customer ID. The link between these two tables is the customer ID, which as previously mentioned is defined as a primary key in the customers table.

Later on, you'll see how to join tables together and define a relationship between them. A join and a relationship essentially mean the same thing: a logical link between two or more tables that can be defined through a specific column or set of columns between the tables.

Foreign/Referencing Key

There will be times when you have two or more tables linked together in a relationship, as demonstrated in the previous section's example, where the link between the customers and transactions tables is the customer ID column. This column returns a unique row in the customers table; hence, it is defined as the primary key of the customers table. However, there has to be a corresponding **foreign** (or **referencing**) **key** in the transactions table to link back to the customers table, which is the customer ID column of the customers table.

When it comes to creating relationships within our example database, you will later see how a foreign key is created that will create a link, or a relationship, between two columns. This link is created through a **constraint**, which is a method SQL Server uses to check the details built into the relationship. From the viewpoint of a foreign key, this constraint, or check, will ensure that the relationship follows the conditions set with it. We'll examine foreign keys in more depth in the "More on Foreign Keys" section.

Candidate/Alternate Key

As mentioned previously, a table can have only one primary key. However, there may be another key that could just as easily be defined as a primary key. This is known as a **candidate key**, as it is a candidate for being the primary key.

There is no logical difference at all between the definition of a candidate key and a primary key. For example, if we have a table that holds spare parts for a General Motors (GM) vehicle, we could have an internal GM part number to use when ordering parts at the head office for various GM branches. This part number would be unique and would likely be used as the primary key. However, a part number is also created by each of the manufacturers, which is unique to them. This, too, could be a primary key if we include the supplier identifier in the database. We can't have two primary keys, and we've chosen the GM part number as the primary key, but we could create a candidate key using the manufacturer identifier and part number.

A Unique Constraint Instead of a Primary Key

This is where having a constraint defined will ensure that unique values can only be entered into columns defined within the constraint. This sounds very much like the previous primary key definition, but there are differences.

A **unique constraint** is not a primary key, but the column or columns defined within the constraint could be a primary key. Also, a unique constraint can contain NULL values, but recall that a primary key cannot. However, NULL is treated as any other value within a column; therefore, the columns used to make a unique constraint must remain unique, including the NULL value, when you're looking to insert or update data. Finally, it is possible to have multiple unique constraints, but you can have only one primary key.

Creating Relationships

A **relationship** in a SQL Server database is a logical link between two tables. It is impossible to have a physical link, although, as you will see later, a physical line is drawn between two tables when designing the database. To have a physical link would mean the actual data linking the two tables would be stored only once in a central location, and that information within the keys linking the tables would be stored more than once, which is just not the case.

When defining a logical relationship, we're informing SQL Server that we'll be linking a primary key from the master table to a foreign key in another table. So already there is a need for two keys: one on each table.

The following sections present specific details about relationships, starting with a look at how relationships work with the concept of referential integrity.

Relationships and Referential Integrity

A relationship can be used to enforce data integrity. In other words, if you are expecting data in one table because there is data in another, you can place a relationship between these two tables to ensure that no SQL command breaks this rule. However, don't confuse referential integrity with other processes that are associated with maintaining data integrity, such as placing checks or default values on columns to ensure that values for a specific column are valid.

Referential integrity revolves around the idea that there are two tables in the database that contain the same information, and it requires that the duplicated data elements are kept consistent. For example, if you have a primary key in one table and a foreign key in another table and both have data that matches exactly, then it is important that both pieces of data either change together or don't change at all. Relationships are not the only way referential integrity can be enforced; you can also use triggers to ensure that data remains valid (we'll examine this further in Chapter 13).

For instance, our example banking system includes the customers and transactions tables. It is not possible to record customer transactions without a customer record. As a result, we have to use referential integrity to enforce data integrity between these two tables, so that a customer record can't be removed from the database while there are customer transaction records for that customer. Similarly, this rule should allow the removal of a customer record when there are no customer transaction records.

Another result of enforcing referential integrity is that it isn't possible for a customer transaction to be entered using a customer reference number that doesn't exist within the customers table. Instead, to enter a customer transaction in this situation, we first have to create the customer record, and then we can carry out the transaction.

Finally, if we had a customer record and related customer transaction records, we couldn't alter the customer reference number in the customer record without first altering the customer transaction records and checking that the reference we're altering the customer transaction records to already exists.

So, there are a number of rules to follow if we want to maintain the integrity of our data. If we so desired, we could use referential integrity to enforce data integrity. However, a flip side to all of this to be aware of is that we can keep data integrity within a system and not use referential integrity. Instead, we can create stored procedures or triggers, which are types of programs within SQL Server, to do this task. We'll look at these topics in Chapters 10 and 13.

Using stored procedures and triggers is a possible but undesirable solution, because it leaves our system open to instances where data integrity is not kept, because of holes within the design of the system or perhaps because a developer doesn't have the correct processing sequence to ensure that all data is always valid. Not only that, but if someone adds data directly to a table, the referential integrity will be lost. That said, having the data integrity checks in an application does lead to less traffic flow over the network, as all the validation is done on the front end.

There is one more important point about referential integrity before we move on to discuss database relationship types: if you want to maintain referential integrity by creating a relationship between two tables, then these two tables must be in the same database. It is not possible to have referential integrity between two databases.

Types of Relationships

Three main relationship types can exist in a database:

- One-to-one
- One-to-many
- Many-to-many

The sections that follow cover each type, so when it comes to creating a relationship, you'll know which one to create, when to create it, and why. We'll start off by looking at the one-to-one relationship, which is perhaps the easiest type of relationship to understand, although it is one of the least used.

One-to-One

This relationship type isn't very common within a working database. Typically, there is no real reason for one record in one table to match just one record in another. This scenario would really only exist, for example, if you were splitting a very large table into two separate tables.

To illustrate the one-to-one relationship, imagine that in our example bank database there is a table that holds PIN numbers for ATM cards, keeping them completely separate from the remainder of the customer records (see Figure 3-1). In most cases, there would be one PIN number record for each customer record, but there may be exceptions—for instance, a high-interest deposit account may not have a card, and therefore there would be no associated PIN number record.

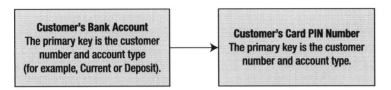

Figure 3-1. *One-to-one relationship*

One-to-Many

Perhaps the most common relationship found in a database is the one-to-many relationship. This is where one master record is linked with zero, one, or more records in a child table.

Using our banking example, say we have a customer master record along with any number of associated transaction records. The number of these transaction records could range from none, which corresponds to when a customer is new to the bank and hasn't made a deposit or performed a transaction, to one or more, which corresponds to when there has been an initial deposit in an account, and then further deposits or withdrawal transactions after that (see Figure 3-2).

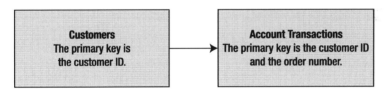

Figure 3-2. *One-to-many relationship*

You'll see this concept in action again in the customer-to-transactions relationship we'll build for our solution.

Many-to-Many

Many-to-many is the final relationship type that can exist in a database. This relationship can happen relatively frequently. In this type of relationship, zero, one, or indeed many records in the master table relate to zero, one, or many records in a child table.

An example of a many-to-many relationship might be where a company has several depots for dispatching goods, seen as the master table, which then dispatch goods to many stores, seen as the child table (see Figure 3-3). The depots could be located and organized so that different depots could all supply the same store, and they could be arranged in groups of produce, frozen, perishables, and bonded. In order for a store to be supplied with a full complement of goods, it would need to be supplied by a number of different depots, which would typically be in different locations.

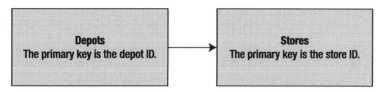

Figure 3-3. *Many-to-many relationship*

When building relationships within a database, it is necessary to have a foreign key. I covered foreign keys briefly earlier in the chapter; let's take a closer look at them in the next section.

More on Foreign Keys

A foreign key is any key on a child table where a column, or a set of columns, can be directly matched with exactly the same number and information from the master table. By using this foreign key, you can build up the data to return via a relationship.

However, a foreign key does not have to map to a primary key on a master table. Although it is common to see a foreign key mapped to a primary key, as long as the key in the master table that is being mapped to is a unique key, you can build a relationship between a master table and a child table.

The whole essence of a foreign key lies in its mapping process and the fact that it is on the child table. A foreign key will exist only when a relationship has been created from the child table to the parent table. But what exactly are the master table and the child tables? To demonstrate, let's refer to our relationship examples. Take, for example, the one-to-many relationship. The master table would be on the left-hand side, or the "one" side of the relationship, and the child table would be on the right-hand side, or the "many" side of the relationship (see Figure 3-4).

Figure 3-4. *Foreign key*

There is one final point to mention concerning foreign keys, relationships, and the master and child tables. It is totally possible for the master table and the child table to be the same table, and for the foreign key and the unique key to both be defined within the same table. This is called a **self-join** or a **reflexive relationship**. You don't tend to see this much within a database, as it is quite an unusual situation, although you could use it to ensure that the data in one column exactly matches the information in another column, just as in any other join.

For example, say you have a table built around customers, and you have two columns, one of which is a parent customer ID, which holds an ID for the head office and is used to link all the branches. If the head office is also seen as valid branch of the conglomerate, the second column could be the specific branch ID, and you could put a link between these two columns so that there is still a valid link for the head office as a branch as well (see Figure 3-5). Another example is in an employees table where all employees reside, with a self-join from an employee back to his or her manager.

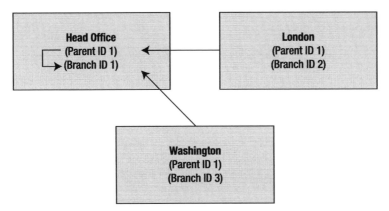

Figure 3-5. *Foreign keys in same table*

Now that we've looked at relationships, let's move on to cover how to normalize the database.

Normalization

Normalizing a database is the science of reducing any duplication of data within tables. You can then build multiple tables related to one another through keys or indexes. The removal of as much duplication of data will lead to smaller, more compact databases. There will be a reduced chance of confusion over which column holding the "same" data is correct or should be modified, and there will also be less overhead involved in having to keep multiple columns of data up to date.

■**Note** Just a reminder that we're still in the logical phase of building our solution, and we're not ready to start building our database within SQL Server.

A database designer should not normalize with impunity, as this may have an effect on speed within the database and the retrieval of data. In good normalization, the removal of the duplication of data will provide faster sorting of data and queries that run faster, thereby improving performance. Although normalization will produce an efficient database, it is possible to overnormalize data by creating too many relationships and too many slim, small tables, so that to retrieve one piece of information requires access to many tables and many joins between these tables. A knowledgeable designer knows when to stop normalizing and does not take things just that stage too far, such as having too many relationships. This knowledge comes with experience and practice mainly, but in our database example, you'll learn where to "stop."

■**Tip** When any reference tables return one row of data without further table references to retrieve that information, that's a signal to stop normalization.

In this section of the chapter, we'll model our example in a method known as **logical modeling**. The purpose of the logical model is to show the data that the application must store to satisfy business requirements. It demonstrates how this data is related and explores any integration requirements with business areas outside the scope of the development project. It is created without any specific computer environment in mind, so no optimization for performance, data storage, and so forth is done.

In logical modeling, the term **entity** is used to mean a conceptual version of a table. As we're still in the logical modeling stage of designing our database, I'll use "entity" rather than "table" in this discussion, since it is less tied to implementation. Also within logical modeling, a column of data is referred to as an **attribute**. To build our logical model, we'll take the information gathered previously in the chapter and implement attributes in our entities. From that, we'll see how we need to alter our design.

The question remains, what should be contained in an entity? Three principles should govern the contents of an entity:

- Each entity should have a unique identifier.
- Only store information that directly relates to that entity.
- Avoid repeating values or columns.

The sections that follow provide more detail about each principle.

Each Entity Should Have a Unique Identifier

It must be possible to find a unique row in each entity. You can do this through the use of a unique identifying attribute or the combination of several attributes. However, no matter which method you use, it must be impossible for two rows to contain the same information within the unique identifying attribute(s).

Consider the possibility that there is no combination of attributes in an entity that can make a row unique, or perhaps you wish to build a single value from a single attribute. SQL Server has a special data type, called a **unique identifier**, that can do this, but a more common solution is to build a column attribute with an integer data type, and then set this up as an **identity** column. You'll learn more about this technique when building the tables in Chapter 5.

Only Store Information That Directly Relates to That Entity

It can be very easy in certain situations to have too much information in one entity and therefore almost change the reason for the existence of the specific entity. Doing so could reduce efficiency in an OLTP system, where duplicate information has to be inserted. It could also lead to confusion when an entity that has been designed for one thing actually contains data for another.

Avoid Repeating Values or Columns

Having attributes of data where the information is an exact copy of another attribute within either the same entity or a related entity is a waste of space and resources. However, what tends to happen is that you have repeated values or attributes within two or more tables, and therefore the information is duplicated. It is in this scenario that you are expected to avoid the repeating values and move them elsewhere.

Normalization Forms

Now that you know what should be contained within an entity, how do you go about normalizing the data? The normalization forms addressed within this chapter are as follows:

- First normal form (1NF)
- Second normal form (2NF)

- Third normal form (3NF)

There are a number of other, "higher" normal forms, but they are rarely used outside academic institutions, so they will not be covered here.

First Normal Form

To achieve 1NF within a database, it is required that you eliminate any repeating groups of information. Any groups of data found to be repeated will be moved to a new table. Looking at each table in turn, we find that we have two tables in our example database that potentially flout the first requirement of 1NF: customers and shares.

Customers

There are two columns with possible repeating values in this table:

- *Title*: A customer's title will be Mr., Miss, Ms., or Mrs., all of which you could put in to a reference table. Some corporations do this; others don't. It all depends on whether you want to restrict what users can enter.
- *Address*: The address should be split out into separate lines, one for each part of the address (e.g., street, district, etc.). It is probably well worth having a reference table for cities, states, and countries, for example.

Shares

There is one column that will possibly repeat: share name. This is really due to the shares table actually doing two jobs: holding details about the share, such as its name and the market ticker, which really are unique; and holding a historical list of share prices. This table actually needs to be split into Share Details and Share Prices, which we'll see happening when we discuss the 3NF.

Second Normal Form

To achieve 2NF, each column within the table must depend on the whole primary key. This means that if you look at any single column within a table, you need to ask if it is possible to get to this information using the whole key or just part of the key. If only part of the key is required, then you must look to splitting the tables so that every column does match the whole key. So, you would look at each column within the table and ask, "Can I reach the information contained within this column just using part of the key?" All of the tables use an ID as the primary key, and only one column will define that ID. Therefore, to break 2NF with this is almost impossible. Where you are more likely to break 2NF is a scenario in which the primary key uses several columns.

If we look at all the tables within our example, every column within each table does require the whole key to find it.

Third Normal Form

To achieve 3NF, you must now have no column that is not defined as a key be dependent on any other column within the table. Further, you cannot have any data derived from other data within the table.

The Customers table does have data derived from another table, with account numbers for each product the customer has bought and financial product details. This means that the account number plus details about the product such as the date opened, how much is paid with each payment, and the product type do not belong in the Customers table. If such information did remain in the table, then Customers would have multiple rows for the same customer. Therefore, this table also now needs to be split into customer details such as name and address, and customer products, such as a row for each product bought with the customer details about that product.

We have now reached full normalization to 3NF of the tables within our database. Let's take a moment to clarify where we are now. Figure 3-6 shows that we're now moving from a logical model to a physical model, where we are physically defining what information is stored where.

Figure 3-6. *Physical database model*

Denormalization

Despite having normalized our data to be more efficient, there will be times when denormalizing the data is a better option. **Denormalization** is the complete opposite of normalization: it is where you introduce data redundancy within a table to reduce the number of table joins and potentially speed up data access. Instances of denormalization can be found in production systems where the join to a table is slowing down queries, or perhaps where normalization is not required (e.g., when working with a system in which the data is not regularly updated).

Just because others say your data should be totally normalized, this is not necessarily true, so don't feel forced down that route. The drawback of denormalizing your data too far, though, is that you'll be holding duplicate and unnecessary information that could be normalized out to another table and then just joined during a query. This will, therefore, create performance issues as well as use a larger amount of data storage space. However, the costs of denormalization can be justified if queries run faster. That said, data integrity is paramount in a system. It's no use having denormalized data in which there are duplications of data where one area is updated when there's a change, and the other area isn't updated.

Denormalization is not the route we want to take in our database example, so now that we have all the data to produce the system, it's time to look at how these tables will link together.

Creating the Sample Database

Let's now begin to create our example database. In this section, we'll examine two different ways to create a database in SQL Server:

- Using the SQL Server Management Studio graphical interface
- Using T-SQL code

Both methods have their own merits and pitfalls for creating databases, as you'll discover, but these two methods are used whenever possible throughout the book, and where you might find one method is good for one task, it might not be ideal for another. Neither method is right or wrong for every task, and your decision of which to use basically comes down to personal preference and what you're trying to achieve at the time. You may find that using T-SQL code for building objects provides the best results, as you will see instantly the different possible selections. However, if the syntax for the commands is not familiar to you, you may well choose to use a wizard or SQL Server Management Studio. Once you become more comfortable with the syntax, then a Query Editor pane might become your favored method.

We'll also examine how to drop a database in SQL Server Management Studio.

Creating a Database in SQL Server Management Studio

The first method of creating a database we'll look at is using SQL Server Management Studio, which was introduced in Chapter 2.

Try It Out: Creating a Database in SQL Server Management Studio

1. Before creating the database, you'll need to start up SQL Server Management Studio.

■**Tip** Throughout the book examples, I'm working on a server called FAT-BELLY using the default installed instance. Replace your server and instance where appropriate.

2. Ensure that you have registered and connected to your server. If the SQL Server service was not previously started, it will automatically start as you connect, which may take a few moments. However, if you have not shut down your computer since the install of SQL Server, then everything should be up and running. SQL Server will only stop if you have shut down your computer and indicated not to start the SQL Server service automatically. To start SQL Server, or conversely, if you want to set up SQL Server not to start automatically when Windows starts, set this either from Control Panel or from the SQL Server Configuration Manager found under Programs ➤ Microsoft SQL Server 2008 ➤ Configuration Tools.

3. In Object Explorer, expand the Databases node until you see either just the system database and database snapshot nodes that always exist, or, on top of these, the individual sample databases you installed earlier in the book. Ensure that the Databases folder is highlighted and ready for the next action, as shown in Figure 3-7.

Figure 3-7. *The Databases node in Object Explorer*

A minimum amount of information is required to create a database:

- The name the database will be given

- How the data will be sorted

- The size of the database

- Where the database will be located

- The name of the files used to store the information contained within the database

SQL Server Management Studio gathers this information using the New Database menu option.

4. Right-click the Databases folder to bring up a context-sensitive menu with a number of different options. Select New Database, as shown in Figure 3-8.

Figure 3-8. *Selecting to create a new database*

5. You are now presented with the New Database screen set to the General tab. First enter the name of the database you want to create—in this case, ApressFinancial. Notice as you type that the two file names in the Database Files list box also populate. This is simply an aid, and the names can be changed (see Figure 3-9). However, you should have a very good reason to not take the names that the screen is creating, as this is enforcing a standard. Once you have finished, click OK to create the database.

Figure 3-9. *General settings in the New Database dialog*

The General dialog within this option collects the first two pieces of information. The first piece of information required is the database name. No checks are done at this point as to whether the database exists (this comes when you click OK); however, there is some validation in the field so that certain illegal characters will not be allowed.

Note Illegal characters for a database name are as follows:

" ' */?:\<> -

Keep your naming standard to alphabetic, numeric, underscore, or dash characters. Also, you may want to keep the database name short, as the database name has to be entered manually in many parts of SQL Server.

Below the database name is the owner of the database. This can be any login that has the authority to create databases. A server in many—but not all—installations can hold databases that belong to different development groups. Each group would have an account that was the database owner, and at this point, you would assign the specific owner. For the moment, let it default to the <default> account, which will be the account currently logged in to SQL Server; you'll learn how to change this later. If you're using Windows authentication, then your Windows account will be your user ID, and if you're using SQL Server authentication, it will be the ID you used at connection time.

The database owner initially has full administration rights on the database, from creating the database, to modifying it or its contents, to even deleting the database. It is normal practice for a database administrator type account to create the database, such as a user that belongs to the Builtin\Administrators group, as this is a member of the sysadmin role, which has database creation rights.

Ignore the check box for Full-Text Indexing. You would select this option if you wanted your database to have columns that you could search for a particular word or phrase. For example, search engines could have a column that hold a set of phrases from web pages, and full-text searching could be used to find which web pages contain the words being searched for.

The File Name entry (off screen to the right in Figure 3-9) is the name of the physical file that will hold the data within the database you're working with. By default, SQL Server takes the name of the database and adds a suffix of _Data to create this name.

Just to the left of the File Name option is the physical path where the files will reside. The files will typically reside in a directory on a local drive. For an installation such as you are completing on a local machine, the path will normally be the path specified by default. That path is to a subfolder under the SQL Server installation directory. If, however, you are working on a server, although you will be placing the files on a local hard drive, the path may be different, so that different teams' installations will be in different physical locations or even on different local hard drives.

The database files are stored on your hard drive with an extension of .MDF—for example, ApressFinancial_Data.MDF. In this case, .MDF is not something used by DIY enthusiasts, but it actually stands for **Master Data File** and is the name of the **primary data file**. Every database **must** have at least one primary data file. This file may hold not only the data for the database, but also the location of all the other files that make up the database, as well as start-up information for the database catalog.

It is also possible to have **secondary data files**. These would have the suffix .NDF. Again, you could use whatever name you wished, and in fact, you could have an entirely different name from the primary data file. However, if you did so, the confusion that would abound is not worth thinking about. So do use the same name, and if you need a third, fourth, and so on, then add on a numerical suffix.

Secondary data files allow you to spread your tables and indexes over two or more disks. The upside is that by spreading the data over several disks, you will get better performance. In a production environment, you may have several secondary data files to spread out your heavily used tables.

▓**Note** As the primary data file holds the database catalog information that will be accessed constantly during the operation of the server, it would be best, in a production environment at least, to place all your tables on a secondary data file.

You would place the file name for a secondary data file in the row below the ApressFinancial_Data entry in the Data Files list box, after clicking the Add button. The File Type column shows whether the file is a data file or a log file, as in a file for holding the data or a file for holding a record of the actions done to the data.

The next column in the grid is titled Filegroup. This allows you to specify the PRIMARY file group and any SECONDARY data file groups for your database. The Filegroup option is a method for grouping logical data files together to manage them as a logical unit. You could place some of your tables in one file group, more tables in another file group, indexes in another, and so on. Dividing your tables and indexes into file groups allows SQL Server to perform parallel disk operations and tasks if the file groups are on different drives.You could also place tables that are not allowed to be modified together in one file group and set the file group to Read-Only. Figure 3-10 shows the dialog for creating a new file group. The top option allows you to create read-only file groups. Finally, when creating a database object, the default file group is the PRIMARY file group. In a production environment—and therefore in a development environment as well, so that it is simpler to move from development through to production—you would create a secondary file group and set it as the default. In this book, we will just keep to the PRIMARY file group for simplicity.

Figure 3-10. *New file group*

> ■**Note** Remember that the PRIMARY file group may hold not only data, but also the system tables, so the PRIMARY file group could fill up purely with information about tables, columns, and so forth.

The next item is the Initial Size (MB) column. The initial size of the database is its size when empty. Don't forget that the database won't be totally empty, and some of the space will be initially taken up with the system tables. It is impossible to say, "I'm creating a database, and the initial size must be *nn*MB"—the database size depends on many factors, such as the number of tables, how much static information is stored, to what size you expect the database to grow, and so on. It would be during the investigation phase that you would try to determine the size that you expect the database to reach over a given period of time. If anything, estimate larger rather than smaller to avoid fragmentation.

Moving on to the next, and possibly most important, area: Autogrowth. This option indicates whether SQL Server will automatically handle the situation that arises if your database reaches the initial size limit. If you don't set this option, you will have to monitor your database and expand its size manually, if and when required. Think of the overhead in having to monitor the size, let alone having to increase the size! It is much easier and less hassle, and much less of a risk, to let SQL Server handle this when starting out. However, do set a maximum size so that you have some emergency disk space available in case it is required.

> ■**Note** In a production environment, or even when you're developing in the future, it will be more common to switch Autogrowth on and fix the size. This prevents your hard drive from filling up and your server from being unable to continue. At least when you fix the maximum size, you can keep some hard drive space in reserve to enable your SQL Server to continue running while the development team tries to clear out unwanted data, but also create an initial smaller size and allow growth if required.

While SQL Server handles increasing the size of the database for you, it has to know by how much. This is where the Autogrowth option comes in. You can let SQL Server increase the database either by a set amount each time in megabytes or by a percentage. The default is By Percent, and at this stage, it doesn't really matter. In our example, the first increase will be 3MB; the second increase will be 3.3MB. For our example, this is sufficient, as there won't be a great deal of data being entered. However, the percentage option does give uneven increases, and if you like order, then By MB is the option for you. If you want to change these options by selecting the autogrowth options button (the ellipsis) to the right of the current setting, you can disable autogrowth of your database in the dialog that appears. You can also, as discussed, alter it to increase by By MB rather than By Percent.

In the autogrowth dialog, the Maximum File Size option sets a limit on how large the database is allowed to grow. The default is "unrestricted growth"—in other words, the only limit is the spare space on the hard drive. This is good, as you don't have to worry about maintaining the database too much. But what if you have a rogue piece of code entering an infinite loop of data? This scenario is rare, but not unheard of. It might take a long time to fill up the hard drive, but fill up the hard drive it will, and with a full hard drive, purging the data will prove troublesome. When it is time to start moving the database to a production environment, ensure the Restrict File Growth (MB) option is set to guard against such problems.

The final column that you will find in the New Database dialog by scrolling to the right is Path. In this column, you define where the database files will reside on your hard drive. If SQL Server is installed on your C drive and none of the paths for the data were changed and you are working on a default instance, then you will find that the default is `C:\Program Files\ Microsoft SQL Server\MSSQL.10.MSSQLSERVER\MSSQL\Data`. Figure 3-9 shows working on a mapped drive that has been given the drive letter C. The command button with the ellipsis (. . .) to the right of the path brings up an explorer-style dialog that allows you to change the location of the database files. For example, if you move to a larger SQL Server installation, moving the location of these files to a server relevant to the needs of your database will probably be a necessity.

The line that has a File Type setting of Log includes the same information as a Data File Type setting, with one or two minor exceptions. The File Name places a suffix of _Log onto the database name, and there is no ability to change the Filegroup column, since the Transaction Log doesn't actually hold system tables, and so would only fill up through the recording of actions. It is possible, however, to define multiple log file locations. Filling the transaction log and not being able to process any more information because the log is full will cause your SQL Server to stop processing. Specifying more than one log location means that you can avoid this problem. The use of a failover log file in larger production systems is advisable.

Let's now move on to discuss the Options area of the New Database dialog (see Figure 3-11).

The first field in the Options area is labeled Collation. We discussed this option in Chapter 1 when installing SQL Server. If you need to alter a collation setting on a database, you can do so, but care is required.

The next setting is Recovery Model. You'll learn about backing up and restoring your database in Chapter 7, and this option forms part of that decision-making process. In development, the best option is to choose the Simple backup mode, as you should have your most up-to-date source being developed and saved to your local hard drive. The three modes are as follows:

- *Full*: Allows the database to be restored to where the failure took place. Every transaction is logged; therefore, you can restore a database backup and then move forward to the individual point in time required using the transaction log.

- *Bulk-Logged*: Minimally logs bulk operations, so if you're performing a bulk operation such as bulk copying into SQL Server, or if you're inserting a bulk of rows of data, then only the action is recorded and not every row is inserted. This will increase performance during these sorts of operations, but if a problem occurs, then recovery can only occur to the end of the last log backup.

- *Simple*: Truncates the transaction log after each database backup. This allows restores to be created to the last successful data backup only, as no transaction log backups are taken. You should not use this mode in a production environment.

The third item in the Options area is Compatibility Level. It is possible to build a database for previous versions of SQL Server, provided you are willing to sacrifice the new functionality. This will allow you to connect to a SQL Server 2005 or earlier–defined database.

Figure 3-11. *Options area of the New Database dialog*

Among the next set of options, the ones of interest to us at the moment are the first five. We'll examine the remaining options when we build the database using T-SQL.

- *Auto Close*: If you want the database to shut down when the last user exits, then set this option to True. The standard practice is a setting of False, and you should have a good reason to set this option to True, especially on a remote server.

- *Auto Create Statistics*: This option relates to the creation of statistics used when querying data. The standard practice is a setting of True; however, in a production environment, especially if you have a nightly or weekly process that generates statistics on your data, you would switch this to False. Creating and updating statistics while your system is being used does increase processing required on your server, and if your server is heavily used for inserting data, then you will find a performance degradation with this option set to True. To clarify, though, it is necessary to balance your choice with how much your system will have to query data.

- *Auto Shrink*: Database and transaction logs grow in size not only with increased data input, but also through other actions, which we'll discuss in more detail in Chapter 7. You can shrink the logical size of the log file through certain actions, some of which can be instigated by T-SQL and some as a by-product of actions being performed.

- *Auto Update Statistics and Auto Update Statistics Asynchronously*: These are more common options to have set to True, even on production servers, although there is still a performance degradation. These options will update statistics as data is inserted, modified, or deleted for tables for use in indexes, and they will also update statistics for columns within a table. We'll discuss indexes further in Chapter 6.

> ▓**Note** It is possible to switch modes, and you may wish to do this if you have a number of bulk-logged operations—for example, if you're completing a refresh of static data.

SQL Server will now perform several actions. First, it checks whether the database already exists; if so, you will have to choose another name. Once the database name is validated, SQL Server does a security check to make sure that the user has permission to create the database. This is not a concern here, since by following this book, you will always be logged on to SQL Server with the proper permissions. Now that you have security clearance, the data files are created and placed on the hard drive. Providing there is enough space, these files will be successfully created, and it is not until this point that SQL Server is updated with the new database details in the internal system tables.

Once this is done, the database is ready for use. As you can see, this whole process is relatively straightforward, and simple to complete. Congratulations!

> ▓**Tip** You need not create the database at this point if you don't want to. There are several other options available to you to save the underlying T-SQL to a file, to the clipboard, or to the Query window. The first two options are very useful as methods of storing actions you're creating to keep in your source code repository, such as Visual Source-Safe. The third option is ideal if you wish to add more options to your database than you have defined within the wizard setup. All of the options enable you to see the underlying code and understand what is required to create a database. We'll look at the code in a moment.

When you return to Object Explorer in SQL Server Management Studio, refresh the contents manually if the explorer hasn't autorefreshed. You will see the new database listed, as shown in Figure 3-12.

Figure 3-12. *The new database within Object Explorer*

SQL Server Management Studio is simply a GUI front end to running T-SQL scripts in the background. As we progress through the book, you'll see the T-SQL generated for each object type we're using, and you'll create the objects graphically, as you've just seen. There are two methods you can use to get the script for this database:

- Notice that at the top of the New Database wizard screen in Figure 3-9, there is a button that generates the script. After you click this button, you can indicate where you would like the script sent to.

- Once the database has been created, you can right-mouse-click and, as shown in Figure 3-13, have the details sent to one of four locations.

Figure 3-13. *Scripting the database from SSMS*

Whichever method you choose to use, the script will be the same, with the exception of a comment line when you create the script in the second option. The script for generating the database from this option is listed here, so we can go through what is happening. The fourth option allows you to schedule a re-creation of the database at a certain point in time. This is ideal to use when building a database from scratch, which you'll sometimes find in a daily job for setting up a test area.

First of all, SQL Server points itself to a known database, as shown in the following snippet. master has to exist; otherwise, SQL Server will not work. The USE statement, which instructs SQL Server to alter its connection to default to the database after the USE statement, points further statements to the master database:

```
USE [master]
```

```
GO
```

Next, the script builds up the CREATE DATABASE T-SQL statement built on the options selected. (We'll walk through the CREATE DATABASE syntax that could be used in the "Creating a Database in a Query Pane" section, as this statement doesn't cover all the possibilities.) Notice in the code that follows that the name of the database is surrounded by square brackets: [ ]. SQL Server does this as a way of defining that the information between the square brackets is to be used similarly to a literal and not as a variable. Also it defines that the information is to be treated as one unit. To clarify, if we want to name the database Apress Financial (i.e., with a space between "Apress" and "Financial"), then we need to have a method of knowing where the name of the database starts and ends. This is where the identifier brackets come in to play.

█Note Recall the Quoted Identifier option that we encountered in Chapter 2, with the T-SQL command SET QUOTED_IDENTIFIER ON/OFF. Instead of using the square brackets, you can define identifiers by surrounding them with double quotation marks using this command. Therefore, anything that has double quotation marks around it is seen as an identifier rather than a literal, if this option is set to ON. To get around this requirement, you can use single quotation marks, as shown in the example, but then if you do have to enter a single quote mark—as in the word "don't"—you would have to use another single quotation mark. So as you can see, this situation can get a bit messy. I prefer to have QUOTED_IDENTIFIER set to OFF to reduce confusion.

The following code shows the code generated by the script for creating the ApressFinancial database:

```
/****** Object:  Database [ApressFinancial]
Script Date: 02/28/2008 21:57:46 ******/
CREATE DATABASE [ApressFinancial] ON  PRIMARY
( NAME = N'ApressFinancial', FILENAME = N'C:\Program Files\
Microsoft SQL Server\
MSSQL10.MSSQLSERVER\MSSQL\DATA\ApressFinancial.mdf' ,
SIZE = 3072KB , MAXSIZE = UNLIMITED, FILEGROWTH = 1024KB )
 LOG ON
( NAME = N'ApressFinancial_log', FILENAME = N'C:\Program Files\
Microsoft SQL Server\
MSSQL10.MSSQLSERVER\MSSQL\DATA\ApressFinancial_log.ldf' ,
SIZE = 1024KB , MAXSIZE = 2048GB , FILEGROWTH = 10%)
GO
```

Have you noticed that every so often there is a GO command statement? This signals to SQL Server—or any other SQL Server utility—that this is the end of a batch of T-SQL statements, and the utility should send the batch of statements to SQL Server. You saw this in Chapter 2 when we were looking at Query Editor's options. Certain statements need to be in their own batch and cannot be combined with other statements in the same batch. To clarify, a GO statement determines that you have come to the end of a batch of statements and that SQL Server should process these statements before moving on to the next batch of statements.

■**Note** GO statements are used only in ad hoc T-SQL, which is what I'm demonstrating here. Later in the book, you'll build T-SQL into programs called stored procedures. GO statements are not used in stored procedures.

Next, we define the new database's compatibility level. This statement defines that the database's base level is SQL Server 2008. It is possible to define SQL Server to an earlier level, as far back as SQL Server 2000, by changing the version number in the parameter @new_cmptlevel. You'll learn more about this code in Chapter 10. Notice, though, that it is a figure of 100 rather than 2008 that you may have been expecting. A base level of 100 actually means 10.0, as in version 10 (100). SQL Server 2000 was version 8, known as compatibility level 80. 2005 was version 9 (90). SQL Server 2008 thus becomes level 100.

```
ALTER DATABASE [ApressFinancial] SET COMPATIBILITY_LEVEL = 100
GO
```

We then can define the remaining database options. The statements to set those options have GO statements separating them. But in this scenario, the GO statements are superfluous. So why are they included? When SQL Server is preparing the wizard, it is safer for it to place GO statements after each statement, as the wizard then doesn't have to predict what the next statement is, and therefore whether the end of the batch of transactions has to be defined.

It is possible to set up a database to allow searching of values within columns of your tables. This is a great utility, if you need it, but it does have a processing overhead when working with your data. There is an IF statement around the following code that enables or disables full text searching. This code is testing whether full texting has been installed or not as part of the current instance. If it has not been installed, then by default the option is disabled.

```
IF (1 = FULLTEXTSERVICEPROPERTY('IsFullTextInstalled'))
begin
EXEC [ApressFinancial].[dbo].[sp_fulltext_database] @action = 'disable'
end
```

There will be times when columns have no data in them. When a column is empty, it is said to contain the special value of NULL. Setting ANSI_NULL_DEFAULT to OFF means that a column's default value is NOT NULL. We'll look at NULL values in Chapter 5 during our table creation discussion. The following statement defines what the default setting is when defining a new column within a table in SQL Server. If you define a new column for a table without defining if it can hold NULL values or not, using the T-SQL ALTER TABLE command, then the column by default will not allow NULL values.

```
ALTER DATABASE [ApressFinancial] SET ANSI_NULL_DEFAULT OFF
GO
```

Still with NULL values, the ANSI standard states that if you are comparing two columns of data that have this special NULL value in them, then the comparison should fail and should not return the rows with NULL values, when you use the equals sign (=) and not equals (<>) operators. Setting ANSI NULL values to OFF alters the standard, so when you do compare two NULL values, the comparison will pass. The following is the statement to use:

```
ALTER DATABASE [ApressFinancial] SET ANSI_NULLS OFF
GO
```

There are columns of characters than can store variable-length data. We'll come across these when we build our table in Chapter 5. If set to ON, this option makes every column of data contain the maximum number of characters, whether you sent through just one character or many more. It is common to have this set to OFF.

```
ALTER DATABASE [ApressFinancial] SET ANSI_PADDING OFF
GO
```

If an ANSI standard warning or error occurs, such as "divide by zero," then switching the ANSI_WARNINGS setting to OFF will suppress these. A value of NULL will be returned in any columns that have the error.

```
ALTER DATABASE [ApressFinancial] SET ANSI_WARNINGS OFF
GO
```

If the ANSI_WARNINGS setting was ON, and you performed a divide by zero, the query would terminate. To change this in combination with ANSI_WARNINGS set to ON, we tell SQL Server not to abort when there's an arithmetic error.

```
ALTER DATABASE [ApressFinancial] SET ARITHABORT OFF
GO
```

If you have a database that is only "active" when users are logged in, then switching the AUTO_CLOSE setting to ON would close down the database when the last user logged out. This is unusual, as databases tend to stay active 24/7, but closing unwanted databases frees up resources for other databases on the server to use if required. One example of when to switch this setting ON is for a database used for analyzing data by users through the day (e.g., one in an actuarial department, where death rates would be analyzed). By then switching it to AUTO_CLOSE, it would ensure there were no connections when a job was run to update the data if the job required there to be no updates to the data while it was processing.

```
ALTER DATABASE [ApressFinancial] SET AUTO_CLOSE OFF
GO
```

SQL Server uses statistics when returning data. If it finds that statistics are missing when running a query, having the following option ON will create these statistics.

```
ALTER DATABASE [ApressFinancial] SET AUTO_CREATE_STATISTICS ON
GO
```

If the volume of data within your database reduces (e.g., if you have a daily or weekly archive process), you can reduce the size of the database automatically by setting the following option ON. It is standard to have the option OFF because the database size will simply increase as data is re-added. It would be switched ON only if a reduction in the database is required—due to disk space requirements, for example—but it is never a good idea for this option to kick in when the database is in use, so really it is best to keep it off.

```
ALTER DATABASE [ApressFinancial] SET AUTO_SHRINK OFF
GO
```

■**Note** It would be better to shrink the database manually by using the DBCC SHRINKDATABASE command.

When data is added or modified to SQL Server, statistics are created that are then used when querying the data. These statistics can be updated with every modification, or they can be completed via a T-SQL set of code at set times. There is a performance reduction as data is inserted, modified, or deleted, but this performance is gained back when you want to return data. Your application being a pure insertion, pure query, or a mix determines whether you'll want this option on. If you have a pure insertion application, you probably want this option switched off, for example, but this is an optimization decision.

```
ALTER DATABASE [ApressFinancial] SET AUTO_UPDATE_STATISTICS ON
GO
```

A **cursor** is a special type of data repository that exists only while the cursor is defined. It's a temporary memory resident table, in essence. A cursor can exist for the lifetime of a program, but if you switch the following setting to ON, when a batch of data is committed or rolled back during a transaction, the cursor will be closed.

```
ALTER DATABASE [ApressFinancial] SET CURSOR_CLOSE_ON_COMMIT OFF
GO
```

A cursor can exist either locally or globally. This means that if GLOBAL is selected for this option, then any cursor created in a program is available to any subprogram that is called. LOCAL, the other option, indicates that the cursor exists only within that program that created it.

```
ALTER DATABASE [ApressFinancial] SET CURSOR_DEFAULT  GLOBAL
GO
```

If you're concatenating character fields and if the following option is ON, then if any of the columns has a NULL value, the result is a NULL.

```
ALTER DATABASE [ApressFinancial] SET CONCAT_NULL_YIELDS_NULL OFF
GO
```

When you're working with some numeric data types, it is possible to lose precision of the numerics. This can occur when you move a floating-point value to a specific numeric decimal point location, and the value you're passing has too many significant digits. If the following option is set to ON, then an error is generated. OFF means the value is truncated.

```
ALTER DATABASE [ApressFinancial] SET NUMERIC_ROUNDABORT OFF
GO
```

As mentioned earlier, when you're defining database names, if there is a space in the name or the name is a reserved word, it is possible to tell SQL Server to ignore that fact and treat the contents of the squared brackets as a literal. You are using **quoted identifiers** when you use the double quotation mark instead of square brackets. We'll delve into this further when inserting data in Chapter 8, as there are a number of details to discuss with this option.

```
ALTER DATABASE [ApressFinancial] SET QUOTED_IDENTIFIER OFF
GO
```

The following option relates to a special type of program called a **trigger**. A trigger can run when data is modified, and one trigger can call another trigger. A setting of OFF means that this cannot take place.

```
ALTER DATABASE [ApressFinancial] SET RECURSIVE_TRIGGERS OFF
GO
```

Service Broker provides developers with a raft of functionality, such as asynchronous processing or the ability to distribute processing over more than one computer. Such a scenario might be heavy overnight batch processing that needs to be completed within a certain time window. By distributing the processing, it could mean that a process that wouldn't have been distributed could finish within that time frame.

```
ALTER DATABASE [ApressFinancial] SET ENABLE_BROKER
GO
```

I mentioned statistics earlier with another option and how they can be updated as data is modified. The following option is similar to AUTO_UPDATE_STATISTICS. If this option is set to ON, the query that triggers an update of the statistics will not wait for the statistics to be created. The statistics update will start, but it will do so in the background asynchronously.

```
ALTER DATABASE [ApressFinancial] SET AUTO_UPDATE_STATISTICS_ASYNC OFF
GO
```

This option governs whether there is a relationship between datetime columns in related tables:

```
ALTER DATABASE [ApressFinancial] SET DATE_CORRELATION_OPTIMIZATION OFF
GO
```

This option defines whether this database is seen as trustworthy regarding what resources it can access and whether SQL Server can trust it not to crash the server, for example. By setting it to OFF, it means that SQL Server will not allow any code developed to have access to external resources, for example.

```
ALTER DATABASE [ApressFinancial] SET TRUSTWORTHY OFF
GO
```

If you build a database that is set for replication—in other words, where data changes are replicated to another server, which you sometimes see for distributed solutions—then this option will define details for this process.

```
ALTER DATABASE [ApressFinancial] SET ALLOW_SNAPSHOT_ISOLATION OFF
GO
```

We will look at this option more when we look at returning data in Chapter 9. The basis of this option, though, is to inform SQL Server how best to work with code that has parameters within it and decide on the best and fastest way to work with that query.

```
ALTER DATABASE [ApressFinancial] SET PARAMETERIZATION SIMPLE
GO
```

The following option defines how the file groups are set: READ_WRITE or READ_ONLY. The use of READ_ONLY is ideal where you have a backup database that users can use to inspect data. The database is an exact mirror of a production database, for example, so it has the security on it set to allow updates to it, but by setting this option to READ_ONLY, you can be sure that no updates can occur.

```
ALTER DATABASE [ApressFinancial] SET READ_WRITE
GO
```

The next option determines how your data can be recovered when a failure such as a power outage happens. In other words, the following option defines the recovery model, as discussed earlier. We'll look at this in more detail when we discuss database maintenance in Chapter 7.

```
ALTER DATABASE [ApressFinancial] SET RECOVERY FULL
GO
```

The following option defines the user access to the database. MULTI_USER is the norm and allows more than one user into the database. The other settings are SINGLE_USER and RESTRICTED_USER, where only people who have powerful privileges can connect. You would set your database to RESTRICTED_USER after a media or power failure, for example, when a database administrator needs to connect to the database to ensure everything is OK.

```
ALTER DATABASE [ApressFinancial] SET  MULTI_USER
GO
```

When you have an I/O error (e.g., a hard drive might be on its way to breaking down), then this option will report an error if checksums don't match:

```
ALTER DATABASE [ApressFinancial] SET PAGE_VERIFY CHECKSUM
GO
```

Finally, the following line is used for controlling whether permissions checks are required when referring to objects in another database:

```
ALTER DATABASE [ApressFinancial] SET DB_CHAINING OFF
```

Dropping the Database in SQL Server Management Studio

To follow the next section properly and build the database using code, it is necessary to remove the database just created. It is also handy to know how to do this anyway, for those times when you have made an error or when you wish to remove a database that is no longer in use. Deleting a database is also known as **dropping** a database.

Try It Out: Dropping a Database in SQL Server Management Studio

1. If SQL Server Management Studio should still be running from our previous example. Expand the nodes until you see the database ApressFinancial.

2. Right-click ApressFinancial to bring up the context menu.

3. Click the Delete option, as shown in Figure 3-14.

4. The dialog shown in Figure 3-15 will display. Select Close Existing Connections, and then click OK.

The first check box, Delete Backup and Restore History Information for Databases, gives you the option of keeping or removing the history information that was generated when completing backups or restores. If you want to keep this information for audit purposes, then uncheck the box.

The second check box is very important. If there is a program running against a database, or if you have any design windows or query panes open and pointing to the database you want to delete, then this option will close those connections. If you are deleting a database, then there really should be no connections there. This is a good check and will prevent accidents from happening, and it also allows any rogue databases to be removed without having to track down who is connected to them.

5. Click OK. The database is now permanently removed.

Figure 3-14. *Deleting a database within SSMS*

Figure 3-15. *Selecting to delete a database in the Delete Object dialog*

When you click the OK button, SQL Server actually performs several actions. First, a command is sent to SQL Server informing it of the name of the database to remove. SQL Server then checks that nobody is currently connected to that database. If someone is connected, through either SQL Server Query Editor or a data access method like ADO.NET, then SQL Server will refuse the deletion. Only if you select Close Existing Connections will this process be overridden

For SQL Server to refuse the deletion, it does not matter if anyone connected to the database is actually doing anything; all that is important is the existence of the connection. For example, if you selected ApressFinancial in Query Editor and then returned to SQL Server Management Studio and tried to drop the database, you would see the error shown in Figure 3-16.

Figure 3-16. *Failed database deletion*

■**Tip** Errors like the one shown in Figure 3-16 provide hyperlinks to documentation that can give you further help.

Once SQL Server has checked that nobody is connected to the database, it then checks that you have **permission** to remove the database. SQL Server will allow you to delete the database if it was your user ID that created it, in which case you own this database and SQL Server allows you to do what you want with it. However, you are not alone in owning the database.

If you recall from Chapter 1, there was mention of the sa account when installing SQL Server. Since it is the most powerful ID and has control over everything within SQL Server, there were warnings about leaving the sa account without any password and also about using the sa account as any sort of login ID in general. This section also mentioned that the sa account was in fact a member of the sysadmin server role. A **role** is a way of grouping together similar users who need similar access to sets of data. Anyone in the sysadmin role has full administrative privileges—and this includes rights to remove any database on the server.

So whether you are logged in as yourself or as sysadmin, take care when using SQL Server Management Studio to drop a database.

Creating a Database in a Query Pane

To use the second method of creating databases, you first need to drop the ApressFinancial database as described in the previous section.

Try It Out: Creating a Database in a Query Pane

1. From the standard toolbar of SQL Server Management Studio, select New Query.

2. In the query pane, enter the following T-SQL script:

```
CREATE DATABASE ApressFinancial ON  PRIMARY
( NAME = N'ApressFinancial',
FILENAME = N'C:\Program Files\Microsoft SQL
Server\MSSQL10.MSSQLSERVER\MSSQL\DATA\
ApressFinancial.mdf' , SIZE = 3072KB ,
MAXSIZE = UNLIMITED, FILEGROWTH = 1024KB )
 LOG ON
( NAME = N'ApressFinancial_log',
FILENAME = N'C:\Program Files\Microsoft SQL
Server\MSSQL10.MSSQLSERVER\MSSQL\DATA\
ApressFinancial_log.ldf' ,
SIZE = 1024KB , MAXSIZE = 2048GB , FILEGROWTH = 10%)
 COLLATE SQL_Latin1_General_CP1_CI_AS
GO
```

3. Execute this code by pressing F5 or Ctrl+E, or by clicking the Execute Query toolbar button.

4. Once the code is executed, you should see the following result:

```
Command(s) completed successfully.
```

How It Works: Creating a Database in Query Editor

The main focus of this section of the chapter is the code listed in the previous exercise: the CREATE DATABASE command.

When placing code in the Query Editor, you're building up a set of instructions for SQL Server to act on. As you progress through the book, you will encounter many commands that you can place in Query Editor, all of which build up to provide powerful and useful utilities or methods for working with data. An in-depth discussion of Query Editor took place in Chapter 2, so if you need to refresh your memory, take a quick look back at the material covered in that chapter.

Before we actually looking at the code itself, we need to inspect the syntax of the CREATE DATABASE command:

```
CREATE DATABASE <database name>
[ON
   ( [ NAME = logical_name, ]
      FILENAME = physical_file_name
    [, FILESIZE = size ]
    [, MAXSIZE = maxsize ]
    [, FILEGROWTH = growth_increment] ) ]
[LOG ON
   ( [ NAME = logical_name, ]
      FILENAME = physical_file_name
    [, FILESIZE = size ]
    [, MAXSIZE = maxsize ]
    [, FILEGROWTH = growth_increment] ) ]
[COLLATE collation_name ]
```

The parameters are as follows:

- database name: The name of the database that the CREATE DATABASE command will create within SQL Server.

- ON: The use of the ON keyword informs SQL Server that the command will specifically mention where the data files are to be placed, as well as their name, size, and file growth. With the ON keyword comes a further list of comma-separated options:

  - NAME: The logical name of the data file that will be used as the reference within SQL Server.

  - FILENAME: The physical file name and full path where the data file will reside.

  - SIZE: The initial size, in megabytes by default, of the data file specified. This parameter is optional, and if omitted, it will take the size defined in the model database. You can suffix the size with KB, MB, GB, or TB (terabytes).

  - FILEGROWTH: The amount that the data file will grow each time it fills up. You can specify either a value that indicates by how many megabytes the data file will grow or a percentage, as discussed earlier when we created a database with SQL Server Management Studio.

- LOG ON: The use of the LOG ON keyword informs SQL Server that the command will specifically mention where the log files will be placed, and their name, size, and file growth.

- NAME: The name of the log file that will be used as the reference within SQL Server.

- FILENAME: The physical file name and full path to where the log file will reside. You must include the suffix .LDF. This could be a different name from the FILENAME specified earlier.

- SIZE: The initial size, in megabytes by default, of the log file specified. This parameter is optional, and if omitted, it will take the size defined in the model database. You can suffix the size with KB, MB, GB, or TB.

- FILEGROWTH: The amount by which the log file will grow each time the data file fills up, which has the same values as for the data file's FILEGROWTH.

- COLLATE: The collation used for the database. Collation was discussed earlier in the chapter when we created a database with SQL Server Management Studio.

It's now time to inspect the code entered into Query Analyzer that will create the ApressFinancial database.

Commencing with CREATE DATABASE, you are informing SQL Server that the following statements are all parameters to be considered for building a new database within SQL Server. Some of the parameters are optional, and SQL Server will include default values when these parameters are not entered. But how does SQL Server know what values to supply? Recall that at the start of this chapter, we discussed the built-in SQL Server databases—specifically, the model database. SQL Server takes the default options for parameters from this database unless they are otherwise specified. Thus, it is important to consider carefully any modifications to the model database.

The database name is obviously essential, and in this case, ApressFinancial is the chosen name.

The ON parameter provides SQL Server with specifics about the data files to be created, rather than taking the defaults. Admittedly, in this instance, there is no need to specify these details, as by taking the defaults, SQL Server would supply the parameters as listed anyway.

This can also be said for the next set of parameters, which deal with the Transaction Log found with LOG ON. In this instance, there is no need to supply these parameters, as again the listed amounts are the SQL Server defaults.

Finally, the collation sequence we specify is actually the default for the server.

Taking all this on board, the command could actually be entered as follows, which would then take all the default settings from SQL Server to build the database:

```
CREATE DATABASE ApressFinancial
```

We can then set the database options as outlined during the discussion of the script earlier in the chapter.

Similarly, if we want to delete the database using T-SQL code, it's a simple case of ensuring that we are not connected within that particular query pane to ApressFinancial via the USE command. Then we use the command DROP followed by the object we want to drop, or delete, and then the name of the object.

```
USE Master
GO
DROP DATABASE ApressFinancial
```

Summary

In this chapter, we looked at designing and building our example database. The steps covered are very important on the development front. The database itself requires careful thought regarding some of the initial settings, but as time moves on and you have a better idea about the volume of data and how people will use the data, you may find you need to alter some of these options. As you move to user acceptance testing, keep an eye on the statistic options mentioned here.

In the next chapter, we'll start adding some meat to the bones of our example database by creating tables to hold data.

CHAPTER 4

■ ■ ■

Security and Compliance

Security is important—more so, in fact, than design, creation, and performance. If your database had no security measures in place, absolutely anyone could come along and steal or corrupt the data, causing havoc to you and your company. And not just in one database, but on every database in every server.

Security can be enforced in many ways on SQL Server: by Windows itself through Windows authentication; by restricting users' access to sensitive data through views; by specifically creating users, logins, and roles that have explicit levels of access; or by encrypting your database, logs, and files.

This chapter will cover some parts of security, although it is impossible to talk about every area of security, mainly because we haven't seen much of SQL Server's contents yet! In Chapter 1, we looked at the difference between Windows authentication and SQL Server authentication, so already you know your options with regard to the type of security you might wish to use. In this chapter, we'll go deeper. You will also learn about the Declarative Management Framework, which is new to SQL Server 2008. In the past, you had to write tools and monitor systems to ensure that any new database created in production was created with the right options. You also had to monitor to make sure items were not being created when they should not be. Now it is possible to create rules on databases, tables, views, and so on to check whether the object in question is compliant with standards defined by the rules. If an object isn't, then you will be notified, and a simple click will allow you to make changes to bring the object back in to alignment.

By the end of this chapter, you will have dealt with

- Logins for individuals and groups
- Roles at the server, database, and application level
- Schemas
- Applying policies to your database to ensure compliance

First of all, you need to understand what **users**, **roles**, and **logins** are.

Logins

The only way anyone can connect to SQL Server is via a login. As discussed in Chapter 1, this doesn't necessarily mean that every user has to have a specific login within SQL Server itself. With Windows authentication, if a user belongs to a specific Windows group, just by belonging to that group, providing that group is contained within SQL Server, the account will have access to SQL Server.

When a database is created, initially only the database owner has any rights to complete any task on that database, whether that be to add a table, insert any data, or view any data. This was the case when we first created our ApressFinancial database in Chapter 3. It is only when the database owner grants permissions to other users that they gain extra access to complete tasks.

It is common practice to create a Windows group and place Windows user accounts into that group. This is how we wish to work with our ApressFinancial system, and so we will create some Windows groups for it. We will group logins depending on which department we are dealing with and what we want to allow each group to do. We will allow some groups to add new financial products and other groups to add customers, and, finally, we'll set up a group for batch processes to add interest and financial transactions. We will create a few of these groups so that later in the book we can see security in action.

▰**Note** If you are running on Windows Vista, then you need to be on either Windows Vista Business or Windows Vista Ultimate.

In Chapter 1, I mentioned that you should log in as an administrator account to install SQL Server. This would mean that you are in the BUILTIN/Administrators group, which is a group defined for the local computer that contains Windows users accounts with administrator rights. We can therefore already connect to SQL Server with this login, which includes VMcGlynn. JThakur could not log in, though. However, by adding this account to a group we will be creating, and then adding that group to SQL Server, we will see how they both can.

▰**Note** The process we are about to go through would be the same if we were adding a single user.

Try It Out: Creating a Group

1. Navigate to your Control Panel, then select Administrative Tools ➤ Computer Management.

2. This brings up a screen that shows different aspects of your computer management. We are interested in selecting Local Users and Groups ➤ Groups. When you do so, you will see that there are already several groups within your computer, as shown in Figure 4-1, as well as a large number of groups already defined for the use of SQL Server. These groups differ from groups that we will be defining for accessing the data.

3. JThakur is a product controller and can add new corporate financial products. Right-click Groups and select New Group. This brings up the New Group screen, as shown in Figure 4-2, where we can add our grouping for our product controllers. Apress_Product_Controllers is the group we'll use in this chapter.

4. By clicking Add, we can then add all the Windows user accounts that we wish to be part of this group. We can either type **JThakur** or click Advanced, which brings up a selection dialog box. Clicking the Check Names button adds the user to the group.

Figure 4-1. *List of groups on the computer*

Figure 4-2. *Adding the first group for our application*

If JThakur were on your company network, you would have to prefix the name with the domain name. For example, if you had a network domain called Apress, and JThakur were on that domain (as opposed to your local computer and therefore your local domain, as is the case for our example), then you would type **Apress\JThakur**. Figure 4-3 shows JThakur is on the FAT-BELLY local domain.

Figure 4-3. *JThakur found, ready to add to our group*

5. Click OK and then click the Create button on the New Group screen. Once you have created the group, you should close the New Group dialog box, as we don't want to create any more groups at the moment. This brings us back to the Computer Management dialog box, where we see our new group added, as shown in Figure 4-4.

Figure 4-4. *New group added*

6. We now need to add this group to SQL Server. Open SQL Server Management Studio and navigate to Security ➤ Logins within the Object Explorer. Once there, click New Login, which brings up the dialog box shown in Figure 4-5.

Figure 4-5. *Creating a new login*

7. Click Search to display the Select User or Group dialog box where we will begin our search for our group, as shown in Figure 4-6. This is very similar to the previous search box we saw but has been defined to search for a user or built-in security principal. However, by default, the search will not search for groups. You need to click Object Types and ensure the Groups option is checked on the screen that comes up.

Figure 4-6. *Searching for groups*

8. This allows you to click Advanced, which then lets you complete the search for the group you want. You need to click on Object Types . . . and select the Groups option. Highlight the following group—Apress_Product_Controllers, in this case—as shown in Figure 4-7, and click OK.

Figure 4-7. *Finding the Apress_Product_Controllers group*

9. This brings us back to the Select User or Group dialog box where we will see our group has been added, as shown in Figure 4-8. We can then click OK.

Figure 4-8. *Group found, ready for adding*

Note We are now back at the new login screen where the group will be populated. If we clicked OK at this point, this would only allow the group to connect to SQL Server and nothing else. Members of this group would therefore not be able to do anything. We also will be ignoring the Credentials section. This is used when a login has to access external SQL Server resources.

10. We need to give this group access to the databases we wish to allow them to use. It is vital that you only allow users or groups of users access to the resources they need and don't use the "allow everything, it's easier" approach that I have seen on my travels. We only want our users to see the ApressFinancial database, so we select that database on the Users Mapped to This Login section of the screen shown in Figure 4-9. For the moment, click the Script button. (When you select this option, it doesn't matter which of the three options you choose when selecting where to put the T-SQL.) We will come back to logins in the next section when we examine roles.

Figure 4-9. *Giving a login access to a database*

11. The SQL generated from Figure 4-9 follows. We will look at it in more detail in a moment when we more closely examine adding a login.

```
USE [master]
GO
CREATE LOGIN [FAT-BELLY\Apress_Product_Controllers]
FROM WINDOWS WITH DEFAULT_DATABASE=[master]
GO
USE [ApressFinancial]
GO
CREATE USER [FAT-BELLY\Apress_Product_Controllers]
FOR LOGIN [FAT-BELLY\Apress_Product_Controllers]
GO
```

12. Going back to SQL Server Management Studio, you can see in Figure 4-10 that we have moved to the Status page. Here we can grant or deny access to SQL Server for a Windows account, SQL Server login, or, in our case, Windows group. The second set of options is for enabling or disabling SQL Server logins. The final set of options, specific to SQL Server authentication, allows an account to be unlocked after it has been locked out.

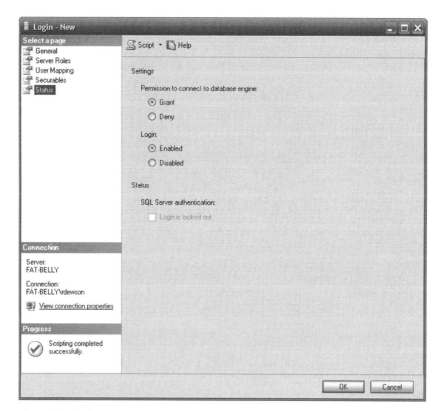

Figure 4-10. *Login status*

13. We can now click OK to add the group. This will complete the addition to SQL Server.

Now that we have created the new group and placed it within SQL Server, we could now switch the user account to JThakur and successfully connect. However, as JThakur, we would only be able to explore the ApressFinancial database we created in Chapter 3. As this is the ideal secure scenario, our task has succeeded in its objective.

Note As I mentioned at the start of this discussion, the process of creating a login would be the same if you wished to add a single user.

For SQL Server authentication, each user needs to be added separately. The process is very similar to that for adding users with Windows authentication, but you must specify a password expiration and enforce password complexity. This forces the Windows password policies for expiration and complexity that exist on the local computer or domain to apply to this login's password.

So now that we have added a login graphically, the same can be achieved via a query pane using T-SQL code. We saw the code generated previously, and we will use it as the basis of our next login creation. This is a very straightforward process, so let's take a look at it next.

Try It Out: Programmatically Working with a Login

1. From SQL Server, select New Query ➤ Database Engine Query. This should bring up an empty query pane similar to the one we saw in Chapter 2.

2. We want to add a second login group. We have available two different methods, and which one we use depends on whether we are going to use Windows authentication or SQL Server authentication. Our first example takes a look at the Windows authentication method. Locate the code from Steps 10 and 11 in the previous "Try It Out: Creating a Group" section (it is repeated here for ease of reference).

```
USE [master]
GO
CREATE LOGIN [FAT-BELLY\Apress_Product_Controllers]
FROM WINDOWS WITH DEFAULT_DATABASE=[master]
GO
USE [ApressFinancial]
GO
CREATE USER [FAT-BELLY\Apress_Product_Controllers]
FOR LOGIN [FAT-BELLY\Apress_Product_Controllers]
GO
```

3. We can now alter this code to create a group that will be defined for users wishing to view customers and their information, probably used in call centers, for example, for the Corporate edition of our software. Also, this time we are going to set the database that will be connected to by default, to our ApressFinancial database. Before entering the following code, we will of course need to add the new group, Apress_Client_Information, within our Computer Management icon found in the Administrative tools of the Control Panel first (see the "Try It Out: Creating a Group" section earlier for more on this). Once you've done this, enter the following code in a new Query Editor window (don't execute it yet):

```
CREATE LOGIN [FAT-BELLY\Apress_Client_Information]
FROM WINDOWS
WITH DEFAULT_DATABASE=[ApressFinancial],
DEFAULT_LANGUAGE=[us_english]
GO
```

The format of this syntax is straightforward. In this case, CREATE LOGIN instructs SQL Server that you want to create a new login called FAT-BELLY\Apress_Client_Information, where FAT-BELLY is the name of the network domain in which the Apress_Client_Information group can be found. You should change the prefix to match your own setup. Here the definition appears surrounded with optional square brackets in case of spaces in the name.

Next, the keywords FROM WINDOWS inform SQL Server that you are creating a login with Windows authentication. After that, you define the name of the database that the login will connect to when a connection is made using WITH DEFAULT_DATABASE. Finally, the second option specifies the default language the connection will use, although it is possible at any time to alter the language using the Set Language option. This allows this group to connect to SQL Server.

4. Once you have placed the code in your query pane, you can execute it by pressing either Ctrl+E or F5 or by clicking the Execute button on the toolbar. Once it finishes executing, you should see the new login in the Security node within the Object Explorer on the left, as shown in Figure 4-11. If you right-click the new login and select Properties, you will see the same screen and details as we saw when we created the login graphically.

Figure 4-11. *Both logins created*

5. We can then give the login access to SQL Server or disable it by using the ALTER LOGIN command. It is also possible to alter the login's default database. In our graphical example, if you check back to Figure 4-5, you will see that the default database was called master. It would be better for the login to connect to the correct database. The following code informs SQL Server that it should connect our login to the ApressFinancial database by default, rather than the master database as defined previously. Remember to change the prefix as appropriate:

```
ALTER LOGIN [FAT-BELLY\Apress_Product_Controllers]
WITH DEFAULT_DATABASE=ApressFinancial
```

6. The final piece in the jigsaw is to grant the Windows account access to the database, which will then allow the login to use the ApressFinancial database. To do this, we need to switch from the master database to the ApressFinancial database with the USE keyword followed by the name of the database.

Using CREATE USER, we can then specify the name of the user we want in our database. The standard procedure is to use the same name as the login, which makes life so much easier when maintaining the system in general. We then use FOR LOGIN to define which server login we want to map to this database user:

```
USE ApressFinancial
GO
CREATE USER [FAT-BELLY\Apress_Client_Information]
FOR LOGIN [FAT-BELLY\Apress_Client_Information]
GO
```

Server Logins and Database Users

As you now know, there are two steps to complete, whether you want to create a SQL Server authentication–based login or a Windows authentication–based login. The first is a server login, which was the first part of creating a login that we went through. A server login is one that, when used, can connect only to the server itself. It cannot use any of the user databases within SQL Server. The second step was creating the database user; in the graphical section that we looked at first, this is when we selected the databases we wanted to use.

Within SQL Server, permissions can be granted at multiple levels, including the server and database level. Examples of server-level permissions include creating new logins or managing server properties. Examples of database permissions include being able to read data from a table or being able to create new tables. One server login can be associated with multiple users in different databases. Generally, when using Windows authentication, a database username is the same as the login name, but this does not have to be the case. It does, however, simplify administration. In this book, we will mostly be dealing with database-level permissions, but we will briefly examine server roles in the following section.

Roles

Three different types of roles exist within SQL Server: fixed server roles, database roles (which refers to the general roles included during installation of SQL Server; component-specific roles such as those for Reporting Services that are added when the component is installed; and user-defined roles), and application roles.

Fixed Server Roles

Within SQL Server, specific predefined roles are set up to allow certain tasks and to restrict other tasks. Someone with the right permissions, such as a system administrator, can assign these roles to any user ID or group of user IDs within SQL Server.

If you look at the Server Roles node in the Object Explorer, you will see a list of roles as shown in Figure 4-12. But what do they mean? You get a little hint if you move to the Server Roles node within SQL Server Management Studio.

Figure 4-12. *Fixed server roles*

■**Note** It is not possible to create your own server role.

These roles, available for anyone to use across the server, can perform the following tasks:

- bulkadmin: Run BULK INSERT statements.
- dbcreator: Create, alter, or drop databases as well as restore them.
- diskadmin: Administer disk files.
- processadmin: Kill a session running T-SQL code.
- public: View any database permission but not alter any.
- securityadmin: Manage logins including passwords for SQL logins and login permissions.
- serveradmin: Administer the server and carry out tasks such as changing options and even starting and shutting down the server.
- setupadmin: Work with more than one server, where the servers are linked and manage the linked server definitions.
- sysadmin: Perform any activity.

Server roles are static objects. They contain groups of actions that operate at the server level rather than at the database level. When creating a new login, you could assign these server roles to it if you wanted the login to carry out server actions as well as any database-related actions, if required.

If your Windows account belongs to the BUILTIN/Administrators group, then it automatically belongs to the sysadmin server role. You can check this yourself by highlighting the sysadmin server role, right-clicking it, and selecting Properties to bring up the dialog box shown in Figure 4-13. You should see BUILTIN/Administrators listed. As more logins are created, they can be added to this role via the Add button.

Although we are not going to alter this for our example database, having Windows XP administrators automatically being administrators for SQL Server can be a bit of a security issue. Many companies batten down their computers so that no user is an administrator of his or her local machine. By doing this, they stop people from adding their own software, shareware, games, or whatever to a machine that is administrated and looked after by a support team.

This helps keep the machine stable, and throughout your organization everyone will know that a piece of software developed on one machine will work on any other. Therefore, users won't have administrator rights on their Windows machine and won't have those rights in SQL Server. This is not the case in all organizations. By leaving the Administrators group in the sysadmin role, everyone who has administrator rights on their PC will have system administrator rights within SQL Server. As the owner of the database, you have now lost control of the security and development of your SQL Server database.

■**Note** Because this book assumes that we're using either a standalone PC or a secure set of users, it is safe to keep the Administrators group. However, you will find that this group is usually removed from database setups to keep the security of the database intact. It is worth keeping in mind that before removing the login, or removing it from the sysadmin role, you should set up a new group or user as a system administrator to prevent locking yourself out.

Figure 4-13. *Members of the sysadmin role*

Database Roles

Database roles deal with actions that are performed at the database level. Actions within SQL Server can be grouped into different types of actions.

Following are the existing database roles installed with SQL Server and what they can or cannot do:

- dbo/db_owner: Specifies the owner of the database
- db_accessadmin: Can manage access to a database for logins
- db_backupoperator: Can back up the database
- db_datareader: Can read data from all user-defined tables
- db_datawriter: Can perform any write actions to user tables
- db_ddladmin: Can perform Data Definition Language (DDL) actions such as creation of tables
- db_denydatareader: Cannot read data from user tables
- db_denydatawriter: Cannot write data from user tables
- db_securityadmin: Can modify database role membership and manage permissions
- public: Can see any database objects that are created with public, or full rights, access (every user that you create will belong to the public database role)

Although you will put the existing database roles to use, you'll find it helpful to create new database roles—a common task in SQL Server—when you want to be very specific about permissions particular users have. You do this by creating a specific database role, and then adding the Windows accounts/Windows groups/SQL Server logins to your role. If you wanted to group several groups together, then you might create a new role.

Application Roles

Databases are written for applications. However, not all databases exist for just one application. Application roles allow you to define one role for accessing a database based on the application that is connecting, rather than having security for different groups of users or single users. Let's look at an example.

Consider a central database that holds client data. This database is in turn accessed from the sales order department, which has its own separate database. The client database is also accessed from the debt recovery department, which also has its own database.

As a database administrator, you may set up user groups for each application. Say you have a Debt Recovery group and a Sales Order Processing group. Debt Recovery would want to see information that was hidden from the Sales Order group, such as how in debt a customer is. But what if a user, such as JThakur, worked in both the debt recovery and sales order departments, in two different part-time jobs, for instance? While working as part of the Sales Order group, JThakur could see information that was not pertinent to that group.

You can set up an application role for Sales Order and another for Debt Recovery, thus removing the conflict of having two different sets of security settings for the one user. Also, when users move departments, you are not wasting time revoking one set of roles to give them a new set of roles for their new department.

An application role overrides any user security settings and is created for giving an application access to SQL Server. Therefore, the Sales Order Processing application would define the access for anybody using it.

An application role has no users; it is used when you wish to define what an application can access within your database and what it cannot. We need to create an application role for examples shown later in this book, so let's do this now.

Try It Out: Creating a New Application Role

1. Navigate to the ApressFinancial database, expand the Security node, right-click Roles, and select New Application Role. In the dialog box that appears, enter a useful role name and a password, as shown in Figure 4-14. This role will be for the banking application through which users will want to look at checks, cash withdrawals, etc.

2. Click Securables in Object Explorer on the left-hand side, and then click Add and then Add Objects. This is how we begin to define what objects we want to assign to this role.

3. In the Add Objects dialog box that appears, leave the options as they are shown in Figure 4-15 and click OK. We have seen this screen a couple of times already, so there is no need to explain it again.

Figure 4-14. *Creating a new application role*

Figure 4-15. *Selecting the type of objects to add*

4. As we don't have much within our database that we can give permissions to just now, select Databases, as shown in Figure 4-16, and click OK. We are going to give this application authority to access our database, but not the ability to do anything (mainly because we don't have anything it can do yet).

Figure 4-16. *Selecting the database*

5. Click Browse. We now see a list of all the databases within the server. As shown in Figure 4-17, select ApressFinancial, as this is the only database this role will access.

Figure 4-17. *ApressFinancial database selected*

6. Clicking OK brings us back to the Select Objects screen, and clicking OK again gets us back to the Securables screen, where we can allow or deny specific actions, as you see in Figure 4-18. Leave everything unchecked for the moment; we will come back to this later in the book when we look at stored procedures in Chapter 10.

Figure 4-18. *Application roles' explicit permission settings*

7. Click OK to finish creating our application role.

Schemas

In the following chapters, we will be creating SQL Server objects to hold and work with our data. We could create these objects so that each could be seen as its own small part of the overall solution. It would make for better organization, though, if objects that could be seen as subsets of the whole solution were grouped together. For example, in our example, we could group share details and share prices together as share information, or group the financial transactions the customer makes using the transactions and transaction types tables together. These groupings could then be used as the basis of security to the underlying data for when a SQL Server connection tries to access the data. These groupings we have just talked about exist in SQL Server 2008 and are called **schemas**. Therefore, a schema is a method of creating a group and placing objects within that group, which can then be used to grant or revoke permissions as a group to SQL Server connections.

Prior to SQL Server 2005, each object was owned by a user account. Whenever a user left, quite often it would mean moving the ownership of objects for that user's account to a new account. As you can imagine, in a very large system this could take hours or even days to complete. Now objects are owned by schemas, and the many objects that exist will be contained within one schema in our very large system. Although a schema will still be owned by a SQL Server account, as we will see when we take a look at the syntax in a moment, the number of schemas should be a fraction of the number of objects, even in very large systems, and therefore moving ownership will be easier and faster.

So by having a schema within our solution and assigning objects to that schema, not only are we improving security, but we are also grouping logical units of the database together, making our solution easier to understand and use.

Creating a schema is very simple, and the syntax is defined as follows:

```
CREATE SCHEMA schema_name AUTHORIZATION owner_name
```

We can now see this in action.

Try It Out: Creating Schemas and Adding Objects

1. Open up a Query Editor window so we can create our first schema. This schema will be used to keep all our transaction details together. Enter the following code:

```
USE ApressFinancial
GO
CREATE SCHEMA TransactionDetails AUTHORIZATION dbo
```

2. When we execute this by pressing F5 or Ctrl+E or by clicking the Execute button, we should see it successfully complete. This will have created a new schema where the owner of the schema is the dbo user. This means that any login with sysadmin privileges will automatically have access to this schema because it maps to the dbo user in all databases. If you execute the code successfully, you'll see the following message:

```
Command(s) completed successfully.
```

3. We can then create further schemas for other groupings, such as one for share details or customer details including products. Enter the following code:

```
CREATE SCHEMA ShareDetails AUTHORIZATION dbo
GO
CREATE SCHEMA CustomerDetails AUTHORIZATION dbo
```

4. Execute this code, which adds the schemas to the database. If you execute the code successfully, you'll see the following message:

```
Command(s) completed successfully.
```

5. If we move to the Object Explorer, we can see our schemas in place, as shown in Figure 4-19.

Figure 4-19. *Schemas applied*

Before You Can Proceed with Your Solution

You have now created a database and gained an understanding of the different roles in SQL Server. Before you can proceed and create objects such as tables, you need to clear a couple of obstacles. After the database, the next objects you will create are tables, which you will learn about in the next chapter. So what security considerations do you need to check before you can do this?

First of all, you must be using a database user account that has the authority to add tables to the specific database you are required to—in this case, ApressFinancial. This is the next security issue we will tackle, and you should keep in mind what you learned in the previous chapter about accounts and roles. You also need to have access to that specific database. Let's look at the issue of access to the database if you are using a user ID that did not create the database.

The database was re-created at the very end of the previous chapter under user ID FAT-BELLY\ RDewson. The user who created the database is the database owner, also known as dbo. So how can you check who created the database if you did not? At the end of the last chapter, I asked you to create the database under your own user ID, which, if you followed the instructions so far and you are a local administrator of the machine SQL Server is installed on, you should have the right privileges within SQL Server to do.

If you are working with SQL Server already installed on a Vista/XP/Windows 2003 machine, you need to ensure that your user ID is set up as an administrator user ID, as demonstrated in Chapter 1, or set up specifically as an administrator within SQL Server.

This next section will demonstrate how you check the identity of the database owner.

Try It Out: Checking the Database Owner

1. Ensure that SQL Server Management Studio is open.

2. Navigate to the database that you wish to check on—in this case, ApressFinancial.

3. Click the ApressFinancial database node in Object Explorer on the left-hand side of the screen once, and then right-click.

4. Select Properties to bring up the Database Properties dialog box shown in Figure 4-20. On the General tab, you will see an item named Owner. This is the fully qualified Vista/XP/Win2K account preceded by the domain or local machine name.

Figure 4-20. *Database Properties*

5. Click Cancel to close this dialog box.

Ownership of tables and other database objects is just as important. If you create a table using the same login ID as that which you created the database with, or use a logon ID that is a member of the sysadmin role that is also implicitly mapped to the dbo user in the database, the table will have a default schema of dbo. However, if you logged in with a different user ID, the table would have that user's default schema as the prefix to the table name, replacing the dbo prefix.

Now that we know who the database owner is, it is up to that user, or another user who has system administration rights (in other words, a login that has the sysadmin server role or has the db_owner database role), to allow any other specified user the ability to create tables within the database. We have a user called JThakur who is not a system administrator, but a developer. Recall we created this user in Chapter 1, and that this user could not log in to SQL Server.

The next section will go through a scenario where, as a developer, JThakur has no rights to create any new items. However, we will rectify this situation in the next section, where we will alter JThakur so that he can connect to SQL Server and create a table.

Try It Out: Allowing a User to Create a Table

1. Log on to SQL Server as a `sysadmin` if required. (However, you are probably already logged in as a sysadmin.) Create a new login by right-clicking the Logins node on the Server Security node and selecting New Login. This brings up the new login screen, which we can populate with the login name of the user by typing in the details of the login, as shown in Figure 4-21. We are also going to allow this user to connect to `ApressFinancial` by default when he or she logs in.

Figure 4-21. *New login*

2. We are not going to assign this user any server roles, but we are going to assign this user to the `db_owner` role, as you see in Figure 4-22. This will allow the user to create tables as well as create and work with other objects and data. We could have selected `db_ddladmin`, but this would only have allowed the user to create objects and not create data.

Figure 4-22. *New login with database access*

3. We now click OK, which will create not only a server login, but also a database user in ApressFinancial for JThakur, as shown in Figure 4-23.

Figure 4-23. *User login accounts*

JThakur is now in a position to log in to SQL Server and create tables in the ApressFinancial database.

Declarative Management Framework

The security of a database does not just involve ensuring that only the correct people can log in to the system and see only the data that they are authorized to see. Security also involves knowing that the basis of the data has met certain defined compliance criteria. This comes under the header of Declarative Management Framework (DMF). SQL Server 2008's DMF allows policies to be defined to ensure that SQL Server objects follow a defined set of rules. These rules are not compulsory, but rather generate warnings showing that you are not in compliance. The DMF also includes tools to rectify such problem situations. The logic behind DMF is for administrators to determine how an installation should be defined with its setup and to then have the ability to enforce the DMF defined if any created installation does not meet the criteria.

There are three aspects to DMF, and you must understand all three before you can make DMF work for you:

Facets: A facet is a grouping that exists to place conditions in to. Facets are prebuilt within SQL Server and expose conditions that can be tested within a policy. Each facet group contains logically combined conditions. One example would be the Login facet, which contains conditions to test whether a login is locked, the default database, the last time the password was altered, whether password expiration is enabled, and so on.

Policies: A policy defines one or more conditions to be applied to a server. Database administrators or even auditors define policies to ensure that specified conditions are met. Historically, one of the largest areas of contention with installations of SQL Server has been that it required the database administrators to write their own stored procedures and schedule them to ensure that every database complied to company policy. Now it is a simple method of defining a condition and letting Service Broker execute and report on the condition. The result is a greater degree of standardization, as well as ease of programming.

Conditions: A condition within DMF is very similar to any other condition. It tests an attribute to make sure that it meets a certain criteria. A number of conditions for your installations will be built up over time, and it is even good practice to set up conditions to test the value of attributes that should be set by default. Such conditions could surround the checking of the ANSI NULL default, for example. Such a condition would then trap any database where, even by accident, the tested value was altered as part of the set up. Conditions need to be part of a policy.

Try It Out: Building a Condition and a Policy

1. Ensure that SQL Server Management Studio is open. There are two ways to progress with this example. It is possible to create a condition and then the policy, or you can create the condition while building the policy. There is no right or wrong way. For this example, you will be building a condition from inside a policy. From within Object Explorer, expand the Management node, followed by the Policy Management node, and then the Policies node. Right-click and select New Policy, as demonstrated in Figure 4-24.

Figure 4-24. *Create a new policy.*

2. You are now presented with an empty Create New Policy screen. Enter a description of **Database ANSI NULL Default** in the name. Below this, you will see the Check Condition combo box, which holds the condition the policy is testing (see Figure 4-25). When you click the down arrow, select New Condition.

Figure 4-25. *Create a new condition.*

3. Clicking the New button takes you to the Create New Condition screen. It is then necessary to enter a name and select the type of facet you wish to create. As we are creating a database condition, select Database under the Facet option, which exposes the facets that are available. We will be testing that the database has been set up with `AnsiNullDefault` set to False, so in the Expression section, select `AnsiNullDefault` from the list of expressions (see Figure 4-26). Then in the Value column, select False from the list of available options. Once complete, click OK.

Figure 4-26. *The New Condition screen with the description and test expression*

4. Clicking OK returns you back to the New Policy screen, which should like the one shown in Figure 4-27. Ensure the Enabled box is selected. The Check Condition combo box should be populated, and in the Against Targets list, the condition should check Every Database as the database server. You could also refine this condition to only databases that are over a certain size or to online databases. At this point, you should see an Exception at the top of the screen. This is a SQL Server exception detailing that this policy has to have an Execution mode that is not On Demand, as you have enabled the policy. If you want to run the condition on demand, then you don't need to have it enabled. While the policy is disabled, an Execution Mode of None is valid.

Figure 4-27. *New Policy screen that sets the Condition*

5. Once you click OK, you should notice both the policy and the condition listed, as shown in Figure 4-28. At this point, nothing has been tested and no policy or condition has been checked against any database.

Figure 4-28. *New policy in Object Browser*

6. Find the ApressFinancial database, and select Properties, as shown in Figure 4-29. You are going to alter the AnsiNullDefault option on the database to break the policy.

Figure 4-29. *Open the database properties.*

7. In the Properties screen of the database, scroll down to the Miscellaneous section and switch ANSI NULL Default to True, as shown in Figure 4-30. Click OK.

Figure 4-30. *Alter the database property to break the condition.*

8. Now that the database is no longer compliant, you need to run the policy and test it. Running the policy normally would be a task scheduled at periodic times, with the results sent to the relevant person. You can schedule the running of a policy by using a job to build the script. You will learn about the use of jobs in Chapter 6 when you see how to back up and restore a database. For the moment, as demonstrated in Figure 4-31, highlight the policy, right-click, and select Test Policy from the pop-up menu.

Figure 4-31. *Find the policy and test it.*

9. You are now presented with a Run Now screen, similar to the one shown in Figure 4-32. When you are ready, click the Check button. You should see similar results to those shown in the figure, which demonstrate that your database is out of policy.

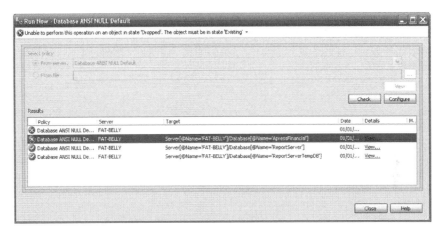

Figure 4-32. *The results of the test in the Run Now window*

10. It is not necessary to close this dialog and step through and find all the times that have failed any policy tests you have. To clean up your database of all policies that you have set up, even if there is just one, as you have built in this example, click the Configure button as seen toward the right in Figure 4-32. This configures the database and sets all the policies to the values set.

11. Run Check again, and you should see a healthy database as demonstrated by the green ticks in Figure 4-33.

Figure 4-33. *All is well with your database.*

Summary

There is a great deal to cover concerning security and its different aspects. I would like to recap everything that we have seen just for one last time to ensure that you understand how everything fits together.

Before you can connect to SQL Server, an administrator of the SQL Server installation must give you permission to connect. In a Windows authentication setup, the administrator would either allow your Windows account or a group that contains your Windows account to connect to SQL Server. He or she can do this by either using the GUI and creating a login via the Security node or using the CREATE LOGIN ... FROM WINDOWS T-SQL statement. If you are in a SQL Server authentication setup, then a user ID and password would be created within SQL Server, again either via the Security/Logins node or by using the CREATE LOGIN ... PASSWORD = 'password' syntax.

Once a connection has been made, you can create a user login within the database using the
CREATE USER ... syntax. This allows either the Windows account or the SQL Server login access to
the database.

It is then possible to place the user into a role: either a predefined role or, more likely, a custom
role that you create. This role can be used to determine what can and cannot be accessed within SQL
Server tables, views, stored procedures, and any other object. Therefore, a role allows groups of users
in one statement to be granted or revoked access to objects within SQL Server. Without roles, as new
people join and as old people leave, or as people move between departments, you would need to
grant or revoke privileges as required—quite an onerous task.

Finally, when creating objects, as you will see in the next few chapters, these objects are owned
by schemas. This allows for groups of objects to belong to a specific schema rather than a specific
user login. This also reduces the overhead of granting privileges and allows the grouping of objects
that belong together, making your application easier to understand.

This chapter continued our coverage of security within SQL Server 2008. At this point in the
book, you now know about SQL Server authentication and Windows authentication, and you have
discovered how to control access to databases. Even during the installation process, the sa login and
password enforcement were discussed on that special account. Our discussions on security are by
no means finished because there are still several areas that we need to explore together, which we
will do as we go through the book.

Security is the most important part of ensuring that your organization continues to have the
ability to work. A security breach could result in lost income and will certainly mean that many
people will be unable to do their work. It can also lead to unfulfilled orders, backlogs, or even fraud-
ulent transactions. Regardless of whether you have the most well-designed database or the most
poorly performing application ever, if you allow the wrong person into the wrong database, the
result will be catastrophic.

■ ■ ■

Defining Tables

Now that we've created the database, it obviously needs to have the ability to store information. After all, without this, what is the point of a database? The first area that needs to be worked on is the table definitions.

To be functional, a database needs at least one table, but it can have many and, depending on the solution you are building, the number of tables can become quite large. Therefore, it is important that you as a developer know as much about tables, their structures, and their contents as possible. The aim of this chapter is to teach just that, so that you have a sound base to work from regarding tables, which you can then use for the creation of other objects associated with tables.

The design of a table is crucial. Each table needs to contain the correct information for its collection of columns to allow the correct relationships to be established. One of the skills of a database developer or administrator is to ensure that the final design is the correct solution, hence avoiding painful alterations once further development of the system is in progress. For example, if we designed a system where the table definitions had some major problems and required columns to be moved around, then every aspect of an application would have to be revisited. This would mean quite a large redesign. We looked at database design in Chapter 3, where we also created the database in which our tables will reside, so we know what tables we need and what data they will store.

So that we can successfully create a table, this chapter will cover the following:

- The definition of a table
- The different types of data that can be stored
- How and where a table is stored
- Creating a table using SQL Server Management Studio and Query Editor
- Dealing with more advanced areas of table creation including
  - How to make a row unique
  - Special data states
- Dealing with pictures and large text data

What Is a Table?

A table is a repository for data, with items of data grouped in one or more columns. Tables contain zero or more rows of information. An Excel spreadsheet can be thought of as a table, albeit a very simple table with few or no rules governing the data. If you look at Figure 5-1, you will see that the first three columns contain data that can be assumed to be first name, last name, and date of birth, but the fourth column is free-format and varies between a hotel room number, a house number, and a flat number. There is no consistency. In fact, in Excel, all the columns could in reality contain any data.

A	B	C	D	E	F	G
Julie	Dewson	01/06/1964	Room 213	Grand Hotel	Regents Park	London
Jitendra	Thakur	02/03/1975	Flat 40	Block 7	Main Drive	
Vic	McGlynn	04/09/1983	80	Woodland Drv		

Figure 5-1. *Excel showing partial address details*

What sets a table inside SQL Server apart from other potential tables is that a SQL Server table will have specific types of data held in each column, and a predetermined type of data defined for a column can never change without affecting every row of data within that column for that table. If you use Excel, in a specific column you could have a character in one row, a number in the next row, a monetary value in the following row, and so on. That cannot happen in a database table. You can store all of these different values, but they would all have to be stored as a data type that holds strings, which defeats the purpose of using a database in the first place.

At the time a table is created, every column will contain a specific data type. Therefore, very careful consideration has to be made when defining a table to ensure that the column data type is the most appropriate. There is no point in selecting a generic data type (a string, for example) to cover all eventualities, as you would have to revisit the design later anyway.

A table's purpose is to hold specific information. The table requires a meaningful name and one or more columns defined, each given a meaningful name and a data type; in some cases, you want to set a restriction on the maximum number of characters that the column can hold.

When it comes time to create a table, you do have to be connected to SQL Server with a login that belongs to the correct server or database role that can create tables, such as sysadmin or db_ddladmin. When you create a table, it has to be owned within the database, and this is done via assigning the table to a schema. Recall Chapter 4, which discusses a schema for grouping objects and as a basis for object security.

Some data types have fixed storage specifications, whereas with other data types, you have to decide for yourself how many characters the maximum will be. If you had a column defined for holding surnames, it would hold character values. There would also be no sense in setting the maximum length of this column at 10 characters, as many surnames are longer than this. Similarly, there would be little sense in saying the maximum should be 1,000 characters. A sensible balance has to be reached. On top of this, though, Microsoft does provide you with the ability to set a maximum value, but the characters entered are stored rather than a fixed amount. These data types are known as variable-length data types and only apply to a few data types. They are detailed in the following sections.

The rows of data that will be held in a table should be related logically to each other. If a table is defined to hold customer information, then this is all it should hold. Under no circumstances should you consider putting information that was not about a customer in the table. It would be illogical to put, for example, details of a customer's orders within it.

SQL Server Data Types

You have learned a great deal about SQL Server before we even create our first table. However, it is essential to know all of this information before creating a table and looking at the security of your database to avoid any ramifications of it all going horribly wrong. You also now know why you have to be careful with users to ensure that they have enough security privileges to build tables. In this section, you will be introduced to the data types that exist within SQL Server. Some of these can be defined as data types for columns within tables, while others are used within T-SQL programs.

We need to cover one last area before you define your first table, and this concerns the types of data that can be stored within a table in SQL Server. Defining a table can be completed either in SQL Server Management Studio, Query Editor, or SQL Server's database designer tool. You can also create a table through a number of other means using third-party developer tools and languages, but these two methods are the ones this book will focus on. We will create the first table with SQL Server Management Studio. This is the Customers table, which will hold details about each customer. But before we can do this, it is necessary to look at the different types of data that can be stored.

Table Data Types

SQL Server has many different data types that are available for each column of data. This section will explain the different data types and help you down the path of choosing the right type for each column. Data types described in this section are known as base data types. Recall when looking at SQL Server scripting options in Chapter 2 that you have the option to convert user data types to base data types. This book only concentrates on base data types; however, it is possible to create your own user data types, and there are advantages to doing so. If you want to have consistency over several tables for a specific column—usually, but not exclusively, on the same server—then it is possible to create a data type, give it a name, and use it when defining a table. For example, you might want all tax identifiers to be defined the same. Once we have covered these base data types, you will see a demonstration of this.

You can use .NET to build more complex data types that also perform extra functionality. See *Pro SQL Server 2005 Assemblies* by Robin Dewson and Julian Skinner (Apress, 2005).

You will find that several data types may look similar, but keep in mind that each data type has a specific use. For example, unless you really need to define characters to be stored as Unicode, then don't use the n prefix data types. Unicode characters use up more space than standard characters due to the potentially wide range of characters that SQL Server has to store. Also, when looking at numbers, if the largest value you will store in a column is 100, then don't go for the data type that will allow the largest number to be stored. This would be a waste of disk space.

Let's take a look at the possible base data types you can use in a table. Afterward, you'll see data types you can use in a program.

char

The char data type is fixed in length. If you define a column to be 20 characters long, then 20 characters will be stored. If you enter fewer than the number of characters defined, the remaining length will be space filled to the right. Therefore, if a column were defined as char (10), "aaa" would be stored as "aaa   ". Use this data type when the column data is to be of fixed length, which tends to be the case for customer IDs and bank account IDs.

nchar

The nchar type is exactly the same as char, but will hold characters in Unicode format rather than ANSI. The Unicode format has a larger character set range than ANSI. ANSI character sets only hold up to 256 characters. However, Unicode character sets hold up to 65,536 different characters. Unicode data types do take up more storage in SQL Server; in fact, SQL Server allocates double the space internally, so unless there is a need in your database to hold this type of character, it is easier to stick with ANSI.

varchar

The varchar data type holds alphanumeric data, just like char. The difference is that each row can hold a different number of characters up to the maximum length defined. If a column is defined as varchar(50), this means that the data in the column can be up to a maximum of 50 characters long. However, if you only store a string of 3 characters, then only 3 storage spaces are used up. This defi-nition is perfect for scenarios where there is no specific length of data—for example, people's names or descriptions where the length of the stored item does not matter. The maximum size of a varchar column is 8,000 characters. However, if you define the column with no size—that is, varchar()—then the length will default to 1.

You can also use another setting that can exceed the 8,000-character limit, by defining the data type with the constant max. You would use this when you believe the data to be below 8,000 characters in length but you want to account for instances when the data may exceed this limit. If you know that you will exceed the 8,000-character limit in at least one row, then use this option. Finally, you should use max for large blocks of text, because it will eventually supersede the text data type.

nvarchar

The nvarchar type is defined in a similar way to varchar, except it uses Unicode and therefore doubles the amount of space required to store the data.

text

The text data type holds data that is longer than 8,000 characters. However, you should not use this data type.

■**Caution** The text data type will be removed in a future release of SQL Server, so you should use varchar(max) instead.

---

ntext

As with the text data type, ntext is the Unicode version and should also not be used.

■**Caution** The ntext data type will be removed in a future release of SQL Server, so you should use nvarchar(max) instead.

---

image

image is very much like the text data type, except it is for any type of binary data, which includes images but could also include movies, music, and so on.

■**Caution** The image data type will be removed in a future release of SQL Server, so you should use varbinary(max) instead.

---

int

The int, or integer, data type is used for holding numeric values that do not have a decimal point (whole numbers). There is a range limit to the value of the numbers held: int will hold any number between the values of –2,147,483,648 and 2,147,483,647.

bigint

A bigint, or big integer, data type is very similar to int, except that much larger numbers can be held. A range of –9,223,372,036,854,775,808 through to 9,223,372,036,854,775,807 can be stored.

smallint

The smallint data type, or small integer, holds small integer numbers in the range of –32,768 through to 32,767. Do take care when defining columns with this data type and make sure there really is no possibility of exceeding these limits. There is always a big danger when creating a column with this data type that you will have to go back and change the data type, so if in doubt, select int.

tinyint

The tinyint, or tiny integer, data type is even smaller than smallint and holds numbers from 0 through to 255. It could be used to hold a numerical value for each US or Canadian state or perhaps every county in the United Kingdom.

decimal/numeric

Both the decimal and numeric data types hold the same precision and ranges of data. The range is from –10 to the power 38 + 1 through to 10 to the power 38 – 1. These are quite large ranges, from –0.00000000000000000000000000000000000001 through to 10,000,000,000,000,000,000,000,000,000. However, do take care with this, as you cannot store 38 digits to the right and left of the decimal point. You can only store up to and including 38 digits. So, the greater the precision required to the right of the decimal point, the fewer digits are left to represent the whole number.

float

The float data type is used for numbers where the decimal point is not fixed. float data types hold very large numbers in the range of –1.79E+308 through 1.79E+308. There is a warning with this data type: the values cannot always be seen as 100% accurate, as they can be approximate. The approximation arises from the way the number is physically stored as binary code. You will have problems where a number ends in .3, .6, or .7. The value stored has to be approximated, or rounded, as some values can't be stored accurately, for they may have more decimal places than can be catered to. A well-known example is the value of Pi.

real

The real data type is very much like float, except that real can store only numbers in the range of –3.40E+38 through 3.40E+38. This data type also holds an approximate value.

money

The money data type is used for holding numeric values up to four decimal places. If you need to use more than four decimal places, you need to look to another data type, such as decimal. This data type doesn't actually store the currency symbol to signify the monetary type, so you should not use this data type for different currencies' values, although you can combine a column using this data type with a second column defining the currency type. The money data type has a range of –922,337,203,685,477.5808 through 922,337,203,685,477.5807. If you need to store the currency symbol of the currency that is held here ($ or USD for dollars, £ or GBP for British pounds, etc.), then you would need to store this separately, as the money data type does not hold the currency symbol. A column defined as money will hold the money to 1/10,000 of a decimal unit, which is a bit of a waste if you are storing the values as Turkish Lira.

smallmoney

This data type is similar to money with the exception of the range, which lies between –214,748.3648 and 214,748.3647.

date

The new date data type has been built to only hold a date from January 1, AD 1 through to December 31, 9999. The format is YYYY-MM-DD. Until this version of SQL Server, it was not possible to hold the date and time, as two separate data types without having to build this yourself using .NET. Therefore, in the past, you were storing unnecessary data. This is a great advancement, as it reduces confusion and gives the correct refinement for the data that the column contains. This was an anomaly until now. In the past, you may not have been sure what the data contained within any column defined with its predecessor, datetime.

datetime

The datetime date type will hold any date and time from January 1, 1753 through to December 31, 9999. However, it stores not only a date, but also a time alongside it. If you just populate a column defined as datetime with a date, a default time of 12:00:00 will be stored as well.

datetime2

Similar to datetime, datetime2 is used to hold a date and a time. The difference is that datetime2 can hold the fractions of a second to a greater precision. It can also store a date from January 1, AD 1 through to December 31, 9999. The format is YYYY-MM-DD hh:mm:ss[.nnnnnnn].

smalldatetime

The smalldatetime data type is very much like datetime, except the date range is January 1, 1900 through to June 6, 2079. The reason for the strange date at the end of the range lies in the binary storage representation of this datetime.

datetimeoffset

If you need to store a date and time relative to a specific date and time zone, then you should define your column with the datetimeoffset data type. The date and time is stored in this data type in Coordinated Universal Time (UTC) value, and then you define the amount of time to add or subtract depending on the time zone that the value should relate to. For example, if you wish to store 6 p.m. on March 24, 2008 in Eastern Standard Time, the value would be 2008-03-24 13:00:00 +05:00, because New York is five hours ahead of UTC. The format for this data type is YYYY-MM-DD hh:mm:ss[.nnnnnnn] [+|-]hh:mm.

time

If you just wish to hold a time based on the 24-hour clock, then you can define a column to use the time data type. The format is hh:mm:ss[.nnnnnnn]. Like the date data type, the time data type was introduced to provide a column with the correct data type for the data that is required to be held. As you can see from the format, the time data type can hold up to a precision of 100 nanoseconds, which is ideal for more precision-based applications than the datetime data type.

hierarchyid

Prior to SQL Server 2008, producing a hierarchy of data could prove complex and usually involved a self-join of the data. Now, however, it is possible to define a column of the hierarchyid data type that allows you to say how a given row sits in the overall hierarchy of rows. This is a complex Common Language Runtime (CLR)–based data type, which is not covered within this book. I recommend *Accelerated SQL Server 2008* by Rob Walters, Michael Coles, Robin Dewson, Fabio Claudio Ferracchiati, Jan Narkiewicz, and Robert Rae (Apress, 2008).

geometry

The geometry data type is a planar CLR data type that allows you to store geographical information in a "flat earth" way. Data within this data type can be one of 11 different geometry measurements, including point, curve, and polygon. It is only possible to store one type of measurement in each column defined, and part of the data stored will be the definition of the type of data.

geography

The geography CLR data type stores "round earth" data. Therefore, data is stored as degrees of latitude and longitude but uses the same type of measurement as the geometry data type.

■**Note** The geometry and geography data types require a chapter, if not a whole book, to understand and deal with fully. They won't be covered within this book.

---

rowversion

rowversion is an unusual data type, as it is used for a column for which you would not be expected to supply a value. The rowversion data type holds a binary number generated by SQL Server, which will be unique for each row within a database. Every time a record is modified, the column with this data type in the record will be modified to reflect the time of modification. Therefore, you can use columns with this data type in more advanced techniques where you want to keep a version history of what has been changed. rowversion used to be called timestamp, and you may come across timestamp in databases created under older versions of SQL Server.

uniqueidentifier

The uniqueidentifier data type holds a Globally Unique Identifier (GUID). It is similar to the timestamp data type, in that the identifier is created by a SQL Server command when a record is inserted or modified. The identifier is generated from information from the network card on a machine, processor ID, and the date and time. If you have no network card, then the uniqueidentifier is generated from information from your own machine information only. These IDs should be unique throughout the world.

binary

Data held in the binary data type is in binary format. This data type is mainly used for data held as flags or combinations of flags. For example, perhaps you want to hold flags about a customer. You need to know whether the customer is active (value = 1), ordered within the last month (value = 2), placed the last order for more than $1,000 (value = 4), or meets loyalty criteria (value = 8). This would add up to four columns of data within a database. However, by using binary values, if a client had a value of 13 in binary, then he would have values 1 + 4 + 8, which means he is active, his last order was more than $1,000, and he meets the loyalty criteria. When you define the column of a set size in binary, all data will be of that size.

varbinary

The varbinary data type is very much like binary, except the physical column size per row will differ depending on the value stored. varbinary(max) can hold values more than 8,000 characters in length and should be used for holding data such as images.

bit

The bit data type holds a value of 0 or 1. Usually, bit is used to determine true (1) or false (0) values.

xml

XML data can be held in its own special data type rather than in a varchar(max) column. There are special query commands that can then be used to query and work with this data. Prior to SQL Server 2005, XML data was almost an afterthought with no data type, and earlier versions of SQL Server had extremely limited functionality to work with the XML data that did exist.

Program Data Types

There are three more data types that can be used within a program, which we will take a look at now.

cursor

Data can be held in a memory-resident state called a **cursor**. It is like a table, as it has rows and columns of data, but that's where the similarity ends. There are no indexes, for example. A cursor is used to build up a set of data for processing one row at a time.

table

A table data type has similarities to both a cursor and a table. It holds rows and columns of data, but the data cannot be indexed. In this case, you deal with the data a "set at a time," like a normal table. We'll look at both the cursor and table data types later in the book, as they are more advanced topics.

sql_variant

It is possible to have a data type that can hold a few different data types. I will be honest: I don't recommend using this data type, as it shows that you are unsure of your data and what type of data to expect. Before putting data into a data type, I feel you need to be sure what type of data you are getting. Although we have sql_variant as a program data type, it can also be used as a column data type, but the same arguments apply. We won't look at this data type any further within this book.

Columns Are More Than Simple Data Repositories

Assigning a data type to a column defines what you expect to hold at that point. But column definitions have more power than just this. It is possible to fill the column with a seed value, or even with no value whatsoever.

Default Values

As a row is added to a table, rather than enforcing developers to add values to columns that could be populated by SQL Server, such as a column that details using a date and time when a row of data was added, it is possible to place a default value there instead. The default value can be any valid value for that data type. A default value can be overwritten and is not "set in stone."

Generating IDENTITY Values

For those readers who have used Microsoft Access, the IDENTITY keyword option is similar to AutoNumber.

When adding a new row to a SQL Server table, you may wish to give this row a unique but easily identifiable ID number that can be used to link a row in one table with a row in another. Within the ApressFinancial database, there will be a table holding a list of transactions that needs to be linked to the customer table. Rather than trying to link on values that cannot guarantee a unique link (first name and surname, for example), a unique numeric ID value gives that possibility, providing it is used in conjunction with a unique index. If you have a customer with an ID of 100 in the Customers table and you have linked to the Transaction table via the ID, you could retrieve all the financial transactions for that customer where the foreign key is 100. However, this could mean that when you want to insert a new customer, you have to figure out which ID is next via some T-SQL code or using a table that just held "next number" identities. But fear not, this is where the IDENTITY option within a column definition is invaluable.

By defining a column using the IDENTITY option, you are informing SQL Server that

- The column will have a value generated by SQL Server.

- There will be a start point (seed).

- An increment value is given, informing SQL Server by how much each new ID should increase.

- SQL server will manage the allocation of IDs.

Normally, a user would not insert the value; instead, SQL Server would create it automatically. However, you can enter explicit values if you use the SET IDENTITY_INSERT option to alter the database setting to ON for the specific table.

You would have to perform all of these tasks if SQL Server did not do so. Therefore, by using this option in a column definition, you can use the value generated to create a solid, reliable, and unique link from one table to another, rather than relying on more imprecise selection criteria.

The Use of NULL Values

When building table definitions, there can be columns defined as NULL and columns that have NOT NULLs, or, if using the Table Designer, you can check or uncheck the Allow Nulls option. These two different statements define whether data must be entered into the column or not. A NULL value means that there is absolutely nothing entered in that column—no data at all. A column with a NULL value is a special data state, with special meaning. This really means that the type of data within the column is unknown.

If a field has a NULL value, no data has been inserted into the column. This also means that you have to perform special function statements within any T-SQL code to test for this value. Take the example of a column defined to hold characters, but where one of the rows has a NULL value within it. If you completed a SQL function that carried out string manipulation, then the row with the NULL value would cause an error or cause the row not to be included in the function without any special processing. However, there are times when the use of NULL is a great advantage.

Why Define a Column to Allow NULL?

So what advantages are there to allowing data columns to hold NULL values? Well, perhaps the largest advantage is that if a field has a NULL value, you know for a fact that nothing has been entered into it. If you couldn't define a column as having NULLs, when a column is defined as numeric and has a value of 0, you could not be sure if it has no value or if it does have a valid value of 0. Using NULL allows you to instantly know that the column has no data and you can then work in that knowledge.

Another advantage is the small space that a NULL column takes up. To be precise, it takes up no space whatsoever, again unlike a 0 or a single space, which do take up a certain amount of space. In this age of inexpensive hard drives, this is less of an issue, but if you extrapolate for a database with a million rows and four columns have a space instead of a NULL, that's 4 million bytes (4MB) of space used up unnecessarily. Also, because a NULL takes up no space, then including NULL values means it will be a lot faster to get the data from the database to where it needs to go to either in a .NET program or back to your T-SQL code for further processing.

There will be more on NULL values in Chapter 8.

Image and Large Text Storage in SQL Server

Storing pictures and large amounts of text is different from storing other kinds of information within SQL Server. Pictures can take up large amounts of space. The following also holds true for large amounts of text.

Several scenarios exist where, by holding large amounts of data, SQL Server and the SQL Server installation will end up running into problems. I'll explain why in a minute, but first of all you will see what you should do in SQL Server to handle such data.

If you wish to store large numbers of images or large amounts of text (by large, I mean more than 1MB), you should store these outside SQL Server on the hard drive in a file volume somewhere on the server.

If you do wish to hold image or binary large object (BLOB) data within a table, then if you define a column as varbinary(max), it is possible to hold up to 2^31 bytes of data, or around 2GB. To store the data outside the table, you would supplement this data type with the FILESTREAM parameter. The database also has to have file streaming enabled, which you complete via a special database command known as a system stored procedure, sp_filestream_configure.Using a FILESTREAM will allow faster reading of the data as opposed to the data being held within the table.

If your application does use images or large amounts of text within a column, then keep a close eye on disk space and where the information is stored. By doing so, you can avoid situations where your SQL Server database stops when the limit of disk space is met on your hard drive or it has no growth options left, whether the data is held in SQL Server or on the server file system.

In Chapter 12, there will be discussions about manipulating and inserting images into the database and how this works. However, keep in mind the information just given so that you can start planning now what solution would be best for your database.

Creating a Table in SQL Server Management Studio

This is the first table in our example application. Every organization has to have a set of customers and will need to store these details. Within this table, we will hold information such as each customer's name and an ID to an external system where addresses are held. The only product that our company has where a customer can have an ongoing cash balance with funds that aren't cleared is a bank account. This means our table will also hold the bank account ID, the current balance, and any amount clearing.

Try It Out: Defining a Table

1. Ensure that SQL Server Management Studio is running.

2. Expand the Object Explorer so that you can see the ApressFinancial database, created in Chapter 3.

3. Expand the ApressFinancial database so that you can see the Tables node, as shown in Figure 5-2.

Figure 5-2. *ApressFinancial with no user tables defined in the Tables node*

4. Right-click the Tables node and select New Table. This will take you into the Table Designer. Figure 5-3 shows how the Table Designer looks when you first enter it.

Figure 5-3. *Creating our first table with no columns as yet*

5. From this screen, you need to enter the details for each column within the table. Enter the first column, CustomerId, in the Column Name column. When naming columns, try to avoid using spaces. Either keep the column names without spaces, like I have done with CustomerId, or use an underscore (_) instead of a space. It is perfectly valid to have column names with spaces. However, to use these columns in SQL code, we have to surround the names by square brackets, [ ], which is very cumbersome.

    At the moment, notice that Column Properties in the middle of Figure 5-3 is empty. This will fill up when you start entering a data type after entering the column name. The Column Properties section is just as crucial as the top half of the screen where you enter the column name and data type.

6. The drop-down combo box that lists the data types is one of the first areas provided by SQL Server to help us with table creation. This way, we don't have to remember every data type there is within SQL Server. By having all the necessary values listed, it is simple enough to just select the most suitable one. In this instance, we want to select bigint, as shown in Figure 5-4.

Figure 5-4. *Selecting our data type*

7. The final major item when creating a column within a table is the Allow Nulls check box option. If you don't check the box, some sort of data must be placed in this column. Leaving the check box in the default state will allow NULL values in the column, which is not recommended if the data is required (name, order number, etc.) or the column(s) are going to be used as the main method to find data within your queries, relationships, or indexes. You can also allow NULLs for numeric columns, so instead of needing to enter a zero, you can just skip over that column when it comes to entering the data. In this instance, we want data to be populated within every row as it will be used within a relationship, so remove the check mark.

8. The Column Properties section for our column will now look like the screen shown in Figure 5-5. Take a moment to peruse this section. We can see the name, whether we are allowing NULLs, and the type of data we are storing. There will be changes to what is displayed depending on the data type chosen.

Figure 5-5. *More in-depth properties for columns*

9. We want this column to be an identity column. If you have not already done so, within the Column Properties area, expand the Identity Specification node, as we need to set the Is Identity property to Yes. This will set the Identity Increment to 1 and the Identity Seed to 1 as well, as shown in Figure 5-6.

Identity Specification	Yes
(Is Identity)	Yes
Identity Increment	1
Identity Seed	1

Figure 5-6. *Defining a column as having an identity*

10. It is now possible to add in a few more columns before we get to the next interesting item, shown in Figure 5-7. Go ahead and do so now. Not everybody will have more than a first name and last name, although some people may have initials. Therefore, we will allow NULL values for any initials they may have. We leave the box checked on the `CustomerOtherInitials` column, as shown in Figure 5-7. We also alter the length of this column to ten characters, which should be more than enough.

FAT-BELLY.Apre...ils.Customers*	Object Explorer Details	
Column Name	Data Type	Allow Nulls
CustomerId	bigint	☐
CustomerTitleId	int	☐
CustomerFirstName	nvarchar(50)	☐
▶ CustomerOtherInitials	nvarchar(10) ▾	☑
CustomerLastName	nvarchar(50)	☐

Figure 5-7. *A column that will allow NULL values*

11. We can now define our final columns, which you see in Figure 5-8. The last column will record when the account was opened. This can be done by setting the default value of the `DateAdded` column. The default value can be a constant value, the value from a function, or a value bound to a formula defined here. For the moment, we will use a SQL Server function that returns the current date and time, `GETDATE()`, as shown in Figure 5-8. Then every time a row is added, it is not necessary for a value to be entered for this column, as SQL Server will put the date and time in for you.

Column Name	Data Type	Allow Nulls
CustomerId	bigint	☐
CustomerTitle	int	☐
CustomerFirstName	nchar(50)	☐
CustomerOtherInitials	nchar(10)	☑
CustomerLastName	nchar(50)	☐
AddressId	bigint	☐
AccountNumber	nchar(15)	☐
AccountTypeId	int	☐
ClearedBalance	money	☐
UnclearedBalance	money	☐
▶ DateAdded	date	☐

Figure 5-8. *The table column definition is now complete.*

> **▓Note** In Chapter 3, when we discussed normalization, we also covered when data should be denormalized. The Customers table is the one place we do need a small amount of denormalization for speed of access. To speed up the process when a client goes to a cash point, we will have a column that holds her account number so that we send a single row of data to the cash point. We can therefore cross-check with her card as well as her cleared and uncleared balance for display. This data will also be held within the CustomerProducts and Transactions tables. If the account number was stored in the CustomerProducts table only, we would have to send two rows of data to the cash machine: one with the account number and one with the balances.

12. Before we save the table, we need to define some properties for it, such as the schema owner. On the right, you should see the Table Properties dialog window, as shown in Figure 5-9. If this is not displayed, you can press F4 or from the menu select View ➤ Properties Window. First of all, give the table a name, Customers, and give the table some sort of description. We then move to the schema owner details. When you click the Schema combo box, it presents you with a list of possible schemas the table can belong to. In Chapter 4, we built the schema we want to use for this table, CustomerDetails.

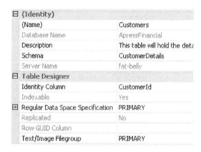

Figure 5-9. *Table properties*

13. Now that we are finished, we can save the table either by clicking the Save toolbar button, which sports a floppy disk icon, or by clicking the X (close) button on the Table Designer to close the window, which should bring up the Save dialog box, asking if we want to save the changes. By clicking Yes, we get a second box asking for the name of the table if we didn't enter a table name in the Table Properties dialog window as shown in Figure 5-10, or the table is saved using the name specified and we are returned to SQL Server Management Studio.

Figure 5-10. *Saving a table that was not given a name*

14. If you now right-click the table and select Properties, you can see important details about the table, as shown in Figure 5-11. The first section details who is currently connected. Then we see the date the table was created, its name, and the schema name of the owner of the table.

Figure 5-11. *Table properties*

15. When you right-clicked to get to Figure 5-11, you will see a list of other options that are available to you, as shown in Figure 5-12:

   - *New Table*: Builds a new table

   - *Design*: Takes you in to the design mode to let you alter a table defenition

   - *Select TOP 1000 Rows*: Displays up to the first 1,000 rows of data

   - *Edit Top 200 Rows*: Allows the first 200 rows to be displayed and can be edited

   - *Script Table As*: Displays several different scripting options, including scripting the table as a CREATE or a DROP, as well as options for SELECTing rows, DELETEing rows, UPDATEing rows, and INSERTing rows

   - *View Dependencies*: Lists out any other stored procedures, views, and objects that use the table

   - *Full-Text Index*: Displays a special type of indexing for text data

   - *Policies*: Lets you view and run policies for the table

   - *Reports*: Creates a custom report for the table

   - *Rename*: Renames a table to a new table

   - *Delete*: Drops the table from the database

   - *Refresh*: Refreshes the list of tables

   - *Properties*: Produces a dialog box with a number of properties about the table

Figure 5-12. *Table properties*

Now that a table has been created in SQL Server Management Studio, let's look at creating a table within the Query pane.

Creating a Table Through the Query Editor

The next table that needs to be created is the one that will hold the details of the financial transactions that each customer has. These transactions will not just be simple money-in and money-out transactions, but will also be those financial transactions involving shares when a dividend is received or a tax credit if the shares are held in a product that is tax-free. We know from our design that details of which product the transaction relates to will be held in a separate table, so we need to create a link between our transaction table and one holding some sort of reference data. It is also necessary to have a link between this table and our CustomerDetails.Customers table. Notice the slight name change as we have now created the table, defined the schema for the table, and attached the schema to the table. This should mean that your naming convention should be schemaname.tablename. Finally, if the transaction relates to shares and is not recording the finances involved, then we need to record that this is the case. To clarify this last point, when a client buys some shares, there will be two records: one for the money leaving the account to buy the shares, and another showing the physical number of shares purchased.

Try It Out: Defining a Table Through Query Editor

1. Ensure that you are pointing to the ApressFinancial database in Query Editor. If you're not, you'llll find that you may be creating the table in the wrong database.

2. In the Query Editor, enter the following code:

```
CREATE TABLE TransactionDetails.Transactions
    (TransactionId bigint IDENTITY(1,1) NOT NULL,
    CustomerId bigint NOT NULL,
    TransactionType int NOT NULL,
    DateEntered datetime NOT NULL,
    Amount numeric(18, 5) NOT NULL,
```

```
ReferenceDetails nvarchar(50) NULL,
Notes nvarchar(max)  NULL,
RelatedShareId bigint NULL,
RelatedProductId bigint NOT NULL)
```

▓Note Notice that when you type this code into the Query Editor, the keywords are colored. For example, CREATE TABLE is in blue, as is NOT NULL. This helps you to avoid typing mistakes.

3. Execute the code by either pressing Ctrl+E or F5 or clicking the toolbar's Execute button.

4. You should now see the following message in the Results pane:

```
The command(s) completed successfully.
```

5. However, you may have received an error message instead. This could be for a number of reasons, from a typing mistake to not having the authority to create tables. I could list every message that you could receive at this point, but I would be doing so for many pages. Taking one example here, as you can see, the error messages generated are usually self-explanatory. This is informing me that I have a typing error on line 5:

```
Msg 102, Level 15, State 1, Line 5
Incorrect syntax near 'NUL'.
```

6. Now move to the Object Explorer. If it is already open, you will have to refresh the Details pane (by right-clicking the Tables node and selecting Refresh). You should then see the TransactionDetails.Transactions table alongside the CustomerDetails.Customers table created previously.

HOW IT WORKS: DEFINING A TABLE THROUGH THE QUERY PANE

Using the Query pane to define a table works very much like SQL Server Management Studio without the graphical aids. Recall that SQL Server Management Studio has prompts for column name, data type, and so on, but here you have to type in every detail. All of the code will be discussed in a moment. However, many people prefer to create a table this way. Having to switch between cursor and keyboard when using the graphical designer can be slower than keying in the details in Query Editor. There is not a lot of time required to create a table this way, and we can build up the table creation as we go along. The query can be saved to a file until it is time to run it and build the table in the database.

Let's now take a look at the T-SQL code that we used to create the table. This code does not include all the options available for creating a table, as there are a large number not used within this book. If you need to use more options or discover what they are, then check in Books Online. When it comes to putting a database solution into a production environment, you should consider these options, although some of them will be for larger enterprise production solutions.

The basic syntax for creating a table is as follows:

```
CREATE TABLE [database_name].[schema_name].table_name
    (column_name data_type [length] [IDENTITY(seed, increment)] [NULL/NOT NULL])
```

There are a greater number of possible options, but for the moment, let's just concentrate on the ones mentioned previously. You should be able to create most tables using this syntax.

The items listed in square brackets in the CREATE TABLE syntax are optional; however, there are times when we will require them. Let me explain. Take the first option, database_name: if you are in the master database and you wish to create a table in the ApressFinancial database, you would have to either switch to that database with the USE command or use the database_name option. Usually you will be in the database where you want to create the table, but this option is ideal when creating code that will be executed unattended. It will ensure that the table is built for the correct database rather than trusting that you are in the right area.

The schema_name option allows us to assign the table to the correct and relevant schema, rather than in the default schema of the user connected.

Next we define the columns. Column name and data type are mandatory. However, depending on the data type, the length is optional. You must prefix the first column with an opening parenthesis (and once you have defined the last column, close the list with a closing parenthesis). Each column should be separated from the previous column by a comma. There is a limit of 1,024 columns for a table. If you get anywhere close to that number, you should sit back and reevaluate your table design, because chances are the design needs to be revised.

Creating a Table: Using a Template

SQL Server has a third method of creating ables, although it is my least favored method. In this section, you will create a table based upon a template that either you define or that comes predefined with SQL Server.

A large number of templates are built into SQL Server Management Studio for everyday tasks. It is also possible to build your own template for repetitive tasks, which is where I can see more power for developers in this area.

Templates can be found in their own explorer window. Selecting View ➤ Template Explorer or pressing Ctrl+Alt+T brings up the Template Explorer window, displayed initially on the right-hand side of SQL Server Management Studio.

Try It Out: Creating a Table Using a Template

1. Expand the Table node on the Template Explorer. About halfway down you will see a template called Create Table, as shown in Figure 5-13. Double-click this to open up a new Query Editor pane with the template for creating a table.

Figure 5-13. *List of templates*

2. Take a close look at the following, which is the listing from the template. A template includes a number of parameters. These are enclosed by angle brackets (<>):

```
-- =========================================
-- Create table template
-- =========================================
USE <database, sysname, AdventureWorks>
GO

IF OBJECT_ID('<schema_name, sysname, dbo>.<table_name,
              sysname, sample_table>', 'U') IS NOT NULL
  DROP TABLE <schema_name, sysname, dbo>.<table_name, sysname,
sample_table>
GO

CREATE TABLE
  <schema_name, sysname, dbo>.<table_name, sysname, sample_table>(
  <column1_name, sysname, c1> <column1_datatype, , int>
  <column1_nullability,, NOT NULL>,
  <column2_name, sysname, c2> <column2_datatype, , char(10)>
  <column2_nullability,, NULL>,
  <column3_name, sysname, c3> <column3_datatype, , datetime>
  <column3_nullability,, NULL>,
  CONSTRAINT <contraint_name, sysname, PK_sample_table>
    PRIMARY KEY (<columns_in_primary_key, , c1>)
)
GO
```

3. By pressing Ctrl+Shift+M, you can alter these parameters to make a set of meaningful code from the template. Do this now, so that the parameters can be altered. Figure 5-14 shows our third table, TransactionDetails. TransactionTypes. The template code as it is only deals with three columns, although it is possible to work with tables of four or more columns. Before choosing to display this screen, you could alter the template code to include the fourth column or as many columns as required, or you could modify the base template if you think that three columns are not enough. When you scroll down, you will see a parameter called CONSTRAINT. You can either leave the details as they are or blank them out; it doesn't matter, as we will be removing that code in a moment.

Figure 5-14. *Template parameters for TransactionTypes*

4. After clicking OK, the code is as follows. The main point of interest is the `IF` statement after switching to the ApressFinancial database. This code queries SQL Server's system tables to check for a TransactionTypes table within the dbo schema. If it does exist, then the DROP TABLE statement is executed. This statement will delete the table defined from SQL Server, if possible. An error message may be displayed if the table has links with other tables or if someone has a lock on it, thus preventing the deletion. We talk about locks in Chapter 8.

```
-- ==========================================
-- Create table template
-- ==========================================
USE ApressFinancial
GO

IF OBJECT_ID('dbo.TransactionTypes', 'U') IS NOT NULL
  DROP TABLE dbo.TransactionTypes
GO

CREATE TABLE dbo.TransactionTypes
(
    TransactionTypeId int NOT NULL,
    TransactionDescription nvarchar(30) NOT NULL,
    CreditType bit NOT NULL,
    CONSTRAINT PK_sample_table PRIMARY KEY (TransactionTypeId)
)
GO
```

5. The full code for the TransactionTypes table follows. Once you have entered it, you can execute it. Note that there are three changes here. First of all, we change the schema name from dbo to the correct schema, TransactionDetails, then we put in the IDENTITY details for the TransactionTypeId column. There is a fourth column to this table, but we are not going to place the fourth column in at this time. We will add it when we take a look at how to alter a table in the section "The ALTER TABLE Statement" later in this chapter. Finally, we remove the CONSTRAINT statement, as we are not creating a key at this time.

```
-- ==========================================
-- Create table template
-- ==========================================
USE ApressFinancial
GO

IF OBJECT_ID('TransactionDetails.TransactionTypes', 'U') IS NOT NULL
  DROP TABLE TransactionDetails.TransactionTypes
GO

CREATE TABLE TransactionDetails.TransactionTypes(
    TransactionTypeId int IDENTITY(1,1) NOT NULL,
    TransactionDescription nvarchar(30) NOT NULL,
    CreditType bit NOT NULL
)
GO
```

Now that we have our third table, we can look at altering the template of the CREATE TEMPLATE, as it would be better to have the IDENTITY parameter there as well as four or five columns.

Creating and Altering a Template

The processes for creating and altering a template follow the same steps. All templates are stored in a central location and are available for every connection to SQL Server on that computer; therefore, templates are not database- or server-restricted. The path to where they reside is

```
C:\Program Files\Microsoft SQL Server\
100\Tools\Binn\VSShell\Common7\IDE\sqlworkbenchnewitems\Sql
```

It is also possible to create a new node for templates from within the Template Explorer by right-clicking and selecting New ➤ Folder.

■**Note** Don't create the folder directly in the Sql folder, as this is not picked up by SQL Server Management Studio until you exit and reenter SQL Server Management Studio.

You could create different formats of templates for slightly different actions on tables. We saw the CREATE TABLE template previously, but what if we wanted a template that included a CREATE TABLE specification with an IDENTITY column? This is possible by taking a current template and upgrading it for a new template.

Try It Out: Creating a Template from an Existing Template

1. From the Template Explorer, find the CREATE TABLE template, right-click it, and select Edit. This will display the template that we saw earlier. Change the comment, and then we can start altering the code.

2. The first change is to add that the first column is an IDENTITY column. We know where this is located from our code earlier: it comes directly after the data type. To add a new parameter, input a set of angle brackets, then create the name of the parameter as the first option. The second option is the type of parameter this is—for example, sysname—which defines that the parameter is a system name, which is just an alias for nvarchar(256). The third option is the value for the parameter; in this case, we will be including the value of IDENTITY(1,1). The final set of code follows, where you can also see a fourth column has been defined with a bit data type.

■**Tip** You can check the alias by running the sp_help_sysname T-SQL command.

```
-- =========================================
-- Create table template with IDENTITY
-- =========================================
USE <database, sysname, AdventureWorks>
GO

IF OBJECT_ID('<schema_name, sysname, dbo>.<table_name, sysname,Â
sample_table>', 'U') IS NOT NULL
  DROP TABLE
    <schema_name, sysname, dbo>.<table_name, sysname, sample_table>
GO
```

```
CREATE TABLE
  <schema_name, sysname, dbo>.<table_name, sysname, sample_table>(
  <column1_name, sysname, c1> <column1_datatype, , int> Â
<identity,,IDENTITY (1,1)>
  <column1_nullability,, NOT NULL>,
  <column2_name, sysname, c2> <column2_datatype, , char(10)>
  <column2_nullability,, NULL>,
  <column3_name, sysname, c3> <column3_datatype, , datetime>
  <column3_nullability,, NULL>,
  <column4_name, sysname, c4> <column4_datatype, , bit>
  <column4_nullability,, NOT NULL>,
  CONSTRAINT <contraint_name, sysname, PK_sample_table>
    PRIMARY KEY (<columns_in_primary_key, , c1>)
)
GO
```

3. Now the code is built, but before we test it, we shall save this as a new template called CREATE TABLE with IDENTITY. From the menu, select File ➤ Save CREATE TABLE.sql As, and from the Save File As dialog box, save this as CREATE TABLE with IDENTITY.sql. This should update your Template Explorer, but if it doesn't, try exiting and reentering SQL Server Management Studio, after which it will be available to use.

The ALTER TABLE Statement

When using the original template, we had created the table with only three columns; therefore, we have an error to correct. Another error we have to change is the schema on TransactionTypes from dbo. One solution is to delete the table with DROP TABLE, but if we had placed some test data in the table before we realized we had missed the column, this would not be ideal. There is an alternative: the ALTER TABLE statement, which allows restrictive alterations to a table layout but keeps the contents. SQL Server Management Studio uses this statement when altering a table graphically, but here I will show you how to use it to add the missing fourth column for our TransactionTypes table.

Columns can be added, removed, or modified using the ALTER TABLE statement. Removing a column will simply remove the data within that column, but careful thought has to take place before adding or altering a column.

There are two scenarios when adding a new column to a table: should it contain NULL values for all the existing rows, or should there be a default value instead? Any new columns created using the ALTER TABLE statement where a value is expected (or defined as NOT NULL) will take time to implement. This is because any existing data will have NULL values for the new column; after all, SQL Server has no way of knowing what value to enter. When altering a table and using NOT NULL, you need to complete a number of complex processes, which include moving data to an interim table and then moving it back. The easiest solution is to alter the table and define the column to allow NULLs, add in the default data values using the UPDATE T-SQL command, and alter the column to NOT NULL.

▦**Note** It is common practice when creating columns to allow NULL values, as the default value may not be valid in some rows.

Try It Out: Adding a Column

1. First of all, open up the Query Editor and ensure that you are pointing to the ApressFinancial database. Then write the code to alter the TransactionDetails.TransactionTypes table to add the new column. The format is very simple. We specify the table prefixed by the schema name we want to alter after the ALTER TABLE statement. Next we use a comma-delimited list of the columns we wish to add. We define the name, the data type, the length if required, and finally whether we allow NULLs or not. As we don't want the existing data to have any default values, we will have to define the column to allow NULL values.

    ```
    ALTER TABLE TransactionDetails.TransactionTypes
    ADD AffectCashBalance bit NULL
    GO
    ```

2. Once we've altered the data as required, we then want to remove the ability for further rows of data to have a NULL value. This new column will take a value of 0 or 1. Again, we use the ALTER TABLE statement, but this time we'll add the ALTER COLUMN statement with the name of the column we wish to alter. After this statement are the alterations we wish to make. Although we are not altering the data type, it is a mandatory requirement to redefine the data type and data length. After this, we can inform SQL Server that the column will not allow NULL values.

    ```
    ALTER TABLE TransactionDetails.TransactionTypes
    ALTER COLUMN AffectCashBalance bit NOT NULL
    GO
    ```

3. Execute the preceding code to make the TransactionDetails.TransactionTypes table correct.

Defining the Remaining Tables

Now that three of the tables have been created, we need to create the remaining four tables. We will do this as code placed in Query Editor. There is nothing specifically new to cover in this next section, and therefore only the code is listed. Enter the following code and then execute it as before. You can then move into SQL Server Management Studio and refresh it, after which you should be able to see the new tables.

```
USE ApressFinancial
GO
CREATE TABLE CustomerDetails.CustomerProducts(
          CustomerFinancialProductId bigint IDENTITY(1,1) NOT NULL,
          CustomerId bigint NOT NULL,
          FinancialProductId bigint NOT NULL,
          AmountToCollect money NOT NULL,
          Frequency smallint NOT NULL,
          LastCollected datetime NOT NULL,
          LastCollection datetime NOT NULL,
          Renewable bit NOT NULL
)
ON [PRIMARY]
GO
```

```
CREATE TABLE CustomerDetails.FinancialProducts(
           ProductId bigint NOT NULL,
           ProductName nvarchar(50) NOT NULL
) ON [PRIMARY]

GO
CREATE TABLE ShareDetails.SharePrices(
           SharePriceId bigint IDENTITY(1,1) NOT NULL,
           ShareId bigint NOT NULL,
           Price numeric(18, 5) NOT NULL,
           PriceDate datetime NOT NULL
) ON [PRIMARY]

GO
CREATE TABLE ShareDetails.Shares(
           ShareId bigint IDENTITY(1,1) NOT NULL,
           ShareDesc nvarchar(50) NOT NULL,
           ShareTickerId nvarchar(50) NULL,
           CurrentPrice numeric(18, 5) NOT NULL
) ON [PRIMARY]

GO
```

Setting a Primary Key

Setting a primary key can be completed in SQL Server Management Studio with just a couple of mouse clicks. This section will demonstrate how easy this actually is. For more on keys, see Chapter 3.

Try It Out: Setting a Primary Key

1. Ensure that SQL Server Management Studio is running and that you have navigated to the ApressFinancial database. Find the ShareDetails.Shares table, right-click it, and select Design. Once in the Table Designer, select the ShareId column. This will be the column we are setting the primary key for. Right-click to bring up the pop-up menu shown in Figure 5-15.

Figure 5-15. *Defining a primary key*

2. Select the Set Primary Key option from the pop-up menu. This will then change the display to place a small key in the leftmost column details. Only one column has been defined as the primary key, as you see in Figure 5-16.

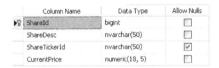

Column Name	Data Type	Allow Nulls
ShareId	bigint	☐
ShareDesc	nvarchar(50)	☐
ShareTickerId	nvarchar(50)	☑
CurrentPrice	numeric(18, 5)	☐

Figure 5-16. *Primary key defined*

3. However, this is not all that happens, as you will see. Save the table modifications by clicking the Save button. Click the Manage Indexes/Keys button on the toolbar. This brings up the dialog box shown in Figure 5-17. Look at the Type, the third option down in the General section. It says Primary Key. Notice that a key definition has been created for you, with a name and the selected column, informing you that the index is unique and clustered (more on indexes and their relation to primary keys in Chapter 6).

Figure 5-17. *Indexes/Keys dialog box*

That's all there is to creating and setting a primary key. A primary key has now been set up on the `ShareDetails.Shares` table. In this instance, any record added to this table will ensure that the data will be kept in `ShareId` ascending order (this is to do with the index, which you will see in Chapter 6), and it is impossible to insert a duplicate row of data. This key can then be used to link to other tables within the database at a later stage.

Creating a Relationship

We covered relationships in Chapter 3, but we've not created any. Now we will. The first relationship that we create will be between the customer and customer transactions tables. This will be a one-to-many relationship where there is one customer record to many transaction records. Keep in mind that although a customer may have several customer records—one for each product he or she has bought—the relationship is a combination of customer and product to transactions because a new CustomerId will be generated for each product the customer buys. We will now build that first relationship.

Try It Out: Building a Relationship

1. Ensure that SQL Server Management Studio is running and that ApressFinancial database is selected and expanded. We need to add a primary key to CustomerDetails.Customers. Enter the code that follows and then execute it:

```
ALTER TABLE CustomerDetails.Customers
ADD CONSTRAINT
    PK_Customers PRIMARY KEY NONCLUSTERED
    (
    CustomerId
    )
WITH( STATISTICS_NORECOMPUTE = OFF, IGNORE_DUP_KEY = OFF,
ALLOW_ROW_LOCKS = ON, ALLOW_PAGE_LOCKS = ON)
ON [PRIMARY]
GO
```

2. Find and select the TransactionDetails.Transactions table, and then right-click. Select Design to invoke the Table Designer.

3. Once in the Table Designer, right-click and select Relationships from the pop-up menu shown in Figure 5-18, or click the Relationships button on the Table Designer toolbar.

      Set Primary Key
      Insert Column
      Delete Column
      Relationships...
      Indexes/Keys...
      Fulltext Index...
      XML Indexes...
      Check Constraints...
      Spatial Indexes...
      Generate Change Script...

Figure 5-18. *Building a relationship*

4. This brings up the relationship designer. As it's empty, you need to click Add. This will then populate the screen as shown in Figure 5-19.

Figure 5-19. *Foreign Key Relationships dialog box*

5. Expand the Tables And Columns Specified node, which will allow the relationship to be built. Notice that there is now an ellipsis button on the right, as shown in Figure 5-20. To create the relationship, click the ellipsis.

Figure 5-20. *Adding tables and columns*

6. The first requirement is to change the name to make it more meaningful. Quite often you will find that naming the key `FK_ParentTable_ChildTable` is the best method, so in this case change it to `FK_Customers_Transactions`, as the `CustomerDetails.Customers` table will be the master table for this foreign key. We also need to define the column in each table that is the link. We are linking every one customer record to many transaction records, and we can do so via the `CustomerId`. So select that column for both tables, as shown in Figure 5-21. Now click OK.

Figure 5-21. *Columns selection*

▨**Note** In this instance, both columns have the same name, but this is not mandatory. The only requirement is that the information in the two columns be the same.

---

7. This brings us back to the Foreign Key Relationships definition screen, shown in Figure 5-22. Notice that at the top of the list items in the grayed-out area, you can see the details of the foreign key we just defined. Within the Identity section, there is now also a description of the foreign key. Ignore the option Enforce for Replication.

Figure 5-22. *Foreign key with description*

8. There are three other options we are interested in that are displayed at the bottom of the dialog box, as shown in Figure 5-23. Leave the options as the defaults.

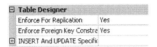

Figure 5-23. *INSERT And UPDATE Specification*

9. Closing this dialog box does not save the changes. Not until you close the Table Designer will the changes be applied. When you do so, you should see the dialog box in Figure 5-24 notifying you that two tables are to be changed. Click Yes to save the changes.

Figure 5-24. *Saving changes*

The relationship is now built, but what about those options we left alone? Let's go through those now.

Check Existing Data on Creation

If there is data within either of the tables, by setting this option to Yes, we instruct SQL Server that when the time comes to physically add the relationship, the data within the tables is to be checked. If the data meets the definition of the relationship, then the relationship is successfully inserted into the table. However, if any data fails the relationship test, then the relationship is not applied to the database. An example of this would be when it is necessary to ensure that there is a customer record for all transactions, but there are customer transaction records that don't have a corresponding customer record, which would cause the relationship to fail. Obviously, if you come across this, you have a decision to make. Either correct the data by adding master records or altering the old records, and then reapply the relationship, or revisit the relationship to ensure it is what you want.

By creating the relationship, you want the data within the relationship to work, therefore you would select No if you were going to go back and fix the data after the additions. What if you still miss rows? Would this be a problem? In the preceding scenario, there should be no transaction records without customer records. But you may still wish to add the relationship to stop further anomalies going forward.

Enforce Foreign Key Constraints

Once the relationship has been created and placed in the database, it is possible to prevent the relationship from being broken. If you set Check Existing Data on Creation from higher up in the dialog box to Yes, then you are more than likely hoping to keep the integrity of the data intact. That option will only check the existing data. It does nothing for further additions, deletions, and more on the data. However, by setting the Enforce Foreign Key Constraints option to Yes, we ensure that any addition, modification, or deletion of the data will not break the relationship. It doesn't stop changing or removing data providing that the integrity of the database is kept in sync. For example, it would be possible to change the customer number of transactions, providing that the new customer number also exists with the `CustomerDetails.Customers` table.

Choosing Delete and Update Rules

If a deletion or an update is performed, it is possible for one of four actions to then occur on the related data, based on the following options:

- *No Action*
- *Cascade*: If you delete a customer, then all of the transaction rows for that customer will also be deleted.
- *Set Null*: If you delete a customer, then if the `CustomerId` column in the `TransactionDetails.Transactions` table could accept `NULL` as a value, the value would be set to `NULL`. In the customers/transactions scenario, we have specified the column cannot accept `NULL` values. The danger with this is that you are leaving "unlinked" rows behind—a scenario that can be valid, but do take care.
- *Set Default*: When defining the table, the column could be defined so that a default value is placed in it. On setting the option to this value, you are saying that the column will revert to this default value—again, a dangerous setting, but potentially a less dangerous option than `SET NULL` as at least there is a meaningful value within the column.

■**Note** If at any point you do decide to implement cascade deletion, then please do take the greatest of care, as it can result in deletions that you may regret. If you implemented this on the `CustomerDetails.Customers` table, when you delete a customer, then all the transactions will be gone. This is ideal for use if you have an archive database to which all rows are archived. To keep your current and online system lean and fast, you could use delete cascades to quickly and cleanly remove customers who have closed their accounts.

Building a Relationship via T-SQL

It is also possible to build a relationship, or constraint, through a T-SQL statement. This would be done using an `ALTER TABLE` SQL statement. This time, a relationship will be created between the `TransactionDetails.Transactions` table and the `ShareDetails.Shares` table. Let's now take a few moments to check the syntax for building a constraint within T-SQL code:

```
ALTER TABLE child_table_name
WITH NOCHECK|CHECK
ADD CONSTRAINT [Constraint_Name]
FOREIGN KEY (child_column_name, ...,)
REFERENCES [master_table_name]([master_column_name, ...,])
```

We have to use an ALTER TABLE statement to achieve the goal of inserting a constraint to build the relationship. After naming the child table in the ALTER TABLE statement, we then decide whether we want the foreign key to check the existing data or not when it is being created. This is similar to the Check Existing Data on Creation option you saw earlier.

Now we move on to building the constraint. To do this, we must first of all instruct SQL Server that this is what we are intending to complete, and so we will need the ADD CONSTRAINT command.

Next, we name the constraint we are building. Again, I tend to use underscores instead of spaces. However, if you do wish to use spaces, which I wholeheartedly do not recommend, then you'll have to surround the name of the key using the [ ] brackets. I know I mentioned this before, but it's crucial to realize the impact of having spaces in a column, table, or constraint name. Every time you wish to deal with an object that has a name separated by spaces, then you will also need to surround it with square brackets. Why make extra work for yourself?

Now that the name of the constraint has been defined, the next stage is to inform SQL Server that a FOREIGN KEY is being defined next. Recall that a constraint can also be used for other functionality, such as creating a default value to be inserted into a column.

When defining the foreign key, ensure that all column names are separated by a comma and surrounded by parentheses. The final stage of building a relationship in code is to specify the master table of the constraint and the columns involved.

The rule here is that there must be a one-to-one match on columns on the child table and the master table, and that all corresponding columns must match on data type.

It is as simple as that. When building relationships, you may wish to use SQL Server Management Studio, as there is a lot less typing involved, and you can also instantly see the exact correspondence between the columns and whether they match in the same order. However, with T-SQL, you can save the code, and it will be ready for deployment to production servers when required.

Try It Out: Using SQL to Build a Relationship

1. In a Query Editor pane, enter the following T-SQL command and execute it by pressing Ctrl+E or F5 or clicking the Execute button:

```
USE ApressFinancial
GO
ALTER TABLE TransactionDetails.Transactions
WITH NOCHECK
ADD CONSTRAINT FK_Transactions_Shares
FOREIGN KEY(RelatedShareId)
REFERENCES ShareDetails.Shares(ShareId)
```

2. You should then see that the command has been executed successfully:

```
The command(s) completed successfully.
```

That's it. The relationship is created in the second batch of T-SQL code, the first batch ensuring that we are pointing to the right database. Once the index is built, it is possible to alter the table to add the relationship.

With our code, although we are executing an ALTER TABLE statement, no columns are being altered, but a constraint is being added. A relationship is a special type of constraint, and it is through a constraint that a relationship is built.

A constraint is, in essence, a checking mechanism, checking data modifications within SQL Server and the table(s) that it is associated with.

Summary

So, now you know how to create a table. This chapter has covered several options for doing so, but there is one point that you should keep in mind when building a table, whether you are creating or modifying it. When creating a table in SQL Server Management Studio, you should always save the table first by clicking the Save toolbar button. If you have made a mistake when defining the table and you close the table, and in doing so save in one action, you will get an error message informing you that an error has occurred, and all your changes will be lost. You will then have to go back in to the Table Designer and reapply any changes made.

Try also to get used to using both SQL Server Management Studio and the Query pane, as you may find that the Query pane gives you a more comfortable feel to the way you want to work. Also, you will find that in the Query pane, you can save your work to a file on your hard drive as you go along. You can also do this within SQL Server Management Studio; however, the changes are saved to a text file as a set of SQL commands, which then need to be run through the Query pane anyway.

CHAPTER 6

■■■

Creating Indexes and Database Diagramming

Now that we've created the tables, we could stop at this point and just work with our data from here. However, this would not be a good decision. As soon as any table contained a reasonable amount of information, and we wished to find a particular record, it would take SQL Server a fair amount of time to locate it. Performance would suffer, and our users would soon get annoyed with the slowdown in speed.

In this scenario, the database is like a large filing cabinet in which we have to find one piece of paper, but there's no clear filing system or form of indexing. If we had some sort of cross-reference facility, then it would likely be easier to find the information we need. And if that cross-reference facility were in fact an index, then this would be even better, as we might be able to find the piece of paper in our filing cabinet almost instantly. It is this theory that we need to put into practice in our SQL Server database tables. Generally, indexing is a conscious decision by a developer who favors faster conditional selection of records over modification or insertion of records.

In this chapter, you'll learn the basics of indexing and how you can start implementing an indexing solution. This chapter will cover the following topics:

- What an index is
- Different types of indexes
- Size restrictions on indexes
- Qualities of a good index and a bad index
- How to build an index in code as well as graphically
- How to alter an index

Let's begin by looking at what an index is and how it stores data.

What Is an Index?

In the previous chapter, you learned about tables, which are, in essence, repositories that hold data and information about data—what it looks like and where it is held. However, a table definition is not a great deal of use in getting to the data quickly. For this, some sort of cross-reference facility is required, where for certain columns of information within a table it should be possible to get to the whole record of information quickly.

If you think of this book, for example, as a table, the cross-reference you would use to find information quickly is the index at the back of the book. You look in the book index for a piece of information, or key. When you find the listing for that information in the index, you'll find it's associated with a page number, or a pointer, which directs you to where you can find the data you're looking for. This is where an index within your SQL Server database comes in.

You define an index in SQL Server so that it can locate the rows it requires to satisfy database queries faster. If an index does not exist to help find the necessary rows, SQL Server has no other option but to look at every row in a table to see if it contains the information required by the query. This is called a table scan, which by its very nature adds considerable overhead to data-retrieval operations.

> ▨**Note** There will be times when a table scan is the preferred option over an index. For example, if SQL Server needs to process a reasonable proportion of rows within a table, sometimes estimated to be around 10 percent or more of the data, then it may find that using a table scan is better than using an index. This is all to say that a table scan isn't wholly a bad thing, but on large tables, it could take some time to process.

When searching a table using the index, SQL Server does not go through all the data stored in the table; rather, it focuses on a much smaller subset of that data, as it will be looking at the columns defined within the index, which is faster. Once the record is found in the index, a pointer states where the data for that row can be found in the relevant table.

There are different types of indexes you can build onto a table. An index can be created on one column, called a **simple index**, or on more than one column, called a **compound index**. The circumstances of the column or columns you select and the data that will be held within these columns determine which type of index you use.

Types of Indexes

Although SQL Server has three types of indexes—clustered, nonclustered, and primary and secondary XML indexes—we will concentrate only on clustered and nonclustered in this book, as XML and XML indexes are quite an advanced topic.

The index type refers to the way the index and the physical rows of data are stored internally by SQL Server. The differences between the index types are important to understand, so we'll delve into them in the sections that follow.

Clustered

A clustered index defines the physical order of the data in the table. If you have more than one column defined in a clustered index, the data will be stored in sequential order according to columns: the first column, then the next column, and so on. Only one clustered index can be defined per table. It would be impossible to store the data in two different physical orders.

Going back to our earlier book analogy, if you examine a telephone book, you'll see that the data is presented in alphabetical order with surnames appearing first, then first names, and then any middle-name initial(s). Therefore, when you search the index and find the key, you are already at the point in the data from which you want to retrieve the information, such as the telephone number. In other words, you don't have to turn to another page as indicated by the key, because the data is right there. This is a clustered index of surname, first name, and initials.

As data is inserted, SQL Server will take the data within the index key values you have passed in and insert the row at the appropriate point. It will then move the data along so that it remains in the same order. You can think of this data as being like books on a bookshelf. When a librarian gets a new book, he will find the correct alphabetical point and try to insert the book at that point. All the books will then be moved within the shelf. If there is no room as the books are moved, the books at the end of the shelf will be moved to the next shelf down, and so on, until a shelf with enough room is found. Although this analogy puts the process in simple terms, this is exactly what SQL Server does.

Do not place a clustered index on columns that will have a lot of updates performed on them, as this means SQL Server will have to constantly alter the physical order of the data and so use up a great deal of processing power.

As a clustered index contains the table data itself, SQL Server would perform fewer I/O operations to retrieve the data using the clustered index than it would using a nonclustered index. Therefore, if you only have one index on a table, try to make sure it is a clustered index.

Nonclustered

Unlike a clustered index, a nonclustered index does not store the table data itself. Instead, a nonclustered index stores pointers to the table data as part of the index keys; therefore, many nonclustered indexes can exist on a single table at one time.

As a nonclustered index is stored in a separate structure—in fact, it is really held as a table with a clustered index hidden from your view—to the base table, it is possible to create the nonclustered index on a different file group from the base table. If the file groups are located on separate disks, data retrieval can be enhanced for your queries as SQL Server can use parallel I/O operations to retrieve the data from the index and base tables concurrently.

When you are retrieving information from a table that has a nonclustered index, SQL Server finds the relevant row in the index. If the information you want doesn't form part of the data in the index, SQL Server will then use the information in the index pointer to retrieve the relevant row in the data. As you can see, this involves at least two I/O actions—and possibly more, depending on the optimization of the index.

When a nonclustered index is created, the information used to build the index is placed in a separate location to the table and therefore can be stored on a different physical disk if required.

■**Caution** The more indexes you have, the more times SQL Server has to perform index modifications when inserting or updating data in columns that are within an index.

Primary and Secondary XML

If you wish to index XML data, which I cover only briefly later in the book, then it would be best to read Books Online, as this topic is beyond the scope of this book.

Uniqueness

An index can be defined as either **unique** or **nonunique**. A unique index ensures that the values contained within the unique index columns will appear only once within the table, including a value of NULL.

SQL Server automatically enforces the uniqueness of the columns contained within a unique index. If an attempt is made to insert a value that already exists in the table, an error will be generated and the attempt to insert or modify the data will fail.

A nonunique index is perfectly valid. However, as there can be duplicated values, a nonunique index has more overhead than a unique index when retrieving data. SQL Server needs to check if there are multiple entries to return, compared with a unique index where SQL Server knows to stop searching after finding the first row.

Unique indexes are commonly implemented to support constraints such as the primary key. Nonunique indexes are commonly implemented to support locating rows using a nonkey column.

Determining What Makes a Good Index

To create an index on a table, you have to specify which columns are contained within the index. Columns in an index do not have to all be of the same data type. You should be aware that there is a limit of 16 columns on an index, and the total amount of data for the index columns within a row cannot be more than 900 bytes. To be honest, if you get to an index that contains more than four or five columns, you should stand back and reevaluate the index definition. Sometimes you'll have more than five columns, but you really should double-check.

It is possible to get around this restriction and have an index that does include columns that are not part of the key: the columns are tagged onto the end of the index. This means that the index takes up more space, but if it means that SQL Server can retrieve all of the data from an index search, then it will be faster. However, to reiterate, if you are going down this route for indexes, then perhaps you need to look at your design.

In the sections that follow, we'll examine some of factors that can determine if an index is good:

- Using "low-maintenance" columns

- Using primary and foreign keys

- Being able to find a specific record

- Using covering indexes

- Looking for a range of information

- Keeping the data in order

Using Low-Maintenance Columns

As I've indicated, for nonclustered indexes the actual index data is separate from the table data, although both can be stored in the same area or in different areas (e.g., on different hard drives). To reiterate, this means that when you insert a record into a table, the information from the columns included in the index is copied and inserted into the index area. So, if you alter data in a column within a table, and that column has been defined as making up an index, SQL Server also has to alter the data in the index. Instead of only one update being completed, two will be completed. If the table has more than one index, and in more than one of those indexes is a column that is to be updated a great deal, then there may be several disk writes to perform when updating just one record. While this will result in a performance reduction for data-modification operations, appropriate indexing will balance this out by greatly increasing the performance of data-retrieval operations.

Therefore, data that is **low maintenance**—namely, columns that are not heavily updated—could become an index and would make a good index. The fewer disk writes that SQL Server has to do, the faster the database will be, as well as every other database within that SQL Server instance. Don't let this statement put you off. If you feel that data within a table is retrieved more often than it is modified, or if the performance of the retrieval is more critical than the performance of the modification, then do look at including the column within the index.

In the example application we're building, each month we need to update a customer's bank balance with any interest gained or charged. However, we have a nightly job that wants to check for clients who have between $10,000 and $50,000, as the bank can get a higher rate of deposit with the Federal Reserve on those sorts of amounts. A client's bank balance will be constantly updated, but an index on this sort of column could speed up the overnight deposit check program. Before the index in this example is created, we need to determine if the slight performance degradation in the updating of the balances is justified by the improvement of performance of the deposit check program.

Primary and Foreign Keys

One important use of indexes is on referential constraints within a table. If you recall from Chapter 3, a referential constraint is where you've indicated that through the use of a key, certain actions are constrained depending on what data exists. To give a quick example of a referential constraint, say you have a customer who owns banking products. A referential constraint would prevent the customer's record from being deleted while those products existed.

SQL Server does not automatically create indexes on your foreign keys. However, as the foreign key column values need to be identified by SQL Server when joining to the parent table, it is almost always recommended that an index be created on the columns of the foreign key.

Finding Specific Records

Ideal candidates for indexes are columns that allow SQL Server to quickly identify the appropriate rows. In Chapter 8, we'll meet the WHERE clause of a query. This clause lists certain columns in your table and is used to limit the number of rows returned from a query. The columns used in the WHERE clause of your most common queries make excellent choices for an index. So, for example, if you wanted to find a customer's order for a specific order number, an index based on customer_id and order_number would be perfect, as all the information needed to locate a requested row in the table would be contained in the index.

If finding specific records is going to make up part of the way the application works, then do look at this scenario as an area for an index to be created.

Using Covering Indexes

As mentioned earlier, when you insert or update a record, any data in a column that is included in an index is stored not only in the table, but also in the indexes for nonclustered indexes. From finding an entry in an index, SQL Server then moves to the table to locate and retrieve the record. However, if the necessary information is held within the index, then there is no need to go to the table and retrieve the record, providing much speedier data access.

For example, consider the ShareDetails.Shares table in the ApressFinancial database. Suppose that you wanted to find out the description, current price, and ticker ID of a share. If an index was placed on the ShareId column, knowing that this is an identifier column and therefore unique, you would ask SQL Server to find a record using the ID supplied. It would then take the details from the index of where the data is located and move to that data area. If, however, there was an index with all of the columns defined, then SQL Server would be able to retrieve the description ticker and price details in the index action. It would not be necessary to move to the data area. This is called a **covered index**, since the index covers every column in the table for data retrieval.

Looking for a Range of Information

An index can be just as useful for finding one record as it can be for searching for a range of records. For example, say you wish to find a list of cities in Florida with names between Orlando and St. Petersburg in alphabetical order. You could put an index on the city name, and SQL Server would go to the index location of Orlando and then read forward from there an index row at a time, until it reached the item after St. Petersburg, where it would then stop. Because SQL Server knows that an index is on this column and that the data will be sorted by city name, this makes it ideal for building an index on a city name column.

It should be noted that SQL Server indexes are not useful when attempting to search for characters embedded in a body of text. For example, suppose you want to find every author in a publisher's database whose last name contains the letters "ab." This type of query does not provide a means of determining where in the index tree to start and stop searching for appropriate values. The only way SQL Server can determine which rows are valid for this query is to examine every row within the table. Depending on the amount of data within the table, this can be a slow process. If you have a requirement to perform this sort of wildcard text searching, you should take a look at the SQL Server full-text feature, as this will provide better performance for such queries.

Keeping the Data in Order

As previously stated, a clustered index actually keeps the data in the table in a specific order. When you specify a column (or multiple columns) as a clustered index, upon inserting a record, SQL Server will place that record in a physical position to keep the records in the correct ascending or descending order that corresponds to the order defined in the index. To explain this a bit further, if you have a clustered index on customer numbers; and the data currently has customer numbers 10, 6, 4, 7, 2, and 5; then SQL Server will physically store the data in the following order: 2, 4, 5, 6, 7, 10. If a process then adds in a customer number 9, it will be physically inserted between 7 and 10, which may mean that the record for customer number 10 needs to move physically. Therefore, if you have defined a clustered index on a column or a set of columns where data insertions cause the clustered index to be reordered, this will greatly affect your insert performance. SQL Server does provide a way to reduce the reordering impact by allowing a fill factor to be specified when an index is created. I will discuss the fill factor shortly; however, this option allows you to define how much of an index leaf will be filled before a new leaf is created. Think of an index leaf as your index card for each cabinet. You know that more items are going to come in, and a few of these may you'll need to add to an index card for that cabinet. You try to estimate how many items you'll need to add, so you leave space on that card to add them on. You're then trying to avoid having to create a new index card.

Determining What Makes a Bad Index

Now that you know what makes a good index, let's investigate what makes a bad index. There are several "gotchas" to be aware of:

- Using unsuitable columns
- Choosing unsuitable data
- Including too many columns
- Including too few records in the table

Using Unsuitable Columns

If a column isn't used by a query to locate a row within a table, then there is a good chance that the column won't need to be indexed, unless it is combined with another column to create a covering index, as described earlier. If this is the case, the index will still add overhead to the data-modification operations but will not produce any performance benefit to the data-retrieval operations.

Choosing Unsuitable Data

Indexes work best when the data contained in the index columns is highly selective between rows. The optimal index is one created on a column that has a unique value for every row within a table, such as a primary key. If a query requests a row based on a value within this column, SQL Server can quickly navigate the index structure and identify the single row that matches the query predicate.

However, if the selectivity of the data in the index columns is poor, the effectiveness of the index will be reduced. For example, if an index is created on a column that contains only three distinct values, the index will be able to reduce the number of rows to just a third of the total before applying other methods to identify the exact row. In this instance, SQL Server would probably ignore the index anyway and find that reading the data table instead would be faster. Therefore, when deciding on appropriate index columns, you should examine the data selectivity to estimate the effectiveness of the index.

Including Too Many Columns

The more columns there are in an index, the more data writing has to take place when a process completes an update or an insertion of data. Although these updates to the index data take a very short amount of time in SQL Server 2008, they can add up. Therefore, each index that is added to a table will incur extra processing overhead, so it is recommended that you create the minimum number of indexes needed to give your data-retrieval operations acceptable performance.

Including Too Few Records in the Table

From a data-performance viewpoint, there is absolutely no need to place an index on a table that has only one row. SQL Server will find the record at the first request, without the need of an index, because it will use a table scan. That said, you may wish to include a primary key that can then be used to enforce data integrity.

This statement also holds true when a table has only a handful of records. Again, there is no reason to place an index on these tables. The reason for this is that SQL Server would go to the index, use its engine to make several reads of the data to find the correct record, and then move directly to that record using the record pointer from the index to retrieve the information. Several actions are involved in this process, as well as passing data between different components within SQL Server. When you execute a query, SQL Server will determine whether it's more efficient to use the indexes defined for the table to locate the necessary rows or to simply perform a table scan and look at every row within the table.

Reviewing Your Indexes for Performance

Every so often, it's necessary for you as an administrator or a developer to review the indexes built on your table to ensure that yesterday's good index is not today's bad index. When a solution is built, what is perceived to be a good index in development may not be so good in production—for example, the users may be performing one task more times than expected. Therefore, it is highly advisable that you set up tasks that constantly review your indexes and how they are performing. This can be completed within SQL Server via its index-tuning tool, the Database Tuning Advisor (DTA).

The DTA looks at your database and a workload file holding a representative amount of information that will be processed, and uses the information it gleans from these to figure out what indexes to place within the database and where improvements can be made. At this point in the book, I haven't actually covered working with data, so going through the use of this tool will just lead to confusion. This powerful and advanced tool should be used only by experienced SQL Server 2008 developers or database administrators.

Getting the indexes right is crucial to your SQL Server database running in an optimal fashion. Spend time thinking about the indexes, try to get them right, and then review them at regular intervals. Review clustering, uniqueness, and especially the columns contained within indexes so that you ensure the data is retrieved as quickly as possible. Finally, also ensure that the order of the columns within the index will reduce the number of reads that SQL Server has to do to find the data. An index where the columns defined are FirstName, LastName, and Department might be better defined as Department, FirstName, and LastName if the greatest number of queries is based on finding someone within a specific department or listing employees of a department. The difference between these two indexes is that in the first, SQL Server would probably need to perform a table scan to find the relevant records. Compare that with the second example, where SQL Server would search the index until it found the right department, and then just continue to return rows from the index until the department changed. As you can see, the second involves much less work.

Creating an Index

Now that you know what an index is and you have an understanding of the various types of indexes, let's proceed to create some in SQL Server. There are many different ways to create indexes within SQL Server, as you might expect. Those various methods are the focus of this section of the chapter, starting with how to use the table designer in SQL Server Management Studio.

The first index we'll place into the database will be on the `CustomerId` field within the `CustomerDetails.Customers` table.

Creating an Index with the Table Designer

As you may recall from the previous chapter, when the `CustomerId` column is set up, SQL Server will automatically generate the data within this field whenever a new record is inserted into this table. This data will never alter, as it uses the `IDENTITY` function for the column. Thus, the `CustomerId` column will be updated automatically whenever a customer is added. An application written in C#, for example, could be used as the user front end for updating the remaining areas of the customer's data, and it could also display specific customer details, but it would not know that the `CustomerId` requires incrementing for each new record, and it would not know the value to start from.

The first index created will be used to find the record to update with a customer's information. The application will have found the customer using a combination of name and address, but it is still possible to have multiple records with the same details. For example, you may have John J. Doe and his son, John J. Doe, who are both living at the same address. Once you have those details displayed on the screen, how will the computer program know which John J. Doe to use when it comes to completing an update?

Instead of looking for the customer by first name, last name, and address, the application will know the `CustomerId` and use this to find the record within SQL Server. When completing the initial search, the `CustomerId` will be returned as part of the set of values, so when the user selects the appropriate John J. Doe, the application will know the appropriate `CustomerId`. SQL Server will use this value to specifically locate the record to update. In the following exercise, we'll add this index to the `CustomerDetails.Customers` table.

Try It Out: Creating an Index Graphically

1. Ensure that SQL Server Management Studio is running and that you have expanded the nodes in the tree view so that you can see the Tables node within the `ApressFinancial` database.

2. Find the first table that the index is to be added to (i.e., the `CustomerDetails.Customers` table). Right-click and select Design. This will bring you into the table designer. Right-click and select Manage Indexes and Keys (see Figure 6-1).

Figure 6-1. *The Manage Indexes and Keys button*

3. The index-creation screen will appear. The screen will look similar to Figure 6-2. Notice that there is a Primary Key already defined. You created this in Chapter 5; in Figure 5-24, you saw the Save dialog when creating a relationship. We defined the `Customers.CustomerDetails` table as the primary key table, and the table had no primary key, so SQL Server created one for us. Click the Add button to create a new index and to set the index's properties.

   The fields in this dialog box are prepopulated, but you are able to change the necessary fields and options that you might wish to use. However, no matter what indexes have been created already, the initial column chosen for the index will always be the first column defined in the table.

Figure 6-2. *The Indexes/Keys dialog*

4. The first area to change is the name of the index. Notice that in the (Name) text box, SQL Server has created a possible value for you. The name is prefixed with `IX_`, which is a good naming system to use. It is also good to keep the name of the table and then a useful suffix, such as the name of the column. In this case, the index will be called `IX_Customers_CustomerId`. It might also be good to place something in the description. However, index names should be self-explanatory, so there really shouldn't be a need for a description.

5. SQL Server has, in this instance, correctly selected `CustomerId` as the column that will make up the index. Also, it has selected that the index will be ascending. For this example, the default sort order is appropriate. The sort order of the index column is useful when creating an index on the columns that will be used in an `ORDER BY` clause of a query when there are multiple columns with differing sort orders. If the sort order of the columns within the index matches the sort order of those columns specified in the `ORDER BY` clause, SQL Server may be able to avoid performing an internal sort, resulting in improved query performance.

■**Tip** If an index is only one column, SQL Server can read the index just as fast in a forward direction as it can backward.

---

6. As indicated earlier when defining the tables, SQL Server generates the value of the `CustomerId` column to be the next number in a sequence when a record is added, as this column uses the `IDENTITY` functionality. This value can't be altered within the table, as the option for creating your own identity values has not been switched on, so taking these two items of information and putting them together, you should be able to deduce that this value will be unique. Therefore, change the Is Unique option to Yes.

7. The final part of creating the index is to look at the Create As Clustered option, which will be set to No (see Figure 6-3). Although this key meets a number of criteria that would mean it was an ideal candidate for a clustered index, such as a high degree of uniqueness and the ability to be used in a range within a query, it's rare to access this table initially by a customer ID. It's more likely that this table will be accessed on the customer checking account AccountNumber held in this table. Finally, the order of the records inserted into SQL Server won't change. And if you scroll down the screen, the Re-compute Statistics for This Index option should remain No.

Note If this were a production environment or if you were creating a system in a development environment to move to a production environment, then you would need to take a couple of other considerations into account. You would need to alter the Filegroup or Partition scheme so that indexes were placed on a different file group, as we discussed earlier. Another area to note is the Fill Factor. I will talk about this at the end of the exercise.

Figure 6-3. *The clustering option in the Indexes/Keys dialog*

8. Click Close and then close the table modification, answering Yes when you are asked if you wish to save the changes. This will add the index to the database.

Building an index in Management Studio is a straightforward procedure, as you have just seen. Although this is the first index that you have created yourself, it took only a few moments, and there were just a couple of areas where you had to do any reasonable amount of decision making. We will cover those areas now.

Choosing the name of the index and the columns to include is easy and is not worth dwelling on. You should know which columns to include from the discussions at the start of the chapter, where we examined the basics of building indexes.

The first major decision you need to make is determining whether a column carries unique values. The column chosen for our first index is an identity column which, if you recall, is a column that cannot have data entered into it by any SQL command, as the data entered in to this column is completed automatically by SQL Server itself. Also, in an identity column, by default no two rows can have the same value. However, there is no automation to stop any attempt to create duplicate keys. Therefore, there is still a need to inform SQL Server that the index will be unique.

Moving on to the Create As Clustered setting, the data in this table would be best held in CustomerId order. This is because each record that is inserted will have a higher CustomerId number than the previous record. Therefore, each time a record is added, it will be added to the end of the table, removing the need for a clustered index. As with the Is Unique option, the Create As Clustered option doesn't need to be selected.

Moving to Fill Factor, this tells SQL Server how much of a page should be filled with index data before SQL Server starts a new page of data to continue with the index. In an index such as this, it would be better to make the fill factor a high percentage, such as 95, as there won't be much movement in having to shuffle index entries, because the data will remain static.

Finally, the Re-compute Statistics option defines whether SQL Server automatically recomputes the statistics on the index when data is modified.

Indexes and Statistics

When retrieving data, SQL Server obviously has to make some decisions as to the best way to get to that data and return it to the query requesting it. Even if an index has been created on a set of columns, SQL Server may determine that it is better and faster to use another method to retrieve the data—through a table scan, perhaps. Or maybe there are a couple of indexes that could be chosen to retrieve the same data. No matter what the scenario, SQL Server has to have some basis of information on which to make sensible and accurate choices. This is where statistics come in.

SQL Server keeps statistics on each column contained within an index. These statistics are updated over a period of time and over a number of inserts or modifications. The specifics of how all of this works in the background, and how SQL Server keeps the statistics up to date, is an advanced topic. What you need to know is that if you alter or build an index on a table that has data in it, and you don't let SQL Server update the statistics on the table, then SQL Server could be using inaccurate information when it is trying to decide how to retrieve the data. It could even mean that the index change you thought would improve performance has in fact made the performance much slower.

That said, it is not always prudent to let SQL Server recompute statistics automatically. SQL Server will do the updates when it feels they are required. This may happen at a busy time of processing; you have no control over when it will happen. However, if SQL Server does update the statistics, the query that caused the update to start will not be impacted, as the statistics will be updated asynchronously if the AUTO_UPDATE_STATISTICS_ASYNC option is switched on.

It may be more efficient to manually update the statistics via a scheduled job and keep all statistic building off. This is what you quite often see within production environments that have a number of inserts and modifications to the data.

The CREATE INDEX Syntax

Creating an index using T-SQL is a lot easier than creating a table. In this section, we'll look only at indexes on tables, although there is an object within SQL Server called a **view** that can also be indexed.

The full syntax for creating an index is not listed here, although you can find it within Books Online once you progress in your SQL Server knowledge. A reduced version will be sufficient while you are learning SQL Server 2008. Most of your indexes will use the following version:

```
CREATE [UNIQUE] [CLUSTERED|NONCLUSTERED]
INDEX index_name
ON table (column [ASC|DESC] [ ,...n ] )
[WITH {IGNORE_DUP_KEY|DROP_EXISTING|SORT_IN_TEMPDB}]
[ON filegroup ]
```

Let's go through each point one by one so that the options in this cut-down version are clear:

- CREATE: Required. This keyword informs SQL Server that you will be building a new object.

- UNIQUE: Optional. If used, this option will inform SQL Server that the columns listed in the index will bring back a single unique row. This is enforced by SQL Server when attempting to insert a duplicate row, as an error message will be returned.

- CLUSTERED *or* NONCLUSTERED: Optional. If neither CLUSTERED nor NONCLUSTERED is explicitly listed, the index will be created as NONCLUSTERED.
- INDEX: Required. This informs SQL Server that the new object will be an index.
- index_name: Required. This is the name of the index being built. This name must be unique for the table, and it is advisable to keep this name unique for the database, using the naming method of IX_table_column discussed earlier.
- ON table: Required. This is the name of the table with which the index is associated. Only one table can be named.
- column: Required. This is the name of the column(s) in the table that we wish to include in the index. This is a comma-separated list.
- ASC: Optional (default). If neither ASC nor DESC is mentioned, then ASC is assumed. ASC informs SQL Server that it should store the column named in ascending sequence.
- DESC: Optional. This informs SQL Server that the column is to be stored in descending order.
- WITH: Optional. It is, however, required if any of the following options have to be used:
    - IGNORE_DUP_KEY: This option is only available when the index is defined as UNIQUE. If this option has not been used earlier, then it is not available to you. I'll explain this further in a moment.
    - DROP_EXISTING: This option is used if there is an existing index of the same name within the database. It will then drop the index before re-creating it. This is useful for performance if you are not actually changing any columns within the index. More on this in a moment.
    - SORT_IN_TEMPDB: When building an index where there is already data within the table, it may be advisable, if the table is a large table, to get the data sorted for the index within the temporary database, tempdb, as mentioned in Chapter 3. Use this option if you have a large table, or if tempdb is on a different hard disk from your database. This option may speed up the building of the index, as SQL Server can simultaneously read from the disk device where the table is located and write to the disk device where tempdb is located.
- ON: Optional. This option is, however, required if you are going to specify a file group. It is not required if you wish the index to be built on the PRIMARY file group.
- filegroup: This is the name of the file group on which the index should be stored. At the moment, there is only one file group set up: PRIMARY. PRIMARY is a reserved word and is required to be surrounded by square brackets, [ ], if used.

Two options need further clarification: IGNORE_DUP_KEY and DROP_EXISTING. We'll look at both in the sections that follow.

IGNORE_DUP_KEY

If you have an index defined as UNIQUE, then no matter how hard you try, you cannot add a new row whose values in the index columns match the values of any current row. However, there are two actions that you can perform, depending on this setting within an index.

When performing multirow inserts, if the IGNORE_DUP_KEY option is specified, then no error will be generated within SQL Server if some of the rows being inserted violate the unique index. Only a warning message will be issued. The rows that violated the unique index are not inserted, although all other rows are inserted successfully.

When performing multirow inserts, if the IGNORE_DUP_KEY option is omitted, then an error message will be generated within SQL Server if some of the rows violate the unique index. The batch will be rolled back, and no rows will be inserted into the table.

■**Caution** The system variable called @@ERROR can be tested after every SQL Server action to see if there has been an error in any item of work or through another error-handling command called Try/Catch. If there has been an error, some sort of error handling within the batch will usually be performed. If you have IGNORE_DUP_KEY, then no error will be produced when there is an attempt to insert a duplicate row, and the batch will run as if everything had been inserted. So, be warned: it may look like everything has worked, but in fact some rows were not inserted!

DROP_EXISTING

When data is being inserted and modified, there will be times when an index bloats to a less than ideal state. Just as an Access database may need to be compacted, indexes within SQL Server also need to be compacted sometimes. Compacting the index will speed up performance and reclaim disk space by removing fragmentation of the index. To compact an index, you re-create the index without actually modifying the columns or, in fact, starting from scratch and having to rebuild the whole index and visit every row within the table.

The DROP_EXISTING clause provides enhanced performance when rebuilding a clustered index compared to a DROP INDEX command followed by a CREATE INDEX command. Nonclustered indexes will be rebuilt every time the clustered index for a table is rebuilt if the columns are included in the clustered index. The name of the clustered index must also remain the same, as must the sort order and the partition the index is built on. Finally, the uniqueness attribute must not change. So, if you drop a clustered index and then re-create it, the existing nonclustered indexes will be rebuilt twice (if they are to be rebuilt): once from the drop and once from the creation. Keep this in mind, as it is crucial if you are working in a time-critical batch window. With the size of table and indexes created, it may only be possible to re-create a clustered index on a weekend.

DROP_EXISTING also allows an existing index to be rebuilt by explicitly dropping and re-creating the index. This is particularly useful for rebuilding primary key indexes. As other tables may reference a primary key, it may be necessary to drop all foreign keys in these other tables prior to dropping the primary key. By specifying the DROP_EXISTING clause, SQL Server will rebuild the index without affecting the primary key constraint.

Creating an Index in Query Editor: Template

Not surprisingly, there is a template within Query Editor that you can use as a basis for creating an index. We'll look at this process first, before we build an index natively in Query Editor, as this creates the basis of the SQL syntax for the creation of the index.

Try It Out: Using a Query Editor Template to Build an Index

1. Ensure that Template Explorer is open (press Ctrl+Alt+T or select View ➤ Template Explorer). Navigate to the Index node and expand it. Select the Create Index Basic node and double-click (see Figure 6-4).

Figure 6-4. *Selecting the Create Index Basic node*

2. A new editor will open with the following code in it. The template that is installed is based on the AdventureWorks example. As you saw in the previous chapter, you can create new templates or modify this one.

```
-- ===============================================
-- Create index basic template
-- ===============================================
USE <database_name, sysname, AdventureWorks>
GO

CREATE INDEX <index_name, sysname, ind_test>
ON <schema_name, sysname, Person>.<table_name, sysname, Address>
(
    <column_name1, sysname, PostalCode>
)
GO
```

3. Alter the template by either changing the code or using the Specify Values for Template Parameters option, which will make the index creating easier. The button should be on the SQL Editor toolbar (see Figure 6-5).

Figure 6-5. *The Specify Values for Template Parameters button*

4. Change the database to the example database, name the index (in this case, it has been named after the table), set schema_name to CustomerDetails, table_name to CustomerProducts, and column_name1 to CustomerId (see Figure 6-6). Then click OK.

5. The code now looks as follows:

```
USE ApressFinancial
GO

CREATE INDEX IX_CustomerProducts
ON CustomerDetails.CustomerProducts
(
    CustomerId
)
GO
```

Figure 6-6. *The Specify Values for Template Parameters dialog*

6. Execute the code by pressing F5 or Ctrl+E, or clicking the Execute toolbar button. You should then see the following success message:

```
Command(s) completed successfully.
```

7. Now that you've completed the process, you'll want to check that the index has actually been created as expected. From within Object Explorer, click the Refresh button on the Object Explorer toolbar or select the Refresh option from the right-click context menu. Navigate to the `CustomerDetails.CustomerProducts` table and expand the Indexes node. This provides you with instant, but limited, information about this index. You can see its name and that it is neither unique nor clustered (see Figure 6-7).

Figure 6-7. *Index for CustomerProducts*

8. You can see a different perspective of the index if you highlight the index, right-click, and select Properties. Figure 6-8 shows you a layout that offers not only a graphical version of the index, but also a list of many other potential options.

Figure 6-8. *The Index Properties dialog*

9. The most interesting tab to view once you have data within the table or once you are in production is the Frag-mentation tab. As data is modified, indexes are also modified. Similar to a hard drive, an index will also suffer from fragmentation of the data within the index. This will slow down your index, and, as mentioned earlier in this chapter, it is important that you continue to check on your indexes to ensure their best possible speed and per-formance. It is possible to correct the fragmentation while users are still using the system. You can do this by ticking the Reorganize Index box shown at the bottom of Figure 6-9. For a slightly more detailed view, highlight the index in Object Explorer, right-click to bring up the submenu, and select Reorganize.

The final way to create an index is by coding the whole index by hand in a Query Editor window, which we will look at in the next section.

Figure 6-9. *Examining index fragmentation*

Creating an Index in Query Editor: SQL Code

In the following exercise, we will create two indexes and a primary key within a Query Editor pane. This will allow us in the next section to build a foreign key between the two tables, TransactionDetails. Transactions and TransactionDetails.TransactionTypes. The code will also demonstrate how to build T-SQL defining options for the index presented during the CREATE INDEX syntax discussion earlier.

■**Note** The code discussion in the following exercise is broken out into three parts before the code execution, in order to make it simpler to follow.

Try It Out: Creating an Index with Query Editor

1. Enter the following code into an empty pane of Query Editor. The first index you will be creating in this section is a uniquely clustered index on the TransactionDetails.TransactionTypes table.

```
USE ApressFinancial
GO
CREATE UNIQUE CLUSTERED INDEX IX_TransactionTypes
ON TransactionDetails.TransactionTypes
(
    TransactionTypeId ASC )
WITH (STATISTICS_NORECOMPUTE  = OFF, SORT_IN_TEMPDB = OFF,
 DROP_EXISTING = OFF, IGNORE_DUP_KEY = OFF, ONLINE = OFF,
 ALLOW_ROW_LOCKS  = ON, ALLOW_PAGE_LOCKS  = OFF)
ON [PRIMARY]
GO
```

2. The second index you'll create is a nonclustered index on the TransactionDetails.Transactions table based on the TransactionType column. You won't make this index clustered, as it would be better to consider either CustomerId or DateEntered as clustered columns.

```
CREATE NONCLUSTERED INDEX IX_Transactions_TType
ON TransactionDetails.Transactions
(
    TransactionType ASC)
WITH (STATISTICS_NORECOMPUTE  = OFF, SORT_IN_TEMPDB = OFF,
DROP_EXISTING = OFF, IGNORE_DUP_KEY = OFF, ONLINE = OFF,
ALLOW_ROW_LOCKS  = ON, ALLOW_PAGE_LOCKS  = OFF)
ON [PRIMARY]
GO
```

3. The final action is to add a primary key to the TransactionDetails.TransactionTypes table. You do this through an ALTER TABLE statement:

```
ALTER TABLE TransactionDetails.TransactionTypes
ADD CONSTRAINT
    PK_TransactionTypes PRIMARY KEY NONCLUSTERED
    (
    TransactionTypeId
    )
WITH (STATISTICS_NORECOMPUTE = OFF, IGNORE_DUP_KEY = OFF,
ALLOW_ROW_LOCKS = ON, ALLOW_PAGE_LOCKS = ON)
ON [PRIMARY]
GO
```

4. You can now execute the preceding code by pressing F5 or Ctrl+E, or clicking the Execute toolbar button. You should then see the following success message:

```
The command(s) completed successfully.
```

As noted, two different indexes are created in this example. The first one is a unique clustered index, based on the identity column of the TransactionDetails.TransactionTypes table. This column was chosen because we will be linking to this table using the TransactionType column. Rarely, if ever, will we link on any other column within this table. The overhead is microscopic, though, due to the few records we will be entering, and it is therefore not really a concern. It also allows us to see where to place the keyword within the example.

The second index, built on the TransactionDetails.Transactions table, cannot be a unique index; there will be multiple entries of the same value because there are multiple transactions for the same type. However, it is still possible to make this index clustered. Changing the transaction type on a transaction will be rare, or, if we had a full audit trail built within our system, we may "ban" such an action. The only way to change a transaction type around this ban would be to cancel the entry, record the cancel action, and create a new entry. However, a clustered index on transaction types will not give us much of a gain in performance, as there will be few queries of data based on transaction type alone. As mentioned earlier, there are better choices for clustering.

What is interesting about this example is that two indexes are created in one execution—albeit in two batch transactions— whereas in the previous examples, only one index was created at a time. Notice the keyword GO between the two CREATE statements creating the index; each index creation has to be completed on its own, without any other SQL statements included. If you need to create more than one index, but you would prefer to build them at the same time, then this may be the solution you need. (Please see Chapter 8 for details on transactions.)

An area we have not yet covered is what happens if you try to create an index twice using the same index name. The preceding indexes have already been created, but if you run the query again, SQL Server will produce error messages informing you that the index already exists. You should see messages like the following:

```
Msg 1913, Level 16, State 1, Line 1
The operation failed because an index or statistics with name
'IX_TransactionTypes'
already exists on table 'TransactionDetails.TransactionTypes'.
Msg 1913, Level 16, State 1, Line 1
The operation failed because an index or statistics with name
'IX_Transactions_TType' already exists on table
'TransactionDetails.Transactions'.
Msg 1779, Level 16, State 0, Line 1
Table 'TransactionDetails.TransactionTypes' already has a primary key
defined on it.
Msg 1750, Level 16, State 0, Line 1
Could not create constraint. See previous errors.
```

Even if you alter the contents of the index and include different columns but still use the same name, it is not possible to create another index with the same name as an existing one.

In the last part of the example, we altered the table so that we could add a primary key. There are different types of CONSTRAINTS that can be defined for a table: column constraints are used for default values, as you saw in the previous chapter, but constraints are also used for primary and foreign keys.

Once again, a couple of new areas were covered in this section, but you now have the information you need to be able to create the most common indexes. Indexes need a lot less coding than tables and can be created quickly and easily. However, if you are adding a new index to an existing table that has a substantial amount of information, adding this new index could take a few minutes to complete, depending on the scenario. It is possible to add indexes while the system is being used and the table or clustered indexes are being updated. This is only available in SQL Server Enterprise Edition, by specifying the index action with the REBUILD WITH (ONLINE = ON) option. Take care when using this option. If anybody tries to access the relevant table while the index is being built, SQL Server will not recognize the index until it has been built, and when working out the best way to access the data, it will ignore this index.

If you are creating the index after removing it for rebuilding statistics, for example, problems may arise if you don't use the ONLINE = ON option. With this option ON, SQL Server will allow access to the table to add or modify data. However, if it is set to OFF, then all actions against the table will have to wait until the index is re-created. This will mean that any part of your system that requires access to the table that the index is being built on will pause while the index is being generated. Therefore, if you are rebuilding an index with the database available, you have to decide which of the two problems that may arise is acceptable.

Dropping an Index

There will be times when an index is redundant and should be removed (i.e., dropped) from a table. Dropping an index is simply a case of executing the DROP INDEX statement, followed by the table name and the index name. Keep in mind that for every index that exists, processing time is required to keep that index up to date for every data modification. Therefore, when an index has been created using the same columns, or when an index is no longer providing speedy data access and is therefore being ignored by SQL Server, it should be dropped.

Note If the index is used by a primary key or unique constraint, you cannot drop it directly. In this case, you must use the DROP CONSTRAINT command. The removal of this constraint will also remove the index from the table.

Try It Out: Dropping an Index in Query Editor

1. If you want to drop the index created in the last section, all you need to do is execute the following code. This will remove the index from SQL Server and also remove any statistics associated with it.

```
USE ApressFinancial
GO
DROP INDEX IX_TransactionTypes ON TransactionDetails.TransactionTypes
```

2. After execution, you should see that everything executed correctly:

```
Command(s) completed successfully.
```

---

3. Don't forget to re-create the index by running the following code:

```
CREATE UNIQUE CLUSTERED INDEX IX_TransactionTypes
ON TransactionDetails.TransactionTypes
(
    TransactionTypeId ASC
) WITH (STATISTICS_NORECOMPUTE  = OFF, SORT_IN_TEMPDB = OFF,
DROP_EXISTING = OFF, IGNORE_DUP_KEY = OFF, ONLINE = OFF,
ALLOW_ROW_LOCKS  = ON, ALLOW_PAGE_LOCKS  = OFF)
ON [PRIMARY]
GO
```

In the next section, we'll examine what's needed to alter an index.

Altering an Index in Query Editor

Unlike with a table, it is not possible to use an ALTER command to change the columns contained in an index. To do this, you first have to drop the index and then re-create it. The DROP command will physically remove the index from the table; therefore, you should ensure that you know what the contents of the index are before you drop the index, if you want to re-create a similar index.

▓**Note** In Management Studio, you can add and remove columns from an index's definition without dropping and re-creating the index, as this is all done for you behind the scenes.

This next exercise demonstrates the steps you need to take to remove an index and then re-create it. You'll learn how to do all of this in two steps, rather than the expected three steps.

Try It Out: Altering an Index in Query Editor

1. First, you want to create an index to retrieve the price of a specific share at a set point in time. The following index will do just that, as you are querying the data using the share ID and the date you want the price for (don't run this code):

```
USE ApressFinancial
GO
CREATE UNIQUE CLUSTERED INDEX IX_SharePrices
ON ShareDetails.SharePrices
(
    ShareId ASC,
    PriceDate ASC
) WITH (STATISTICS_NORECOMPUTE  = OFF, SORT_IN_TEMPDB = OFF,
DROP_EXISTING = OFF, IGNORE_DUP_KEY = OFF, ONLINE = OFF,
ALLOW_ROW_LOCKS  = ON, ALLOW_PAGE_LOCKS  = OFF)
ON [PRIMARY]
GO
```

2. However, it would be better to have the PriceDate descending, so that the latest price is at the top, because asking for this information is a query. By including this column, SQL Server would read only one row rather than an increasing number as more prices were created. It would also be advantageous to include the Price itself to avoid a second read to retrieve that column of information from the clustered index.

▓**Note** Remember, clustered indexes hold the data, not pointers to the data. However, in this instance, without the Price column, a second read would be performed.

```
CREATE UNIQUE CLUSTERED INDEX IX_SharePrices
ON ShareDetails.SharePrices
(
    ShareId ASC,
    PriceDate DESC,
    Price
```

```
) WITH (STATISTICS_NORECOMPUTE  = OFF, SORT_IN_TEMPDB = OFF,
DROP_EXISTING = OFF, IGNORE_DUP_KEY = OFF, ONLINE = OFF,
ALLOW_ROW_LOCKS  = ON, ALLOW_PAGE_LOCKS  =
OFF, DROP_EXISTING = OFF) ON [PRIMARY]
```

Note If you did accidentally run the first set of code, change to DROP_EXISTING = ON.

3. Now execute the code using your chosen method, and you should see the following results:

```
The command(s) completed successfully.
```

By using the DROP_EXISTING clause of the CREATE INDEX command, you can then perform the modification in one execution rather than two. This will drop the index and re-create it.

Note Take care when building indexes. It is possible to use the same columns in the same order more than once, thus creating the same index twice, but under two different index names. This is a waste of time and will place unnecessary overhead on SQL Server. However, when including key column(s) from a clustered index in a nonclustered index, because the row pointer is actually the clustered index key, SQL is smart enough not to store the information twice in the nonclustered index, and you can explicitly define the order of the clustered index keys as they are used in the nonclustered index.

There are more indexes to build, but we'll take a look at these later.

When an Index Does Not Exist

As the amount of data in your database expands, expansion may occur in areas that are unexpected. The application originally built with your database could have extensions, so your original database design and index decisions may not still be 100% correct. The underlying problem is that queries are happening within your database against data for which a suitable index doesn't exist.

When SQL Server accesses data, it uses its query optimizer to generate what is termed a **query plan**. A query plan is a plan of actions that SQL Server uses to perform the query you have built against the data. The query plan could consist of several steps that SQL Server performs to execute your query and produce the results you require. You will see an overview of query plans when I discuss advanced T-SQL in Chapter 12. When you look at a query plan, you'll need to decide which is the best index to use to perform the query filtration.

Diagramming the Database

Now that the database has been built, the tables have been created, the indexes have been inserted, and relationships link some of the tables, it's time to start documenting. To help with this, SQL Server offers us the database diagram tool, which is the topic of this section.

One of the most tedious aspects of creating documentation is often the task of documenting tables and showing how they relate to one another in a diagram. Done manually, such work is tedious indeed, and the results are difficult to keep up to date. A database diagram tool, however, can do the work very quickly and simply, with one caveat: if more than one person is using the database diagram tool on the same database, and there are two sets of changes to be applied to the same table, the person who saves his or her changes last will be the person who creates the final table layout. In other words, the people who save before the last person will lose their changes. Therefore, I advise that you develop a database solution using the diagramming tool only on single-developer applications. At all other times, use it as a tool for understanding the database.

As you developed tables within your database, hopefully you will have commented the columns and tables as you have gone along to say what each column and table is. This is a major part of documentation anyway, although a database-naming convention should make your solution self-documenting to an extent. Provided that you comment columns and tables at the start, it will be less of a chore to add in further comments when you add new columns. If you do have comments on each of your columns within a table, then this will help overall with the documentation shown within the diagram.

This said, SQL Server's database diagram feature is more than just a documentation aid. This tool provides us with the ability to develop and maintain database solutions. It is perhaps not always the quickest method of building a solution, but it is one that allows the entire solution to be completed in one place. Alternatively, you can use it to build up sections of a database into separate diagrams, breaking the whole solution into more manageable parts, rather than switching between nodes in Management Studio.

Database Diagramming Basics

In the book so far, with the creation of databases, tables, indexes, and relationships, as much documentation as SQL Server will allow should have so far been maintained. However, there is no documentation demonstrating how the tables relate to one another within the database. This is where the database diagram comes to the forefront.

A database diagram is a useful and easy tool to build simple but effective documentation on these aspects. You build the diagram yourself, and you control what you want to see within the diagram. When you get to a large database solution, you may want diagrams for sections of the database that deal with specific aspects of the system, or perhaps you want to build a diagram showing information about process flows. Although there are other external tools to do this, none is built into SQL Server that can allow diagrams to be kept instantly up to date.

A diagram will only show tables, columns within those tables, and the relationships between tables in a bare form. You will also see a yellow "key," which denotes a primary key on the table where one has been defined, but that is all the information displayed. It is possible to define the information that is to be displayed about the columns in the table, whether it is just the column name or more in-depth information, such as a column's data type and length, comments, and so on. However, to display more than just the bare essentials, a little bit of work is required.

Although the diagram shows the physical and logical attributes of the database that is being built or has been built, it also allows developers and administrators to see exactly what is included with the database at a glance and how the database fits together.

In the next section, we'll delve a bit deeper into what the SQL Server database diagram is all about.

The SQL Server Database Diagram Tool

Management Studio's database diagram tool aids in the building of diagrams that detail aspects of the database that a developer wishes to see. Although it is a simple and straightforward tool, and it's not as powerful as some other tools on the market for building database diagrams, it is perfect for SQL Server.

For example, one of the market leaders in database design tools is a product called ERWin. ERWin is a powerful database utility that not only builds diagrams of databases, but also provides data dictionary language output, which can be used to build database solutions. Through links such as OLE DB data providers, these tools can interact directly with databases and so can be used as a front end for creating databases. They can also, at the same time, keep the created source in alignment and under control from a change control perspective, not only ensuring that the code exists within the database, but also issuing a command to create a new database quickly, if necessary. An example of where this might be useful is when you're creating a new test database. If you want to go further than the SQL Server database diagram tool provides (you'll learn about the tool's boundaries in this chapter), then you should be looking at more powerful tools, which can cost a great deal of money.

SQL Server's database diagram utility offers more than just the ability to create diagrams. As mentioned earlier, it can also be used as a front end for building database solutions. Through this utility, SQL Server allows you to add and modify tables, build relationships, add indexes, and do much more. Any changes built in the tool are held in memory until they are committed using a save command within the tool. However, there are limitations to its overall usefulness.

First of all, the biggest restriction of any diagram-based database tool comes down to the amount of screen space available to view the diagram. As soon as your database solution consists of more than a handful of tables, you will find yourself scrolling around the diagram, trying to find the table you are looking for.

Second, you cannot add stored procedures, schemas, users, views, or any object that is not a table. Other products allow you to include these objects, or they may even build some of them for you.

Finally, for the moment, when altering any of the information you can change within this tool, you are usually using the same dialogs and screens as you would in Management Studio.

As you will see as you go through the chapter, the database diagram tool is quite powerful in what it can achieve, but there are some areas of concern that you have to be aware of when working with diagrams. Keep in mind that the database diagram tool is holding all the changes in memory until you actually save the diagram.

For example, if you have a database diagram open, and a table within that diagram is deleted outside of the diagram, perhaps in Query Editor or Management Studio by yourself or another valid user ID, then one of two things can happen. First, if you have unsaved changes to the deleted table, saving your diagram will re-create the table, but don't forget that through the earlier deletion, all the data will be removed. If, however, you have no changes pending to that table, then the table will not be re-created. When you come to reopen the diagram, the table will have been removed.

With several developers working on the database at once, any changes made from the diagramming tool of your Management Studio will not be reflected in any other developer's diagram until his changes are saved and his diagrams are refreshed. If you have multiple diagrams open, and you alter a table and insert or remove a column, then this will reflect immediately in all the open diagrams within your own Management Studio only. Don't forget this is an in-memory process, so this process can't reflect on anyone else's diagrams until the changes are saved and the diagrams are refreshed.

Also, if you remove an object in your diagram, when you then save the diagram, the object will be removed and any changes completed by others will be lost. Effectively, the last person who closes his or her diagram wins!

To summarize, if you use the database diagram tool, use it with care. Because many of the processes are in memory, you could inadvertently cause problems.

The Default Database Diagram

Although it's not mandatory, I do feel every SQL Server database solution should have a default database diagram built into it so that any developer—new or experienced—can instantly see how the database being inspected fits together.

A default database diagram should include every table and every relationship that is held for that database. Unlike other diagrams that may take a more sectionalized view of things, the default database diagram should be all-encompassing.

As mentioned earlier, it is imperative that you keep this diagram up to date. You will notice this statement repeated a few times in this chapter. Don't use the default diagram as the source of development for your database solution. The default diagram includes all the tables, which means that if you're using the database diagram tool for development, you are potentially logically locking out all other users from touching any other table as part of their development, in case their changes are lost. Only update the diagram with tables and relationships once they have been inserted in the database. We'll look at this in more detail later when we discuss the dangers of using the database diagram tool as a source of development.

Now that you know what diagrams are and what the tool is, it's time to create the first diagram for this database.

Try It Out: Creating a Database Diagram

1. Ensure that SQL Server Management Studio is running and that the ApressFinancial database is expanded so that you see the Database Diagrams and Tables nodes. Select the Database Diagrams node and then right-click. Choose Install Diagram support (see Figure 6-10).

Figure 6-10. *Creating a new database diagram*

2. If this is the first diagram you are creating for the database, you'll need to install support objects. Without them, you cannot create the diagram, so click Yes at the next dialog prompt (see Figure 6-11).

Figure 6-11. *Installing diagramming support*

3. The first screen you'll see when creating the diagram is the Add Table dialog (see Figure 6-12). Select all of the tables listed, as you want to use all the tables in your diagram, and then click Add. This will "empty" the screen. Click Close.

Figure 6-12. *Selecting tables*

4. After a few moments, you will be returned to Management Studio, but with the database diagram now built. The diagram will not show all the tables at this point and will be very large. You can reduce the size through the Size combo box in the diagramming toolbar, as shown in Figure 6-13.

Figure 6-13. *The Size combo box*

5. You'll then see a diagram similar to that shown in Figure 6-14. (Don't be surprised if the layout is different, though.)

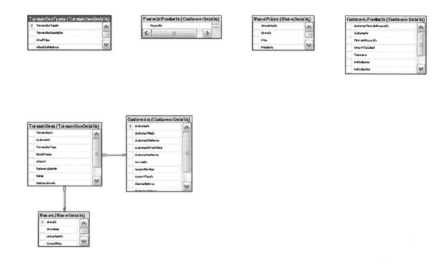

Figure 6-14. *Tables with relationships built so far*

That's all there is to building a basic diagram.

The Database Diagram Toolbar

Let's next take a look at the toolbar and how each of the buttons works within the diagram. The whole toolbar is shown in Figure 6-15.

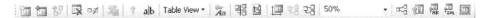

Figure 6-15. *Database diagram toolbar*

The first button is the New Table button, as shown in the following image. You click this button to create a new table within the database designer, which is a similar process to that shown in Chapter 5. The difference is that you need to use the Properties window for each column rather than have the properties at the bottom of the table designer.

When building the diagram, you selected every table. If you hadn't done so and you wanted to add a table added since you created the diagram, clicking the Add Table button (see the following image) would bring up the Add Table dialog shown earlier to add in any missing tables.

The Add Related Tables button, shown next, adds tables related to the selected table in the designer.

It is also possible to delete a table from a database from the designer using the following button.

If you just wish to remove the database from the diagram rather than the database, then you can use the next button to accomplish this. You would use this button, for example, if a table no longer formed part of the "view" the database diagram was built for.

Any changes made to the database within the designer can be saved as a script. Use the following Generate Change Script button to accomplish this.

If you wish to set a column to be the primary key, select the relevant column within a table and click the Set Primary Key button (shown next).

It is possible to create a place within the diagram to put ad hoc text. Use the following New Text Annotation button to do this.

Each table displayed is set to a standard layout. It is possible to change this to a different predefined layout or to create your own custom view. The following Table View button enables you to change the layout or create your own custom version.

Relationships that exist between tables will, by default, show as a line. However, it is possible to show the name of the relationship as a label by clicking the following button.

Diagrams are ideal methods of documenting the database. Diagrams can be printed for meetings, discussions about future development, and so on. The following button shows the **page breaks** in pages that will be printed.

Page breaks in diagrams remain as they were first set up until they are recalculated. You are able to view the page breaks, arrange your tables accordingly, and then recalculate the page breaks based on the new layout. Clicking the following button will do this recalculation for you.

Tables can be expanded or shrunk manually, but when you select one or more tables using the Ctrl button, click the relevant tables, and then click the following button, you can resize the tables to a uniform size.

It is possible, by clicking the following button, to rearrange tables that have been selected and let SQL Server make the arrangement choices.

It is possible to rearrange the tables shown in the diagram. SQL Server will do its best to get the best layout for the tables and relationships when you click the following button. This button is only enabled when tables are selected.

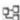

In Chapter 5, you saw how to build a relationship between two tables. The button you use to do this appears next. This button brings up the same dialog as you saw in that chapter. This button is the same as the previous button, but is available all the time.

You have already come across the remaining buttons in the previous chapter.

Summary

We've covered yet another major building block in creating a SQL Server solution. The last few chapters have shown you how to store data, and in this chapter, you've learned about indexes and how to use them to quickly and efficiently retrieve the data stored in the table.

There are many types of indexes, and choosing the right one at the right time to complete the right job is quite an art. This chapter has taken you through the steps to decide which columns will make an efficient index, and then build those columns in the right type of index to make the most of the information.

This chapter also covered database diagramming. Database diagrams should initially be thought of as a form of documentation. Keep in mind, though, that the database diagram tool may expand in future versions of SQL Server to become much more sophisticated and powerful than it is now—although even now it is quite a powerful utility.

■**Tip** Remember, those who save last, save the changes.

Don't be caught off guard by the fact that changes in the diagram are not applied until the diagram is saved, and that your changes could overwrite another's changes. If you're using the database diagram tool for development in any sort of multiuser environment, take the greatest of care when completing updates (in fact, try to avoid them altogether). Unless you split your database solution into multiple diagrams, with any table being found in at most one diagram, don't use the database designer as a development tool.

CHAPTER 7

■■■

Database Backups, Recovery, and Maintenance

Now that we have created a major part of the database in the previous chapters, and before moving on to inserting and manipulating the data, this is a good point to take a moment to back up the database, just so that if things go wrong, it will be possible to recover back to a stable point.

What is abundantly clear when working with any sort of system where data is held is that there must be a comprehensible and workable backup and recovery strategy in place for when things go wrong. The recovery may also be required to cater to problems from a hardware failure to an act of God. In any of these instances, we may move to an **offsite location**, which is a building a safe distance away from our current building housing the computing equipment. That is quite a dramatic step and is a decision that would be taken at a higher level of authority than we probably have; however, we must create a backup of our system and store it according to the recommendations of our board of directors, whether they are for in-house or offsite storage. Companies have gone bust because a good and secure backup storage plan wasn't in place when their building burned down, for example. This is, of course, a worst-case scenario, and there are times that moving out of the current building to a second secure location is not necessary.

This chapter looks at different backup strategies that can be implemented by you as a developer or an administrator and shows you how to implement them. I also show you scenarios where the database is in use 24 hours a day, 7 days a week, and how you need to form a backup strategy around such scenarios. From there, I show you how to perform an ad hoc backup of the database as well as scheduled transaction log backups. I make it clear in this chapter when you would perform both of these types of backups and when they would be useful. Of course, after the backup, you have to test that the backup can be restored. Generally, this backup is restored onto a nonproduction system. Some companies have complete environments established to test their disaster-recovery scenarios.

What you have to realize, and what will be demonstrated, is that there are different methods of taking backups depending on what you are trying to achieve. The most common scenarios are discussed and demonstrated in this chapter, but you will also get to look at database maintenance plans.

It is imperative that you get the correct backup strategy in place and that it works. This point will be repeated throughout the chapter.

So, in this chapter you will learn about:

- Backup strategies
- When a problem might occur during the backup and restore process
- How to take a database offline and then bring it back online
- How to create a backup
- Different media for building a backup and what needs to be considered

- The transaction log and how to back it up

- When to back up the data, and when to back up the transaction log

- Scheduling backups, and what happens if the server isn't running at the scheduled time

- Restoring a database

- Detaching and attaching a database

- Working with users still attached to the database when you need them not to be connected

- Building SQL statements for backing up the database structure, and when it is useful to have them

- Building a maintenance plan and when to use it

- Implementing Database Mail in your maintenance plan

Transaction Logs

Data within the database is stored, of course, on your hard drive, or on a hard drive on a server. Imagine the work involved on the disk controller, and imagine the work SQL Server has to do every time data is added, amended, or removed. Writing data is a slow process compared to other memory-based processes, so inevitably, SQL Server slows down every time data is written. A good comparison is to think how long it takes you to insert, modify, or erase a sentence, even using MS Word, compared to how long it takes you to read a sentence. What if part of the way through writing the data, a power outage occurred and you had no uninterruptible power supply (UPS) in place? What a mess you would be in, not knowing what had been written to disk and therefore your tables within your database, and what hadn't!

It is also possible in SQL Server to update several tables at once. How would you work around the fact that some of the tables had been updated, but when it came to updating a specific table, the update failed? Well, this is where transaction logs come into play. Transactions themselves are covered in Chapter 8, but very simply, a **transaction** is a single unit of work that can contain one or more table modifications that are either all successful and committed to the database or, if some are unsuccessful, all discarded. It is also possible to roll back a transaction so that no changes are made to the database, which can either be invoked by SQL Server or by issuing a specific T-SQL command. But you must be wondering what all this has to do with a transaction log, and you're probably even wondering what a transaction log is. Before we move on, there is one last area of background information we need to discuss first.

The **log file** is a complex item that contains virtual, logical, and physical log files, but to keep it simple, the transaction log has a physical size—in other words, it is like any other file on the hard drive. The transaction log increases in size as necessary to accommodate the transactions. It is a wraparound file. This means that when SQL Server reaches the end of the file as defined by the size when it was set up, it wraps around to the beginning again, looking for free space to use. This allows it to wrap around without increasing in size when there is free logical transaction space. The logical transaction log is "contained" within the physical transaction log and is determind by a physical point in the physical log file at where the last checkpoint or truncation action occurred, and it continues until the next checkpoint or truncation point occurs. Virtual log files are files of no fixed size and are built internally by SQL Server as part of the physical creation of the transaction log.

Every database within a SQL Server instance has its own transaction log. Every time SQL Server is requested to do any data modifications—whether these are additions, deletions, or modifications—a record is kept of the action. There are several reasons for this.

First of all, a piece of code could in fact do several different updates at once, either to different rows of data or to rows of data in different tables or even databases. If one of the updates fails, for example, when you are attempting to place ASCII characters into a column that only allows numerics, then you may wish to return the values in all the updated fields to their original value. This is called **rolling back** a transaction. SQL Server achieves this, in part, by looking at the data held in the transaction log. However, any successful action where all the updates are valid could be permanently stored on file—a process called **committing** a transaction.

As more and more actions are placed in the transaction log, it will become full. Some of these actions will still be within a transaction, and others may form part of a completed transaction ready to be committed to the database. At certain points, SQL Server will want to remove all the actions it can to relieve some space in the transaction log for further actions. One point could be when the transaction log reaches 70% full. SQL Server would then issue a **checkpoint**. The use of a checkpoint ensures that any data modifications are actually committed to the database and not held in any buffers, so that if a problem occurs, such as a power failure, there is a specific point that you can start from. Therefore, at the end of a checkpoint transaction, you know the database is in a consistent and valid state. As SQL Server knows that at a checkpoint all is well within the database, there is no need to keep the completed transactions recorded in the transaction log stored up to the checkpoint. SQL Server therefore issues a truncation of the transaction log to remove these records, minimizing the size of the log on the computer. This is known as **truncating** the transaction log. It is thus necessary to ensure that you have a large enough transaction log defined to hold the largest valid uncommitted transaction, as these transactions obviously will not be truncated. A transaction log can become full with a rogue query as well—that is, one that is coded incorrectly and keeps adding more and more uncommitted transactions. When the transaction log reaches 70%, there is nothing to checkpoint and eventually the transaction log will fill up, and your SQL Server will stop. This is where you will need the help of an experienced database administrator.

If you have a power failure, you might have to "replay" all the work completed since the last backup, and in certain scenarios, you could use the transaction log to do this. When a data modification is completed via a T-SQL command, the details are recorded first in the transaction log. These changes are flushed to disk and therefore no longer in memory, before SQL Server starts to make changes to the tables that you are affecting. SQL Server doesn't write data immediately to disk. It is kept in a **buffer cache** until this cache is full or until SQL Server issues a checkpoint, and then the data is written out. If a power failure occurs while the cache is still filling up, then that data is lost. Once the power comes back, though, SQL Server would start from its last checkpoint state, and any updates after the last checkpoint that were logged as successful transactions will be performed from the transaction log.

■**Note** A **disk cache** is a space in the system that holds changes to the tables within the database. This allows a whole block of data to be written at once, saving on the slow process of disk head movement.

Transaction logs are best kept, if at all possible, on a hard drive separate from that holding the data. The reason for this is that data is written serially when it is written to a transaction log. Therefore, if nothing else is on the hard drive except the transaction log, the disk heads will be in the right place to continue writing each time. This is a minor overhead, but if performance is an issue, this is worth considering.

Backup Strategies

Backing up a database, no matter how large or small, should form part of your database solution. Even if a backup is taken only once a week or even once a month, it is crucial that you sit down and decide which backup strategy is right for you. Much of this decision lies in the hands of the product owners for your company, since they must weigh the risk they're willing to take against the cost of minimizing that risk. Many different strategies can be adopted within your overall main backup strategy, depending on days of the week or perhaps periods within the month.

Based on the strategy that you choose, you have to decide what type of backup you need. **Full database backups** take a complete snapshot of a database at any given point. A **differential backup** backs up only the data that has changed since the last full backup. Finally, a **transaction log backup** backs up only the data in the transaction log, which consists of transactions that were recently committed to the database. All of these types of backups can be done while your SQL Server is online and while users are actively hitting your database. To be able to restore a database to any point in time, you have to use a combination of these backup types.

When determining your backup strategy, first look at your application and ask yourself the following questions:

- How much of the data can be lost, if any, at any point of failure? In other words, how crucial is it that no data is lost?

- How often is the data updated? Do you need regular backups from a performance viewpoint as well as a recovery viewpoint? For historical databases that have their data modified only periodically, you would, at most, complete a backup postpopulation.

- Do you need to back up all the data all of the time, or can you do this periodically, and then only back up the data that has altered in the meanwhile?

- How much data needs to be backed up, and how long do you need to keep the copies of the backups?

- In the event of catastrophic failure, how long will it take to completely rebuild the database, if it's even possible?

Many more questions can be asked, but for the moment, these are the most crucial questions that need answers. If you can afford to allow data updates to be lost, then you need a straightforward periodic database backup—for example, you need to back up the whole database once a week. This is simple and easy to complete and requires little thought. However, this scenario is rare and is usually found in data-warehousing systems or those with a large amount of static data that can be rebuilt.

Looking at the next question, if a large number of updates are taking place, then a more complex solution is required. For every data modification, a record is kept in the transaction log file, which has a limited amount of space. This amount of space was defined when you set up the database as a fixed maximum size or, if you are allowing it to grow unrestrictedly, equals the amount of hard drive there is. If you back up and clear the transaction log file, this will free up the space logically initially and also aid performance. This is known as **logical log truncation**. The smaller the active part of the transaction log file, the better. The more transactions there are in the transaction log file, the longer it will take to recover from a corrupt database. This is due to the fact that a restore will have to restore the data and then every transaction log backup to the point of failure. That is, each transaction log will have to be restored to update the database, not just the latest log file. If you have multiple small files and they are held on media that has to be mounted each time, such as a tape, then you will have to take mounting time into consideration as well.

The third question, though, covers the real crux of the problems. If you need to back up all the data each time, how often will that need to take place? This could well be every night, and many production systems do just this. By completing a full data backup every night, you are allowing yourself to be in a state where only one or two restores may need to occur to get back to a working state in a disaster scenario. This would be the data backup, followed by the single transaction log backup, if one was taken in the meantime. This is much better than having one data backup to be restored, and then a log file for every day since the data file backup. What happens if the failure is on a Friday at lunchtime and you completed your last whole database backup on a Saturday evening? That would take one data file and six transaction log file restores to complete.

Sit down and take stock. As often as you can, take a full database backup, then take a differential backup, followed by transaction log backups. However, you have to weigh the time that a full backup takes against a differential backup or a transaction log; how much processing time you have to complete these backups; and the risk level of having to complete, for example, six transaction log restores.

The problem is, there is no universally right answer. Each situation is different, and it is only through experience, which comes from testing your solution thoroughly, that you find out what is best for your situation.

Whatever your backup strategy, the best possible scenario is to complete a backup when nobody is working within the database. If there are times when you can make the database unavailable, then this is an ideal opportunity to take the backup. Although SQL Server can perform full backups while the database is online and active, you will gain performance benefits by having an inactive database. The first example, shortly, demonstrates one method of doing this.

When Problems May Occur

Obviously, when taking a backup, it must work; otherwise, you have wasted your time, but crucially, you are leaving your database and organization in a vulnerable position if the backup fails. If you have time within your backup window to verify that a backup has been successful, then you must do it. As you will see, SQL Server gives you different options for doing this. It cannot be stressed strongly enough that verifying a backup is just as crucial as taking the backup in the first place. There have been situations where a backup has been taken every night; however, no one has noticed that the backup has failed. When there is a hardware failure, there's no backup to use as a restore on a new machine. In one case I know of, almost a week's worth of data was lost. Luckily, the weekend backups had succeeded; otherwise, the company would have been in a major data loss situation. The cause of the failed backups was that the tapes being inserted for the backup were not large enough to hold the backup being performed. Therefore, the tapes became full, and the backup failed. Obviously, this company failed not only to verify the backup, but also to have processes in place to check that its backup strategy was still working after a period of implementation. The only sure and positive way of ensuring a backup has succeeded is to restore the database to a specific restore test location and check the data. Although you will see SQL Server does have a method of checking a backup, this still isn't a guarantee that the backup worked. Do take time to complete regular restores to a location to test that everything is OK.

You should always review your backup strategy on a regular basis. Even better, put in place jobs that run each day that give some sort of space report so that it is possible to instantly see that a potential problem is looming. SQL Server Reporting Services is a new tool that would be ideal for producing and distributing space reports to database administrators and developer owners alike.

Taking a Database Offline

SQL Server does not have to be offline to perform a backup, as you will see as we go through the book and work through creating SQL Server–defined backups using wizards and T-SQL. In most environments, you will not have the luxury of taking a database offline before backing it up, because users are constantly making data changes. Backing up a database can take a long time, and the longer it takes, the longer users cannot be working with the data while it is offline.

By taking your database offline, you do not have to use SQL Server to perform the backup. This strategy is one where you take a disk backup, which means the hard drive is backed up, rather than a specific database within a server. However, don't forget that by taking your database offline, you will have to take a backup of the directory using some sort of drive backup.

If you have your database on a server, no doubt some sort of server backup strategy is in place, and so your database will be backed up fully and successfully through this method; if you can take your database "out of service" in time for those backups, then you should do so. This does allow you to think about your SQL Server deployment strategy. If you have several databases that can be taken offline as part of the backup, then it is worth considering whether they can all reside on the same physical server, and you can set your server backup times accordingly. However, this is a rare scenario, and even rarer within a production environment. Taking the database offline means taking your database out of service. Nobody can update or access the data, modify table structures, and so on. In this next section, we will take ApressFinancial offline, allowing a physical backup to be taken. Just to reiterate and clarify: this is being demonstrated only to complete your knowledge of backups, and it is rare that you will perform this action in a live scenario.

Try It Out: Taking a Database Offline

1. Open SQL Server Management Studio and open a Query Editor pane. Enter and execute the following code:

```
USE master
GO
ALTER DATABASE ApressFinancial
SET OFFLINE
```

2. Try to click some of the nodes for the ApressFinancial database—for example, the Tables node. As shown in Figure 7-1, we are reminded that the database is offline and therefore cannot be viewed or modified. We are also not able to access the database through any application such as Query Editor.

Figure 7-1. *The database is offline and therefore unable to be opened.*

To take a database offline, SQL Server must be able to gain exclusive access to the database. This means that no user can be in the database when we issue the command. If users are connected, then the query will continue to execute until all users are disconnected.

As said earlier, that's all there is to it. Our database is now no longer available for any updates or modifications, so we can back it up using any backup utility that takes files from a hard drive.

If you have to restore from a backup completed this way, don't forget to take the database offline first, then restore from the backup, and then bring the database back online, ready for use:

```
USE master
go
ALTER DATABASE ApressFinancial
SET ONLINE
```

There is one area to note when using backup strategies that employ these methods. If you have a server backup that runs, for example, at 0200 hours, do you fancy getting up every night, just before 2 a.m., taking the database offline, and then bringing the server back up once the backup is complete? No—not many people would. Of course, there are installations where people are working through the night, so this is less of a problem, but what if they are busy? Or forget? Then your whole backup will fail because the files are in use, and therefore the server will not back up these files.

So let's now look at a more friendly method of backing up the data by using SQL Server instead.

Backing Up the Data

The majority of readers will use SQL Server to back up the database. By using SQL Server, we are keeping the backup of the database under the control of an automated process that can control its own destiny, and as you will find out later, it can also control the system when things go wrong.

The backup will be split into two parts. The first part, which will be covered here, will be when we perform the backup manually each time. Obviously, this means we have to be available to perform the backup, but this can be rectified quite easily. Once this has been covered, the next section will show you how to schedule a backup to run at a specific time, which relieves us of needing to be available to complete a backup at the specified time.

Let's start by looking at the manual backup.

Try It Out: Backing Up the Data

1. Ensure SQL Server Management Studio is running. Find our database, right-click, select Tasks, and then click Back Up.

2. This brings up the SQL Server Back Up Database dialog box. Take a moment to peruse this dialog box. As Figure 7-2 shows, a lot appears on this screen, which will be dealt with a section at a time.

Figure 7-2. *Backing up a database (Full Recovery mode)*

Although we have chosen our own database to back up, we could alter which database by changing the value in the combo box. Next is the backup type, of which we have three options to choose from: Full, Differential, and Transaction Log.

The first possibility, full backup, is straightforward. Selecting the Full option ensures that the whole database will be backed up. All the tables, the data, and so on are backed up if we use this option. We also back up enough of the transaction log (transactions committed via code, but not physically applied to the relevant tables at the point of backup). This backup would be seen as any starting point for a restore from a database failure.

The second possibility is the differential backup, also known as an incremental backup. Use the Differential backup option when the circumstances are such that a full backup is either not required or not possible. This just performs a backup on data changed since the last backup. For example, we may take a full backup on the weekend and then a differential backup every night. When it comes to restoring, we would restore the weekend full backup, and then add to that the latest differential backup taken from that point. A word of warning here: if you do take a week's worth of differential backups, and you back up to magnetic tape rather than a hard drive, do keep at least enough different tapes for each differential backup. Therefore, use a complete backup when necessary and then in the interim, use a differential backup.

The last possibility, the transaction log backup, should be used as the most frequent method of backup providing that the database is not in Simple Recovery mode. As data is modified, details of the modifications are stored in the transaction log. These remain in place until an action "truncates" the transaction log, which means that the transaction log will increase constantly in size if not in Simple Recovery. When you issue a transaction log backup, you are just backing up the trans-action log, which issues a checkpoint, and all committed transactions are stored onto the backup. This means that if a system failure occurs, you will restore from a full backup, then from your differential backups for the week, and finally from any transaction log backups after that point.

You are probably wondering why you can't just use differential backups. Transaction logs can fill up during the working day, or perhaps you have set differential backups to happen weekly because there is so little data modification. However, you do need to account for when a transaction log may fill up before you reach the next differential backup. By taking a backup of the transaction log, this is a great deal faster than the other two methods. Certainly in heavily used databases, you may have several transaction log backups in the day. You see how to do this using T-SQL after we take our first full backup. At least one backup must exist before we can take a transaction log backup, as we need a point at which the transaction log can roll committed transactions forward from.

■**Note** If we were backing up the master database, then the only option that would be available to us would be a complete database backup via the Full option.

A name and a description of your backup are always useful. You will create different backups over time, so a good description is always something that will help at a later date. I recommend that you use some sort of date and time as part of the description, as this will make it easier to find, and which mode of backup you have chosen.

Different types of backups will have different expiry dates. This means that after the defined date, the media you have stored your backup on will allow the data to be overwritten if using SQL Server (you can't delete the file manually!). For example, you might have a weekly full backup that you want to keep three instances of, and then the first full backup of the month you may wish to keep for six months, or even longer if it is a database that you must keep for government leg-islation. In this option, you can retain the backup for a set number of days (for example, 21 days) or for a set period of time (a specific date covers for uneven days in a month, or a year, for example).

A default destination is defined, which might be more than acceptable. It will be on our hard drive, in a location below where our data is. It is best to have a directory set aside for backups so that they are easy to find, perhaps with a name such as SQL Server Backups. However, this is not recommended in production. What if the hard drive fails? We can gain a substantial performance improvement by backing up the database to a separate disk or to a RAID 1 drive if one is available. This is because data is written to the backup file in a sequential manner. It is also advisable to give the backup file a mean-ingful name. In this instance, it has been given the name of the database, ApressFinancial.

3. Move to the Options tab, as shown in Figure 7-3, where we can define what options we want to happen as part of this backup.

Figure 7-3. *Database backup options*

The first section of this dialog box deals with what you want to happen on second and subsequent backups. The first time the backup is run, it creates the backup files, but when you run subsequent backups, do you want to append to the current data or overwrite it? If this is a full backup, then you may overwrite, as you should be placing this full backup over an old nonrequired backup. However, if this is a differential backup, where it is perhaps the second or third of the week, then you will append to the existing backup set. This will be after the previous differential backups and means that if you need to do a restore, all the backups will be one after another and therefore will provide the fastest retrieval.

The Check Media Set Name option forces the backup to check that where the data is going to be backed up to is still a valid name and, if appending, that the data set has not expired.

You use the Back Up to a New Media Set, and Erase All Existing Backup Sets option when any previous backups are no longer required. This is ideal when moving the database from development to either user testing or even production, and you don't want to be able to restore from an incorrect backup. There is no point in wishing to restore a production server from a development backup, after all.

The second section deals with the reliability of the backup. It is possible to simply back up the data and trust that everything worked perfectly, meaning no data transmission errors occurred between your SQL Server and the backup device, or that no errors occurred when writing the data. A situation such as this is unusual, but there will be times when it does happen. Do you trust that those times will occur when you will not need a backup? I suggest this is something you cannot and should not rely on. Therefore, although it will increase the amount of time the backup takes, it is good to choose one of the two options in this section. The first option allows a verification of the backup where SQL Server compares what has been backed up with what it expects to have been backed up, and the second option allows for checksum processing whereby SQL Server performs a mathematical calculation on the data to back up, which generates a checksum that can then be compared once the data has been transmitted from SQL Server to the backup device. If you select the second option, you can also specify whether to continue if you get a checksum error.

If you are doing a transaction log backup, the next area of the dialog box will be enabled. You can logically shrink the trans-action log by removing all entries that have just been backed up by selecting the first option, Truncate the Transaction Log. To save processing time, the physical transaction log is not shrunk. The second option, Back Up the Tail of the Log, is used when there has been some sort of database corruption. If you wish to back up transaction log records that have not been backed up prior to performing a restore to correct the corruption, then you would use this option. To clarify, a database becomes corrupt, and you need to be able to restore up to the last backup, then add all the transactions that have occurred since the last backup. By executing a backup of the tail of the log, you can restore the database and then use this tail log backup to add the missing transactions.

The penultimate area of the dialog box is available if you are using tapes as your backup medium. You can eject the tape once the backup has finished. This is a useful option, as the computer operators would know to remove the tape for dispatch to the safe backup area. The second option, which specifies a rewind, is useful for full backups. On differential backups, however, SQL Server would be halted when running the next backup while the tape device got to the right place on the tape to continue the backup.

Finally, it is possible to set the compression level for the backup. This is ideal to keep space taken for each backup to a minimum. Notice that by default, it takes the compression level set for the server, but it's possible to overwrite this with a new setting. If you do use compressed backups, then you will save on I/O and the backup operation will complete in less time, but completing the compression will increase the amount of processing SQL Server is using. It is possible to reduce the priority of completing a compressed backup so that it doesn't affect SQL Server by using the resource governor. This is an advanced topic and not covered in this book.

Clicking OK starts the backup. Once the backup is finished, you should see the dialog box shown in Figure 7-4.

Figure 7-4. *A successful backup*

The first backup of the ApressFinancial database has now taken place and should have been successful. If we now move to the directory on the hard drive where the backup took place, then we will see the ApressFinancial file.

Recall that it was mentioned earlier that a company lost a week's worth of data. It had set up the option to append to media, the tape had become full, and the administrator had not set up the proper scenario to alert someone when a problem occurred. So there was not just one failure in the system, but two; however, it still highlights that if you are using the option to append to media, you must check that enough room is available on the medium that you are appending to for the backup to succeed.

Creating a backup of your database and the data is the most crucial action in building a database solution. Get it wrong, and you may as well go home. Well, not quite, but if (or when) things go wrong, and you don't have a valid or recent enough backup that is acceptable to the users of your database, it will take a long time for you as a developer to recover from that situation and get back to the excellent working relationship you had beforehand.

The backup taken in the preceding example is the simplest backup to perform. It is a complete backup of our particular SQL Server database, and it happens while we are watching. If it goes wrong, we will instantly see and be able to deal with it. However, most backups do not happen when you are there and instead happen throughout the night. In the next section, you will see more about scheduling jobs and how to schedule a task to run through the night. However, it doesn't cover what to do when things go wrong. This is a difficult area to discuss and should be integrated with our database maintenance plan, which is covered later in this chapter in the section "Creating a Database Maintenance Plan." This example demonstrates how to complete a backup manually rather than as an automated process.

Before moving on, there are a couple more points concerning backups that you must keep in mind, and it is recommended strongly that these directions be followed. First of all, keep a regular and up-to-date backup of the master and msdb system databases. SQL Server very rarely becomes corrupted, but it can happen for any number of reasons, from a hard drive failure to a developer altering the database in error. It really doesn't matter, but if you don't have a backup of the master database, you could find yourself in trouble. However, be warned. Restoring the master database should not be performed unless you really have to, and only if you are experienced with SQL Server. Restoring the master database is not like restoring other databases, and it has to be completed outside SQL Server Management Studio. This book quite deliberately does not cover having to restore the master database, since it is a very advanced topic. If you wish to know more, then take a look at Books Online for more details.

When it comes to the msdb database and when to back it up, it could be that a daily backup is required. If you recall, this database holds job schedules and other information pertinent to the SQL Server Agent for scheduling. If you have jobs that run each day, and you need to keep information about when jobs were run, a daily backup may be required. However, if you only wish to keep a backup of jobs that are set up and there is no need to know when certain jobs ran and whether they were successful or not, then perhaps look at backing up this database weekly.

The model database should be backed up if any details within the model database have been altered. This should be pretty infrequent, and therefore backing up this database need not be as regular as any other database; once a week is probably frequent enough.

Backing up tempdb is not necessary, as this should be seen as a transient database, which has no set state. Therefore, it would be very unusual to back up this database.

■**Note** When SQL Server is restarted, tempdb is dropped and is re-created as part of the startup process.

As you can see, it is not just your own databases that need to be considered and remembered when it comes to dealing with your backup strategy. A database within SQL Server is not an insular arrangement and affects the system databases just as much. If in doubt, back it up more frequently than is required!

Backing Up the Database Using T-SQL

Now that we have backed up the database using the wizard, it is useful to demonstrate performing a backup with T-SQL. These commands and statements can be used within a stored procedure that can be scheduled to run at required intervals as part of an overnight task.

There are two different types of backups. It is possible to back up either the database or specific file groups or files that are part of the database. The code for the database backup follows. The highlighted code demonstrates which of the two possible options is the optional default used when neither option is specified:

```
BACKUP DATABASE { database_name | @database_name_var }
TO < backup_device > [ ,...n ]
[ [ MIRROR TO < backup_device > [ ,...n ] ] [ ...next-mirror ] ]
[ WITH
    [ BLOCKSIZE = { blocksize | @blocksize_variable } ]
    [ [ , ] { CHECKSUM | NO_CHECKSUM } ]
    [ [ , ] { STOP_ON_ERROR | CONTINUE_AFTER_ERROR } ]
```

```
    [ [ , ] DESCRIPTION = { 'text' | @text_variable } ]
    [ [ , ] DIFFERENTIAL ]
    [ [ , ] EXPIREDATE = { date | @date_var }
    | RETAINDAYS = { days | @days_var } ]
    | { COMPRESSION | NO_COMPRESSION }
    [ [ , ] PASSWORD = { password | @password_variable } ]
    [ [ , ] { FORMAT | NOFORMAT } ]
    [ [ , ] { INIT | NOINIT } ]
    [ [ , ] { NOSKIP | SKIP } ]
    [ [ , ] MEDIADESCRIPTION = { 'text' | @text_variable } ]
    [ [ , ] MEDIANAME = { media_name | @media_name_variable } ]
    [ [ , ] MEDIAPASSWORD = { mediapassword | @mediapassword_variable } ]
    [ [ , ] NAME = { backup_set_name | @backup_set_name_var } ]
    [ [ , ] { NOREWIND | REWIND } ]
    [ [ , ] { NOUNLOAD | UNLOAD } ]
    [ [ , ] STATS [ = percentage ] ]
    [ [ , ] COPY_ONLY ]
]
```

If instead you just wish to back up specific files or file groups, the difference in the code is high-lighted in the BACKUP DATABASE statement shown here:

```
BACKUP DATABASE { database_name | @database_name_var }
    <file_or_filegroup> [ ,...f ]
TO <backup_device> [ ,...n ]
[ [ MIRROR TO <backup_device> [ ,...n ] ] [ ...next-mirror ] ]
[ WITH
    [ BLOCKSIZE = { blocksize | @blocksize_variable } ]
    [ [ , ] { CHECKSUM | NO_CHECKSUM } ]
    [ [ , ] { STOP_ON_ERROR | CONTINUE_AFTER_ERROR } ]
    [ [ , ] DESCRIPTION = { 'text' | @text_variable } ]
    [ [ , ] DIFFERENTIAL ]
    [ [ , ] EXPIREDATE = { date | @date_var }
    | RETAINDAYS = { days | @days_var } ]
    | { COMPRESSION | NO_COMPRESSION }
    [ [ , ] PASSWORD = { password | @password_variable } ]
    [ [ , ] { FORMAT | NOFORMAT } ]
    [ [ , ] { INIT | NOINIT } ]
    [ [ , ] { NOSKIP | SKIP } ]
    [ [ , ] MEDIADESCRIPTION = { 'text' | @text_variable } ]
    [ [ , ] MEDIANAME = { media_name | @media_name_variable } ]
    [ [ , ] MEDIAPASSWORD = { mediapassword | @mediapassword_variable } ]
    [ [ , ] NAME = { backup_set_name | @backup_set_name_var } ]
    [ [ , ] { NOREWIND | REWIND } ]
    [ [ , ] { NOUNLOAD | UNLOAD } ]
    [ [ , ] STATS [ = percentage ] ]
    [ [ , ] COPY_ONLY ]
```

I can now give a brief description of all the options that are available. We looked at some of these options previously with the Back Up Database dialog box. Seeing these descriptions allows you to compare options within T-SQL and within the backup dialog boxes:

- `database_name | @database_name_var`: Either the name of a database or a local variable that gives the name of the database to back up.

- `file_or_filegroup`: The name of the file or file group to back up.

- `backup_device`: The name of the logical or physical backup device to use.

- `MIRROR TO`: The backup file is mirrored to two to four different file locations.

- `BLOCKSIZE`: The block size to use. For example, if backing up to CD-ROM, then you would set a block size of 2048.

- `CHECKSUM | NO_CHECKSUM`: Specifies whether to perform checksum calculations to ensure the transmission of data.

- `STOP_ON_ERROR | CONTINUE_AFTER_ERROR`: Specifies whether to stop on a checksum error or not.

- `DESCRIPTION`: A description of the backup.

- `DIFFERENTIAL`: If this is a differential backup, then specify this option. Without this option, a full backup is taken.

- `EXPIREDATE`: The date the backup expires and is therefore available to be overwritten.

- `RETAINDAYS`: The number of days the backup will be kept before the system will allow it to be overwritten.

- `COMPRESSION`: Lets you compress your backup and reduce the amount of space taken.

■**Note** Compression backups are only available on the Developer and Enterprise editions of SQL Server. If you don't define this option, then the server instance setting will be used. You can change it at the server level via the `sp_configure` system stored procedure.

- `PASSWORD`: The password associated with the backup. This must be supplied when interrogating the backup for any restore operation. There is no strong encryption on this option, so there is the potential that it could be broken easily.

- `FORMAT | NOFORMAT`: Specifies whether to format the storage medium or not.

- `INIT | NOINIT`: Keeps the media header created with the format but erases the contents.

- `NOSKIP | SKIP`: If you want to skip the checking of `expiredate` or `retaindays` when using the media set, then select the `SKIP` option. Otherwise, `expiredate` and `retaindays` will be checked.

■**Note** A **media set** is an ordered set of backups on the same disk or tape.

- `MEDIADESCRIPTION`: Gives a description to the media set.

- `MEDIANAME`: Names the media set.

- `MEDIAPASSWORD`: Gives the media set its password.

- `NAME`: Names the backup set.

- `NOREWIND | REWIND`: Specifies whether to rewind a tape or not.

- `NOUNLOAD | UNLOAD`: Specifies whether the tape is unloaded or kept on the tape drive.

- STATS [= percentage]: SQL Server provides a message at this percentage interval telling you how much of the approximate backup has completed. It's useful for gauging the progress of long-running backups.
- COPY_ONLY: Tells SQL Server that this is a copy of the data. It cannot be used as a full backup point for differential backups, as the differential backups will be in line with the last "pure" full backup. This option is ideal if you take weekly backups for dumping the data to a user test region, as it will not affect the production backup process.

The only remaining option is for files or file groups where you can name the file or file group that the backup is for. The preceding options do not change for files or file groups.

Try It Out: Backing Up the Database Using T-SQL for a Full and Differential Backup

1. Open up a fresh Query Editor window. It doesn't matter which database it is pointing to, as the BACKUP DATABASE statement defines the database we will be working with.

2. The T-SQL that we need for our full backup follows. Enter the code (keeping the name of where the backup is located via the TO DISK option and the WITH NAME option all on one line). Notice that there are no options defined for several of the options, as we are taking the default.

```
BACKUP DATABASE ApressFinancial
TO DISK = 'C:\Program Files\Microsoft SQL
Server\MSSQL10.MSSQLSERVER\MSSQL\Backup\
ApressFinancial.bak'
WITH NAME = 'ApressFinancial-Full Database Backup',
SKIP,
NOUNLOAD,
STATS = 10
```

3. Execute the code, and you will see results similar to those that follow. The main points to notice are the stats messages that come out in approximations of 10 percentage points. It then lists the number of data pages backed up and the number of log pages backed up. The on file part of the message details which file within the media set the backup now is. In this case, this is the third backup. You will possibly see on file 2 unless a second or subsequent backup has been taken in the meantime. The final message is the one of greatest interest, as it shows that the backup was successful, and it displays the amount of time taken.

```
13 percent processed.
22 percent processed.
31 percent processed.
40 percent processed.
54 percent processed.
63 percent processed.
72 percent processed.
81 percent processed.
90 percent processed.
Processed 176 pages for database 'ApressFinancial', file 'ApressFinancial'
on file 2.
100 percent processed.
Processed 1 pages for database 'ApressFinancial', file 'ApressFinancial_log'
on file 2.
BACKUP DATABASE successfully processed 177 pages in 0.380 seconds (3.815 MB/sec).
```

4. Although useful to see, not many of the options were used. However, Figure 7-5 shows the next backup of the database to be taken, which is a differential backup. We will not allow this backup to expire until 60 days have elapsed, as shown in Figure 7-5. We will also be adding this differential backup to the full backup. At the end of the screen shots, don't back up, but click the Generate Script button which will place the T-SQL equivalent code in a new query window where you will then be asked to run it.

Figure 7-5. *Backing up a database (differential)*

5. Figure 7-6 shows that we are appending to the same media set as the full backup and that we have included some reliability checking. Make sure your version matches the figure.

6. The code that would be the equivalent of these two figures has been split in two. The first part is the differential backup. Again, ensure that the TO DISK, DESCRIPTION, and NAME options are all on the same line of the Query Editor window pane.

```
BACKUP DATABASE [ApressFinancial] TO  DISK =
N'C:\Program Files\Microsoft SQL Server\MSSQL10.MSSQLSERVER\MSSQL\
Backup\ApressFinancial.bak'
WITH  DIFFERENTIAL ,
DESCRIPTION = 'This is a differential backup',
RETAINDAYS = 60, NOFORMAT, NOINIT,
MEDIANAME = N'ApressBackup',
NAME = N'ApressFinancial-Differential Database Backup',
NOSKIP, NOREWIND, NOUNLOAD,  STATS = 10, CHECKSUM
GO
```

Figure 7-6. *Options for backing up a database (differential)*

7. The second part is where the reliability checking takes place. This is more complex T-SQL than we have covered, so for the moment just trust that it works and that it does what it is supposed to. You will encounter this code once more when looking at more complex T-SQL later in the book in Chapter 11. However, the basis of the code is that a check is made in the msdb database to retrieve the last backup set that was taken, that we do a "restore" of the database as verification only without actually restoring any data, and that the restore can complete successfully. If it can't verify the backup set or that the restore is OK, then you will get an error message.

```
declare @backupSetId as int
select @backupSetId = position
from msdb..backupset
where database_name=N'ApressFinancial'
and backup_set_id=
    (select max(backup_set_id)
      from msdb..backupset
      where database_name=N'ApressFinancial' )
if @backupSetId is null
begin
raiserror(N'Verify failed. Backup information for database ''ApressFinancial''
not found.', 16, 1)
end
RESTORE VERIFYONLY FROM
```

```
DISK = N'C:\Program Files\Microsoft SQL Server\MSSQL10.MSSQLSERVER
\MSSQL\Backup\ApressFinancial.bak'
WITH  FILE = @backupSetId,
NOUNLOAD,
NOREWIND
```

8. When the code is executed, you will see something like the results that follow. Again, they contain details of the amount of data backed up as well as which file number on the media set the backup is.

```
19 percent processed.
39 percent processed.
58 percent processed.
78 percent processed.
97 percent processed.
Processed 40 pages for database 'ApressFinancial',
file 'ApressFinancial' on file 3.
100 percent processed.
Processed 1 pages for database 'ApressFinancial',
file 'ApressFinancial_log' on file 3.
BACKUP DATABASE WITH DIFFERENTIAL successfully processed 41 pages
in 0.433 seconds (0.774 MB/sec).
The backup set on file 3 is valid.
```

Transaction Log Backup Using T-SQL

You can back up not only the data, but also, and just as importantly, the transaction log for the database. Just to recap, the transaction log is a file used by databases to log every transaction, including DML actions such as rebuilding indexes. In other words, every data modification that has taken place on any table within the database will be recorded within the transaction log. The transaction log is then used in many different scenarios within a database solution, but where it is most useful, from a database recovery point of view, is when a database crashes. In this case, the transaction log can be used to move forward from the last data backup, using the transactions listed within the transaction log.

If a database crash occurs, then the full and differential backups will only take you to the last valid backup. For data entered since that point, the only way to restore the information is to then "replay" the transactions that were committed and recorded as committed in the transaction log. Any actions that were in progress at the time of the failure that were within a transaction that was still in progress would have to be rerun from the start.

So, to clarify, if you were in the process of deleting data within a table and the power was switched off, you would use your full and differential backups to restore the data. You would then use the information within the transaction log to replay all successful transactions, but because the delete had not been successful, the table would have all the data still within it.

Backing up the transaction log is a good strategy to employ when a large number of updates occur to the data through the day. A transaction log backup should take place at set times throughout the day depending on how large the transaction log has grown and how crucial it was to get your system back up and running after any unexpected outage. When a transaction log is backed up, the transaction log itself is logically shrunk in size so that the transaction log is kept small. It also gives you point-in-time recoverability; this means that you can quickly restore to any time in the past where the transaction was backed up.

Backing up a transaction log is similar to backing up a database. The full syntax is as follows and really only differs from a database backup by using the LOG keyword instead of DATABASE and the options NO_TRUNCATE and NORECOVERY/STANDBY:

```
BACKUP LOG { database_name | @database_name_var }
{
    TO <backup_device> [ ,...n ]
[ [ MIRROR TO <backup_device> [ ,...n ] ] [ ...next-mirror ] ]
    [ WITH
    [ BLOCKSIZE = { blocksize | @blocksize_variable } ]
    [ [ , ] { CHECKSUM | NO_CHECKSUM } ]
    [ [ , ] { STOP_ON_ERROR | CONTINUE_AFTER_ERROR } ]
    [ [ , ] DESCRIPTION = { 'text' | @text_variable } ]
    [ [ ,] EXPIREDATE = { date | @date_var }
    | RETAINDAYS = { days | @days_var } ]
    | { COMPRESSION | NO_COMPRESSION }
    [ [ , ] PASSWORD = { password | @password_variable } ]
    [ [ , ] { FORMAT | NOFORMAT } ]
    [ [ , ] { INIT | NOINIT } ]
    [ [ , ] { NOSKIP | SKIP } ]
    [ [ , ] MEDIADESCRIPTION = { 'text' | @text_variable } ]
    [ [ , ] MEDIANAME = { media_name | @media_name_variable } ]
    [ [ , ] MEDIAPASSWORD = { mediapassword | @mediapassword_variable } ]
    [ [ , ] NAME = { backup_set_name | @backup_set_name_var } ]
    [ [ , ] NO_TRUNCATE ]
    [ [ , ] { NORECOVERY | STANDBY = undo_file_name } ]
    [ [ , ] { NOREWIND | REWIND } ]
    [ [ , ] { NOUNLOAD | UNLOAD } ]
    [ [ , ] STATS [ = percentage ] ]
    [ [ , ] COPY_ONLY ]
    ]
}
```

Now let's look at the options not covered earlier when looking at backing up the database:

- LOG: Determines that we wish to produce a backup of the transaction log rather than a backup of a database or files/file groups.

- NO_TRUNCATE: Doesn't truncate the log after the backup. If the database is corrupt, using this option will allow the backup to be attempted at least. Without this option, you will get an error message.

- NORECOVERY | STANDBY: After the backup, the database will be in a state whereby it looks to anyone trying to connect as if it is still being restored.

■**Note** The LOG options NO_TRUNCATE and NORECOVER | STANDBY are used when the database is corrupt and you wish to back up the transaction log prior to performing a restore.

Try It Out: Backing Up the Transaction Log Using T-SQL

1. In a Query Editor pane, enter the following T-SQL code. This backs up the transaction log to the same media set as the full and differential backups. While developing and learning SQL Server, this is a valid scenario, and in some production setups you may want to back up to the same place as your daily full backup. However, the downside is that if you take several transaction log backups between each differential backup and full backup, then SQL Server will have to "skip" these if they were not required as part of the restore operation. On a tape drive, this could cause significant overhead. In this scenario, you would be better off saving the transaction log files to a different media set.

```
BACKUP LOG ApressFinancial
TO DISK = 'C:\Program Files\Microsoft SQL
Server\MSSQL10.MSSQLSERVER\MSSQL\Backup\
ApressFinancial.bak'
WITH NOFORMAT, NOINIT,
NAME = N'ApressFinancial-Transaction Log Backup',
SKIP, NOREWIND, NOUNLOAD,
STATS = 10
```

2. This code replicates the Truncate the Transaction Log option, as shown in Figure 7-7. Execute the code.

Figure 7-7. *Backing up a transaction log*

3. After execution, you should see output similar to the following, where the transaction log has been successfully backed up and placed on file 4:

```
100 percent processed.
Processed 4 pages for database 'ApressFinancial', file
'ApressFinancial_log' on file 4.
BACKUP LOG successfully processed 4 pages in 0.135 seconds (0.235 MB/sec).
```

Restoring a Database

Now that the data has been backed up, what if you need to complete a restore? As has been mentioned, there are two scenarios where a restore could be required: from a backup or when a media failure occurs. The second type of restore is not one you wish to perform, but you could set it up by creating a long-running transaction and then simply switching your computer off—not one of life's greatest ideas to do deliberately! This book therefore will not be demonstrating this option, and it is not really for a beginner to attempt. However, I will discuss the concept within this section of the chapter. The first option, a simple restore, is easy to replicate and perform, and this will be the option we will be looking at.

You can choose between two means to restore the database: SQL Server Management Studio and T-SQL. This is a scenario that you hope you will never perform in a production environment, but it will happen. If you just need a restore within the development environment to remove test data and get back to a stable predefined set of data to complete the testing, then this next section should help you. It might also be that you do a weekly refresh of your user test region from a production backup. Before completing the restore, let's first modify the ApressFinancial database to prove that the restore works, as there is no data within the database yet to prove the restore has worked by that method. Keep in mind, however, that a restore will restore not only the data structures, but also the data, the permissions, and other areas of the database not yet covered in the book—for example, views, stored procedures, and so on.

Restoring Using SQL Server Management Studio

The restore demonstrated in the following example will be a complete database restore of our ApressFinancial database. In other words, it will restore all the full and differential backups taken.

Try It Out: Restoring a Database

1. Add a new column to the ShareDetails.Shares table using the following code in a Query Editor pane:

```
USE ApressFinancial
GO
ALTER TABLE ShareDetails.Shares
ADD DummyColumn varchar(30)
```

2. Once you have confirmed that the column has been added by looking in the Object Explorer, we can now use the backup we finished earlier to restore the database, which will remove the changes we have just completed. From the Object Explorer window, select the ApressFinancial database, right-click, and select Tasks ➤ Restore ➤ Database. This brings up the dialog box shown in Figure 7-8. It is possible to change the database you wish to restore by changing the name in the To Database combo box or by simply overwriting the name that is there. The second option, To a Point in Time, is used if you are restoring the database as well as rolling forward changes recorded in the transaction log. This situation is similar to the scenario mentioned earlier about a power failure or hard drive failure. As we are not doing this here, leave this option as it is. When taking a backup, details are stored in msdb, but it is possible to restore a database from a backup that is not in msdb. For example, if you are rebuilding a server due to corruption, and msdb was one of the databases corrupted, it is necessary to have the option of finding a backup file and restoring from that instead. Or perhaps the last full backup taken is not the backup you wish to restore. This might occur in a development scenario where you wish to restore to a backup before major changes were done that you wish to remove. There would be no transaction log involved or required to be involved, therefore restoring to a point in time would not be a valid scenario. This is where you could use the From Device option. By selecting this option and clicking the ellipsis to the right, you can navigate to any old backup files. Finally, you can click which of the items in the backup you wish to restore. The default is all files to be selected, as you can see in Figure 7-8. The settings shown will give us a backup that is as fresh as possible (the Most Recent Possible value for the To a Point in Time setting).

Figure 7-8. *Restoring a database—General tab*

3. Moving to the Options page, shown in Figure 7-9, there are a number of points to consider:

- *Overwrite the Existing Database*: This is the most likely option to be enabled for a normal restore. You would disable it if you wished to create a restore on the same server but where the restore would alter the name of the database. You cannot have any items not backed up within the transaction log; if you do, the restore will fail.

- *Preserve the Replication Settings*: A more advanced option for when a database is sending changes to another database. For the time being, leave this option disabled.

- *Prompt Before Restoring Each Backup*: If you wish a prompt message before each restore file is activated, then select this. This is ideal if you need to swap media over.

- *Restrict Access to the Restored Database*: You may wish to check out the database after a restore to ensure the restore is what you wish, or in a production environment to run further checks on the database integrity.

- *Restore the Database Files As*: This grid allows you to move or rename the MDF and LDF files.

- *Leave the Database Ready to Use*: This option defines whether users can immediately connect and work with the data after the restore. If a transaction is in progress, such as deleting rows within a table, then the connection could occur once the deletion has been rolled back and the table is back in its "original" state.

- *Leave the Database Non-operational*: With this option, you can indicate that the database has been partially restored and you are unsure if you need to perform additional actions. If a transaction is in progress, such as deleting a table, then whatever has been deleted will still be deleted and will not be rolled back.

- *Leave the Database in Read-Only Mode*: A combination of the first two options. If a transaction is in progress, such as deleting rows in a table, then the connection could occur once the deletion has been rolled back. However, the changes are also kept in a separate file, so that any of these actions that have been rolled back can be reapplied. This might happen if there are several actions within a transaction and some can be reapplied.

Figure 7-9. *Restoring a database—Options tab*

4. Once you have the option settings you require, a quick click of OK performs the restore. You should see the message in Figure 7-10. If you then move back to the database after clicking OK, you will see that the column we just added has been "removed" when you look in Object Explorer.

Figure 7-10. *Restore successful*

Restoring Using T-SQL

Using the wizard is a pretty fast way to restore a database, and when under pressure, it may even be the best way forward. However, it is not the most flexible way of performing a restore, as some options that are available via T-SQL are not in this wizard. Some of these options were covered when we performed a backup, such as performing checksums when transferring data from the media device back to the database or unloading media at the end of the restore. If there is also a password on the backup medium, this option is not available within the wizard, but you can use passwords with T-SQL. Being comfortable building a restore via T-SQL is important in becoming a more proficient and professional developer or administrator.

The syntax for restoring a database is similar to that for database backups. After looking at the syntax, we will then go through the options you will not be familiar with.

```
RESTORE DATABASE { database_name | @database_name_var }
[ FROM <backup_device> [ ,...n ] ]
[ WITH
    [ { CHECKSUM | NO_CHECKSUM } ]
    [ [ , ] { CONTINUE_AFTER_ERROR | STOP_ON_ERROR } ]
    [ [ , ] FILE = { file_number | @file_number } ]
    [ [ , ] KEEP_REPLICATION ]
    [ [ , ] MEDIANAME = { media_name | @media_name_variable } ]
    [ [ , ] MEDIAPASSWORD = { mediapassword |
                      @mediapassword_variable } ]
    [ [ , ] MOVE 'logical_file_name' TO 'operating_system_file_name' ]
               [ ,...n ]
    [ [ , ] PASSWORD = { password | @password_variable } ]
    [ [ , ] { RECOVERY | NORECOVERY | STANDBY =
          {standby_file_name | @standby_file_name_var }
    } ]
    [ [ , ] REPLACE ]
    [ [ , ] RESTART ]
    [ [ , ] RESTRICTED_USER ]
    [ [ , ] { REWIND | NOREWIND } ]
    [ [ , ] STATS [ = percentage ] ]
    [ [ , ] { STOPAT = { date_time | @date_time_var }
    |  STOPATMARK = { 'mark_name' | 'lsn:lsn_number' }
             [ AFTER datetime ]
    |  STOPBEFOREMARK = { 'mark_name' | 'lsn:lsn_number' }
             [ AFTER datetime ]
    } ]
    [ [ , ] { UNLOAD | NOUNLOAD } ]
]
```

The options we have not yet covered are as follows:

- KEEP_REPLICATION: When working with replication, consider using this option. Replication is when changes completed in one database are automatically sent to another database. The most common scenario is when you have a central database replicating changes to satellite databases, and possibly vice versa.

- MOVE: When completing a restore, the MDF and LDF files that are being restored have to be placed where they were backed up from. However, by using this option, you can change that location.

- RECOVERY | NORECOVERY | STANDBY: These three options are the same, and in the same order, as their counterparts (in parentheses) in the wizard:

- RECOVERY (Leave the Database Ready to Use): This option defines that after the restore is finished, users can immediately connect to and work with the data. If a transaction is in progress, such as updating rows in a table, then not until the updates have been rolled back and therefore the table is back in its "original" state will connections to the database be allowed.

- NORECOVERY (Leave the Database Non-operational): With this option, you are indicating that the database has been partially restored, and you are unsure whether you need to perform additional actions. If a transaction is in progress, such as inserting rows in a table, then the insertions will *not* be rolled back. This allows additional restores to get to a specific point in time.

- STANDBY (Leave the Database in Read-Only Mode): A combination of the first two options. If a transaction is in progress, such as deleting rows in a table, then the deletion will be rolled back. However, the changes are also in a separate file, so that any of these actions that have been rolled back can be reapplied. This might happen if several actions occurred within a transaction and some can be reapplied.

- REPLACE: This works the same as the wizard option Overwrite the Existing Database.

- RESTART: If a restore is stopped partway through, then using this option will restart the restore at the point it was stopped.

- RESTRICTED_USER: Use this with the RECOVERY option to only allow users in specific restricted groups to access the database. Use this to allow further checking by a database owner, or by the dbowner, dbcreator, or sysadmin roles.

- STOPAT | STOPATMARK | STOPBEFOREMARK: Used to specify a specific date and time at which to stop the restore.

The syntax for restoring the transaction log is exactly the same, with the only difference being the definition: you are completing a LOG rather than a DATABASE restore:

```
RESTORE LOG { database_name | @database_name_var }
    <file_or_filegroup_or_pages> [ ,...f ]
[ FROM <backup_device> [ ,...n ] ]
[ WITH
   [ { CHECKSUM | NO_CHECKSUM } ]
   [ [ , ] { CONTINUE_AFTER_ERROR | STOP_ON_ERROR } ]
   [ [ , ] FILE = { file_number | @file_number } ]
   [ [ , ] KEEP_REPLICATION ]
   [ [ , ] MEDIANAME = { media_name | @media_name_variable } ]
   [ [ , ] MEDIAPASSWORD = { mediapassword | @mediapassword_variable }        ]
   [ [ , ] MOVE 'logical_file_name' TO 'operating_system_file_name' ]
             [ ,...n ]
   [ [ , ] PASSWORD = { password | @password_variable } ]
   [ [ , ] { RECOVERY | NORECOVERY | STANDBY =
          {standby_file_name | @standby_file_name_var } }
   ]
   [ [ , ] REPLACE ]
   [ [ , ] RESTART ]
   [ [ , ] RESTRICTED_USER ]
   [ [ , ] { REWIND | NOREWIND } ]
   [ [ , ] STATS [=percentage ] ]
   [ [ , ] { STOPAT = { date_time | @date_time_var }
   | STOPATMARK = { 'mark_name' | 'lsn:lsn_number' }
             [ AFTER datetime ]
```

```
    |  STOPBEFOREMARK = { 'mark_name'  |  'lsn:lsn_number' }
            [ AFTER datetime ]
  } ]
  [ [ , ] { UNLOAD  |  NOUNLOAD } ]
]
```

Try It Out: Restoring Using T-SQL

1. Open up an empty Query Editor pane and enter the following code. This will add the column that we want to see "removed" after a restore.

```
USE ApressFinancial
GO
ALTER TABLE ShareDetails.Shares
ADD DummyColumn varchar(30)
```

2. Now replace this code with the restore code that follows. Don't execute any of the code just yet, as this piece of code is the first part only. Recall that when performing the backups, FILE 2 was the FULL backup taken. This is what the first restore will do.

▌Note Ensure that the FROM DISK option is all on one line. Also recall that FILE = 2 may be FILE = 3 or any other number, depending on the backups taken, and this may be the case with different file numbers as you progress.

```
USE Master
GO
RESTORE DATABASE [ApressFinancial]
FROM  DISK = 'C:\Program Files\Microsoft SQL
Server\MSSQL10.MSSQLSERVER\MSSQL\Backup\
ApressFinancial.bak' WITH  FILE = 2,
NORECOVERY,  NOUNLOAD,  REPLACE,  STATS = 10
GO
```

3. Continue the code with the second part of the restore, which will be the differential backup restore. This uses FILE 3 from the backup set.

```
RESTORE DATABASE [ApressFinancial]
FROM  DISK = 'C:\Program Files\Microsoft SQL
Server\MSSQL10.MSSQLSERVER\MSSQL\Backup\
ApressFinancial.bak' WITH  FILE = 4,
NORECOVERY,  NOUNLOAD,  REPLACE,  STATS = 10
GO
```

4. The final part of the restore operation is to restore the transaction log file. Once all this code is in, you can run it all.

```
RESTORE LOG [ApressFinancial]
FROM  DISK = 'C:\Program Files\Microsoft SQL
Server\MSSQL10.MSSQLSERVER\MSSQL\Backup\
ApressFinancial.bak' WITH  FILE = 5,
NOUNLOAD,  STATS = 10
```

5. Once the code has fully executed, you should see results similar to those listed here:

```
13 percent processed.
22 percent processed.
31 percent processed.
40 percent processed.
54 percent processed.
63 percent processed.
72 percent processed.
81 percent processed.
90 percent processed.
100 percent processed.
Processed 176 pages for database 'ApressFinancial', file 'ApressFinancial'
on file 2.
Processed 1 pages for database 'ApressFinancial',
file 'ApressFinancial_log' on file 2.
RESTORE DATABASE successfully processed 177 pages in 0.284 seconds
(5.105 MB/sec).
24 percent processed.
48 percent processed.
72 percent processed.
97 percent processed.
100 percent processed.
Processed 32 pages for database 'ApressFinancial', file 'ApressFinancial'
on file 3.
Processed 1 pages for database 'ApressFinancial',
file 'ApressFinancial_log' on file 3.
RESTORE DATABASE successfully processed 33 pages in 0.066 seconds
(4.088 MB/sec).
100 percent processed.
Processed 0 pages for database 'ApressFinancial', file 'ApressFinancial'
on file 4.
Processed 4 pages for database 'ApressFinancial',
file 'ApressFinancial_log' on file 4.
RESTORE LOG successfully processed 4 pages in 0.013 seconds (2.441 MB/sec).
```

We can now move back to the ShareDetails.Shares table and check that the column added has now been removed. You may have to perform a refresh within Object Explorer first to see the changes.

Restoring a database in production will in most instances take place under pressure, as the database will have become corrupt or been inadvertently damaged. The production system is obviously down and not working, and we have irate users wanting to know how long before the system will be up. This is hopefully the worst-case scenario, but it is that sort of level of pressure that we will be working under when we have to restore the database. Therefore, having the correct backup strategy for your organization based on full, differential, and transaction log backups is crucial. Full database backups for a system that requires high availability so that the restore takes the least amount of time may be what you need.

Detaching and Attaching a Database

Now that we can back up and restore a database, we have other methods available for dealing with the database. There may be a time in the life of our SQL Server database when we have to move it from one server to another, or in fact just from one hard drive to another. For example, perhaps we currently have ApressFinancial on our C drive, and this is getting full, so we would like to move our database to another hard drive. Or perhaps we are moving from an old slower server to a new faster server or a server on a better network. By detaching and reattaching the database, we can do this simply and easily.

I would like to make a couple of points here; they may seem straightforward and really obvious, but better to mention them than cause problems at a later stage. First of all, no updates can be occurring, no jobs can be running, and no users can be attached. Secondly, just in case, take a full backup before moving the database. This may add time to the process, but it is better to be safe than sorry. Ensure that where you are moving the database to has enough disk space, not only for the move, but also for expected future growth; otherwise, you will be moving your database twice. You should not attach your database to a server without immediately completing a backup on the new server afterward; this way, you can ensure that the databases are protected in their new state.

Detaching a database physically removes the details from the SQL Server `master` and `msdb` databases, but does not remove the files from the disk that it resides on. However, detaching the database from SQL Server then allows you to safely move, copy, or delete the files that make up the database, if you so desire. This is the only way that a database should be physically removed from a server for moving it.

Detaching and Attaching Using SQL Server Management Studio

We'll start by using SSMS to detach and attach a database.

Try It Out: Detaching a Database

1. First of all, it is necessary to ensure that nobody is logged in to the database, and even if someone is, that the user is not doing any updates. For the moment, I want you to ignore this and to have a connection. Ensure that SQL Server Management Studio is running and that there is a Query Editor pane with a connection to the `ApressFinancial` database. Find the `ApressFinancial` database in Object Explorer and ensure that is selected. Right-click and select Tasks ➤ Detach.

2. This brings up the Detach Database dialog box for the `ApressFinancial` database, as shown in Figure 7-11. We haven't removed all the connected users, so you can do this by selecting the Drop Connections check box. The second option, Update Statistics, means that the SQL Server statistics for indexes and so on will be updated before the database is detached. The information is stored separately from the other data files in SQL Server, so selecting this option ensures that when the database is detached that the files are not lost and therefore don't need re-creating. The status is Not Ready due to the message indicating that there is still "2 Active connection(s)." Although you only have one Query Editor open, the second connection is for the T-SQL IntelliSense.

3. In this example select the Drop Connections box. However, in a production environment, this could be very dangerous, so you should not select it without some thought. You can then click OK to finish detaching the database.

That's it. The database is detached, is no longer part of SQL Server, and is ready to be removed or even deleted. If you check the Object Explorer in SQL Server Management Studio, you will see that the database is no longer listed.

Detaching a database, although seemingly a simple and innocuous operation, has the potential to be fraught with problems and worries. As the example demonstrated, ensuring that there are no users attached to the database at the time of detaching is not as easy as it first may seem. Setting up the database options to eliminate connections or to stop updates is only possible once everyone has been removed from connections to the database. There is no easy way of removing connections safely, as you never know what an application with a connection to the database is doing. You could remove a connection that is in the middle of processing. If you are going down the route of detaching the database, though, there is an obvious reason to do this, such as moving servers and removing the database, so you would have a plan of action to do this. Users would have been notified days or weeks in advance, and the database owner would have coordinated a date and time when nobody should be connected. Also, the database owner would be around if there were any problems, and he or she could make the decision to kill any connections left hanging around.

Figure 7-11. *Detaching a database*

Detaching the database is a process that removes entries within the SQL Server system tables to inform SQL Server that this database is no longer within this instance of SQL Server and therefore cannot be used. It is as simple as that. If you are removing the database completely, then you will need to delete the files from the directory they were created in.

It is possible to detach the database using a system stored procedure, although this does not let you kill the connections. This has to be done via a T-SQL command.

We need to reattach the database before being able to demonstrate this, so let's do that now. This would occur on our new SQL Server instances after physically moving the files.

Try It Out: Attaching a Database

1. Within Object Explorer, highlight the Databases node, right-click, and select Attach.

2. This brings up the Attach Databases dialog box, shown in Figure 7-12. To add a database, click Add.

Figure 7-12. *Options for attaching a database*

3. This brings up the Locate Database Files explorer, shown in Figure 7-13. You can use this like other Windows Explorers to locate where your database MDF files are. Once you find the database you want to reattach, highlight it and then click OK.

Figure 7-13. *Locating the database to attach*

4. This brings you back to the Attach Databases dialog box with the details filled in, as you see in Figure 7-14. Take a moment to look over the information in this dialog box. Any problems will be detailed in the Messages column. It is possible to attach more than one database, but it is best to do databases one at a time.

5. This then leaves us to click OK to reattach the database. Moving to Object Explorer, you should see your database at the bottom of the list, where it will remain until the explorer is refreshed.

Attaching a database involves informing SQL Server of the name and the location of the data files and the transaction log files. This data can be placed anywhere on a computer, but it is recommended you place the data in a sensible location. For example, the folders tempfiles or tobedeleted sport extreme names, but do demonstrate the unsuitability that should be avoided.

When moving the data from one physical server to another, the data does not need to be in a subdirectory of Microsoft SQL Server installation found under Program Files. In fact, in production environments, this is the last place you would locate the data. You would generally want to keep these files away from any program files or the pagefile.sys file, because SQL Server's performance can be maximized when these files are separated. However, for the purpose of this book, placing the data in the DATA directory under the instance of SQL Server is perfectly valid and acceptable.

Once the two data files have been copied, it is a simple process of using a couple of mouse clicks to attach these files into the instance. What happens in the background, very basically, is that SQL Server takes the name of the database and the location of the data files and places them into internal tables that are used to store information about databases. It then scans the data files to retrieve information, such as the names of the tables, to populate the system tables where necessary.

Figure 7-14. *Database located, preparing to attach*

The main point to keep in mind is the database owner (see Chapters 1, 2, and 5). It is just as important to use a valid database owner and not the sa login when attaching a database as it is when creating a database. The database, when it is attached, will be given the owner of the login attaching the database.

Detaching and Attaching Using T-SQL

Detaching and attaching a database is an ideal way to move a database from one server to another as part of an overall solution. It's clean and simple and ideal if you are rolling out a "base" database to many client sites, but it's not the only way of doing it. Detaching a database is simply removing it logically from a server, but keeping the physical files. This then allows these files to be moved to anywhere, from another hard drive to a DVD, for further copying to a client computer if need be, and then reattaching the database at the other end.

Detaching a database removes entries from the master and msdb databases. The physical backup files will still be there, so if you do need to complete a restore after a detach and reattach, then you can use the From Device option in the Restore Wizard to define the full location in the RESTORE T-SQL command to get to those files.

Note Detaching a database can only be done by a member of the db_owner role.

```
sp_detach_db [ @dbname= ] 'dbname'
    [ , [ @skipchecks= ] 'skipchecks' ]
    [ , [ @KeepFulltextIndexFile= ] 'KeepFulltextIndexFile' ]
```

The options are straightforward, with each being optional. If they are not supplied, then the default value is mentioned within the following bulleted list:

- dbname: The name of the database to detach. If this option is missed, then no database will be detached.

- skipchecks: NULL (the default) will update statistics. true will skip the updating of statistics.

- KeepFulltextIndexFile: true (the default) will keep all the full text index files that have been generated with this database.

Note **Full text index files** are special files that hold information about data set up for full-text searching, which is an area outside the scope of this book. Basically, full-text searching gives the ability to search on all text in a column or multiple columns of data, and is also functionality used by search engines.

You might be expecting that you would use a stored procedure called sp_attach_db to reattach the database. This command does exist, but it will be made obsolete in future versions of SQL Server. The correct syntax is a "specialized" CREATE DATABASE command:

```
CREATE DATABASE database_name
    ON <filespec> [ ,...n ]
    FOR { ATTACH [ WITH <service_broker_option> ]
        | ATTACH_REBUILD_LOG }
```

The syntax is easy to follow. The first option, ON, specifies the name of the primary database file to attach, which has the mdf suffix. We will ignore the second option, <service_broker_option>, as this is for a more advanced database.

The third option, ATTACH_REBUILD_LOG, is for situations where you wish to attach a database but at least one transaction log file is missing. Specifying this option rebuilds the transaction log. No database can be attached when SQL Server believes that there are missing files. If you do use this option, then you will lose the full, differential, and transaction log backup chains that exist on SQL Server, so complete a full backup after attaching to reestablish the backup baseline. This option tends to be used when you deliberately wish to lose the transaction log file, such as a read-only version of the database for reporting purposes.

Note If you receive any error messages, then reattach *all* files associated with the database, not just the main primary file.

We can now detach and reattach ApressFinancial.

Try It Out: Detaching and Reattaching a Database

1. The first test we will do is to try to detach ApressFinancial while there are still active connections so that we can see what happens. Open up a Query Editor pane and point it to ApressFinancial database. Then open a second pane and enter the sp_detach_db code as follows. Once you have done so, execute the code. Take note that we are explicitly moving this connection to a "safe" system database, away from the database we wish to detach.

```
USE master
GO
sp_detach_db 'ApressFinancial'
```

2. The results you will see will be similar to the following:

```
Msg 3703, Level 16, State 2, Line 1
Cannot detach the database 'ApressFinancial' because it is currently in use
```

3. Close the Query Editor pane opened earlier and any other Query Editor panes that have connections pointing to ApressFinancial and then try rerunning the code again. This time you should see the following message:

```
Command(s) completed successfully.
```

4. You can also achieve the same result within the code and without needing to close your panes. If you run the following code and move back to a pane that had a connection, you will be presented with a reconnection pane. Once connected, if your default database is not ApressFinancial, then you won't be able to change to that database until you move out of single-user mode or use the pane that had the following code within it:

```
ALTER DATABASE ApressFinancial
SET SINGLE_USER WITH ROLLBACK IMMEDIATE
```

5. Change SINGLE_USER to MULTI_USER once you test the following code:

```
ALTER DATABASE ApressFinancial
SET MULTI_USER
```

6. Now that the database has been detached, we need to reattach it, simulating a move to a new server. Enter the following code in the same Query Editor pane. Replace the FILENAME parameters with the path to where your database is located and ensure that the path is all on one line.

```
CREATE DATABASE ApressFinancial
ON (FILENAME='C:\Program Files\Microsoft SQL Server\MSSQL.2\MSSQL\
Data\ApressFinancial.MDF')
FOR ATTACH
```

7. After executing the code, you should see the following message:

```
Command(s) completed successfully.
```

You have now successfully detached and reattached the database.

Producing SQL Script for the Database

This section demonstrates a different method of backing up the structure of the database and the tables and indexes contained within it by using T-SQL commands to complete this.

■**Note** Only the structure will be generated as T-SQL commands; no data will be backed up—only the schema that is needed to re-create the actual database can be scripted here.

The usefulness of this procedure is limited and is really only helpful for keeping structure backups or producing an empty database, but it is useful to know rather than going through the process of copying the database with all the data when the data is not required.

This method tends to be used to keep the structure within a source repository such as Visual SourceSafe. It is also useful for setting up empty databases when moving from development to testing or into production.

Try It Out: Producing the Database SQL

1. Ensure that SQL Server Management Studio is running and that you have expanded the server so that you can see the ApressFinancial database. Right-click, and select Tasks ➤ Generate Scripts. This brings up the wizard shown in Figure 7-15 that allows the database to be scripted. Every attached database will be listed. Select ApressFinancial and click Next.

■**Note** You can select the check box at the bottom of the screen, which will script all the objects if you wish. This will enable the Finish button so that you can go straight to the end.

Figure 7-15. *Scripting—selecting the database*

2. On the second screen are a number of options about the scripting. Take a moment to look them over. Most of these options should be clear to you from the setup options we have covered in setting up the database so far. A bulleted list at the end of the example clarifies the options for you. Figure 7-16 shows the default settings. Click Next.

Figure 7-16. *Options for the script*

3. As shown in Figure 7-17, you are presented with a list of objects that you could script. At the bottom of the dialog is a Select All option. Press this, as we want to script everything. Once you have the options you wish to script, click Next. You will then be taken through each object group one at a time. Within each screen there will be a list of possible objects you wish to script. For example, Figure 7-18 demonstrates what you will see when you get to the dialog for the stored procedures. Every stored procedure within the database will be listed. As you go through each dialog, click Select All and click Next.

▨**Note** The Script Statistics option significantly increases the time taken to generate the script. Leave this option off in most cases; it is really only useful when moving from a user test environment that is very similar to how the system will work in production.

Figure 7-17. *Options selected for scripting*

Figure 7-18. *Scripting for every stored procedure*

4. After you have been presented with the dialogs for all the objects in the database of the areas selected in Figure 7-16, where you should have selected every object, you are now presented with the screen shown in Figure 7-19. This allows you specify how the script should be saved. There are three possibilities. Choose to script to a new Query Editor and then select Next.

Figure 7-19. *Where to store the script*

5. This brings you to a summary screen, shown in Figure 7-20, where you can expand what has been selected. You may find that this screen is not of much use, as there are so few screens within this wizard. However, you can use it for categorizing what objects are to be scripted. Take a moment to investigate this screen.

Figure 7-20. *Script summary*

6. Click Finish. The wizard will start to generate the script. At the end, you will see a summary of how the script production went. Any errors will be within the Message column on the right, as shown in Figure 7-21.

Figure 7-21. *Generating the script*

The options available to you within the wizard are detailed here:

- *Append to File*: If you set this to true, then SQL Server will append the script to the file selected instead of over-writing it.

- *Continue Scripting on Error*: If there are any problems in producing the script, you can decide if you wish to continue scripting or not.

- *Convert UDDTs to Base Types*: As part of SQL Server, you can change the base data types, such as int, to your own named type, so you could name a "copy" of int as myint. This is a bit more advanced, but if you do this, then selecting true will convert myint back to int.

- *Generate Script for Dependent Objects*: A very useful option. If there are any dependencies on what you are wanting to script and you haven't selected that object to script, then there will be problems rebuilding the object later. Selecting true means that these dependent objects will also be scripted.

- *Include Descriptive Headers*: This includes a date-time stamp as well as a short descriptive header of each object as it is reached within the script.

- *Include If NOT EXISTS*: If you select all the objects to be scripted and set this to true, SQL Server will put a test around each object so that if that object is already in the database when the script is run, it won't be created. There will be no test for specific columns when scripting a table, but there will be a test for the table itself.

- *Script Behavior*: You can generate a script for creating items or dropping items.

- *Script Collation*: If you wish the SQL Server collation to be scripted, enable this option. This is useful if you are unsure of the collation the script will then be run against.

- *Script Database Create*: This specifies whether you wish a CREATE DATABASE statement to be scripted or not.

- *Script Defaults*: We have some default values that will be set on columns when rows are added. Setting this to true will set these defaults.

- *Script Extended Properties*: Extra properties can be placed on every SQL Server object. These will be scripted if you select true.

- *Script Logins*: This scripts all Windows and SQL Server authentication logins.

- *Script Object-Level Permissions*: Each object will have permissions on who can do what. For example, on a table, you can set up permissions on who can add, delete, or select the data. This option includes these options.

- *Script Owner*: This scripts the owner of the database if specified.

- *Script Statistics*: This specifies whether to script the SQL Server column and index statistics. It avoids rebuilding them when re-creating the database using the script; however, it increases the time taken to build the script as well as the size of the script.

- *Script USE DATABASE*: Between each object, this specifies whether to script a USE database statement or not. It's ideal if used with scripting-dependent objects.

- *Script Check Constraints*: This script checks constraints.

- *Script Foreign Keys*: Any foreign keys are scripted.

- *Script Full-Text Indexes*: If you have any full-text indexes, this indicates whether you want to script them or not.

- *Script Indexes*: This specifies whether to script table and view indexes.

- *Script Primary Keys*: This dictates whether to script primary keys or not.

- *Script Triggers*: For any trigger, this specifies whether you wish these to be within the script.

- *Script Unique Keys*: Any unique keys are scripted.

This concludes our look at the different methods of backing up, restoring, moving, and scripting databases. While this covers every way of ensuring your database structure and data should never be lost, you still need to maintain the database on a regular basis. This is what we will take a look at in the next section of this chapter.

Maintaining Your Database

At this point, we have now created a backup and performed a restore of the example database. We have also covered the different methods to back up and restore the database. However, we have no real plan for regular maintenance and detection and reporting of problems in our database strategy. Any jobs for backup of the database or transaction log that we have demonstrated so far are held as single units of work called **steps**. Not only that, there is nothing in place that will look after the data and indexes held within the database to ensure that they are still functioning correctly and that the data is still stored in the optimal fashion. Without a process that runs regularly, we would need to perform all of this by hand regularly and check the results each time. What a waste of time, and boring to boot!

This section will demonstrate building a plan and then checking on the plan after it has run to ensure that all has gone well with it. This plan will perform regular backups and checks on the database and keep it in optimum health. This section will then show you how to set up the ability to e-mail results.

To do this, we will use the Database Maintenance Wizard, which will monitor corruption within the database, optimize how the data is stored, and back up both the database and transaction logs. Finally, the wizard will schedule all of this to occur at regular intervals. You will also see how to set up and configure SQL Server Database Mail.

Some areas of this chapter, like the backup screens, are straightforward, as they were covered earlier in the chapter; however, this now brings the whole maintenance of the database into one wizard.

Creating a Database Maintenance Plan

Now that the database is up and built and the tables are there, it really is time to start considering a whole database maintenance plan before data is entered. This will cover database corruption through to inadvertent errors in development. Even though corruption is rare in SQL Server, it can be caused when SQL Server loses power abruptly, for example, or through hardware issues such as a motherboard failure or someone removing the network cable.

There are many areas to building a maintenance plan, and this section covers a lot of them. One or two areas are only touched on, as they are quite advanced and will not be covered in this book. You will still need a little background so that you can see how crucial this area is, and we can move on to those more advanced areas a bit later on.

A single maintenance plan can be built for one database or several databases. A single plan can be set up for system databases and all user databases by selecting those options at the start of the Database Maintenance Wizard. However, it is recommended that you create a plan for all system databases, but have a separate maintenance plan for each separate user database. The logic behind this is that each user database will have its own needs, its own overnight routines, and even its own people for callout when things go wrong. Even if you are a one-man band, each user database should still have a maintenance plan. Therefore, in keeping with this, only the ApressFinancial database will be selected.

Once the plan has been built, it will be stored within SQL Server, but will have been built as a SQL Server Integration Services (SSIS) job. This is a technique within SQL Server for running several tasks in sequence with conditions, which also has the ability to work with errors that occur. SSIS could take up a whole book in itself, but building the plan and seeing what is generated will demonstrate the very basics of what it can achieve.

Maintenance plans use extended stored procedures, which are disabled by default. This means that until extended stored procedures are enabled, it is not possible to build a maintenance plan. To demonstrate how you can enable this option via T-SQL, you will use a system stored procedure in the first step to do this.

There are two methods to building a database maintenance plan: you can either use a wizard or select options from a multitabbed screen.

Try It Out: Creating a Database Maintenance Plan

1. This is a potentially two-stage process. First, configure the server to show advanced options, then reconfigure the server and set it to true, as detailed by the number 1, the option Agent XPs. Enter and execute the following code:

```
sp_configure 'show advanced options', 1
GO
RECONFIGURE;
GO
sp_configure 'Agent XPs', 1
GO
RECONFIGURE
GO
```

2. You should now see the following output, which is generated from the sp_configure statements:

```
Configuration option 'show advanced options' changed from 0 to 1.
Run the RECONFIGURE statement to install.
Configuration option 'Agent XPs' changed from 0 to 1.
Run the RECONFIGURE statement to install.
```

3. From the Object Explorer, find the Management Node and expand it, and you should find Maintenance Plans as the top item. Right-click and select the second option, Maintenance Plan Wizard. This starts the wizard.

4. Figure 7-22 shows the first screen of the wizard. Once you have read it, click Next.

Figure 7-22. *Maintenance Plan Wizard, first screen*

5. Enter a suitable name and description for the maintenance plan. You can then choose the server that the maintenance plan is on. This covers instances when your Management Studio is connected to more than one server. For example, if you have a connection to your ISP that you have a SQL Server installation on, and the ISP wants you to set up your own maintenance plan, you would change the server to that location. More likely, you will need to do this when you are maintaining more than one server at your company installation The server you are connected to will be the default. Select the authentication method you wish the plan to connect to the server as, as shown in Figure 7-23. It is possible to run tasks under either separate schedules or one schedule. Choose separate schedules when you want to space the tasks out or run them simultaneously. Choose a single schedule for the entire plan when you want to run the tasks synchronously. This is the option you want to take at this time.

6. At the bottom of the screen shown in Figure 7-23, it is possible to either set the Schedule to a date and time or leave the plan with no schedule and to run it manually. The aim is to run this automatically, so click the Change button. You will now see the screen shown in Figure 7-24. The scheduling of the data optimization should be at a quiet time, and unless the database is updated heavily, this maintenance plan choice will not be required frequently. Running a maintenance plan can be quite intense for the server and should only be done during low-usage hours. For the sake of ApressFinancial, it could be as infrequent as monthly; however, in the initial setup of the database, while the input of data might be heavy, set this up as a weekly task for now. Once done, click OK, and then click Next when you return back to the screen shown in Figure 7-23.

Figure 7-23. *Selecting the server for the maintenance plan*

Figure 7-24. *Defining the schedule*

7. The next screen brings you to a set of choices of actions that you wish the plan to perform. In our plan, we will be performing every action with the exception of cleaning up the history of the database backup and restores. We will add this option later when showing how to modify a plan. Select the options as shown in Figure 7-25, and click Next. Each of the options are briefly described here:

- *Check Database Integrity*: This executes SQL Server database integrity checks on the data and structure of the database both physical and logical.

- *Shrink Database*: The transaction log is truncated and logically shrunk. The database is also shrunk.

- *Reorganize Index*: As data is inserted and deleted, fragmentation of indexes can take place. This reorganizes the index a bit like completing a disk defrag.

- *Rebuild Index*: Instead of just reorganizing the indexes, it is possible to drop and re-create them.

- *Update Statistics*: Statistics are kept to aid the execution of queries. These can get out of date if you don't have the option set to keep these up to date, and this option can update them at this point.

- *Clean Up History*: This removes historical information such as job history for a set period of time.

- *Execute SQL Server Agent Job*: This executes a predefined SQL Server agent job. At present, there are no jobs in the database, so this option cannot be selected.

- *Back Up Database (Full)*: As discussed earlier, this backs up the full database.

- *Back Up Database (Differential)*: As discussed earlier, this backs up the changes since the last full backup.

- *Back Up Database (Transaction Log)*: As discussed earlier, this backs up just the transaction log.

- *Maintenance Cleanup Task*: This cleans up any transient files left over after the task has completed.

Figure 7-25. *Options for the maintenance plan*

8. This then brings us to a summary of the options that have been selected. It is now possible to move the options to a different order if you wish. As you can see in Figure 7-26, the Back Up Database (Full) option has been moved up to the start. This is in case any of the following options fail and cause corruption. This is a decision that you have to make as any restore may require a rerun of the commands after the full backup. Once you have the order you want, click Next.

Figure 7-26. *Options order for the maintenance plan*

9. The wizard then moves on and takes each task one at a time and gives you a dialog box containing options available for that task. The first option we have is a full backup, as shown in Figure 7-27. Most of this is very similar to the backup we completed earlier. However, it is possible to select specific databases or all databases as part of this plan. Select the Specific Databases option to be taken to a second large pop-up screen where you can define them.

10. When you choose to back up specific databases, Figure 7-28 appears. Here you can select—only for this task within the plan—which database or set of databases you want to work with. You will get this screen for every task option, so I will only show it this once. It is best to have separate maintenance plans for the user databases and one separate maintenance plan for the system databases. This splits up the workload not only into sizable, useful, and easy-to-understand units of work, but also into logical components as each database may have a different maintenance plan. You will also have different requirements for the system databases from the user-defined databases. It is preferable not to select the All User Databases option because SQL Server will automatically begin running the maintenance plan on databases that may have been added without your knowledge, and may not be under your "ownership." For our example, select the ApressFinancial database after clicking the These Databases radio button. Click OK. The full list of choices is as follows:

- *All Databases*: Specifies all system and user databases

- *System Databases*: Ignores all user databases, such as ApressFinancial

- *All User Databases*: Ignores any system-defined database, such as master, model, and so on

- *These Databases*: Allows you to select which system and user databases you wish to use

Figure 7-27. *Defining the database backup*

Figure 7-28. *Selecting the database to use*

11. By clicking Next in the subsequent screen, which you see in Figure 7-29, we move on to the next task in the list where SQL Server performs a special SQL Server command that checks the integrity of the database to see that everything is in a stable and noncorrupt state.

Figure 7-29. *Database integrity check*

12. Moving on, we can define when to reduce the logical or physical size of our database through the screen shown in Figure 7-30. This can be thought of like a defrag of your hard drive. The Return Freed Space to Operating System option will shrink the database if it has space it is not fully using. After you select this option, you will be given the opportunity to still leave a given percentage of space free for database growth. Do not fully shrink the database to 0% of free space or your performance will be worse, as the database will have to grow automatically.

Tip The preceding isn't the best process to perform or be encouraged. You should have autogrow kicking in, but you should try to size the database adequately to cope with normal operation. Performance will be better with unused space rather than autogrow kicking in as well.

13. Click Next to bring up the Define Reorganize Index Tag screen, shown in Figure 7-31. As data is added, modified, and deleted, indexes, like tables, can also require reorganizing, which you can do through this screen. Again, this is like a hard drive defrag where there are gaps or data out of order, and by reorganizing indexes you can ensure that SQL Server is able to access the data as fast as possible. This option, which should be completed at least weekly for a high data modification system, only moves index pages.

Figure 7-30. *Shrinking the database*

Figure 7-31. *Reorganizing the database*

14. Click Next to bring up the screen shown in Figure 7-32. This next screen deals with individual rows of indexes. Before we go on, note that there is no real point to reorganizing and reindexing in the same maintenance plan. You should do only one or the other. Which option you should choose comes down to the amount of fragmentation within an index. If fragmentation is low—below 30%, typically—then you should perform a reorganization. If fragmentation is greater, then it is best to reindex. Indexes exist on tables and views and become more defragmented than whole pages of data on a high data modification system. Like the previous option, rebuilding indexes should be completed on a regular basis, probably weekly; however, if your batch window allows you to perform this more frequently, then look to do so. When rebuilding indexes, you can define with a certain amount of free space to allow for increases and mid-index insertions on each index page. This is a bit like inserting lines of text in a book. If you think you are going to do this, then leaving gaps at the end of the page allows for these rows to be added. Failure to leave enough means shuffling data from that page through to the end of the book.

Within the advanced options, the main option of interest to you while you are learning SQL Server is Sort Results in tempdb. You could be low on disk space because when you built your database, you set it to grow no larger than a specific size. Couple this with a situation where your indexes are so fragmented that they take up more space than they will post-defragmentation. This could be because you have a large number of gaps due to deletions of rows within the index or modifications on a clustered index causing rows to be moved. When rebuilding indexes, this would by default be completed within the database the rebuild is for. The "old" indexes are kept until the new indexes are built. If there is not enough space to store them, it would not be possible to rebuild the index unless you physically increased the size of the database. This is not a simple process. Therefore, by using the option to rebuild the new indexes within tempdb, you do not need to increase your database size. Also, the tempdb will not be used as intensively. Therefore, it might also be faster to rebuild your indexes within that database. This is an option you may use a great deal.

Figure 7-32. *The options for rebuilding an index*

15. Move on to the Define Update Statistics Task screen, shown in Figure 7-33, by clicking Next. As has been mentioned before, as data is created, modified, and deleted, SQL Server keeps statistics on that data to aid data retrieval. These can become out of date either because you have set up your database not to keep statistics updated automatically or because the statistics naturally become out of date. Therefore, we can re-create those statistics with the plan. Statistics are not only kept for indexes but also for data within individual columns.

■**Tip** The Auto Update Statistics database option is normally on; although this does mean more processing for SQL Server, the increase is minimal, and you'll rarely notice any impact.

Figure 7-33. *Updating the database statistics*

16. The next two screens you have seen discussed earlier in the chapter in connection with differential and transaction log backups. Set the differential and transaction log backup screens as required, which brings you through to the Define Maintenance Cleanup Task screen shown in Figure 7-34. This screen defines the cleanup actions of the maintenance task when it runs. This is ideal to ensure that your maintenance plans don't take up unwanted and unnecessary space and are easy to view and monitor.

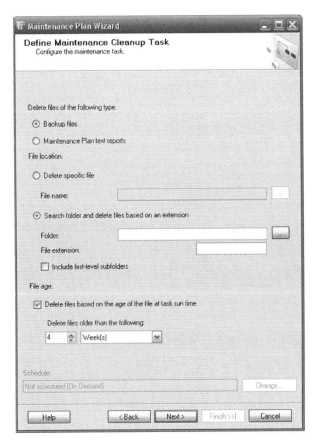

Figure 7-34. *Ensuring the maintenance task is cleaned up efficiently*

17. The next task, illustrated in Figure 7-35, involves choosing where to write out the details of the maintenance plan and each step's success or failure. For the moment, place the output in a report. Later in the chapter, you will see how to mail that report from SQL Server.

18. Similar to when we produced a script for the database, clicking Next brings up a summary of what will be performed within the plan (see Figure 7-36). Here you can review what will be completed, and with the number of different options that will be performed, it is a good place to complete a double-check. Clicking Finish produces the maintenance plan itself.

Figure 7-35. *Ensuring the maintenance task is cleaned up efficiently*

Figure 7-36. *Completing the plan*

19. Once the plan is within `msdb` database, you should see the completed screen shown in Figure 7-37.

20. It is possible to execute the plan outside of the maintenance plan schedule. The maintenance plan created previously can now be found under the Management/Maintenance Plan nodes in Object Explorer. Right-click the nodes to bring up the pop-up menu shown in Figure 7-38. Selecting Execute starts the plan immediately. Do so now.

21. While the plan is executing, the dialog box shown in Figure 7-39 is displayed.

Figure 7-37. *Maintenance plan created successfully*

Figure 7-38. *Maintenance plan pop-up menu*

Figure 7-39. *Maintenance plan executing*

22. In Figure 7-40, you can see the log that has been created for the maintenance plan once that plan has been completed. You can view this log by selecting View ➤ History from the same pop-up menu used to execute the plan. On the left, you can view other logs that are generated within SQL Server.

Figure 7-40. *Log file viewer showing the maintenance plan has run*

Setting Up Database Mail

It would be better to be notified about jobs that have failed rather than having to monitor each job as it processes manually. One of the ways to do this would be to build a maintenance job to mail out results of its work. It is possible in SQL Server 2008 to use SMTP mail to send out notifications from your server. This means that you don't need to install a MAPI client, such as Microsoft Outlook, because SMTP processing is contained within a Windows install. The fact that you don't need another product on the server has benefits in terms of making your server more stable. To supplement stability, SMTP runs in a process outside SQL Server. Even if there are SMTP issues, SQL Server should not be affected if the STMP process stops for any reason.

On top of this, SQL Server comes with built-in system stored procedures and functionality to use SMTP to send out mail. These features are collectively called *Database Mail*.

This section will detail how to set up and test Database Mail. You will see how to implement Database Mail within the maintenance task created in the preceding section.

Try It Out: Setting Up Database Mail

1. To configure Database Mail, you need to create a Mail Profile for SQL Server to use. SQL Server Agent must be running to be able to create a Mail Profile. (If SQL Server Agent is not running, as denoted by a red square, then highlight it, right-click, and select Start.) Find the Database Mail node under the Management node. Right-click, and select Configure Database Mail, as shown in Figure 7-41.

Figure 7-41. *The Configure Database Mail pop-up menu option*

2. By selecting Configure Database Mail, you start the Database Mail Configuration Wizard. As usual, the first screen is a Welcome screen, shown in Figure 7-42. Click Next.

Figure 7-42. *Initial wizard welcome screen*

3. Figure 7-43 shows the first screen of the configuration. This screen allows you to complete one of three tasks. As there are no existing mail accounts set up either via SQL Server or the Windows Control Panel's Mail option, you require the first Configuration Task option. If you already have on your server a mail account you wish to use, then select the second option. The third option lets you change the options if you already have Database Mail set up. Click Next.

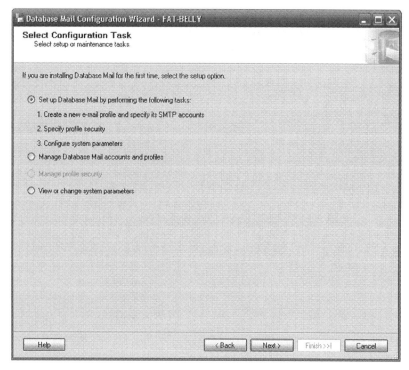

Figure 7-43. *Create or manage a new profile and system parameters*

4. Database Mail would normally be enabled via a system stored procedure, sp_configure 'Database Mail XPs'. If it is not enabled, then a helpful message is shown, as you can see in Figure 7-44. The dialog in Figure 7-44 also allows you to enable the feature. If you see this dialog, then click Yes.

Figure 7-44. *Database Mail has not been enabled via SAC.*

8. You are now at the screen for the public and private profiles. A public profile is one that has been created for any login to use in sending an e-mail from within SQL Server. We will use that option for simplicity, as shown in Figure 7-48. However, you should use a private profile when you have decided on your SQL Server implementation strategy, as its use is restricted to specific roles within the database. Private profiles are the more secure option and would prevent someone from deliberately or inadvertently sending out a mass e-mail from your server. The final action would be to make the profile the default mail profile so that you don't have to define the specific profile each time. If you do decide on a public profile as part of your setup, then you could be opening your organization up to mass mailings via a rogue piece of code if you define the profile as the default. Select the public profiles option with care.

Figure 7-48. *Private profile screen detailing private mail access only*

9. The last screen, shown in Figure 7-49, details the system parameters for mailing. These are the same system parameters that you can alter through the third option that you saw in Figure 7-43. The parameters include:

- *Account Retry Attempts*: Determines the number of times to attempt to send a mail before marking the mail as failed to deliver.

- *Account Retry Delay (Seconds)*: Determines how long to wait before trying to send a mail again.

- *Maximum File Size (Bytes)*: Limits the size of mail that can be delivered to prevent large files being sent out. If you're sending out reports as well as job notifications, you may want to set up two profiles—one with a larger maximum file size than the other.

- *Prohibited Attachment File Extensions*: Defines which file extensions are prohibited. Obviously, you don't wish your database to send out dangerous e-mail or even e-mail containing executables that are protected.

- *Database Mail Executable Minimum Lifetime (Seconds)*: It's always best to shut down processes that are not required on a server to free up as many resources as possible. This option defines the number of seconds that Database Mail will continue to run while waiting on any new mail to process before shutting down. If the number's too low, resources will be used to start and stop frequently, so don't reduce this figure too much.

- *Logging Level*: When an e-mail is sent, fails to send, or is queued to send, these actions can be logged within the msdb database. Three possible logging levels for Database Mail can be used to track these and other scenarios:

- *Normal*: Only logs any errors regarding sending your mail.

- *Extended*: Logs errors, warnings, and information about your mail.

- *Verbose*: Logs everything Database Mail does. This is the best setting to use when setting up Database Mail for the first time so that any errors generated from this wizard or your first executions are logged. However, the logging at this level is severe and not recommended to remain in force for extended periods, as it creates a large msdb.

10. When you're done, click Next.

Figure 7-49. *System parameters for Database Mail*

11. You will see a summary screen similar to Figure 7-50. When you click Finish, SQL Server processes the wizard and adds the profile to the Mail icon within the Control Panel window.

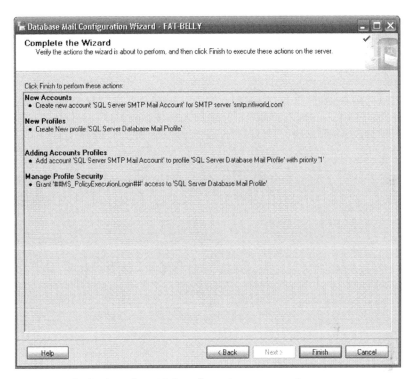

Figure 7-50. *The final Database Mail configuration screen, ready to process*

12. Providing everything has been created correctly, you should see a dialog similar to Figure 7-51. No mail testing is completed at this point, so to do that part of the setup, click Close. The next action will be to test out your setup.

Figure 7-51. *The account profile and details created successfully*

13. Now that your Database Mail is set up, send a test e-mail to check out your SMTP settings, connection, and so on. From the Database Mail node, right-click, and select Send Test E-Mail from the pop-up menu, as shown in Figure 7-52.

Figure 7-52. *The pop-up dialog to check for sending a test e-mail*

14. This then shows you a dialog similar to the one in Figure 7-53, which has been populated with the details of the test e-mail to send. If you have more than one profile, select each profile in turn to test them out and ensure they're working. Once completed, click Close.

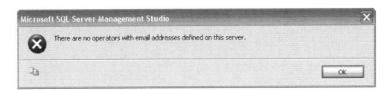

Figure 7-57. *Reporting and logging*

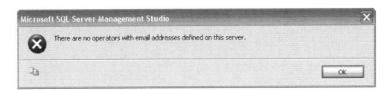

Figure 7-58. *No operators*

6. From Object Explorer, find the SQL Server Agent node, probably at the bottom of the list. Expand the node, and find an item called Operators. Right-click, and select New Operator, as you can see in Figure 7-59.

Figure 7-59. *Selecting to create a new operator*

7. This brings up a New Operator dialog screen. As you can see in Figure 7-60, not only can you send an e-mail, but you can also do a network send message, providing that this is enabled on your network, and a pager ping. Enter the details as shown in Figure 7-60. This operator is used to send out an e-mail from our maintenance plan to my e-mail address. Once you have entered your own e-mail address, click OK.

Figure 7-60. *A new operator screen*

8. Return to the Reporting and Logging screen. Now when you select the report to send to an e-mail, all will be well, and the first operator (if you defined any more) will be selected. When you see a screen similar to Figure 7-61, click OK. Close the maintenance plan and save the changes.

9. You can now execute your maintenance plan. You should receive an e-mail detailing either a success or a failure of the job.

Figure 7-61. *Setting up the reporting to send an e-mail*

Summary

You have seen a great deal in this chapter that is crucial to ensuring that your database is always secure if there are any unforeseen problems. As a manager drummed into me, the unexpected will always happen, but you must always be able to recover from it, no matter what. Therefore, regular backups that are known to work and even the occasional "disaster recovery test" should be done to ensure that you can restore when something unexpected happens. No matter what your managing director says, it is the data of a company that is its most important asset, not the people. Without the data, a company cannot function. If you cannot ensure that the data will be there, then the company will be in a very dangerous position.

As part of this maintenance plan, it is also necessary to be notified of problems so that you're aware of them and can deal with them quickly and efficiently. A database mail account is perfect for this, as it can notify you of problems in a process out of SQL Server.

CHAPTER 8

■■■

Working with the Data

We have now built our tables, set up the relationships, and backed up our solution, so we are ready to start inserting our data. The many tables within the database cover a number of different types of data that can be stored, ranging from characters and numbers to images and XML. This chapter will show you how to insert data into columns defined with all of these data types.

Not all the tables will be populated with data at this point. We will insert data in other tables later on in the book when different functionality of SQL Server is being demonstrated. Although data is being inserted, the database is still at the stage of being set up, as we are inserting static information at this point in the examples we are building together. To clarify, static data is data that will not change once it has been set up, although there may be further additions to this data at periodic intervals such as when a new share is created.

Not everyone who is allowed to access our database may, or should, be allowed to insert data directly into all of the tables. Therefore, you need to know how to set up the security to grant permission to specific user logins for inserting the data. The only people who really ought to be adding data directly to tables rather than using controlled methods such as stored procedures in production, for example, are special accounts like dbo accounts. In development, any developer should be able to insert data, but any login who would be testing out the application should not have that authority. You will see the reasons for this when we look at the security of adding data later in this chapter, and you will learn about alternative and more secure methods when we look at stored procedures and views.

Once we have set up users correctly, it is time to demonstrate inserting data into SQL Server. It is possible to insert data using SQL commands through Query Editor or through SQL Server Management Studio. Although both of these tools will have the same final effect on the database, each works in its own unique way.

When inserting data, you don't have to insert data into every column necessarily. We take a look at when it is mandatory and when it is not. There are many different ways to avoid inserting data into every column. This chapter will demonstrate the various different methods you can use to avoid having to use NULL values and default values. By using these methods, you are reducing the amount of information it is necessary to include with a record insertion. This method of inserting data uses special commands within SQL Server called **constraints**. You will see how to build a column constraint through T-SQL in Query Editor as well as in SQL Server Management Studio.

The T-SQL INSERT Command Syntax

Before it is possible to insert data using T-SQL code, you need to be familiar with the INSERT command and its structure.

The INSERT command is very simple and straightforward in its most minimal form, which is all that is required to insert a record.

```
INSERT [INTO]
   {table_name|view_name}
   [{(column_name,column_name,...)}]
   {VALUES (expression, expression, ...)}
```

Obviously, we are required to start the command with the type of action we are trying to perform—for example, insert data. The next part of the command, INTO, is optional. It serves no purpose, but you will find some do use it to ensure their command is more readable. The next part of the statement deals with naming the table or the view that the insertion has to place the data into. If the name of the table or view is the same as that of a reserved word or contains spaces, we have to surround that name with square brackets or double quotation marks, although as mentioned earlier in the book, it is best to try to avoid names with spaces. However, if you do need to, it is better to use square brackets, because there will be times you wish to set a value such as Acme's Rockets to a column data, which can be added easily by surrounding it by double quotation marks, as covered in the discussion of SET QUOTED_IDENTIFIER OFF earlier in the book.

I cannot stress enough that really, there is nothing to be gained by using reserved words for table, views, or column names. Deciding on easy-to-use and unambiguous object names is part of a good design.

Column names are optional, but it is best practice to list them to help to have reliable code, as this ensures that data is only inserted into the columns into which you want it to be inserted. Therefore, it will be necessary to place the column names in a comma-delimited list. The list of column names must be surrounded by parentheses: ( ). The only time that column names are not required is when the INSERT statement is inserting data into every column that is within the table in the same order as the column names are laid out in the table. However, this is a potentially dangerous scenario. If you build an INSERT command which you then save and use later, you expect the columns to be in a specific order because that is the way they have always been. If someone then comes along and adds a new column, or perhaps alters the order, your query or stored procedure will either not work or give erroneous results, as values will be added to the wrong columns. Therefore, I recommend that you always name every column in anything but a query, which is built, run once, and thrown away.

The VALUES keyword, which precedes the actual values to be entered, is mandatory. SQL Server needs to know that the following list is a list of values, not a list of columns. Therefore, you have to use the VALUES keyword, especially if you omit the list of columns as explained previously.

You will have a comma-separated list surrounded by parentheses covering the values of data to insert. There has to be a column name for every value to be entered. To clarify, if there are ten columns listed for data to be entered, then there must be ten values to enter.

Finally, it is possible to insert multiple rows of data from the one INSERT statement. You can do this by surrounding each row you want to add with its own separate parentheses: ( ). You will see this in action later in the chapter. As with a single-row addition, it is necessary to have the same number of columns either as the table you are inserting into, if you are not defining the columns in the INSERT statement, or as the INSERT statement if you are defining the list. Now that the INSERT command is clear, it's time to move on and use it.

INSERT SQL Command

The first method of inserting data is to use the INSERT SQL command as described previously. This example will insert one record into the ShareDetails.Shares table using Query Editor. When inserting the data, the record will be inserted immediately without any opportunity to roll back changes. This command does not use any transaction processing to allow any changes to take place. You will also see with this example how Query Editor can aid you as a developer in building the SQL command for inserting a record. Let's dive straight in and create the record.

Try It Out: Query Editor Scripting

1. Ensure that you have a Query Editor window open, connected to our ApressFinancial database, and that you are logged in with an account that has insert permissions on the ShareDetails.Shares table (this will be any member of the administrator's or database owner's role).

2. Right-click against the ShareDetails.Shares table, select Script Table As ➤ INSERT To ➤ New Query Editor Window.

3. This will bring up the following code. SQL Server covers itself concerning the use of reserved words, spaces in names, and so on, by surrounding every object name with square brackets. It also fully qualifies the table name with the database name and schema owner—in this case, ShareDetails. Moving to the values, you can see the column name repeated so that when altering the values, if the table has a large number of columns, you know which column you are working with. The final part in the jigsaw is an indication to the data type and length to aid you as well.

```
INSERT INTO [ApressFinancial].[ShareDetails].[Shares]
           ([ShareDesc]
           ,[ShareTickerId]
           ,[CurrentPrice])
     VALUES
           (<ShareDesc, nvarchar(50),>
           ,<ShareTickerId, nvarchar(50),>
           ,<CurrentPrice, numeric(18,5),>)
```

4. We need to place a modification at the top of this code, just to ensure that Query Editor has a setting to allow double quotes to be used to surround strings. This was covered in Chapter 5 when discussing database options. To cover yourself, though, you can always place the following code at the start of queries where quotation marks will be used. There is one hidden downfall that will be covered at the end. Notice as well that a GO command is included at the end of the SET command. This is because we want this command to take place in its own batch. Some commands need their own batch, while others don't. Some that do need their own batch are transaction-based commands, as you will see later in the book.

```
SET QUOTED_IDENTIFIER OFF
GO
```

5. By altering the code within the Query Editor pane, you will see that the next section of code actually inserts the data into the ShareDetails.Shares table. Notice that no GO statement is included at the end of this code. It is not necessary because there is only one INSERT and no other commands that need to form part of this same batch.

```
SET QUOTED_IDENTIFIER OFF
GO
INSERT INTO [ApressFinancial].[ShareDetails].[Shares]
           ([ShareDesc]
           ,[ShareTickerId]
           ,[CurrentPrice])
     VALUES
           ("ACME'S HOMEBAKE COOKIES INC",
            'AHCI',
            2.34125)
```

6. Now that all the information has been entered into the Query Editor pane, it is time to execute the code. Press F5 or Ctrl+E, or click the execute button on the toolbar. You should then see the following result, which indicates that there has been one row of data inserted into the table:

```
(1 row(s) affected)
```

After executing the code, the first record of information is placed into the database in the ShareDetails.Shares table. It is simple and straightforward. All the columns have been listed, and a value has been inserted. Because the name had a single quotation mark within it, it is simpler to surround the name with double quotation marks. However, to make sure that this string was not seen as an identifier, we have to switch that option off.

SQL Server Management Studio has the ability to create template scripts for several T-SQL commands. Templates, which you saw earlier in the book, hold parameter placeholders that require modification to build up the whole command. Template scripts differ from actual templates, as the information created within Query Editor for these templates is for one command only. Therefore, what you are actually seeing is the template for a one-line script.

When using the scripting options within Query Editor, it is possible to build the script as you have just seen for inserting a record into the ShareDetails.Shares table, and save the T-SQL within a new Query Editor pane, to a file, or even to a clipboard. This would then allow the data to be reinserted instantaneously should the table be deleted. To an extent, scripting to files or a clipboard is not as useful as scripting to a Query Editor pane. By scripting to files or a clipboard, you would need to move back into these files to make the necessary changes for data insertion. As you saw, when the script is placed in the Query Editor pane, the table and the columns are listed, but obviously the values need to be altered. This would have to be completed in a file or a clipboard by reopening these contents and making modifications after the event.

The scripting template does build the whole INSERT command and lists all the columns as well as—in the VALUES section of the command—the name of the column and its data type definition. From there, it is easier to know what value is expected within the INSERT command line.

The example mentions that using SET QUOTED_IDENTIFIER OFF does have one hidden downfall: in many cases, when using T-SQL commands, it is possible to surround reserved words with double quotation marks, rather than square brackets; however, with the QUOTED_IDENTIFIER set to OFF, you will only be able to surround reserved words with square brackets. If you had QUOTED_IDENTIFIER set to ON, then you could not have put ACME'S in the name; the code would have to have been written with two single quotation marks. Therefore, the code would have had to look like the following:

```
INSERT INTO [ApressFinancial].[ShareDetails].[Shares]
           ([ShareDesc]
           ,[ShareTickerId]
           ,[CurrentPrice])
      VALUES
           ('ACME''S HOMEBAKE COOKIES INC',
            'AHCI',
            2.34125)
```

Now that you know how to construct an INSERT statement, it is time to look at how you need not define all the columns within a table.

It is not always necessary to define columns with a value when inserting rows of data. This next section looks at two of these methods: using default values and allowing a NULL value. As you have just seen in our first examples, we specified every column in the table within the INSERT statement. You are now probably wondering whether you have to specify every column every time a record is inserted into a table. The answer is no. However, there are a few areas to be aware of.

Default Values

The first method for avoiding having to enter a value is to set a column or a set of columns with a default value. We set up the CustomerDetails.Customers table to have a default value when creating the tables in Chapter 5. Default values are used when a large number of INSERTs for a column would have the same value entered each time. Why have the overhead of passing this information, which would be the column name plus the value, through to SQL Server, when SQL Server can perform the task quickly and simply for you? Network traffic would be reduced and accuracy ensured as the column information would be completed directly by SQL Server. Do note, though, that a default value is not a mandatory value that will always be stored in a column. It is just a value that you think is the best value to use in the event that no other value is supplied.

Although it has been indicated that default values are best for a large number of INSERTs, it can also be argued that this need not be the case. Some people feel that all that is required is a significant number of rows to be affected from a default value setting for the use of default values to be an advantage. It does come down to personal preference as to when you think setting a default value will be of benefit. However, if there are times when you wish a column to have an initial value when a row is inserted with a specific value, then it is best to use a default value.

In the next section's example, where we'll build up our next set of INSERT statements, I will demonstrate how a default value will populate specific columns. When creating the CustomerDetails. Customers table, we created a column that is set up to be populated with a default value: the DateAdded column. In this column, we call a SQL Server reserved function, GETDATE(). This function gets the date and time from the operating system and returns it to SQL Server. By having this within a column default value, it is then inserted into a record when a row is added.

Using NULL Values

The next method for avoiding having to fill in data for every column is to allow NULL values in the columns. We did this for some columns when defining the tables. Ensuring that each column's Allow Nulls option is checked can ensure this is true for all our columns. If you take a look at Figure 8-1, you'll see that one of the columns in the ShareDetails.Shares table, ShareTickerId, does allow a NULL value to be entered into the column.

Column Name	Data Type	Allow Nulls
ShareId	bigint	☐
ShareDesc	nvarchar(50)	☐
ShareTickerId	nvarchar(50)	☑
CurrentPrice	numeric(18, 5)	☐
		☐

Figure 8-1. *NULLs selected on a column*

Therefore, the previous example could have placed data only in the ShareDesc and CurrentPrice fields if we'd wanted, as ShareId is an IDENTITY column and is auto-filled. If the ShareDetails.Shares record had only been inserted with those two columns, the command would have looked like the following T-SQL:

```
INSERT INTO [ApressFinancial].[ShareDetails].[Shares]
        ([ShareDesc]
        ,[CurrentPrice])
    VALUES
        ("ACME'S HOMEBAKE COOKIES INC",
         2.34125)
```

Figure 8-2 shows what the data would have looked like had we used the preceding T-SQL instead of the code in the previous section.

ShareId	ShareDesc	ShareTickerId	CurrentPrice
1	ACME'S HOMEB...	NULL	2.34125

Figure 8-2. *Insert with NULL*

To see the same result as in Figure 8-2, you would view this table in SQL Server Management Studio. This is covered shortly, as unfortunately we are in the chicken-and-egg scenario of showing an area before it has been discussed. As you can see, the columns that had no data entered have a setting of NULL. A NULL setting is a special setting for a column. The value of NULL requires special handling within SQL Server or applications that will be viewing this data. What this value actually means is that the information within the column is unknown; it is not a numeric or an alphanumeric value. Therefore, because you don't know if it is numeric or alphanumeric, you cannot compare the value of a column that has a setting of NULL to the value of any other column, and this includes another NULL column.

■**Note**   One major rule involving NULL values: a primary key cannot contain any NULL values.

Try It Out: NULL Values and SQL Server Management Studio Compared to T-SQL

1. Ensure that SQL Server Management Studio is running and that you are logged in with an account that allows the insertion of records. Any of our users can do this.

2. Expand the ApressFinancial node in Object Explorer so you can see the CustomerDetails.Customers table. Right-click this table and select Open Table.

3. In the main pane on the right, you should now see a grid similar to Figure 8-3. This grid would usually show all the rows of data that are within the table, but as this table contains no data, the grid is empty and ready for the first record to be entered. Notice that a star appears on the far left-hand side. It will change to an arrow shortly. This is the record marker and denotes which record the grid is actually pointing to and working with for insertion. The arrow denotes which record you are viewing, and when the marker changes to a pencil, it denotes that you are writing data in that row, ready for updating the table—perhaps not so relevant in this instance, but very useful when several records are displayed.

	CustomerId	CustomerTitleId	CustomerFirstN...	CustomerOther...	CustomerLastN...	AddressId	AccountNumber
✱	NULL	NULL	NULL	NULL	NULL	NULL	NULL

Figure 8-3. *No data held within the table*

4. It is a simple process to enter the information into the necessary columns as required. However, if you don't enter the data into the correct columns, or leave a column empty when in fact it should have data, you will receive an error message. The first column, CustomerId, is protected, as this is an IDENTITY column, but if you enter Mr into the CustomerTitleId column, then you will see something similar to the message shown in Figure 8-4 when moving to another cell. This message is informing you that CustomerTitleId is expecting an integer data type and that what was entered was not of that type.

Figure 8-4. *Invalid data type*

5. Now press the down arrow, after altering `CustomerTitleId` to the correct data type, to indicate that you have finished creating this customer and wish to create the next. This of course means that some columns that have to be populated aren't, and SQL Server tells you so, as you see in Figure 8-5. I wanted to create a row that was full of `NULL` values, but I can't. The error message indicates that `CustomerFirstName` has not been set up to allow a `NULL` value, and we need to put some data in there.

Figure 8-5. *Trying to insert a row with NULL when NULLs are not allowed*

6. Clicking OK allows you back into the grid where the whole row can be populated with the correct information. Notice that we can miss out placing any data in the `CustomerOtherInitials` column. After populating our grid, click the down arrow, and our grid should resemble Figure 8-6. The thing to notice is that although this is the first record entered, the `CustomerId` is set to 2. Whether insertion of a record is successful or not, an identity value is generated. Therefore, `CustomerId` 1 was generated when we received the second error as we were trying to move on to a new row. It is at this point that SQL Server tried to complete the insertion. It does not attempt an insertion when moving between cells, so therefore, no identity number will be created. This can and will cause gaps within your numbering system. You can see how valuable using defaults as initial values for columns can be. Where the real benefit of using default values comes is in ensuring that specific columns are populated with the correct default values. As soon as we move off from the new row, the default values are inserted and ready to be modified. There is now a record of when the record was added, ideal for auditing. After we look at inserting a row with T-SQL, we will see what we might be able to do about this.

CustomerId	CustomerTitleId	CustomerFirstN...	CustomerOther...	CustomerLastN...	AddressId	AccountNumber	AccountTypeId
2	1	Robin	NULL	Dewson	1333	18176111	1
NULL	NULL	NULL	NULL	NULL	NULL	NULL	NULL

Figure 8-6. *The populated grid*

> **Note** By having an IDENTITY column, every time a record is entered or an attempt is made to enter a record and all the *data entered* is of valid data types—whether this is through SQL Server Management Studio or an INSERT statement—the column value within the table will be incremented by the Identity Increment amount.

7. Now open up a Query Editor window and enter the following code. This code will replicate the first part of this example in which we entered the wrong data type.

```
USE ApressFinancial
GO
INSERT INTO CustomerDetails.Customers (CustomerTitleId) VALUES ('Mr')
```

8. Now execute this by pressing Ctrl+E or F5 or clicking the execute button on the toolbar. This code will generate an error because, once again, this is the wrong data type.

```
Msg 245, Level 16, State 1, Line 1
Conversion failed when converting the varchar value 'Mr' to data type int.
```

9. Change the code to replicate our second attempt at entering a row where the data type for the title is now correct but we are still missing other values.

```
USE ApressFinancial
GO
INSERT INTO CustomerDetails.Customers (CustomerTitleId) VALUES (1)
```

10. Now execute this by pressing Ctrl+E or F5 or clicking the execute button on the toolbar. This code will generate a different error, informing us this time that we didn't allow a NULL into the CustomerFirstName column, and therefore we have to supply a value.

```
Msg 515, Level 16, State 2, Line 1
Cannot insert the value NULL into column 'CustomerFirstName', table
'ApressFinancial.CustomerDetails.Customers'; column does not allow nulls.
INSERT fails.
The statement has been terminated.
```

11. This final example will work successfully. However, note that the CustomerLastName is before that of the CustomerFirstName column. This demonstrates that it is not necessary to name the columns within the insertion in the same order as they are defined within the table. It is possible to place the columns in any order you desire.

```
INSERT INTO CustomerDetails.Customers
(CustomerTitleId,CustomerLastName,CustomerFirstName,
CustomerOtherInitials,AddressId,AccountNumber,AccountType,
ClearedBalance,UnclearedBalance)
VALUES (3,'Mason','Jack',NULL,145,53431993,1,437.97,-10.56)
```

12. This time when you execute the code, you should see the following results, indicating the record has been inserted successfully:

```
(1 row(s) affected)
```

13. Now let's go back and view the data to see what has been entered. Find the `CustomerDetails.Customers` table in Object Explorer again. Right-click the table and select Open Table. The table now has two rows with two gaps in what we want our ideal ascending sequence to be, as you see in Figure 8-7.

CustomerId	CustomerTitleId	CustomerFirstN...	CustomerOther...	CustomerLastN...	AddressId	AccountNumber	AccountTyp:
2	1	Robin	NULL	Dewson	1333	18176111	1
5	3	Jack	NULL	Mason	145	53431993	1

Figure 8-7. *Second customer inserted*

That is all there is to it. It's just as simple as using SQL Server Management Studio, but you did get more informative error messages. We now have a slight problem in that already there are two gaps in the table. This can be remedied easily within Query Editor, which we'll do in the next section.

DBCC CHECKIDENT

The DBCC commands can be used for many different operations, such as working with IDENTITY columns. If you find that when testing out IDENTITY columns, you receive a number of errors, and the identity number has jumped up farther than you wished, it is possible to reset the seed of the IDENTITY column so that Query Editor starts again from a known point. The syntax for this command is very simple:

```
DBCC CHECKIDENT ('table_name'[,{NORESEED |{RESEED[,new_reseed_value]}}])
```

The following elaborates on the three areas of the syntax that may need explanation:

- The name of the table that you wish to reset the identity value for is placed in single quotation marks.

- You can then use NORESEED to return back what SQL Server believes the current identity value should be—in other words, what the current maximum identity value is within the IDENTITY column.

- The final option is the one we are interested in. You can reseed a table automatically by simply specifying the RESEED option with no value. This will look at the table defined and will reset the value to the current maximum value within the table. Or optionally, you can set the column of the table to a specific value by separating the value and the option RESEED by a comma.

If you use RESEED and there are currently no records in the table, but there had been in the past, then the value will still be set to the last value entered, so take care.

Resetting the seed for an IDENTITY column, though, does have a danger, which you need to be aware of. If you reset the point to start inserting values for the IDENTITY column back past the greatest number on the given table, you will find that there is the potential of an error being produced. When a value that already exists is generated from an INSERT after resetting the IDENTITY column value, then you will receive an error message informing you that the value already exists. To give an example, you have a table with the values 1, 2, 5, 6, 7, and 8, and you reset the IDENTITY value back to 2. You insert the next record, which will correctly get the value 3, and the insertion will work. This will still work the same with the next insertion, which will receive the value 4. However, come to the next record, and there will be an attempt to insert the value 5, but that value already exists; therefore, an error will be produced. However, if you had reset the value to 8—the last value successfully entered—then everything would have been OK.

As we do not have the value 1 for the first row in the `CustomerDetails.Customers` table, it would be nice to correct this. It also gives a good excuse to demonstrate CHECKIDENT in action. The code that follows will remove the erroneous record entry and reset the seed of the IDENTITY column back to 0, to a value indicating that no records have been entered. We will then reenter the customer information via T-SQL. Enter the following code, place the code into Query Editor, and execute it. The first line removes the record from CustomerDetails.Customers, and the second line resets the identity. Don't worry too much about the record deletion part, as deleting records is covered in detail later in the chapter in the "Deleting Data" section.

```
DELETE FROM CustomerDetails.Customers
DBCC CHECKIDENT('CustomerDetails.Customers',RESEED,0)
INSERT INTO CustomerDetails.Customers
(CustomerTitleId,CustomerFirstName,CustomerOtherInitials,
CustomerLastName,AddressId,AccountNumber,AccountType,
ClearedBalance,UnclearedBalance)
VALUES (1,'Robin',NULL,'Dewson',1333, 18176111,1,200.00,2.00)
INSERT INTO CustomerDetails.Customers
(CustomerTitleId,CustomerLastName,CustomerFirstName,
CustomerOtherInitials,AddressId,AccountNumber,AccountType,
ClearedBalance,UnclearedBalance)
VALUES (3,'Mason','Jack',NULL,145,53431993,1,437.97,-10.56)
```

When the code is run, you should see the following information output to the Query Results pane:

```
(2 row(s) affected)
Checking identity information: current identity value '5', current column value '0'.
DBCC execution completed. If DBCC printed error messages, contact your system
administrator.

(1 row(s) affected)

(1 row(s) affected)
```

Column Constraints

A constraint is essentially a check that SQL Server places on a column to ensure that the data to be entered in the column meets specific conditions. This will keep out data that is erroneous, and therefore avoid data inconsistencies. Constraints are used to keep database integrity by ensuring that a column only receives data within certain parameters.

We have already built a constraint on the CustomerDetails.Customers table for the default value for the column DateAdded. If you go to Object Explorer, right-click, select Script Table As ➤ Create To, and put the output in a new query window, you will see the following line from that output. So a constraint is used for setting a default value.

```
[DateAdded] [datetime] NULL CONSTRAINT
[DF_Customers_DateAdded]  DEFAULT (getdate()),
```

Constraints are used to not only insert default values, but also validate data as well as primary keys. However, when using constraints within SQL Server, you do have to look at the whole picture, which is the user graphical system with the SQL Server database in the background. If you are using a constraint for data validation, some people will argue that perhaps it is better to check the values inserted within the user front-end application rather than in SQL Server. This has some merit, but what also has to be kept in mind is that you may have several points of entry to your database. This could be from the user application, a web-based solution, or other applications if you are building a central database. Many people will say that all validation, no matter what the overall picture is, should always be placed in one central place, which is the SQL Server database. Then there is only one set of code to alter if anything changes. It is a difficult choice and one that you need to look at carefully.

You have two ways to add a constraint to a table. You saw the first when creating a default value as we built a table via SQL Server Management Studio in Chapter 5.

To build a constraint via code, you need to use the ALTER TABLE command, no matter what type of constraint this is. The ALTER TABLE command can cover many different alterations to a table, but in this instance, the example just concentrates on adding a constraint. This makes the ALTER TABLE statement easy, as the only real meat to the clause comes with the ADD CONSTRAINT syntax. The next example will work with the CustomerDetails.CustomerProducts table, and you will see three different types of constraints added, all of which will affect insertion of records. It is worth reiterating the adding of a default value constraint again, as this will differ from the DateAdded column on the CustomerDetails.Customers table. Once the constraints have been added, you will see them all in action, and how errors are generated from erroneous data input.

Try It Out: Altering a Table for a Default Value in Query Editor

1. Ensure that Query Editor is running. Although all the examples deal with the CustomerDetails. CustomerProducts table, each constraint being added to the table will be created one at a time, allowing a discussion for each point to take place. In the Query Editor pane, enter the following code to add a primary key to the CustomerDetails.CustomerProducts table. This will place the CustomerFinancialProductId column within the key, which will be clustered.

```
USE ApressFinancial
GO
ALTER TABLE CustomerDetails.CustomerProducts
ADD CONSTRAINT PK_CustomerProducts
PRIMARY KEY CLUSTERED
(CustomerFinancialProductId) ON [PRIMARY]
GO
```

2. Next we add a CHECK constraint on the AmountToCollect column. The CustomerDetails. CustomerProducts table is once again altered, and a new constraint called CK_CustProds_AmtCheck is added. This constraint will ensure that for all records inserted into the CustomerDetails.CustomerProducts table from this point on, the score must be greater than 0. Notice as well that the NOCHECK option is mentioned, detailing that any records already inserted will not be checked for this constraint. If they have invalid data, which they don't, then the constraint would ignore them and still be added.

```
ALTER TABLE CustomerDetails.CustomerProducts
WITH NOCHECK
ADD CONSTRAINT CK_CustProds_AmtCheck
CHECK ((AmountToCollect > 0))
GO
```

3. Moving on to the third constraint to add to the CustomerDetails.CustomerProducts table, we have a DEFAULT value constraint. In other words, this will insert a value of 0 to the Renewable column if no value is entered specifically into this column. This signifies that the premium collected is a one-off collection.

```
ALTER TABLE CustomerDetails.CustomerProducts WITH NOCHECK
    ADD CONSTRAINT DF_CustProd_Renewable
    DEFAULT (0)
    FOR Renewable
```

4. Execute the three batches of work by pressing F5 or Ctrl+E or clicking the execute button on the toolbar. You should then see the following result:

```
The command(s) completed successfully.
```

---

5. There are two methods to check that the code has worked before adding in any data. Move to Object Explorer in Query Editor. This isn't refreshed automatically, so you do need to refresh it. You should then see the three new constraints added—two under the Constraints node and one under the Keys node—as well as a display change in the Columns node, as shown in Figure 8-8.

Figure 8-8. *CustomerDetails.CustomerProducts table details*

6. Another method is to move to SQL Server Management Studio, find the CustomerDetails.CustomerProducts table, right-click it, and select Design. This brings us into the Table Designer, where we can navigate to the necessary column to check out the default value—in this case, Renewable. Also notice the yellow key against the CustomerFinancialProductId signifying that this is now a primary key, as shown in Figure 8-9.

Figure 8-9. *Default value constraint on column Renewable*

7. Move to the Table Designer toolbar and click the Manage Check Constraints button, shown here:

8. This will display the Check Constraints dialog box, shown in Figure 8-10, where we will see the AmountToCollect column constraint displayed. We can add a further constraint by clicking the Add button. Do so now.

Figure 8-10. *Check Constraints dialog box*

9. This will alter the Check Constraints dialog box to allow a new check constraint to be added, as you see in Figure 8-11. This check will ensure that the LastCollection date is greater than the value entered in another column. Here we want to ensure that the LastCollection date is equal to or after the LastCollected date. Recall that LastCollection defines when we last took the payment, and LastCollected defines when the last payment should be taken.

Figure 8-11. *Adding a new constraint in the Check Constraints dialog box*

10. The expression we want to add, which is the test the constraint is to perform, is not a value or a system function like GETDATE(), but rather a test between two columns from a table, albeit the same table we are working with. This is as simple as naming the columns and the test you wish to perform. Also, at the same time, change the name of the constraint to something meaningful. Your check constraint should look something like what appears in Figure 8-12. Afterward, click Close, which will add the constraint to the list, although it has not yet been added to the table. It is not until the table is closed that this will happen, so do that now.

Figure 8-12. *LastCollection constraint in the Check Constraints dialog box*

11. Now it's time to test the constraints to ensure that they work. First of all, we want to check the AmountToCollect constraint. Enter the following code, which will fail, because the amount to collect is a negative amount:

```
INSERT INTO CustomerDetails.CustomerProducts
(CustomerId,FinancialProductId,AmountToCollect,Frequency,
LastCollected,LastCollection,Renewable)
VALUES (1,1,-100,0,'24 Aug 2005','24 Aug 2008',0)
```

12. When you execute the code in Query Editor, you will see the following result. Instantly, you can see that the constraint check (CK_CustProds_AmtCheck) has cut in and the record has not been inserted.

```
Msg 547, Level 16, State 0, Line 1
The INSERT statement conflicted with the CHECK constraint
"CK_CustProds_AmtCheck". The conflict occurred in database
"ApressFinancial", table "CustomerDetails.CustomerProducts",
column 'AmountToCollect'.
The statement has been terminated.
```

13. We alter this now to have a positive amount, but change the LastCollection so that we break the CK_CustProd_LastColl constraint. Enter the following code:

```
INSERT INTO CustomerDetails.CustomerProducts
(CustomerId,FinancialProductId,AmountToCollect,Frequency,
LastCollected,LastCollection)
VALUES (1,1,100,0,'24 Aug 2008','23 Aug 2008')
```

14. When the preceding code is executed, you will see the following error message:

```
Msg 547, Level 16, State 0, Line 1
The INSERT statement conflicted with the CHECK constraint
"CK_CustProd_LastColl". The conflict occurred in database
"ApressFinancial", table "CustomerDetails.CustomerProducts".
The statement has been terminated.
```

Adding a constraint occurs through the ALTER TABLE statement as has just been demonstrated. However, the ADD CONSTRAINT command is quite a flexible command and can achieve a number of different goals.

The preceding example uses ADD CONSTRAINT to add a primary key, which can be made up of one or more columns (none of which can contain a NULL value), and also to insert a validity check and a set of default values. The only option not covered in the example is the addition of a foreign key, but this is very similar to the addition of a primary key.

The first constraint added is the primary key, which we saw in Chapter 5. The second constraint definition builds a column check to ensure that the data entered is valid.

```
ADD CONSTRAINT constraint_name CHECK (constraint_check_syntax)
```

The syntax for a CHECK constraint is a simple true or false test. When adding in a constraint for checking the data, the information to be inserted is valid (true) or invalid (false) when the test is applied. As you will see, using mathematical operators to test a column against a single value or a range of values will determine whether the data can be inserted.

Notice in the example that the ADD CONSTRAINT command is preceded with a WITH NOCHECK option on the ALTER TABLE statement. This informs SQL Server that any existing data in the table will not be validated when it adds the table alteration with the constraint, and that only data modified or inserted after the addition of the constraint will be checked. If you do wish the existing rows to be checked, then you would use the WITH CHECK option. The advantage of this is that the existing data is validated against that constraint, and if the constraint was added to the table successfully, then you know your data is valid. If any error was generated, then you know that there was erroneous data, and that you need to fix that data before being able to add the constraint. This is just another method of ensuring that your data is valid.

Finally, for adding a default value, the ADD CONSTRAINT syntax is very simple.

```
ADD CONSTRAINT constraint_name
DEFAULT default_value
FOR column_to_receive_the_value
```

The only part of the preceding syntax that requires further explanation is the default_value area. default_value can be a string, a numeric, NULL, or a system function (for example, GETDATE(), which would insert the current date and time). So the default value does not have to be fixed; it can be dynamic.

Inserting Several Records at Once

It is now necessary to enter a few more customers so that a reasonable amount of data is contained within the CustomerDetails.Customers table to work with later in the book. We need to do the same with several other tables as well, such as TransactionDetails.TransactionTypes, CustomerDetails.CustomerTransactions, and so on. This section will prove that no extra or specialized processing is required when inserting several records. When working with data, there may be many times that several records of data are inserted at the same time. This could be when initially populate a table or when testing. In this sort of situation where you are repopulating a table, it is possible to save your query to a text file, which can then be reopened in Query Editor and executed without having to reenter the code. This is demonstrated at the end of the upcoming example.

This next example will demonstrate inserting several records. The work will be completed in batches. There is no transaction processing surrounding these INSERTs, and therefore each insertion will be treated as a single unit of work, which either completes or fails.

▓**Note** A transaction allows a number of INSERTs or modifications to be treated as one unit, and if any insertion fails within the transaction, all the units will be returned back to their original value, and no insertions will take place. Transactions will be discussed in more detail in the upcoming "Transactions" section.

Try It Out: Insert Several Records At Once

1. Ensure that SQL Server Query Editor is up and running. In the Query Editor window, enter the following code. In this example, several customers will be added through only one INSERT statement.

```
INSERT INTO CustomerDetails.Customers
(CustomerTitleId,CustomerFirstName,CustomerOtherInitials,
CustomerLastName,AddressId,AccountNumber,AccountType,
ClearedBalance,UnclearedBalance)
VALUES (3,'Bernie','I','McGee',314,65368765,1,6653.11,0.00),
(2,'Julie','A','Dewson',2134,81625422,1,53.32,-12.21),
(1,'Kirsty',NULL,'Hull',4312,96565334,1,1266.00,10.32)
```

2. Now just execute the code in the usual way. You will see the following output in the results pane. This indicates that three rows of information have been inserted into the database, one at a time.

```
(3 row(s) affected)
```

Retrieving Data

This section of the chapter will demonstrate how to view the data that has been placed in the tables so far. Many ways of achieving this are available, from using SQL Server Management Studio to using T-SQL commands, and as you would expect, they will all be covered here.

The aim of retrieving data is to get the data back from SQL Server using the fastest retrieval manner possible. We can retrieve data from one or more tables through joining tables together within our query syntax; all of these methods will be demonstrated.

The simplest method of retrieving data is using SQL Server Management Studio, and we will look at this method first. With this method, you don't need to know any query syntax: it is all done for you. However, this leaves you with a limited scope for further work.

You can alter the query built up within SQL Server Management Studio to cater to work that is more complex, but you would then need to know the SELECT T-SQL syntax; again, this will be explained and demonstrated. This can become very powerful very quickly, especially when it comes to selecting specific rows to return.

The results of the data can also be displayed and even stored in different media, like a file. It is possible to store results from a query and send these to a set of users, if so desired.

Initially, the data returned will be in the arbitrary order stored within SQL Server. This is not always suitable, so another aim of this chapter is to demonstrate how to return data in the order that you desire for the results. Ordering the data is quite an important part of retrieving meaningful results, and this alone can aid the understanding of query results from raw data.

Retrieving images is not as straightforward as retrieving normal rows of data, so I'll cover this in Chapter 12 along with other advanced T-SQL techniques.

Starting with the simplest of methods, let's look at SQL Server Management Studio and how easy it is for us to retrieve records. We have partially covered this earlier when inserting rows.

Using SQL Server Management Studio to Retrieve Data

The first area that will be demonstrated is the simplest form of data retrieval, but it is also the least effective. Retrieving data using SQL Server Management Studio is a very straightforward process, with no knowledge of SQL required in the initial stages. Whether you want to return all rows, or even when you want to return specific rows, using SQL Server Management Studio makes this whole task very easy. This first example will demonstrate how flexible SQL Server Management Studio is in retrieving all the data from the CustomerDetails.Customers table.

Try It Out: Retrieving Data Within SQL Server Management Studio

1. Ensure that SQL Server Management Studio is running. Navigate to the ApressFinancial database and click the Tables node; this should list all the tables in the right-hand pane. Find the CustomerDetails.Customers table, right-click it to bring up the pop-up menu, and select Select Top 1000 Rows. This instantly opens up a new Query Editor window pane like the one shown in Figure 8-13, which shows all the rows that are in the CustomerDetails. Customers table. But how did SQL Server get this data? Let's find out (the secret may already be there, depending on the options for SQL Server).

CustomerId	CustomerTitleId	CustomerFirstN...	CustomerOther...	CustomerLastN...	AddressId	AccountNumber	AccountTypeId
1	1	Robin	*NULL*	Dewson	1333	187612311	1
2	3	Jack	*NULL*	Mason	145	53431993	1
3	3	Bernie	I	McGee	314	65368765	1
4	2	Julie	A	Dewson	2134	81625422	1
5	1	Kirsty	*NULL*	Hull	4312	96565334	1

Figure 8-13. *CustomerDetails.Customers table retrieving data*

2. Above the results, you will see the SELECT T-SQL statement used to return the data. You can see what was produced in Figure 8-14.

```
/****** Script for SelectTopNRows command from SSMS ******/
SELECT TOP 1000 [CustomerId]
      ,[CustomerTitleId]
      ,[CustomerFirstName]
      ,[CustomerOtherInitials]
      ,[CustomerLastName]
      ,[AddressId]
      ,[AccountNumber]
      ,[AccountType]
      ,[ClearedBalance]
      ,[UnclearedBalance]
      ,[DateAdded]
  FROM [ApressFinancial].[CustomerDetails].[Customers]
```

Figure 8-14. *Output displayed via the SQL window*

3. You can alter the number next to the top clause if you want to return a fewer or a greater number of rows, and then reexecute the query.For this first time, alter this to 3, and you should see something similar to Figure 8-15. This will return a maximum of three rows. If we entered a value of 100, we would only get five rows returned, as that is the maximum number of rows in the table at this moment in time. You would use this perhaps when you don't know the number of records within a table, but you are only interested in a maximum number of 100 if there are more. This would be when you want to look at just a small selection of content in columns within a table.

	CustomerId	CustomerTitleId	CustomerFirstN...	CustomerOther...	CustomerLastN...	AddressId	AccountNumber	AccountTypeId
▶	1	1	Robin	NULL	Dewson	1333	187612311	1
	2	3	Jack	NULL	Mason	145	53431993	1
	3	3	Bernie	1	McGee	314	65368765	1
*	NULL	NULL	NULL	NULL	NULL	NULL	NULL	NULL

Figure 8-15. *Three rows returned*

So now that you know how to return data from SQL Server Management Studio, let's look at using T-SQL in more detail as well as the T-SQL statement you will probably use most often: SELECT.

The SELECT Statement

If we wish to retrieve data for viewing from SQL Server using T-SQL commands, then the SELECT statement is the command we need to use. This is quite a powerful command, as it can retrieve data in any order, from any number of columns, and from any table that we have the authority to retrieve data from. It can also perform calculations on that data during data retrieval and even include data from other tables! If the user does not have the authority to retrieve data from a table, then you will receive an error message similar to that which you saw earlier in the chapter informing the user that permission is denied. SELECT has a lot more power than even the functions mentioned so far, but for the moment, let's concentrate on the fundamentals.

Let's take some time to inspect the simple syntax for a SELECT statement.

```
SELECT [ ALL | DISTINCT ]
[ TOP expression [ PERCENT ] [ WITH TIES ] ]
    {
                *
    | { table_name | view_name | alias_name }.*
    | { column_name | [ ] expression | $IDENTITY | $ROWGUID }
    [ [ AS ] column_alias ]
    | column_alias = expression
    } [ ,...n ]
FROM table_name | view_name alias_name
WHERE filter_criteria
ORDER BY ordering_criteria
```

The following list breaks down the SELECT syntax, explaining each option. More explanation will be given throughout the chapter as well.

- SELECT: Required—this informs SQL Server that a SELECT instruction is being performed; in other words, we just want to return a set of columns and rows to view.

- ALL|DISTINCT: Optional—we want to return either all of the rows or only distinct, or unique, rows. Normally, you do not specify either of these options.

- TOP expression/PERCENT/WITH TIES: Optional—you can return the top number of rows, which, as you remember, will be in an arbitary order unless you use an ORDER BY. You can also add the word PERCENT to the end: this means that the top n percent of records will be returned. If PERCENT is not specified, all the records will be returned (unless specific column names are given). WITH TIES can only be used with an ORDER BY. If you specify you want to return TOP 10 rows, and the 11th row has the same value as the 10th row on those columns that have been defined in the ORDER BY, then the 11th row will also be returned. It's the same for subsequent rows, until you get to the point that the values differ.

- *: Optional—by using the asterisk, you are instructing SQL Server to return all the columns from all the tables included in the query. This is not an option that should be used on large amounts of data or over a network. Especially if it is busy, you really should not do this against production data. By using this, we are bringing back more information than is required. Wherever possible, we should name the columns instead.

- table_name.*|view_name.*|alias_name.*: Optional—similar to *, but you are defining which table, if the SELECT is working on more than one table. When working with more than one table, this is known as a JOIN, and this option will be demonstrated in Chapter 11 when we take a look at joins.

- column_name: Optional but recommended; not required if * is used—this option is where we name the columns that we wish to return from a table. When naming the columns, it is always a good idea to prefix the column names with their corresponding table names. This becomes mandatory when we are using more than one table in our SELECT statement and instances where there may be columns within different tables that share the same name.

- expression: Optional—we don't have to return columns of rows within a SELECT. We can return a value, a variable, or an expression.

- $IDENTITY: Optional—will return the value from the IDENTITY column.

- $ROWGUID: Optional—will return the value from the ROWGUID column.

- AS: Optional—we can change the column header name when displaying the results by using the AS option.

- `FROM table_name|view_name`: Required—we have to inform SQL Server where the information is coming from.

- `WHERE filter_clause`: Optional—if we want to retrieve rows that meet specific criteria, we need to have a `WHERE` clause specifying the criteria to use to return the data. The `WHERE` clause tends to contain the name of a column on the left-hand side of a comparison operator, such as =, <, >, and either another column within the same table, or another table, a variable, or a static value. There are other options that the `WHERE` statement can contain, where more advanced searching is required, but on the whole, these comparison operators will be the main constituents of the clause.

- `ORDER BY ordering_criteria`: Optional—the data will be returned arbitrarily from the table if no `ORDER BY` clause is specified. Ascending (`ASC`) or descending (`DESC`) is defined for each column, not defined just once for all the columns within the `ORDER BY`. Sorting is completed once the data has been retrieved from SQL Server but before any command such as `TOP`.

Keep in mind that when building a `SELECT` statement, you do not have to name all the columns. In fact, you should only retrieve the columns that you do wish to see; this will reduce the amount of information sent over the network. There is no need to return information that will not be used.

Naming the Columns

When building a `SELECT` statement, it is not necessary to name every column if you don't want to see every column. You should only return the columns that you need. It is very easy to slip into using * to return every column, even when running one-time-only queries. Try to avoid this at all costs; typing out every column name takes time, but when you start dealing with more-complex queries and a larger number of rows, the few extra seconds are worth it.

Now that you know not to name every column unless required, and to avoid using *, what other areas do you need to be aware of? First of all, it is not necessary to name columns in the same order that they appear in the table—it is quite acceptable to name columns in any order that you wish. There is no performance hit or gain from altering the order of the columns, but we may find that a different order of the columns might be better for any future processing of the data.

When building a `SELECT` statement and including the columns, if the final output is to be sent to a set of users, the column names within the database may not be acceptable. For example, if you are sending the output to the users via a file, then they will see the raw result set. Or if you are using a tool such as Crystal Reports to display data from a `SELECT` statement within a SQL Server stored procedure, then naming the columns would help there as well. The column names are less user friendly, and some column names will also be confusing for users; therefore, it would be ideal to be able to alter the names of the column headings. Replacing the SQL Server column headings with the new alias column headings desired, in either quotation marks or square bracket delimiters, is easily accomplished with the `AS` keyword. There is more on this in the next section.

Now that you know about naming the columns, let's take a look at how the SQL command can return data.

The First Searches

This example will revolve around the `CustomerDetails.Customers` table, making it possible to demonstrate how all of the different areas mentioned previously can affect the results displayed.

Try It Out: The First Set of Searches

1. Ensure that Query Editor is running and that you are within the ApressFinancial database. In the Query Editor pane, enter the following SQL code:

```
Select * From CustomerDetails.Customers
```

2. Execute the code using Ctrl+E, F5, or the execute button on the toolbar. You should then see something like the results shown in Figure 8-16.

	CustomerId	CustomerTitleId	CustomerFirstName	CustomerOtherInitials	CustomerLastName	AddressId	AccountNumber	AccountTyp...
1	1	1	Robin	NULL	Dewson	1333	187612311	1
2	2	3	Jack	NULL	Mason	145	53431993	1
3	3	3	Bernie	I	McGee	314	65368765	1
4	4	2	Julie	A	Dewson	2134	81625422	1
5	5	1	Kirsty	NULL	Hull	4312	96565334	1

Figure 8-16. *Customers listing*

3. This is a simple SELECT command returning all the columns and all the rows from the CustomerDetails. Customers table, as you have just seen. Let's now take it to the next stage where specific column names will be defined in the query, which is a much cleaner solution. In this instance from the CustomerDetails.Customers table, we would like to return a customer's first name, last name, and the current account balances. This would mean naming CustomerFirstName, CustomerLastName, and ClearedBalance as the column names in the query. The code will read as follows:

```
SELECT CustomerFirstName,CustomerLastName,ClearedBalance
FROM CustomerDetails.Customers
```

4. Now execute this code, which will return the results shown in Figure 8-17. As you can see, not every column is returned.

	CustomerFirstName	CustomerLastName	ClearedBalance
1	Robin	Dewson	200.00
2	Jack	Mason	437.97
3	Bernie	McGee	6653.11
4	Julie	Dewson	53.32
5	Kirsty	Hull	1266.00

Figure 8-17. *Specific columns returned*

5. As you have seen from the examples so far, the column names, although well named from a design viewpoint, are not exactly suitable if we had to give this to a set of users. Using the same query as before, a couple of minor modifications are required to give the columns aliases. The first alias name is in quotes, as it contains a space. Notice the last column also does not have AS specified because this keyword is optional.

```
SELECT CustomerFirstName As 'First Name',
CustomerLastName AS 'Surname',
ClearedBalance Balance
FROM CustomerDetails.Customers
```

6. Execute this, and the displayed output changes—much more friendly column names, as you see in Figure 8-18.

Figure 8-18. *Friendly column names*

The first SELECT statement demonstrates the fact that in most SQL Server instances, whether we use upper- or lowercase doesn't matter to our queries; however, some language installations are case sensitive. When installing SQL Server, if we chose a SQL collation sequence that was case sensitive, as denoted by CS within the suffix of the collation name— SQL_Latin1_General_Cp437_CS_AS, for instance—then the first SELECT query would generate an error. The collation sequence for SQL Server was chosen in Chapter 1 when we installed the application. Changing a collation sequence within SQL Server is a very difficult task that requires rebuilding parts of SQL Server, so this book won't move into that area.

▓**Tip** It is strongly recommended, and considered best practice, that you use the correct casing when using queries. Not only does this avoid confusion, but it also means that if you do switch to a case-sensitive installation, then it will not be necessary to alter the query.

Moving back to the first query, this query will select all columns and all rows from the CustomerDetails.Customers table, ordered according to how the database sees it—as you can see in Figure 8-18, it has quite plainly done this.

Looking at the second and third query examples, the columns returned have been reduced to just three columns: the customer's first and last names and the cleared balance amounts. All the rows are still being returned. In the last example, notice that after two of the three columns, there is an AS keyword. This signifies that the following literal is to be used as the column heading; note that if we wish to use two words separated by spaces, we must surround these words by identifiers, whether they be quotation marks, as in our example, or square brackets.

Now that the basics of the SELECT statement have been covered, we will next look at the methods within Query Editor to display output in different manners.

Varying the Output Display

There are different ways of displaying the output: from a grid, as we have seen; from a straight text file; still within a Query Editor pane; or as pure text, just like a tabulated Word file. You may have found the results in the previous exercise laid out in a different format than shown previously, depending on how you initially set up Query Editor. In the results so far, you have seen the data as a grid. This next section will demonstrate tabular text output, otherwise known as Results in Text, as well as outputting the data to a file. Let's get right on with the first option, Results in Text.

Try It Out: Putting the Results in Text and a File

1. You should still be in Query Editor. From the Query menu option, select Results To ➤ Results in Text, or press Ctrl+T. Figure 8-19 shows the other options available from the Results To menu.

Figure 8-19. *Sending the results to different places*

2. If we run the same query as earlier (the code is detailed again here), we will be able to see the difference. Once the code is entered, execute it.

```
SELECT CustomerFirstName As 'First Name',
CustomerLastName AS 'Surname',
ClearedBalance Balance
FROM CustomerDetails.Customers
```

3. Examine the output, which should resemble Figure 8-20. As you can see, the output has changed a great deal. No longer is the output in a nice grid where the columns have been shrunk to a more manageable size, but each column's data takes up, and is displayed to, the maximum number of characters that each column could contain. This obviously stretches out the display, but from here we can see easily how large each column is supposed to be.

```
First Name                                       Surname                                       Balance
----------------------------------------------   -------------------------------------------   -----------------
Robin                                            Dewson                                        200.00
Jack                                             Mason                                         437.97
Bernie                                           McGee                                         6653.11
Julie                                            Dewson                                        53.32
Kirsty                                           Hull                                          1266.00

(5 row(s) affected)
```

Figure 8-20. *Results as text*

4. There will be times, though, when users require output to be sent to them. For example, they may wish to know specific details from a set of records, and so you build a query and save the results to a file to send to them. Or perhaps they want output to perform some analysis of data within a Microsoft Excel spreadsheet. Again, this can be achieved from the Query menu by selecting Results To ➤ Results to File, or Ctrl+Shift+F. Specify sending results to a file and rerun the code. Once the code has been executed, a Save Results dialog box like the one in Figure 8-21 will appear: this could show any folder location initially—in this case, it shows the folder for results I have set up on my computer.

Figure 8-21. *Locating where to save the results*

5. So now that you know how to save to different locations, move back to displaying the output to a grid by pressing Ctrl+D.

You now know how to return data, but what happens if you don't want every row and you want to select which rows to display? We'll look at that next.

Limiting the Search: the Use of WHERE

You have a number of different ways to limit the search of records within a query. Some of the most basic revolve around the three basic relational operators: <, >, and = (less than, greater than, and equal to). There is also the use of the keyword NOT, which could be included with these three operators; however, NOT does not work as in other programming languages that you may have come across: this will be demonstrated within the example in this section so you know how to use the NOT operator successfully.

All of these operators can be found in the WHERE clause of the SELECT statement used to reduce the number of records returned within a query.

■**Note** You may come across some legacy code where you will find that the WHERE statement is used to join two tables together to make the results look as if they came from one table. For some databases, this is the "standard" way to join two tables; however, with SQL Server, the WHERE statement is purely used as a filter method.

Try It Out: The WHERE Statement

1. First of all to use a different table, let's enter some more rows in to the ShareDetails.Shares table. Enter and execute the following code. Figure 8-22 shows the query and the results.

```
INSERT INTO ShareDetails.Shares
(ShareDesc, ShareTickerId,CurrentPrice)
VALUES ('FAT-BELLY.COM','FBC',45.20),
('NetRadio Inc','NRI',29.79),
('Texas Oil Industries','TOI',0.455),
('London Bridge Club','LBC',1.46)
```

```
INSERT INTO ShareDetails.Shares
  (ShareDesc, ShareTickerId,CurrentPrice)
  VALUES ('FAT-BELLY.COM','FBC',45.20),
  ('NetRadio Inc','NRI',29.79),
  ('Texas Oil Industries','TOI',0.455),
  ('London Bridge Club','LBC',1.46)
```

Messages

FAT-BELLY(FAT-BELLY\rdewson): (4 row(s) affected)

Figure 8-22. *The results of entering several rows*

2. The requirement for this section is to find the current share price for FAT-BELLY.COM. We restrict the SELECT statement so that only the specific record comes back by using the WHERE statement, as can be seen in the following code:

```
SELECT ShareDesc,CurrentPrice
FROM ShareDetails.Shares
WHERE ShareDesc = 'FAT-BELLY.COM'
```

3. Execute this code, and you will see that the single record for FAT-BELLY.COM is returned, as shown in Figure 8-23.

	ShareDesc	CurrentPrice
1	FAT-BELLY.COM	45.20000

Figure 8-23. *The results of limiting the search*

4. To prove that we are working within an installation that is not case sensitive from a data perspective (unless you installed a different collation sequence from that described in Chapter 1), if you perform the following query, you will get the same results as displayed in Figure 8-23:

```
SELECT ShareDesc,CurrentPrice
FROM ShareDetails.Shares
WHERE ShareDesc = 'FAT-BELLY.COm'
```

▓**Note** As you can see, this may not always be what you want, because you may want your data to be case sensitive. If you do, then query code will also become case sensitive.

5. You have seen WHERE in action using the equals sign; it is also possible to use the other relational operations in the WHERE statement. The next query demonstrates how SQL Server takes the WHERE condition and starts returning records after the given point. This query provides an interesting set of results. Enter the code as detailed here:

```
SELECT ShareDesc,CurrentPrice
FROM ShareDetails.Shares
WHERE ShareDesc > 'FAT-BELLY.COM'
AND ShareDesc < 'TEXAS OIL INDUSTRIES'
```

6. Once done, execute the code and check the results, which should resemble Figure 8-24.

	ShareDesc	CurrentPrice
1	NetRadio Inc	29.79000
2	London Bridge Club	1.46000

Figure 8-24. *Shares output*

7. Let's now bring in another option in the WHERE statement that allows us to avoid returning specific rows. This can be achieved in one of two ways: the first is by using the less than and greater than signs; the second is by using the NOT operator. Enter the following code, which will return all rows except FAT-BELLY.COM. Run both sets of code at once. This will return two sets of output, known as multiple result sets.

```
SELECT ShareDesc,CurrentPrice
FROM ShareDetails.Shares
WHERE ShareDesc <> 'FAT-BELLY.COM'

SELECT ShareDesc,CurrentPrice
FROM ShareDetails.Shares
WHERE NOT ShareDesc = 'FAT-BELLY.COM'
```

8. Executing this code will produce the output shown in Figure 8-25. Notice how in neither sets of output FAT-BELLY.COM has been listed.

	ShareDesc	CurrentPrice
1	ACME'S HOMEBAKE COOKIES INC	2.34125
2	NetRadio Inc	29.79000
3	Texas Oil Industries	0.45500
4	London Bridge Club	1.46000

	ShareDesc	CurrentPrice
1	ACME'S HOMEBAKE COOKIES INC	2.34125
2	NetRadio Inc	29.79000
3	Texas Oil Industries	0.45500
4	London Bridge Club	1.46000

Figure 8-25. *Multiple output*

As you have seen, it is possible to limit the number of records to be returned via the WHERE clause; we can return records up to a certain point, after a certain point, or even between two points with the use of an AND statement. It is also possible to exclude rows that are not equal to a specific value or range of values by using the NOT statement or the <> operator.

When the SQL Server data engine executes the T-SQL SELECT statement, it is the WHERE statement that is dealt with before any ordering of the data, or any limitation placed on it concerning the number of rows to return. The data is inspected, where possible using an index, to determine whether a row stored in the relevant table matches the selection criteria within the WHERE statement, and if it does, to return it. If an index cannot be used, then a full table scan will be performed to find the relevant information.

Table scans can present a large performance problem within your system, and you will find that if a query has to perform a table scan, then data retrieval could be very slow, depending on the size of the table being scanned. If the table is small with only a small number of records, then a table scan is likely to retrieve data more quickly than the use of an index. However, table scanning and the speed of data retrieval will be the biggest challenge you will face as a SQL Server developer. With data retrieval, it is important to bear in mind that whenever possible, if you are using a WHERE clause to limit the records returned, you should try to specify the columns from an index definition in this WHERE clause. By doing this, you will be giving the query the best chance for optimum performance.

As discussed in Chapter 7, getting the index right is crucial to fast data manipulation and retrieval. If you find you are forever placing the same columns in a WHERE clause, but those columns do not form part of an index, perhaps this is something that should be revisited to see whether any gain can come from having the columns be part of an index.

For any table, ensuring that the WHERE clause is correct is important. As has been indicated from a speed perspective, using an index will ensure a fast response of data. This gains greater importance with each table added, and even more importance as the size of each table grows.

Finally, by ensuring the WHERE statement filters out the correct rows, you will ensure that the required data is returned, the right results are displayed, and less data is sent across the network, as the processing is done on the server and not the client. Also, having the appropriate indexing strategy helps with this as well.

It is also possible to return a specific number of rows, or a specific percentage of the number of rows, as you saw when displaying rows in SQL Server Management Studio. These statements are discussed next, with a short code example demonstrating each in action. First of all, we will look at a statement that does not actually form part of the SELECT command itself.

SET ROWCOUNT n

SET ROWCOUNT n is a totally separate command from the SELECT statement and can in fact be used with other statements within T-SQL. What this command will do is limit or reset the number of records that will be processed for the session that the command is executed in.

> **▒Note** Caution should be exercised if you have any statements that also use a TOP command, described in a moment.

The SET ROWCOUNT n function stops the processing of the SELECT command once the number of rows defined has been reached. The difference between SET ROWCOUNT and SELECT TOP n is that the latter will perform one more internal instruction to that of the former. Processing halts immediately when the number of records processed through SET ROWCOUNT is reached. However, by using the TOP command, all the rows are returned internally, the TOP n rows are selected from that group internally, and these are then passed for display. Returning a limited number of records is useful when you want to look at a handful of data to see what values could be included, or perhaps you wish to return a few rows for sampling the data.

You can set the number of rows to be affected by altering the number, n, at the end of the SET ROWCOUNT function. This setting will remain in force only within the query window in which the command is executed, or within the stored procedure in which the command is executed.

To reset the session so that all rows are taken into consideration, you would set the ROWCOUNT number to 0.

Try It Out: SET ROWCOUNT

1. In Query Editor, enter the following code into a new Query Editor pane; once entered, execute it:

```
SET ROWCOUNT 3
SELECT * FROM ShareDetails.Shares
SET ROWCOUNT 0
SELECT * FROM ShareDetails.Shares
```

2. You should see two result sets, as shown in Figure 8-26. The first will return three rows from the ShareDetails. Shares table. The second result set will return all rows from ShareDetails.Shares.

Figure 8-26. *Limiting the output via rowcount*

TOP n

This option, found within the SELECT statement itself, will return a specific number of rows from the SELECT statement, and is very much like the SET ROWCOUNT function for that reason. In fact, the TOP n option is the preferred option to use when returning a set number of rows, as opposed to the SET ROWCOUNT function. The reason behind this is that TOP n only applies to that query command; however, by using SET ROWCOUNT n, you are altering all commands until you reset SQL Server to act on all rows through SET ROWCOUNT 0.

■**Caution** Although it is possible to use TOP n without any ORDER BY statement, it is usual to combine TOP with ORDER BY. When no order is specified, the rows returned are arbitrary, and if you want consistent results, then ordering will provide this. If you are not concerned about which rows are returned, then you can avoid using ORDER BY.

Any WHERE statements and ORDER BY statements within the SELECT statement are dealt with first, and then, from the resultant records, the TOP n function comes into effect. This will be demonstrated with the following example.

Try It Out: TOP n

1. In Query Editor, enter the following code into a new Query Editor pane; once entered, execute it:

```
SELECT TOP 3 * FROM ShareDetails.Shares
SET ROWCOUNT 3
SELECT TOP 2 * FROM ShareDetails.Shares
SET ROWCOUNT 2
SELECT TOP 3 * FROM ShareDetails.Shares
SET ROWCOUNT 0
```

2. The code returns three result sets, as shown in Figure 8-27. Take a moment to peruse these result sets. The first set is just the top three records that are taken from an arbitrary order SQL Server has chosen. The second will only return two records, even though the ROWCOUNT is set to 3. The third result set takes into account the ROWCOUNT setting, as this is the lesser value this time. Therefore, again, only two records are returned.

Figure 8-27. *A mixture of TOP and rowcount*

TOP n PERCENT

TOP n PERCENT is very similar to the TOP n clause with the exception that instead of working with a precise number of records, it is a percentage of the number of records that will be returned. Keep this in mind, as it is not a percentage of the number of records within the table. Also, the number of records is rounded up; therefore, as soon as the percentage moves over to include another record, then SQL Server will include this extra record.

You see more of this option in Chapter 9, which discusses the building of views.

String Functions

A large number of system functions are available for manipulating data. This section looks purely at the string functions available for use within a T-SQL command; later in the book, we will look at some more functions that are available to us. Following are the functions that are used in the next example:

- LTRIM/RTRIM: These perform similar functionality. If you have a string with leading spaces, and you wish to remove those leading spaces, you would use LTRIM so that the returned varchar value would have a nonspace character as its first value. If you have trailing spaces, you would use RTRIM. You can only use this function with a data type of varchar or nvarchar, or a data type that can be implicitly converted to these two data types, or with a data type converted to varchar or nvarchar using the CAST SQL Server function.

- CAST: This specialized function converts one data type to another data type. I don't cover this within the book. If you wish to convert data types, check on the command in Books Online, which can be found by selecting Help in Query Editor.

- LEFT/RIGHT: This function returns the leftmost or rightmost characters from a string. Passing in a second parameter to the function will determine the number of characters to return from whichever side of the string. The LEFT and RIGHT functions accept any data type except text or ntext expressions to perform the string manipulation, implicitly converting any noncharacter data type or varchar or nvarchar, and returning a varchar or nvarchar data type as a result.

Try It Out: String Functions

1. Enter the code that follows into an empty Query Editor window. Alter the output to text format by pressing Ctrl+T. Notice the use of the + operator within the SELECT query. This will concatenate the strings defined within the query into one single string value.

Note Unlike with some programming languages, you cannot use the & character, as this has a totally different meaning in SQL Server.

```
SELECT CustomerFirstName + ' ' + CustomerLastName AS 'Name',
ClearedBalance Balance
FROM CustomerDetails.Customers
```

2. Execute this code, which produces the output shown in Figure 8-28.

```
Results
Name                                                                          Balance
-----------------------------------------------------------------------       --------------
Robin Dewson                                                                  200.00
Jack Mason                                                                    437.97
Bernie McGee                                                                  6653.11
Julie Dewson                                                                  53.32
Kirsty Hull                                                                   1266.00

(5 row(s) affected)
```

Figure 8-28. *Concatenating results*

3. As you can see, it's a bit unwieldy. The Name column heading goes far wider than is required. There is a complex way of getting this right, but a much simpler method is to use the LEFT command. The sum of the width of the two columns gives this column width displayed in the output; by using the LEFT command, it is possible to achieve something better. Clear the Query Editor pane and enter the following code:

```
SELECT LEFT(CustomerFirstName + ' ' + CustomerLastName,50) AS 'Name',
ClearedBalance Balance
FROM CustomerDetails.Customers
```

4. Execute the preceding code. This produces the results shown in Figure 8-29. What the preceding query has done is to reduce the output to the first 50 characters starting from the left.

```
Results

Name                                               Balance
-------------------------------------------------- ----------------------
Robin Dewson                                       200.00
Jack Mason                                         437.97
Bernie McGee                                       6653.11
Julie Dewson                                       53.32
Kirsty Hull                                        1266.00

(5 row(s) affected)
```

Figure 8-29. *Concatenating results and reducing the width*

5. The best way is to remove all trailing spaces from the first name and surname concatenated columns is the RTRIM command. The following code does this, although the output in the text layout doesn't. This is because SQL Server still doesn't know what the maximum size of the concatenation will be, and it has to believe that the maximum number of characters of the sum of the two columns could still be displayed. However, in truth, the amount of data returned will be minimal. Therefore, this is a great method of reducing the amount of data passed over a network.

```
SELECT RTRIM(CustomerFirstName + ' ' + CustomerLastName) AS 'Name',
ClearedBalance Balance
FROM CustomerDetail.Customers
```

In all of our examples thus far, as you know, rows are returned in an arbitrary order. We look now at how this can be changed.

Order! Order!

Of course, retrieving the records in any order SQL Server desires may not always be what you desire. However, it is possible to change the order in which you return records. This is achieved through the ORDER BY clause, which is part of the SELECT statement. The ORDER BY clause can have multiple columns, even with some being in ascending order and others in descending order.

If you should find that you are repeatedly using the same columns within an ORDER BY clause, or that the query is taking some time to run, you should consider having the columns within the query as an index. (Indexes were covered in Chapter 6.)

Ordering the data will of course increase processing time, but it is used as a necessity to display the data in the correct order. Ordering on varchar columns also takes longer than numeric columns.

> **■Note** Ordering takes place after the filtering of rows but before the TOP command, so you could still be ordering a large set of rows before returning the top few you may need.

Let's now take a look at building a query that uses an ORDER BY clause.

Try It Out: Altering the Order

1. Clear the query window in Query Editor and set the display option back to showing a grid by pressing Ctrl+D. Once complete, enter the following code into the Query Editor pane. This will return the data in the ascending (the default) order of the cleared balance of our customers.

```
SELECT LEFT(CustomerFirstName + ' ' + CustomerLastName,50) AS 'Name',
ClearedBalance Balance
FROM CustomerDetails.Customers
ORDER BY Balance
```

2. Execute the code; this will produce the results shown in Figure 8-30.

	Name	Balance
1	Julie Dewson	53.32
2	Robin Dewson	200.00
3	Jack Mason	437.97
4	Kirsty Hull	1266.00
5	Bernie McGee	6653.11

Figure 8-30. *Altering the order by balance*

3. We can also complete the same query, but have the cleared balance in descending order rather than ascending order. This is simply done by placing DESC after the column name. Change your code as detailed here:

```
SELECT LEFT(CustomerFirstName + ' ' + CustomerLastName,50) AS 'Name',
ClearedBalance Balance
FROM CustomerDetails.Customers
ORDER BY Balance DESC
```

4. Execute the code; this will produce the results shown in Figure 8-31.

	Name	Balance
1	Bernie McGee	6653.11
2	Kirsty Hull	1266.00
3	Jack Mason	437.97
4	Robin Dewson	200.00
5	Julie Dewson	53.32

Figure 8-31. *Making the order in descending sequence*

The LIKE Operator

It is possible to use more advanced techniques for finding records where a mathematical operation doesn't quite fit; for example, say someone is trying to track down a customer, but doesn't know the customer's full name or does know the first part of his or her surname but doesn't know how to spell the full name.

Suppose you know that the surname ends in "Glynn" as in the first customer we added, but you don't know if it starts with Mc, Mac, or even M. So how would this be put into a query? There is a keyword that you can use as part of the WHERE statement, called LIKE. This will use pattern matching to find the relevant rows within a SQL Server table using the information provided.

The LIKE operator can come with one of four operators, which are used alongside string values that you want to find. Each of the four operators is detailed in the following list. They can be used together, and using one does not exclude using any others.

▓**Note** LIKE is NOT case sensitive unless you have the SQL Server instance set to a collation that is case sensitive.

- %: This would be placed at the end and/or the beginning of a string. The best way to describe this is through an example; if you were searching the customers who had the letter "a" within their surname, you would search for "%a%", which would look for the letter "a," ignoring any letters before and after the letter "a", and just checking for that letter within the first name column.

- _: This looks at a string, but only for a single character before or after the position of the underscore. Therefore, looking in the first name column for "_a" would return any customer who has two letters in his or her first name where the second letter is an "a." In our example, no records would be returned. However, if you combined this with the % sign and searched for "_a%," then you would get back Jason Atkins, Ian McMahon, and Ian Prentice. You would not get back Vic McGlynn, because "a" is not the second letter.

- [ ]: This lets you specify a number of values or a range of values to look for. For example, if you were looking in the player's first name for the letters "c-f," you would use LIKE "%[c-f]%".

- [^...]: Similar to the preceding option, this one lists those items that do not have values within the range specified.

The best way to learn how to use LIKE is to see an example.

Try It Out: The LIKE Operator

1. We are going to try and find Bernie McGee via the CustomerLastName column. We know the name ends with Gee. The code that follows will search all of the customer rows looking for anything prefixing Gee.

```
SELECT CustomerFirstName + ' ' + CustomerLastName
FROM CustomerDetails.Customers
WHERE CustomerLastName LIKE '%Gee'
```

2. Execute the code; this will give the results shown in Figure 8-32.

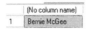

Figure 8-32. *Using the LIKE operator*

3. We can also go to extremes using the LIKE operator—for example, seeing which players have the letter "n" anywhere in their name. The code for this is shown here:

```
SELECT CustomerFirstName + ' ' + CustomerLastName AS [Name]
FROM CustomerDetails.Customers
WHERE CustomerFirstName + ' ' + CustomerLastName LIKE '%n%'
```

4. When you execute this, you should get the results shown in Figure 8-33: four customers are returned, as they have an "n" somewhere in their name.

Figure 8-33. *Using LIKE to search for customers with "n" in their name*

5. Why would we want to go to such lengths? Would it not have been possible to use the Name alias, which is a combination of the first name and last name columns? Well, unfortunately not—the code we might expect to use would look something like the following:

```
SELECT CustomerFirstName + ' ' + CustomerLastName AS [Name]
FROM CustomerDetails.Customers
WHERE [Name] LIKE '%n%'
```

6. Execute this code. Instead of the success messages that we have become used to, an error message will be returned. We can only search on real column names, not aliases.

```
Msg 207, Level 16, State 1, Line 3
Invalid column name 'Name'.
```

▓**Note** There may be times that you'll want to take data from a table in one database on one server and insert the data into another table in another database on another server. A typical scenario might be when data has been inadvertantly deleted, but you have a backup on another database. By using a SELECT statement and many string actions, it is possible to build up a result set of INSERT statements. You can then store these to a text file, which you can use to run against in another database. An short code example would be:

```
SELECT "INSERT (Column1) VALUES ("'+column1+"'") FROM Table1
```

Creating Data: SELECT INTO

The topic discussed in this section is quite an advanced area to be getting into, but it's not too advanced to be covered within this book. It is possible to create a new table within a database by using the INTO keyword, like that found in INSERT INTO, within a SELECT statement, providing, of course, you have the right database permissions to create tables in the first place. First of all, it is necessary to clarify the syntax of how the SELECT INTO statement is laid out; we simply add the INTO clause after the column names, but before the FROM keyword. Although the following section of code shows just one table name, it is possible to create a new table from data from one or more tables.

```
SELECT *|column1,column2,...
INTO new_tablename
FROM tablename
```

The INTO clause is crucial to the success of the creation of the new table. The SELECT statement will fail if there is a table already in existence with the same name for the same table owner. This will be demonstrated within the example.

The table generated will consist of the columns returned from the built SELECT statement, whether that is all the columns from the table mentioned within the FROM statement or a subset. The new table will also contain only the rows returned from the SELECT statement. To clarify, this command is creating a new table using the structure within the SELECT statement. There will be no keys, constraints, relationships, or in fact any other facet of SQL Server, except a new table. Hence, creating tables using SELECT...INTO should only be done with care.

Two tables can exist with the same name within a database, providing that they have different schemas. The tables in ApressFinancial all have the database owner as their owner, but it is possible for a CustomerDetails.Customers table to exist for an owner like VMcGlynn.

▓**Note** Although possible, having two tables of the same name but different owners is *not* recommended, as it causes confusion.

Let's look at the INTO statement in action.

Try It Out: SELECT INTO

1. In an empty Query Editor window, enter the following code:

   ```
   SELECT CustomerFirstName + ' ' + CustomerLastName AS [Name],
   ClearedBalance,UnclearedBalance
   INTO CustTemp
   FROM CustomerDetails.Customers
   ```

2. Execute the code. This will return the following message in the results pane:

```
(5 row(s) affected)
```

---

3. If we now move to Object Explorer on the left-hand side (if Object Explorer is no longer there, press F8) and complete a refresh, you should see a new table in the expanded Tables node, called dbo.CustTemp, as shown in Figure 8-34.

Figure 8-34. *New table created with SELECT INTO*

You should use the INTO clause with care. For instance, in this example, security has not been set up for the table, and we are also creating tables within our database that have not been through any normalization or development life cycle. It is also very easy to fill up a database with these tables if we are not careful. However, it is a useful and handy method for taking a backup of a table and then working on that backup while testing out any queries that might modify the data. Do ensure, though, that there is enough space within the database before building the table if you do use this technique.

■**Note** It is best to avoid using SELECT INTO in a production environment unless you really do need to keep the table permanently. If you do need to build a temporary table, then you may wish to use tempdb by writing your INTO clause as INTO tempdb..CustTemp.

Who Can Add, Delete, and Select Data

In this chapter, we inserted a certain amount of data into tables. All went well, and the data was inserted and selected easily. This was due to using the same connection that created the database. This does not mean that anyone who has access to our database could also add data as easily as we can. In Chapter 1, we set up several different users for the system. To recap, here are the users and their authority:

- *RDewson*: Administrator/database owner
- *JThakur*: Database owner
- *VMcGlynn*: Administrator
- *sa*: Administrator, SQL Server's default system administrator login

We want to prove that not all users can or should be able to do anything against our data. If any new user is created and given authority to connect to ApressFinancial, then providing this user is not an administrator on the local machine, he or she will not be able to view, insert, or delete any data. We do have a limited user in JThakur, although we did give this user db_owner rights earlier in the book to demonstrate his connection. This was a short-term solution that is now no longer is valid.

We need to refine this user so that we can restrict exactly what the user can do. In the following example, we will remove the db_owner role and give JThakur SELECT permissions on the ShareDetails.Shares table only. You will then see this in action.

Try It Out: Refining Permissions

1. Within Object Explorer, expand the Security node, and then the Users node. Find FAT-BELLY\JThakur, right-click it, and select Properties.

2. This will bring up the Database User dialog box. As shown in Figure 8-35, deselect the db_owner role that you will see as being checked.

Figure 8-35. *Removing database owner role*

3. Move to the Securables options for this user. In this area, shown in Figure 8-36, it is possible to define the exact privileges that this user can have, and can even pass on to other users. At present, the options are blank, but we can add objects by clicking the Add button.

Figure 8-36. *Securables tab, preparing to add objects*

4. This brings up the Add Objects dialog box. We want to refine who we are going to give the SELECT privilege to in the ShareDetails schema. Select this schema in the combo box as shown in Figure 8-37 and click OK.

Figure 8-37. *Defining only the ShareDetails schema*

5. When we return to the Securables dialog box, as shown in Figure 8-38, we will see two tables defined: ShareDetails.SharePrices and ShareDetails.Shares. Below that is a list of Explicit Permissions, which at the moment reflects the ShareDetails.SharePrices table. Nothing is selected; therefore, at present, if we applied the actions performed up to this point, JThakur would be unable to perform anything on this table (or any other table, as we had removed db_owner).

Figure 8-38. *Detailing the ShareDetails schema objects*

6. Change the Securables list to the ShareDetails.Shares table. Then in the Explicit Permissions area grant Select permissions by checking the check box as shown in Figure 8-39. I will explain this section in more detail shortly. Once done, click OK, which will then apply these changes to JThakur.

Figure 8-39. *Allowing the user to only select from ShareDetails.Shares*

7. Now switch to JThakur on your computer, and connect to SQL Server 2008. Create a new Query Editor window. If you do a SELECT * FROM ShareDetails.Shares, then you will get a list of the shares that exist. This is because you have SELECT permissions. However, if you try to INSERT some data, as shown in Figure 8-40, then you will see an error.

▓**Note** You may find that JThakur cannot log on. If this is the case, then executing the following code will allow JThakur to connect:

```
USE [master]
GO
CREATE LOGIN [FAT-BELLY\JThakur] FROM WINDOWS
WITH DEFAULT_DATABASE=[ApressFinancial]
GO
```

```
insert into ShareDetails.Shares (ShareDesc, ShareTickerId, CurrentPrice)
Values ('Test Share','TS',1)
```

🔲 Messages

```
Msg 229, Level 14, State 5, Line 2
INSERT permission denied on object 'Shares', database 'ApressFinancial', schema 'ShareDetails'.
```

Figure 8-40. *JThakur cannot insert data.*

There are three different options in the Securables dialog box for explicit permissions. These are GRANT, WITH GRANT, and DENY. Although we are looking at tables here, the same options are possible with other objects that we come across within SQL Server.

- GRANT: This grants the user or role access on that action on the defined table.

- WITH GRANT: This also grants the user or role access on that action on the defined table. However, anyone with this option can also pass on the permission to other users or roles.

- DENY: This explicitly denies any user or role the action against the table.

By setting up different roles and placing users in those roles, you should now know which users can access the data and how to set up groups of users to protect your data. Of course, it is normal practice to set up several roles within your database for each area of the business. There would be a role for supervisors, perhaps another for line managers, another for directors, and so on. It all depends on your database and the solution you are providing as to how many different roles are required. But from this, it is simpler to control access to the data.

Updating Data

Now that data has been inserted into our database, and you have seen how to retrieve this information, it is time to look at how to modify the data, referred to as **updating the data**, and the different methods of deletion.

Ensuring that you update the right data at the right time is crucial to maintaining data integrity. You will find that when updating data, and also when removing or inserting data, it is best to group this work as a single, logical unit, called a **transaction**, thereby ensuring that if an error does occur, it is still possible to return the data back to its original state. This section describes how a transaction works and how to incorporate transactions within your code. When looking at transactions, we will only be taking an overview of them. We will look at the basics of a transaction and how it can affect the data.

Deleting data can take one of two forms. The first is where a deletion of the data is logged in the transaction log. This means that if there is a failure of some sort, the deletion can be backed out. The second is where the deletion of the data is minimally logged. Knowing when to use each of these actions can improve performance of deletions.

This discussion aims to ensure that you

- Know the syntax of the UPDATE command

- Are competent at updating data within a SQL Server table

- Are aware of transactions and how to use them effectively within SQL Server

- Understand the dangers when transactions are nested

- Know the syntax for the DELETE command

- Know how to use this command in T-SQL

- Are aware of the pitfalls of the TRUNCATE command

First of all, let's take a look at the syntax for the UPDATE command.

The UPDATE Command

The UPDATE command will update columns of information on rows within a single table returned from a query that can include selection and join criteria. The syntax of the UPDATE command has similarities to the SELECT command, which makes sense, as it has to look for specific rows to update, just as the SELECT statement looks for rows to retrieve. You will also find that before doing updates, especially more complex updates, you need to build up a SELECT statement first and then transfer the JOIN and WHERE details in to the UPDATE statement. The syntax that follows is in its simplest form. Once you become more experienced, the UPDATE command can become just as complex and versatile as the SELECT statement.

```
UPDATE
    [ TOP ( expression ) [ PERCENT ] ]
    [[ server_name . database_name . schema_name .
    | database_name .[ schema_name ] .
    | schema_name .]
table_or_viewname
    SET
        { column_name = { expression | DEFAULT | NULL }
        | column_name { .WRITE ( expression , @Offset , @Length ) }
        | @variable = expression
        | @variable = column = expression [ ,...n ]
        } [ ,...n ]
    [FROM { <table_source> } [ ,...n ] ]
    [ WHERE { <search_condition>]
```

The first set of options we know from the SELECT statement. The tablename clause is simply the name of the table on which to perform the UPDATE. Moving on to the next line of the syntax, we reach the SET clause. It is in this clause that any updates to a column take place. One or more columns can be updated at any one time, but each column to be updated must be separated by a comma.

When updating a column, there are four choices that can be made for data updates. This can be through a direct value setting, a section of a value setting providing that the recipient column is varchar, nvarchar, or varbinary, the value from a variable, or a value from another column, even from another table. We can even have mathematical functions or variable manipulations included in the right-hand clause, have concatenated columns, or have manipulated the contents through STRING, DATE, or any other function. Providing that the end result sees the left-hand side having the same data type as the right-hand side, the update will then be successful. As a result, we cannot place a character value into a numeric data type field without converting the character to a numeric value.

If we are updating a column with a value from another column, the only value that it is possible to use is the value from the same row of information in another column, provided this column has an appropriate data type. When we say "same row," remember that when tables are joined together, this means that values from these joined tables can also be used as they are within the same row of information. Also, the expression could also be the result of a subquery.

The FROM table source clause will define the table(s) used to find the data to perform the update on the table defined next to the UPDATE command. Like SELECT statements, it is possible to create JOIN statements; however, you must define the table you are updating within the FROM clause.

Finally, the WHERE condition is exactly as in the SELECT command, and can be used in exactly the same way. Note that omitting the WHERE clause will mean the UPDATE statement will affect every row in the table.

Updating Data Within Query Editor

To demonstrate the UPDATE command, the first update to the data will be to change the name of a customer, replicating when someone changes his or her name due to marriage or deed, for example. This uses the UPDATE command in its simplest form, by locating a single record and updating a single column.

Try It Out: Updating a Row of Data

1. Ensure that Query Editor is running and that you are logged in with an account that can perform updates. In the Query Editor pane, enter the following UPDATE command:

```
USE ApressFinancial
GO
UPDATE CustomerDetails.Customers
SET CustomerLastName = 'Brodie'
WHERE CustomerId = 1
```

2. It is as simple as that! Now that the code is entered, execute the code, and you should then see a message like this:

```
(1 row(s) affected)
```

3. Now enter a SELECT statement to check that Robin Dewson is now Robin Brodie. For your convenience, here's the statement, and the results are shown in Figure 8-41:

```
SELECT * FROM CustomerDetails.Customers
WHERE CustomerId = 1
```

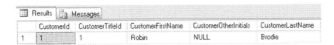

Figure 8-41. *Robin Dewson is now Robin Brodie.*

4. Now here's a little trick that you should know, if you haven't stumbled across it already. If you check out Figure 8-42, you will see that the UPDATE code is still in the Query Editor pane, as is the SELECT statement. No, we aren't going to perform the UPDATE again! If you highlight the line with the SELECT statement by holding down the left mouse button and dragging the mouse, then only the highlighted code will run when you execute the code again.

Figure 8-42. *How to execute only specific code*

Note On executing the highlighted code, you should only see the values returned for the SELECT statement as we saw previously, and no results saying that an update has been performed.

5. It is also possible to update data using information from another column within the table, or with the value from a variable. This next example will demonstrate how to update a row of information using the value within a variable, and a column from the same table. Notice how although the record will be found using the CustomerLastName column, the UPDATE command will also update that column with a new value. Enter the following code and then execute it:

```
DECLARE @ValueToUpdate VARCHAR(30)
SET @ValueToUpdate = 'McGlynn'
UPDATE CustomerDetails.Customers
   SET CustomerLastName = @ValueToUpdate,
       ClearedBalance = ClearedBalance + UnclearedBalance ,
       UnclearedBalance = 0
 WHERE CustomerLastName = 'Brodie'
```

6. You should then see the following output:

```
(1 row(s) affected)
```

7. Now let's check what has happened. You may be thinking that the update has not happened because you are altering the column that is being used to find the record, but this is not so. The record is found, then the update occurs, and then the record is written back to the table. Once the record is retrieved for updating, there is no need for that value to be kept. Just check that the update occurred by entering and executing the following code:

```
SELECT CustomerFirstName, CustomerLastName,
ClearedBalance, UnclearedBalance
FROM CustomerDetails.Customers
WHERE CustomerId = 1
```

You should now see the alteration in place, as shown in Figure 8-43.

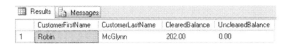

Figure 8-43. *Updating multiple columns*

8. Now let's move on to updating columns in which the data types don't match. SQL Server does a pretty good job when it can to ensure the update occurs, and these following examples will demonstrate how well SQL Server copes with updating an integer data type with a value in a varchar data type. The first example will demonstrate where a varchar value will successfully update a column defined as integer. Enter the following code:

```
DECLARE @WrongDataType VARCHAR(20)
SET @WrongDataType = '4311.22'
UPDATE CustomerDetails.Customers
    SET ClearedBalance = @WrongDataType
WHERE CustomerId = 1
```

9. Execute the code; you should see the following message when you do:

```
(1 row(s) affected)
```

10. The value 4311.22 has been placed into the ClearedBalance column for CustomerId 1. SQL Server has performed an internal data conversion (known as an implicit data type conversion) and has come up with a money data type from the value within varchar, as this is what the column expects, and therefore can successfully update the column. Here is the output as proof:

```
SELECT CustomerFirstName, CustomerLastName,
ClearedBalance, UnclearedBalance
FROM CustomerDetails.Customers
WHERE CustomerId = 1
```

Figure 8-44 shows the results of updating the column.

	CustomerFirstName	CustomerLastName	ClearedBalance	UnclearedBalance
1	Robin	McGlynn	4311.22	0.00

Figure 8-44. *Updating a column with internal data conversion*

11. However, in this next example, the data type that SQL Server will come up with is a numeric data type. When we try to alter an integer-based data type, bigint, with this value, which we can find in the AddressId column, the UPDATE does not take place. Enter the following code:

```
DECLARE @WrongDataType VARCHAR(20)
SET @WrongDataType = '2.0'
UPDATE CustomerDetails.Customers
    SET AddressId = @WrongDataType
WHERE CustomerId = 1
```

12. Now execute the code. Notice when we do that SQL Server generates an error message informing you of the problem. Hence, never leave data conversions to SQL Server to perform. Try to get the same data type updating the same data type. We look at how to convert data within Chapter 12.

```
Msg 8114, Level 16, State 5, Line 3
Error converting data type varchar to bigint.
```

Updating data can be very straightforward, as the preceding examples have demonstrated. Where at all possible, use a unique identifier—for example, the `CustomerId`—when trying to find a customer, rather than a name. There can be multiple rows for the same name or other type of criteria, but by using the unique identifier, you can be sure of using the right record every time. To place this in a production scenario, we would have a Windows-based graphical system that would allow you to find details of customers by their name, address, or account number. Once you found the right customer, instead of keeping those details to find other related records, you would keep a record of the unique identifier value instead.

Getting back to the `UPDATE` command and how it works, first of all SQL Server will filter out from the table the first record that meets the criteria of the `WHERE` statement. The data modifications are then made, and SQL Server moves on to try to find the second row matching the `WHERE` statement. This process is repeated until all the rows that meet the `WHERE` condition are modified. Therefore, if using a unique identifier, SQL Server will only update one row, but if the `WHERE` statement looks for rows that have a `CustomerLastName` of Dewson, multiple rows could be updated (Robin and Julie). So choose your row selection criteria for updates carefully.

But what if you didn't want the update to occur immediately? There will be times when you will want to perform an update, and then check that the update is correct before finally committing the changes to the table. Or when doing the update, you'll want to check for errors or unexpected data updates. This is where transactions come in, and these are covered next.

Transactions

A **transaction** is a method through which developers can define a unit of work logically or physically that, when it completes, leaves the database in a consistent state. A transaction forms a single unit of work, which must pass the ACID test before it can be classified as a transaction. The ACID test is an acronym for Atomicity, Consistency, Isolation, and Durability:

- *Atomicity*: In its simplest form, all data modifications within the transaction must be both accepted and inserted successfully into the database, or none of the modifications will be performed.

- *Consistency*: Once the data has been successfully applied, or rolled back to the original state, all the data must remain in a consistent state, and the data must still maintain its integrity.

- *Isolation*: Any modification in one transaction must be isolated from any modifications in any other transaction. Any transaction should see data from any other transaction either in its original state or once the second transaction has completed. It is impossible to see the data in an intermediate state.

- *Durability*: Once a transaction has finished, all data modifications are in place and can only be modified by another transaction or unit of work. Any system failure (hardware or software) will not remove any changes applied.

Transactions within a database are a very important topic, but also one that requires a great deal of understanding. This chapter covers the basics of transactions only. To really do justice to this area, we would have to deal with some very complex and in-depth scenarios, covering all manner of areas such as triggers, nesting transactions, and transaction logging, which is beyond the scope of this book.

A transaction can be placed around any data manipulation, whether it is an update, insertion, or deletion, and can cater to one row or many rows, and also many different commands. There is no need to place a transaction around a `SELECT` statement unless you are doing a `SELECT...INTO`, which is of course modifying data. This is because a transaction is only required when data manipulation occurs such that changes will either be committed to the table or discarded. A transaction could cover several UPDATE, DELETE, or INSERT commands, or indeed a mixture of all three. However, there is one very large warning that goes with using transactions (see the Caution note).

▨**Caution** Be aware that when creating a transaction, you will be keeping a hold on the whole table, pages of data, or specific rows of information in question, and depending upon how your SQL Server database is set up to lock data during updates, you could be stopping others from updating any information, and you could even cause a **deadlock**, also known as a **deadly embrace**. If a deadlock occurs, SQL Server will choose one of the deadlocks and kill the process; there is no way of knowing which process SQL Server will select.

A deadlock is where two separate data manipulations, in different transactions, are being performed at the same time. However, each transaction is waiting for the other to finish the update before it can complete its update. Neither manipulation can be completed because each is waiting for the other to finish. A deadlock occurs, and it can (and will) lock the tables and database in question. So, for example, transaction 1 is updating the customers table followed by the customer transactions table. Transaction 2 is updating the customer transactions table followed by the customers table. A lock would be placed on the customers table while those updates were being done by transaction 1. A lock would be placed on the customer transactions table by transaction 2. Transaction 1 could not proceed because of the lock by transaction 2, and transaction 2 could not proceed due to the lock created by transaction 1. Both transactions are "stuck." So it is crucial to keep the order of table updates the same, especially where both could be running at the same time.

It is also advisable to keep transactions as small, and as short, as possible, and under no circumstances hold onto a lock for more than a few seconds. We can do this by keeping the processing within a transaction to as few lines of code as possible, and then either roll back (that is, cancel) or commit the transaction to the database as quickly as possible within code. With every second that you hold a lock through a transaction, you are increasing the potential of trouble happening. In a production environment, with every passing millisecond that you hold on to a piece of information through a lock, you are increasing the chances of someone else trying to modify the same piece of information at the same time and the possibility of the problems that would then arise.

There are two parts that make up a transaction: the start of the transaction and the end of the transaction, where you decide if you want to commit the changes or revert back to the original state. We will now look at the definition of the start of the transaction, and then the T-SQL commands required to commit or roll back the transaction. The basis of this section is that only one transaction is in place, and that you have no nested transactions. Nested transactions are much more complex and should only really be dealt with once you are proficient with SQL Server. The statements we are going through in the upcoming text assume a single transaction; the COMMIT TRAN section changes slightly when the transaction is nested.

BEGIN TRAN

The T-SQL command, BEGIN TRAN, denotes the start of the transaction processing. From this point on, until the transaction is ended with either COMMIT TRAN or ROLLBACK TRAN, any data modification statements will form part of the transaction.

It is also possible to suffix the BEGIN TRAN command with a name of up to 32 characters in length. If you name your transaction, it is not necessary to use the name when issuing a ROLLBACK TRAN or a COMMIT TRAN command. The name is there for clarity of the code only.

COMMIT TRAN

The COMMIT TRAN command commits the data modifications to the database permanently, and there is no going back once this command is executed. This function should only be executed when all changes to the database are ready to be committed.

ROLLBACK TRAN

If you wish to remove all the database changes that have been completed since the beginning of the transaction—say, for example, because an error had occurred—then you could issue a ROLLBACK TRAN command.

So, if you were to start a transaction with BEGIN TRAN and then issue an INSERT that succeeds, and then perhaps an UPDATE that fails, you could issue a ROLLBACK TRAN to roll back the transaction as a whole. As a result, you roll back not only the UPDATE changes, but also, because they form part of the same transaction, the changes made by the INSERT, even though that particular operation was successful.

To reiterate, keep transactions small and short. Never leave a session with an open transaction by having a BEGIN TRAN with no COMMIT TRAN or ROLLBACK TRAN. Ensure that you do not cause a deadly embrace.

If you issue a BEGIN TRAN, then you *must* issue a COMMIT TRAN or ROLLBACK TRAN transaction as quickly as possible; otherwise, the transaction will stay around until the connection is terminated.

Locking Data

The whole area of locking data, how locks are held, and how to avoid problems with them, is a very large complex area and not for the fainthearted. However, it is necessary to be aware of locks, and at least have a small amount of background knowledge about them so that when you design your queries, you stand a chance of avoiding problems.

The basis of locking is to allow one transaction to update data, knowing that if it has to roll back any changes, no other transaction has modified the data since the first transaction did.

To explain this with an example, let's say you have a transaction that updates the CustomerDetails. Customers table and then moves on to update the TransactionDetails.Transactions table, but hits a problem when updating the TransactionDetails.Transactions table. The transaction must be safe in the knowledge that it is only rolling back the changes it made and not changes made by another transaction. Therefore, until all the table updates within the transaction are either successfully completed or have been rolled back, the transaction will keep hold of any data inserted, modified, or deleted.

However, one problem with this approach is that SQL Server may not just hold the data that the transaction has modified. Keeping a lock on the data that has just been modified is called **row-level locking**. On the other hand, SQL Server may be set up to lock the database, which is known as **database-level locking**, found in areas such as backups and restores. The other levels in between are row, page, and table locking, and so you could lock a large resource, depending on the task being performed.

This is about as deep as I will take this discussion on locks, so as not to add any confusion or create a problematic situation. SQL Server handles locks automatically, but it is possible to make locking more efficient by developing an effective understanding of the subject and then customizing the locks within your transactions.

Updating Data: Using Transactions

Now, what if, in the first update query of this chapter, we had made a mistake or an error occurred? For example, say we chose the wrong customer, or even worse, omitted the WHERE statement, and therefore all the records were updated. These are unusual errors, but quite possible. More common errors could result from where more than one data modification has to take place and succeed, and the first one succeeds but a subsequent modification fails. By using a transaction, we would have had the chance to correct any mistakes easily, and could then revert to a consistent state. Of course, this next example is nice and simple, but by working through it, the subject of transactions will hopefully become a little easier to understand and appreciate.

Try It Out: Using a Transaction

1. Make sure Query Editor is running for this first example, which will demonstrate COMMIT TRAN in action. There should be no difference from an UPDATE without any transaction processing, as it will execute and update the data successfully. However, this should prove to be a valuable exercise, as it will also demonstrate the naming of a transaction. Enter the following code:

```
SELECT 'Before',ShareId,ShareDesc,CurrentPrice
  FROM ShareDetails.Shares
 WHERE ShareId = 3
BEGIN TRAN ShareUpd
UPDATE ShareDetails.Shares
   SET CurrentPrice = CurrentPrice * 1.1
 WHERE ShareId = 3
COMMIT TRAN
SELECT 'After',ShareId,ShareDesc,CurrentPrice
  FROM ShareDetails.Shares
 WHERE ShareId = 3
```

Notice in the preceding code that COMMIT TRAN does not use the name associated with BEGIN TRAN. The label after BEGIN TRAN is simply that, a label, and it performs no functionality. It is therefore not necessary to then link up with a similarly labeled COMMIT TRAN.

2. Execute the code. Figure 8-45 shows the results, which list out the Shares table before and after the transaction.

	[No column name]	ShareId	ShareDesc	CurrentPrice
1	Before	3	NetRadio Inc	29.79000

	[No column name]	ShareId	ShareDesc	CurrentPrice
1	After	3	NetRadio Inc	32.76900

Figure 8-45. *Updating with a transaction label and a COMMIT TRAN*

3. We are now going to work through a ROLLBACK TRAN. We will take this one step at a time so that you fully understand and follow the processes involved. Note in the following code that the WHERE statement has been commented out with --. By having the WHERE statement commented out, hopefully you'll have already guessed that every record in the ShareDetails.Shares table is going to be updated. The example needs you to execute all the code at once, so enter the following code into your Query Editor pane, and then execute it. Note we have three SELECT statements this time—before, during, and after the transaction processing.

```
SELECT 'Before',ShareId,ShareDesc,CurrentPrice
  FROM ShareDetails.Shares
-- WHERE ShareId = 3
BEGIN TRAN ShareUpd
UPDATE ShareDetails.Shares
```

```
        SET CurrentPrice = CurrentPrice * 1.1
-- WHERE ShareId = 3
SELECT 'Within the transaction',ShareId,ShareDesc,CurrentPrice
  FROM ShareDetails.Shares
ROLLBACK TRAN
SELECT 'After',ShareId,ShareDesc,CurrentPrice
  FROM ShareDetails.Shares
-- WHERE ShareId = 3
```

4. The results, as you see in Figure 8-46, show us exactly what has happened. Take a moment to look over these results. The first list shows the full set of rows in the ShareDetails.Shares table prior to our UPDATE. The middle recordset shows us the BEGIN transaction where we have updated every share, and the final listing shows the data restored back to its original state via a ROLLBACK TRAN.

	(No column name)	ShareId	ShareDesc	CurrentPrice
1	Before	1	ACME'S HOMEBAKE COOKIES INC	2.34125
2	Before	2	FAT-BELLY.COM	45.20000
3	Before	3	NetRadio Inc	32.76900
4	Before	4	Texas Oil Industries	0.45500
5	Before	5	London Bridge Club	1.46000

	(No column name)	ShareId	ShareDesc	CurrentPrice
1	Within the transaction	1	ACME'S HOMEBAKE COOKIES INC	2.57538
2	Within the transaction	2	FAT-BELLY.COM	49.72000
3	Within the transaction	3	NetRadio Inc	36.04590
4	Within the transaction	4	Texas Oil Industries	0.50050
5	Within the transaction	5	London Bridge Club	1.60600

	(No column name)	ShareId	ShareDesc	CurrentPrice
1	After	1	ACME'S HOMEBAKE COOKIES INC	2.34125
2	After	2	FAT-BELLY.COM	45.20000
3	After	3	NetRadio Inc	32.76900
4	After	4	Texas Oil Industries	0.45500
5	After	5	London Bridge Club	1.46000

Figure 8-46. *Updating with transaction label and a ROLLBACK TRAN*

Nested Transactions

Let's look at one last example before moving on. It is possible to nest transactions inside one another. We touch on this enough for you to have a good understanding on nested transactions, but this is not a complete coverage, as it can get very complex and messy if you involve save points, stored procedures, triggers, and so on. The aim of this section is to give you an understanding of the basic but crucial points of how nesting transactions work.

Nested transactions can occur in a number of different scenarios. For example, you could have a transaction in one set of code in a stored procedure, which calls a second stored procedure that also has a transaction. We will look at a simpler scenario where we just keep the transactions in one set of code.

What you need to be clear about is how the ROLLBACK and COMMIT TRAN commands work in a nested transaction. First of all, let's see what we mean by nesting a simple transaction. The syntax is shown here, and you can see that two BEGIN TRAN statements occur before you get to a COMMIT or a ROLLBACK:

```
BEGIN TRAN
    Statements
    BEGIN TRAN
        Statements
    COMMIT|ROLLBACK TRAN
COMMIT|ROLLBACK TRAN
```

As each transaction commences, SQL Server increments a running count of transactions it holds in a system variable called @@TRANCOUNT. Therefore, as each BEGIN TRAN is executed, @@TRANCOUNT increases by 1. As each COMMIT TRAN is executed, @@TRANCOUNT decreases by 1. It is not until @@TRANCOUNT is at a value of 1 that you can actually commit the data to the database. The code that follows might help you to understand this a bit more.

Enter and execute this code and take a look at the output, which should resemble Figure 8-47. The first BEGIN TRAN increases @@TRANCOUNT by 1, as does the second BEGIN TRAN. The first COMMIT TRAN marks the changes to be committed, but does not actually perform the changes because @@TRANCOUNT is 2. It simply creates the correct BEGIN/COMMIT TRAN nesting and reduces @@TRANCOUNT by 1. The second COMMIT TRAN will succeed and will commit the data, as @@TRANCOUNT is 1.

```
BEGIN TRAN ShareUpd
    SELECT '1st TranCount',@@TRANCOUNT
    BEGIN TRAN ShareUpd2
        SELECT '2nd TranCount',@@TRANCOUNT
        COMMIT TRAN ShareUpd2
    SELECT '3rd TranCount',@@TRANCOUNT
COMMIT TRAN -- It is at this point that data modifications will be committed
SELECT 'Last TranCount',@@TRANCOUNT
```

	(No column name)	(No column name)
1	1st TranCount	1

	(No column name)	(No column name)
1	2nd TranCount	2

	(No column name)	(No column name)
1	3rd TranCount	1

	(No column name)	(No column name)
1	Last TranCount	0

Figure 8-47. *Showing the @@TRANCOUNT*

▓**Note** After the last COMMIT TRAN, @@TRANCOUNT is at 0. Any further instances of COMMIT TRAN or ROLLBACK TRAN will generate an error.

If in the code there is a ROLLBACK TRAN, then the data will immediately be rolled back no matter where you are within the nesting, and @@TRANCOUNT will be set to 0. Therefore, any further ROLLBACK TRAN or COMMIT TRAN instances will fail, so you do need to have error handling, which we look at in Chapter 11.

Try to avoid nesting transactions where possible, especially when one stored procedure calls another stored procedure within a transaction. It is not "wrong," but it does require a great deal of care.

Now that updating data has been completed, the only area of data manipulation left is row deletion, which we look at now.

Deleting Data

Deleting data can be considered very straightforward, especially compared to all of the other data manipulation functions covered previously, particularly transactions and basic SQL. However, mistakes made when deleting data are very hard to recover from. Therefore, you must treat deleting data with the greatest of care and attention to detail, and especially test any joins and filtering via a SELECT statement before running the delete operation.

Deleting data without the use of a transaction is almost a final act: the only way to get the data back is to reenter it, restore it from a backup, or retrieve the data from any audit tables that had the data stored in them when the data was created. Deleting data is not like using the recycle bin on a Windows machine: unless the data is within a transaction, it is lost. Keep in mind that even if you use a transaction, the data will be lost once the transaction is committed. That's why it's very important to back up your database before running any major data modifications.

This section of the chapter will demonstrate the DELETE T-SQL syntax and then show how to use this within Query Editor. It is also possible to delete records from the results pane within SQL Server Management Studio, which will also be demonstrated.

However, what about when you want to remove all the records within a table, especially when there could be thousands of records to remove? You will find that the DELETE command takes a very long time to run, as each row to delete is logged in the transaction log, thus allowing transactions to be rolled back. Luckily, there is a command for this scenario, called TRUNCATE, which is covered in the section "Truncating a Table" later in the chapter. However, caution should be exercised when using this command, and you'll see why later.

First of all, it is necessary to learn the simple syntax for the DELETE command for deleting records from a table. Really, things don't come much simpler than this.

DELETE Syntax

The DELETE command is very short and sweet. To run the command, simply state the table you wish to delete records from, as shown here:

```
DELETE
[FROM] tablename
WHERE where_condition
```

The FROM condition is optional, so your syntax could easily read

```
DELETE tablename
WHERE where_condition
```

There is nothing within this command that has not been covered in other chapters. The only area that really needs to be mentioned is that records can only be deleted from one table at a time, although when looking for rows to delete, you can join to several tables, as you can with SELECT and UPDATE.

Now that you've seen the DELETE syntax, let's dive right in with an example.

Using the DELETE Statement

Recall we created a table with the SELECT INTO command called CustTemp. Rather than delete data from the main tables created so far, we'll use this temporary table in this section of the book.

We'll use transactions a great deal here to avoid having to keep inserting data back into the table. It's a good idea to use transactions for any type of table modification in your application. Imagine that you're at the ATM and you are transferring money from your savings account to your checking account. During that process, a transaction built up of many actions is used to make sure that your money doesn't credit one system and not the other. If an error occurs, the entire transaction will roll back, and no money will move between the accounts.

Let's take a look at what happens if you were to run this statement:

```
BEGIN TRAN
    DELETE CustTemp
```

When this code runs, SQL Server opens a transaction and then tentatively deletes all the records from the CustTemp table. The records are not actually deleted until a COMMIT TRAN statement is issued. In the interim, though, SQL Server will place a lock on the rows of the table, or if this was a much larger table, SQL Server may decide that a table lock (locking the whole table to prevent other modifications) is better. Because of this lock, all users trying to modify data from this table will have to wait until a COMMIT TRAN or ROLLBACK TRAN statement has been issued and completed. If one is never issued, users will be blocked. This problem is one of a number of issues frequently encountered in applications when analyzing performance issues. Therefore, never have a BEGIN TRAN without a COMMIT TRAN or ROLLBACK TRAN.

So, time to start deleting records.

Try It Out: Deleting Records

1. Enter the following commands in an empty Query Editor pane. They remove all the records from our table within a transaction, prove the point by trying to list the rows, and then roll back the changes so that the records are put back into the table.

```
BEGIN TRAN
    SELECT * FROM CustTemp
    DELETE CustTemp
    SELECT * FROM CustTemp
ROLLBACK TRAN
SELECT * FROM CustTemp
```

2. Execute the code. You should see the results displayed in Figure 8-48. Notice that the number of records in the CustTemp table before the delete is five, then after the delete the record count is tentatively set to zero. Finally, after the rollback, it's set back to five. If we do not issue a ROLLBACK TRAN command in here, we would see zero records, but other connections would be blocked until we did.

Figure 8-48. *Deletion of all rows that were rolled back*

3. Let's take this a step further and only remove the last three records of the table. Again, this will be within a transaction. Alter the preceding code as indicated in the following snippet. Here we are using the TOP command to delete three random rows. This is not the best way to delete rows, as in virtually all cases you will want to control the deletion.

```
BEGIN TRAN
    SELECT * FROM CustTemp
    DELETE TOP (3) CustTemp
    SELECT * FROM CustTemp
ROLLBACK TRAN
SELECT * FROM CustTemp
```

4. Execute the code, which should produce the results shown in Figure 8-49.

Figure 8-49. *Deletion of three rows that were rolled back*

Truncating a Table

All delete actions caused by DELETE statements are recorded in the transaction log. Each time a record is deleted, a record is made of that fact. If you are deleting millions of records before committing your transaction, your transaction log can grow quickly. Recall from earlier in the chapter the discussions about transactions; now think about this a bit more. What if the table you are deleting from has thousands of records? That is a great deal of logging going on within the transaction log. But what if the deletion of these thousands of records is, in fact, cleaning out all the data from the table to start afresh? Or perhaps this is some sort of transient table? Performing a DELETE would seem to have a lot of overhead when you don't really need to keep a log of the data deletions anyway. If the action failed for whatever reason, you would simply retry removing the records a second time. This is where the TRUNCATE TABLE command comes into its own.

By issuing a TRUNCATE TABLE statement, you are instructing SQL Server to delete every record within a table, without any logging or transaction processing taking place. In reality, minimal data is logged about what data pages have been deallocated and therefore removed from the database. This is in contrast to a DELETE statement, which will only deallocate and remove the pages from the table if it can get sufficient locks on the table to do this. The deletion of the records can be almost instantaneous, and a great deal faster than using the DELETE command. This occurs not only because of the differences with what happens with the transaction log, but also because of how the data is locked at the time of deletion. Let's clarify this point before progressing.

When a DELETE statement is issued, each row that is to be deleted will be locked by SQL Server so that no modifications or other DELETE statements can attempt to work with that row. Deleting hundreds or thousands of rows is a large number of actions for SQL Server to perform, and it will take time to locate each row and place a lock against it. However, a TRUNCATE TABLE statement locks the whole table. This is one action that will prevent any data insertion, modification, or deletion from taking place.

> **Note** A TRUNCATE TABLE statement will delete data from a table with millions of records in only a few seconds, whereas using DELETE to remove all the records on the same table would take several minutes.

The syntax for truncating a table is simple:

```
TRUNCATE TABLE [{database.schema_name.}]table
```

> **Caution** Use the TRUNCATE TABLE statement with extreme caution: there is no going back after the transaction is committed outside of a transaction; you cannot change your mind. Also, every record is removed: you cannot use this command to selectively remove some of the records. If you are within a transaction, you can still use the ROLLBACK command.

One "side effect" to the TRUNCATE TABLE clause is that it reseeds any identity columns. For example, say that you have a table with an identity column that is currently at 2,000,000. After truncating the table, the first inserted piece of data will produce the value 1 (if the seed is set to 1). If you issue a DELETE command to delete the records from the table, the first piece of data inserted after the table contents have been deleted will produce a value of 2,000,001, even though this newly inserted piece of data may be the only record in the table!

One of the limitations with the TRUNCATE TABLE command is that you cannot issue it against tables that have foreign keys referencing them. For example, the Customers table has a foreign key referencing the Transactions table. If you try to issue the following command:

```
TRUNCATE TABLE CustomerDetails.Customers
```

you will receive the following error message:

```
Msg 4712, Level 16, State 1, Line 1
Cannot truncate table 'customers' because it is being referenced
by a FOREIGN KEY constraint.
```

Dropping a Table

Another way to quickly delete the data in a table is to just delete the table and re-create it. Don't forget that if you do this, you will need to also re-create any constraints, indexes, and foreign keys. When you do this, SQL Server will deallocate the table, which is minimally logged. To drop a table in SQL Server, issue the following command:

```
DROP TABLE table_name
```

As with TRUNCATE TABLE, DROP TABLE cannot be issued against a table that has a foreign key referencing it. In this situation, either the foreign key constraint referencing the table or the referencing table itself must first be dropped before it is possible to drop the original table.

Summary

This chapter has taken a look at how to insert and then retrieve data on a set of tables in the simplest form. Later in the book, we will return to retrieving data with more complex language as well as working with data from more than one table within the single query.

We have taken a look at NULL values and default values, and we've seen how to insert data within columns defined with these settings and constraints. You should also be comfortable with getting information from tables using different searching, filtering, and ordering criteria.

Updating data can go wrong, and does, especially when you are working in a live environment and you wish to update data that is in flux. In such a scenario, getting the correct rows of information to update and then actually updating them is akin to a fine art.

Therefore, surrounding any of your work with a transaction will prevent any costly and potentially irretrievable mistakes from taking place, so always surround data modifications or deletions with a transaction. With data inserts, it is not quite so critical that you surround your work with a transaction, although it is recommended. For example, if you are inserting data within a test environment and the data insertion is easily removed if you have part of the insertion wrong, then perhaps it's not overly critical to use a transaction; although to be safe, really and truly, I still recommend that you use a transaction.

Updating columns within a table is very straightforward. As long as the data type defined for the column to update is the same as, or is compatible with, the data type of the column, variable, or static value that is being used to update this column, then you will have no problem. For example, you can update a varchar column with char data type values. However, it is not possible to update an integer column with a varchar value that has a noninteger value without converting the varchar value to an integer. But don't be fooled, you can update a varchar with an integer or numeric data type.

The DELETE command in this chapter completes the commands for data retrieval and manipulation. From this point, SQL Server is your oyster, and there should be no stopping you now. Deleting data is a very straightforward process—perhaps too straightforward—and with no recycle bin, you really do have to take care. Having to reinstate data is a lot harder than having to remove records inserted incorrectly or changing back modifications completed in error.

Whenever deleting data (no matter how small the recordset is), it is strongly recommend that a transaction be used, as this chapter has demonstrated, and also that a SELECT statement be included to check your work.

Finally, the removal of every record within a table was also shown, along with the dire warnings if you got it wrong. Really, only use the TRUNCATE TABLE command in development or with the utmost extreme care within production.

So where can you go from here? The next chapter will look at views of data.

CHAPTER 9

■■■

Building a View

A view is a virtual table that, in itself, doesn't contain any data or information. All it contains is the query that the user defines when creating the view. You can think of a view as a query against one or more tables that is stored within the database. Views are used as a security measure by restricting users to certain columns or rows; as a method of joining data from multiple tables and presenting it as if it resides in one table; and by returning summary data instead of detailed data. Another use for a view is to provide a method of accessing the underlying data in a manner that provides the end user with a business layout. For example, you will see within this chapter the building of a view that shows customer details along with enriched transaction details, thus making it easier for anyone interrogating your data who has no knowledge of the underlying data model to access useful information.

Building a simple view is a straightforward process and can be completed in SQL Server Management Studio or a Query Editor pane using T-SQL within SQL Server. Each of these tools has two options to build a view, and this chapter will cover all four options so that you become conversant with building a view no matter which tool is currently at hand.

To give things a bit more bite in this chapter, a query within a query, known as a subquery, will also be demonstrated, along with how to build a subquery to create a column.

Finally, placing an index on a view can speed up data retrieval, but it also can give performance problems as well. An index on a view is not quite as straightforward as building an index on a table.

The aim of this chapter is to

- Make you aware of what a view is.

- Inform you as to how views can improve a database's security.

- Show how to encrypt your view so that the source tables accessed cannot be seen.

- Demonstrate building a view using

  - Management Studio View Designer

  - Management Studio Create a View Wizard

  - A Query Editor pane and T-SQL

- Show how to join two tables within a view.

- Demonstrate subqueries within a view.

- Build an index on a view and give the reasons as to why you would or would not do this.

Why a View?

There will be times when you'll want to group together data from more than one table, or perhaps only allow users to see specific information from a particular table, where some of the columns may contain sensitive or even irrelevant data. A view can take one or more columns from one or more tables and present this information to a user, without the user accessing the actual underlying tables. A view protects the data layer while allowing access to the data. All of these scenarios can be seen as the basis and reason for building a view rather than another method of data extraction. If you are familiar with Microsoft Access, views are similar to Access queries. Because a view represents data as if it were another table—a virtual table in fact—it is also possible to create a view of a view.

Let's take a look at how a view works. As you know, we have a customer table that holds information about our customers such as their first name, last name, account number, and balances. There will be times when you'll want your users to have access to only the first and last names, but not to the other sensitive data. This is where a view comes into play. You would create a view that returns only a customer's first and last name but no other information.

Creating a view can give a user enough information to satisfy a query he or she may have about data within a database without that user having to know any T-SQL commands. A view actually stores the query that creates it, and when you execute the view, the underlying query is the code that is being executed. The underlying code can be as complex as required, therefore leaving the end user with a simple SELECT * command to run with perhaps a small amount of filtering via a simple WHERE statement.

From a view, in addition to retrieving data, you can also modify the data that is being displayed, delete data, and in some situations, insert new data. There are several rules and limitations for deleting, modifying, and inserting data from multitable views, some of which will be covered in the "Indexing a View" section later in the chapter.

However, a view is not a tool for processing data using T-SQL commands, like a stored procedure is. A view is only able to hold one query at a time. Therefore, a view is more like a query than a stored procedure. Just as with a stored procedure or a query within a Query Editor pane, you can include tables from databases that are running on different servers. Providing the user ID has the necessary security credentials, it is possible to include tables from several databases.

So to summarize, a view is a virtual table created by a stored SQL statement that can span multiple tables. Views can be used as a method of security within your database, and they provide a simpler front end to a user querying the data.

Later in the chapter, you will see how to build a view and how all of these ideas are put into practice. Before we get to that, let's look in more depth at how a view can be used as a security vehicle.

Using Views for Security

Security is always an issue when building your database. So far, the book has covered the different database-provided roles, when to use them, how to set up different types of roles, and how useful they are. You also saw in Chapter 8 how to assign a user only SELECT rights and not any other rights such as INSERT. By restricting all users from accessing or modifying the data in the tables, you will then force everyone to use views and stored procedures to complete any data task. (There will be more on stored procedures in the next chapter.)

However, by taking a view on the data and assigning which role can have select access, update access, and so on, you are protecting not only the underlying tables, but also particular columns of data. This is all covered in the discussions involving security in this chapter.

Security encompasses not only the protection of data, but also the protection of your system. At some point as a developer, you will build a view and then someone else will come along and remove or alter a column from an underlying table that was used in the view. This causes problems; however, this chapter will show you how to get around this problem and secure the build of a view so that this sort of thing doesn't happen.

Imagine that you have a table holding specific security-sensitive information alongside general information—an example would be where you perhaps work for the licensing agency for driver's licenses and alongside the name and address, there is a column to define the number of fines that have had to be paid. As you can see, this is information that should not be viewed by all employees within the organization. So, what do you do?

The simplest answer is to create a view on the data where you exclude the columns holding the sensitive data. In this way, you can restrict access on the table to the bare minimum of roles or logins, and leave either a view or a stored procedure as the only method of data retrieval allowed. This way, the information returned is restricted to only those columns that a general user is allowed to see.

It is also possible to place a WHERE statement within a view to restrict the rows returned. This could be useful when you don't wish all employee salaries to be listed: perhaps excluding the salaries of the top executives would be advised!

All these methods give you, as a developer, a method for protecting the physical data lying in the base tables behind the views. Combine this with what you learned about roles and restricting table access, and you can really tighten the security surrounding your data. With more and more companies embracing initiatives like Sarbanes-Oxley, where security should be so tight a company can be defined as having secure data, views are a great method of getting toward this goal.

Another method of securing views is to encrypt the view definition, which we explore next.

Encrypting View Definitions

As well as restricting access to certain tables or columns within a database, views also give the option of encrypting the SQL query that is used to retrieve the data. Once a view is built and you are happy that it is functioning correctly, you would release that view to production; it is at this point that you would add the final area of security—you would encrypt the view.

The most common situation where you will find views encrypted is when the information returned by the view is of a privileged nature. To expand further, not only are you using a view to return specific information, you also don't wish anyone to see how that information was returned, for whatever reason. You would therefore encrypt the SQL code that makes up the view, which would mean that how the information was being returned would not be visible.

There is a downside to encrypting a view: once the process of encryption is completed, it is difficult to get back the details of the view. There are tools on the Internet that can decrypt an encrypted view. When you encrypt a view, the view definition is not processed via encryption algorithms, but is merely obfuscated—in other words, changed so that prying eyes cannot see the code. These tools can return the obfuscation back to the original code. Therefore, if you need to modify the view, you will find that it is awkward. Not only will you have to use a tool, but you will also have to delete the view and re-create it, as it will not be editable. So, if you build a view and encrypt it, you should make sure that you keep a copy of the source somewhere. This is why it is recommended that encrypted views should be used with care and really should only be placed in production, or at worst, in user testing.

Always keep a copy of the original view, before encryption, in the company's source-control system—for example, Visual SourceSafe—and make sure that regular backups are available.

Now that we have touched upon the security issues behind views, it is time to start creating views for the database solution that we are building together.

Creating a View: SQL Server Management Studio

The first task for us is to create a view using SQL Server Management Studio. This is perhaps the simplest solution, as it allows us to use drag-and-drop to build the view. This may be the slowest method for creating a new view, but it does give us the greatest visual flexibility for building the view, and this may also be the best method for dealing with views that already exist and require only minor modifications.

The View Designer can aid you in the design of a view or the modification of any view already built. For example, it can assist if you are trying to build a complex view from a simple view, or it can even be used as a trial-and-error tool while you are gaining your T-SQL knowledge.

However, enough of the background—let's take a look at how the View Designer works. In this example, we will be making a view of `ShareDetails.Shares`.

Try It Out: Creating a View in SQL Server Management Studio

1. Ensure that SQL Server Management Studio is running and that the `ApressFinancial` database is expanded.

2. Find the Views node, and right-click it—this brings up the pop-up menu shown in Figure 9-1; from there, select New View.

Figure 9-1. *Creating a new view*

3. The next screen you will see is the View Designer, with a modal dialog box on top presenting a list of tables that you can add to make the view. The background is pretty empty at the moment (move the dialog box around if you need to). It is within the View Designer that you will see all of the information required to build a view. There are no tables in the view at this time, so there is nothing for the View Designer to show. For those of you who are familiar with Access, you will see that the View Designer is similar to the Access Query Designer, only a bit more sophisticated! We want to add our table, so moving back to the modal dialog box, shown in Figure 9-2, select Shares (ShareDetails), click Add, and then click Close to remove the dialog box.

Figure 9-2. *Selecting the tables for your view*

4. Take a moment to see how the View Designer has changed, as illustrated in Figure 9-3. Notice that the background Query Designer area has been altered, the ShareDetails.Shares table has been added, and the beginnings of a SELECT statement now appear about two thirds of the way down the screen. By adding a table, the Query Designer is making a start to the view you wish to build.

Figure 9-3. *The basic view*

5. There are four separate parts to the View Designer, each of which can be switched on or off for viewing via the toolbar buttons on top. Take a look at these toolbar buttons, as shown close up in Figure 9-4. The first button brings up the top pane—the diagram pane—where you can see the tables involved in the view and can access them via the leftmost toolbar button. The next button accesses the criteria pane, where you can filter the information you want to display. The third button accesses the SQL pane, and the fourth button accesses the results pane. As with Query Editor, here you also have the ability to execute a query through the execute button (the one with the red exclamation point). The final button relates to verifying the T-SQL. When building the view, although the T-SQL is created as you build up the view, you can alter the T-SQL code, and this button will verify any changes.

Figure 9-4. *View toolbar buttons*

6. We will see the ShareDetails.Shares table listed in the top part of the Query Designer (the diagram pane) with no check marks against any of the column names, indicating that there are not yet any columns within the view. What we want is a view that will display the share description, the stock market ticker ID, and the current price. If we wanted all the columns displayed, we could click the check box next to * (All Columns), but for our example, just place checks against the last three columns, as shown in Figure 9-5. Notice as you check the boxes how the two areas below the table pane alter. The middle grid pane lists all the columns selected and gives you options for sorting and giving the column an alias name. The bottom part is the underlying query of the columns selected. The finished designer will look as shown in Figure 9-5.

Figure 9-5. *Our view with the columns selected*

7. We are going to change the details in the column grid now to enforce sorting criteria and to give the column aliases. This means that if a user just does SELECT * from the view, then he or she will receive the data in the order defined by the view's query by default. It also means that some of the column names will have been altered from those of the underlying table. We want to ensure that the shares come out from the view in ascending name order. Move to the Sort Type column and click in the row that corresponds to ShareDesc. Select Ascending, as shown in Figure 9-6.

Figure 9-6. *Placing an order on the data*

8. In the next column, Sort Order, if we were defining more than one column to sort, we would define the order to sort the columns in. Select the value 1 in this value. However, we still need to add the aliases, which are found in the second column of the grid. Notice the third column, CurrentPrice. To make this column more user friendly, we make the name Latest Price, with a space. When we type this and tab out of the column, it becomes [Latest Price], as you see in Figure 9-7; SQL Server places the square brackets around the name for us because of the space.

Figure 9-7. *Alias with identifier*

9. Scrolling to the right of the screen would allow us to define a filter for the view as well. This is ideal if we want to restrict what a user can see. Although sort orders can be changed by the T-SQL that calls the view, filters placed within the view cannot return more data than the view allows. So going back to our salary example mentioned earlier, this would be where we would restrict users to not seeing the MD's salary. In our example, we will only list those shares that have a current price—in other words, where `CurrentPrice` is greater than 0, as shown in Figure 9-8.

Column	Alias	Table	Output	Sort Type	Sort Order	Filter
ShareDesc		Shares (Sh...	☑			
ShareTickerId		Shares (Sh...	☑			
CurrentPrice	[Latest Price]	Shares (Sh...	☑			> 0

Figure 9-8. *Filtering the data*

10. Notice the Query Editor pane, which now has the filter within it as well as the sorting order. Also take a look at the diagram pane and how the table display has been altered, as you see in Figure 9-9.

Figure 9-9. *The table with the view options applied*

11. Moving back to the T-SQL in the SQL pane, what about the `TOP (100) PERCENT` clause? Where did that come from? First of all, if you specify an order in a view, then by default SQL Server will place the `TOP (100) PERCENT` clause within the SQL, just as you saw in Chapter 8. It can be used if the table is very large and you don't want to allow users to return all the data on a production system, as it would tie up resources. You can also remove that clause from the Query Editor pane if you want; this will unlink your query from the designer and the Properties window, but you would also need to remove the `ORDER BY`. The `ORDER BY` is only here for the `TOP` clause, and the data can be returned after the `TOP` number has been chosen by SQL Server in random order. If the user of the view required a specific order, then an `ORDER BY` would be required when using the view. A final point to notice is how the column aliases are defined. The physical column is named followed by `AS` and then the alias.

■**Note** The AS when defining aliases is optional.

```
SELECT TOP (100) PERCENT
    ShareDesc AS Description,
    ShareTickerId AS Ticker,
    CurrentPrice AS [Latest Price]
FROM ShareDetails.Shares
WHERE (CurrentPrice > 0)
ORDER BY ShareDesc
```

12. If you wish to remove the TOP clause, it would be better to do this within the Properties window, shown in Figure 9-10, usually found on the bottom right of SQL Server Management Studio; however, you would also need to remove the sorting. If it's not there, it can be found by selecting View ➤ Toolbox from the menu or by pressing F4. Within the properties, we can give the view a description—very useful—but we can also remove the TOP clause by setting Top Specification to No. We can also define whether this view is read-only by setting Update Specification to No.

Figure 9-10. *The properties of a view*

13. We do need to change some of the properties in the view definition, as shown in Figure 9-11. First of all, it is better to give the view a description. Also, like a table, a view should belong to a schema. This can be from an existing schema, or if you have a view traversing more than one table, you may have a schema to cater to that scenario. In our case, it fits into the ShareDetails schema.

14. We think the view is complete, but we need to test it out. By executing the query with the execute button (the one sporting the red exclamation point), we will see the results in the results pane.

15. Now that the view is complete, it is time to save it to the database. Clicking the close button will bring up a dialog box asking whether you want to save the view. Click Yes to bring up a dialog box in which you give the view a name. You may find while starting out that there is a benefit to prefixing the name of the view with something like vw_ so that you know when looking at the object that it's a view. Many organizations do use this naming standard; however, it is not compulsory, and SQL Server Management Studio makes it clear what each object is. The naming standard comes from a time when tools did not make it clear what object belonged to which group of object types. Once you have the name you wish, as shown in Figure 9-12, click OK.

Figure 9-11. *Populated properties of a view*

Figure 9-12. *Naming the view*

16. This will bring us back to SQL Server Management Studio, where we will see the view saved (see Figure 9-13).

Figure 9-13. *Finding a view in Object Explorer*

We have now created our first view on the database. However, this method of building a view could be seen as a bit slow and cumbersome for something so simple. What if we wanted to combine two tables, or a view and another table?

Creating a View Using a View

Creating a view that uses another view is as straightforward as building a view with a table. The downside of building a view with a view is that it cannot be indexed for faster execution. Therefore, depending on what the T-SQL of the final view is, data retrieval may not be as fast as it could be with an index. Also, by having a view within a view, you are adding increased complexity when debugging or profiling performance. Therefore, consider including the T-SQL from the selected view in this new view.

In this example, we will build a view of share prices using the vw_CurrentShares view created previously. In reality, we would use the ShareDetails.Shares table along with ShareDetails.SharesPrices for the reasons just discussed.

Try It Out: Creating a View with a View

1. From SQL Server Management Studio Object Explorer, find Views, right-click, and select New View. The Add Table dialog box comes up as before (see Figure 9-14). From the Tables tab, select SharePrices(ShareDetails).

Figure 9-14. *Add a table.*

2. Move to the Views tab; there should only be one view, shown in Figure 9-15, as that is all we have created. Select the view, click Add, and then click Close.

Figure 9-15. *Adding a view*

3. The View Designer will now look similar to Figure 9-16, with two tables and the SQL showing a new type of join, a CROSS JOIN.

▦**Note** A CROSS JOIN will take every row in one table and join it with every row in the second table. We look at these in Chapter 12.

Figure 9-16. *With more than one object, how the basic view looks*

4. We want to place an INNER JOIN between the table and the view where for each share we get all the share prices only. At this moment in time, we cannot do this, as vw_CurrentShares does not have a share ID column. We therefore have to modify the vw_CurrentShares view. Keep what you have built in the View Designer, and move back to the Object Explorer. Find vw_CurrentShares, right-click, and this time select Design, as shown in Figure 9-17.

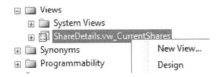

Figure 9-17. *Modifying a view for a join*

5. From the View Designer, click the ShareId column, as shown in Figure 9-18. This will then include the ShareId column in the view as the last column. You can use the criteria pane to move this column if you wish.

Figure 9-18. *Selecting the column*

6. Close this dialog box, which will bring up the Save Changes dialog box, as shown in Figure 9-19. Click Yes to save the changes.

Figure 9-19. *Saving the modifications*

7. We can now move back to our original View Designer, and you can now see the new column in the view, as shown in Figure 9-20; there should be no need to refresh the screen.

Figure 9-20. *The view with the "new" column*

8. It is very easy to link the two tables together by dragging a column from one table to a column in another table. This is very similar to how the relationships are built in the Database Designer, as we saw earlier in the book. First of all, click the ShareId column in the vw_CurrentShares view. Keeping the mouse button down, drag the mouse pointer from the vw_CurrentShares view over to the ShareId column in the ShareDetails. SharePrices table and then release it. The View Designer should now look like Figure 9-21. We have not really created a relationship in the truest sense of the word—this is simply the relationship between the columns for the purpose of this query. We can see one gray line, which shows which fields are used for the join.

Figure 9-21. *The view with the JOIN completed*

9. Select `Price` and `PriceDate` from the `ShareDetails.SharePrices` table and `ShareDesc` from the vw_Shares view, as shown in Figure 9-22. `ShareId` would already be selected in the `SharePrices` table from the drag-and-drop join from the previous step.

Figure 9-22. *How the view with a JOIN looks*

10. The final part to this view creation is to build the sort orders. We want the result to be in the order of ascending description, but we want the most recent price first and the first price last. Figure 9-23 shows the criteria pane with these options.

Figure 9-23. *Sorting with ascending and descending items*

11. Moving to the SQL pane, note the code shows the columns, as well as the `INNER JOIN` of the two `ShareId` columns, and finally the ordering of the data for the `TOP` clause.

```
SELECT TOP (100) PERCENT
ShareDetails.SharePrices.Price, ShareDetails.SharePrices.PriceDate,
ShareDetails.vw_Shares.Description
FROM ShareDetails.SharePrices INNER JOIN ShareDetails.vw_Shares ON
  ShareDetails.SharePrices.ShareId = ShareDetails.vw_Shares.ShareId
ORDER BY ShareDetails.vw_Shares.Description,
ShareDetails.SharePrices.PriceDate DESC
```

12. Before we can execute to test the view, we need to add some data to the ShareDetails.SharePrices details. Just because we are completing one action doesn't preclude us from performing another action within another Query Editor window. Click the New Query button on the toolbar if it is not visible, and then from the menu select File ➤ New ➤ Query with Current Connection. In the code window that comes up, enter the following code and then execute to insert the data:

```
USE ApressFinancial
GO
INSERT INTO ShareDetails.SharePrices (ShareId, Price, PriceDate)
VALUES (1,2.155,'1 Aug 2008 10:10AM')
INSERT INTO ShareDetails.SharePrices (ShareId, Price, PriceDate)
VALUES (1,2.2125,'1 Aug 2008 10:12AM')
INSERT INTO ShareDetails.SharePrices (ShareId, Price, PriceDate)
VALUES (1,2.4175,'1 Aug 2008 10:16AM')
INSERT INTO ShareDetails.SharePrices (ShareId, Price, PriceDate)
VALUES (1,2.21,'1 Aug 2008 11:22AM')
INSERT INTO ShareDetails.SharePrices (ShareId, Price, PriceDate)
VALUES (1,2.17,'1 Aug 2008 14:54')
INSERT INTO ShareDetails.SharePrices (ShareId, Price, PriceDate)
VALUES (1,2.34125,'1 Aug 2008 16:10')
INSERT INTO ShareDetails.SharePrices (ShareId, Price, PriceDate)
VALUES (2,41.10,'1 Aug 2008 10:10AM')
INSERT INTO ShareDetails.SharePrices (ShareId, Price, PriceDate)
VALUES (2,43.22,'2 Aug 2008 10:10AM')
INSERT INTO ShareDetails.SharePrices (ShareId, Price, PriceDate)
VALUES (2,45.20,'3 Aug 2008 10:10AM')
```

13. We can now navigate back to the View Designer window. Execute the code within the view's code window by pressing the execute button, and you should see the results displayed in Figure 9-24.

ShareId	Price	PriceDate	ShareDesc
1	2.34125	01/08/2008 16:...	ACME'S HOMEB...
1	2.17000	01/08/2008 14:...	ACME'S HOMEB...
1	2.21000	01/08/2008 11:...	ACME'S HOMEB...
1	2.41750	01/08/2008 10:...	ACME'S HOMEB...
1	2.21250	01/08/2008 10:...	ACME'S HOMEB...
1	2.15500	01/08/2008 10:...	ACME'S HOMEB...
2	45.20000	03/08/2008 10:...	FAT-BELLY.COM
2	43.22000	02/08/2008 10:...	FAT-BELLY.COM
2	41.10000	01/08/2008 10:...	FAT-BELLY.COM

Figure 9-24. *View test results.*

14. Assign the view to the ShareDetails schema in the view's Properties window, as shown in Figure 9-25.

15. The final action is to save the view. As before, click the close button and save the view as vw_SharePrices.

Now that we have built views using the designer, it's time to build one with T-SQL.

Figure 9-25. *Setting the view schema*

CREATE VIEW Syntax

Very quickly, you will find that creating a view using T-SQL is the better way forward. It is just as fast as building a view using the designer.

```
CREATE VIEW [ schema_name . ] view_name [ (column [ ,...n ] ) ]
[ WITH <view_attribute> [ ,...n ] ]
AS select_statement [ ; ]
[ WITH CHECK OPTION ]
<view_attribute> ::= {[ ENCRYPTION ][ SCHEMABINDING ][ VIEW_METADATA ]}
```

The basic CREATE VIEW syntax is very simple and straightforward. The following syntax is the most basic syntax of the CREATE VIEW statement and is the one used most often:

```
CREATE VIEW [database_name.][schema_name.]view_name
WITH {ENCRYPTION | SCHEMABINDING}
AS
SELECT_statement
```

Taking a look at the first section of the syntax, notice that the name of the view can be prefixed with the name of the schema and the name of the database to which it belongs; however, the database name and the schema are optional. Providing that we are in the correct database and are logged in with the ID we wish to create the view for, the database_name and schema_name options are not required, especially if the logon has the desired schema as their default, as the options will be assumed from the connection details. For production views, rather than views used purely by a single SQL Server user, it is recommended that they be built by the database owner. If the view is built by a nondatabase owner, then when someone tries to execute the view, that user will need to prefix the name of the view with the login of the person who created it.

Following on from these options, we build the query, typically formed with a SELECT statement that makes up the view itself. As you saw in the previous example, the SELECT statement can cover one or many tables or views, many columns, and as many filtering options using the WHERE statement as you wish. We cannot reference any temporary variable or temporary table within a view, or create a new table from a view by using the INTO clause. To clarify, it is not possible to have a SELECT column INTO newtable.

The ENCRYPTION option will take the view created and encrypt the schema contained so that the view is secure and no one can see the underlying code or modify the contents of the SELECT statement within. However (I know I keep repeating this, but it is so important), do keep a backup of the contents of the view in a safe place in development in case any modifications are required.

The SCHEMABINDING option ensures that any column referenced within the view cannot be dropped from the underlying table without dropping the view built with SCHEMABINDING first. This, therefore, keeps the view secure with the knowledge that there will be no run-time errors when columns have been altered or dropped from the underlying table, and the view is not altered in line with those changes. If you try to remove a column from the table that is contained within a schema bound view, for example, then you will receive an error. There is one knock-on effect when using SCHEMABINDING: all tables or other views named within the SELECT statement must be prefixed with the name of the schema of the table or view, even if the owner of these objects is the same as the schema of the view.

Let's go back to the two options that will be used less often, the first being WITH CHECK OPTION. If the view is being used as the basis of completing updates to the underlying table, then any modification call, such as UPDATE/DELETE/INSERT, will still make the data visible through the view.

▓**Note** Even with WITH CHECK OPTION defined, if the data is modified directly in the table, it won't be verified against any views defined with the underlying tables. Also, if the view uses TOP, then WITH CHECK OPTION cannot be defined.

The final possible option, VIEW_METADATA, exposes the view's metadata if you are calling the view via ODBC, OLE DB, and so on—in other words, from a program that is external to SQL Server.

Now that you are aware of the basic syntax for creating a view, the next example will take this knowledge and build a new view for the database.

Creating a View: a Query Editor Pane

Another method for creating views is by using T-SQL code in a Query Editor pane—in my experience, the fastest and best option. This can be a faster method for building views than using SQL Server Management Studio, especially as you become more experienced with T-SQL commands. This section will demonstrate the T-SQL syntax required to create a view, which you will soon see is very straightforward.

The SELECT statement forms the basis for most views, so this is where most of the emphasis is placed when developing a view. By getting the SELECT statement correct and retrieving the required data, it can then be easily transformed into a view. This is how the view in the following example is created, so let's look at building a view using T-SQL and a Query Editor pane. In the following example, we will create a view that returns a list of transactions for each customer with some customer information.

Try It Out: Creating a View in a Query Editor pane

1. Ensure that a SQL Server Query Editor pane is running and that there is an empty Query Editor pane. First of all, let's get the T-SQL correct. We need to link in three tables: the CustomerDetails.Customers table to get the name and address, the TransactionDetails.Transactions table so we can get a list of transactions for the customer, and finally the TransactionDetails.TransactionTypes table so that each transaction type has its full description. The code is as follows:

```
SELECT c.AccountNumber,c.CustomerFirstName,c.CustomerOtherInitials,
tt.TransactionDescription,t.DateEntered,t.Amount,t.ReferenceDetails
FROM CustomerDetails.Customers c
JOIN TransactionDetails.Transactions t ON t.CustomerId = c.CustomerId
JOIN TransactionDetails.TransactionTypes tt ON
  tt.TransactionTypeId = t.TransactionType
ORDER BY c.AccountNumber ASC, t.DateEntered DESC
```

2. Once done, execute the code by pressing F5 or Ctrl+E or clicking the execute button.

3. We can now wrap the `CREATE VIEW` statement around our code. Execute this code to store the view in the `ApressFinancial` database. As there is an `ORDER BY` clause, we need to add to the query a `TOP` statement, so we have `TOP 100 Percent`.

```
CREATE VIEW CustomerDetails.vw_CustTrans
AS
SELECT TOP 100 PERCENT
c.AccountNumber,c.CustomerFirstName,c.CustomerOtherInitials,
tt.TransactionDescription,t.DateEntered,t.Amount,t.ReferenceDetails
FROM CustomerDetails.Customers c
JOIN TransactionDetails.Transactions t ON t.CustomerId = c.CustomerId
JOIN TransactionDetails.TransactionTypes tt ON
  tt.TransactionTypeId = t.TransactionType
ORDER BY c.AccountNumber ASC, t.DateEntered DESC
```

This view is a straightforward view with no `ENCRYPTION` or `SCHEMABINDING` options. The remainder of the `SELECT` statement syntax is very straightforward.

Creating a View: SCHEMABINDING

The following example will bind the columns used in the view to the actual tables that lie behind the view, so that if any column contained within the view is modified, an error message will be displayed and the changes will be cancelled. The error received will be shown so that we can see for ourselves what happens.

First of all, let's build the view before going on to discuss the background. This view is going to list products for customers, therefore linking the `Customers.CustomerProducts` and `CustomerDetails.FinancialProducts` tables.

Try It Out: Creating a View with SCHEMABINDING

1. Create a new Query Editor pane and connect it to the `ApressFinancial` database. We can then create the T-SQL that will form the basis of our view.

```
SELECT c.CustomerFirstName + ' ' + c.CustomerLastName AS CustomerName,
c.AccountNumber, fp.ProductName, cp.AmountToCollect, cp.Frequency,
cp.LastCollected
FROM CustomerDetails.Customers c
JOIN CustomerDetails.CustomerProducts cp ON cp.CustomerId = c.CustomerId
JOIN CustomerDetails.FinancialProducts fp ON
  fp.ProductId = cp.FinancialProductId
```

2. We need some test data within the system to test this out. This is detailed in the following code. Enter this code and execute it:

```
INSERT INTO CustomerDetails.FinancialProducts (ProductId,ProductName)
VALUES (1,'Regular Savings'),
 (2,'Bonds Account'),
 (3,'Share Account'),
 (4,'Life Insurance')
INSERT INTO CustomerDetails.CustomerProducts
(CustomerId,FinancialProductId,
AmountToCollect,Frequency,LastCollected,LastCollection,Renewable)
VALUES (1,1,200,1,'31 October 2008','31 October 2025',0),
 (1,2,50,1,'24 October 2008','24 March 2009',0),
 (2,4,150,3,'20 October 2008','20 October 2008',1),
 (3,3,500,0,'24 October 2008','24 October 2008',0)
```

3. Test out that the SELECT T-SQL works as required by executing it. The results you get returned should look similar to Figure 9-26.

	CustomerName	AccountNumber	ProductName	AmountToCollect	Frequency	LastCollected
1	Robin McGlynn	187612311	Regular Savings	200.00	1	2008-10-31 00:00:00.000
2	Robin McGlynn	187612311	Bonds Account	50.00	1	2008-10-24 00:00:00.000
3	Bernie McGee	65368765	Share Account	500.00	0	2008-10-24 00:00:00.000
4	Jack Mason	53431993	Life Insurance	150.00	3	2008-10-20 00:00:00.000

Figure 9-26. *Testing schema binding in T-SQL*

4. We now need to create the CREATE VIEW. First of all, we are completing a test to see whether the view already exists within the system catalogs. If it does, then we DROP it. Then we define the view using the WITH SCHEMABINDING clause. The other change to the T-SQL is to prefix the tables we are using with the schema that the tables come from. This is to ensure that the schema binding is successful and can regulate when a column is dropped.

```
IF EXISTS(SELECT TABLE_NAME FROM   INFORMATION_SCHEMA.VIEWS
     WHERE  TABLE_NAME = N'vw_CustFinProducts'
        AND  TABLE_SCHEMA = N'CustomerDetails')
   DROP VIEW CustomerDetails.vw_CustFinProducts
GO
CREATE VIEW CustomerDetails.vw_CustFinProducts WITH SCHEMABINDING
AS
SELECT c.CustomerFirstName + ' ' + c.CustomerLastName AS CustomerName,
c.AccountNumber, fp.ProductName, cp.AmountToCollect, cp.Frequency,
cp.LastCollected
FROM CustomerDetails.Customers c
JOIN CustomerDetails.CustomerProducts cp ON cp.CustomerId = c.CustomerId
JOIN CustomerDetails.FinancialProducts fp ON
  fp.ProductId = cp.FinancialProductId
```

5. Once done, execute the code by pressing F5 or Ctrl+E or clicking the execute button. You should then see the following message:

```
The command(s) completed successfully.
```

6. Now that our `vw_CustFinProducts` view is created, which we can check by looking in the SQL Server Management Studio Object Explorer, it is possible to demonstrate what happens if we try to alter a column used in the view so as to affect one of the underlying tables. Enter the following code, and then execute it:

```
ALTER TABLE CustomerDetails.Customers
ALTER COLUMN CustomerFirstName nvarchar(100)
```

7. You will then see in the Results pane two error messages: the first shows that an alteration has been attempted on the `CustomerDetails.Customers` table and has been disallowed and names the view stopping this, and the second shows that the alteration failed.

```
Msg 5074, Level 16, State 1, Line 1
The object 'vw_CustFinProducts' is dependent on column 'CustomerFirstName'.
Msg 4922, Level 16, State 9, Line 1
ALTER TABLE ALTER COLUMN CustomerFirstName failed because one or more
objects access this column.
```

Indexing a View

Views can be indexed just as tables can be indexed. Rules in choosing columns to make indexes on a view are similar to those for a table. There are also some major requirements you need to meet before you can index a view. I will show you these first so that you are aware of which views can be indexed and what you have to do with your view.

When building indexes on views, the first index to be created must be a unique clustered index. Once such an index has been built, additional nonclustered indexes on this view can then be created. This can also be taken further, in that if we have a view with subsequent indexes on it, and we drop the unique clustered index, then all of the other indexes will automatically be dropped. Also, if we drop the view, as we would expect, the indexes are also dropped.

The view that the index is to build on must only contain tables and cannot contain views. The tables must all come from one database, and the view must also reside in that database and have been built with the `SCHEMABINDING` option.

As you saw when creating our database, certain options can be switched on or off. The following options must be set to `ON` while creating an index. These options need only be set to `ON` for that session and therefore would precede the `CREATE INDEX` statement.

```
SET ANSI_NULLS ON
SET ANSI_PADDING ON
SET ANSI_WARNINGS ON
SET CONCAT_NULL_YIELDS_NULL ON
SET ARITHABORT ON
SET QUOTED_IDENTIFIER ON
```

On top of this, the `NUMERIC_ROUNDABORT` option must be set to `OFF`.

```
SET NUMERIC_ROUNDABORT OFF
```

Finally, the view itself cannot have `text`, `ntext`, or `image` columns defined in it. In Chapter 11, we'll look at how to group data through a clause called `GROUP BY`. If you have grouping within your view, then the columns used to group data are the only columns that can be in the first index.

Although these seem like they could be quite restrictive requirements, the upside is that indexing views also comes with major speed implications. If a view remains without an index, every time that the view is executed, the data behind the view, including any joins, is rebuilt and executed. However, as the first index is a clustered index, this is similar to a clustered table index, and the data will be retrieved at index-creation time and stored in that order. Also, like table indexes, when the data is modified, then the index will receive the updates as well. Therefore, if SQL Server can use the clustered index, there will be no need to run the query again.

SQL Server will use any indexes that you have on the tables when building the views. Indexing a view is most beneficial when the data in the underlying tables is not changing frequently and when the view is executed often. Keep in mind that a view is taking information from other tables and is not a table itself, and therefore any updates to the underlying tables will not be reflected in the view until the view is rerun.

By placing an index on a view, the columns named within the index are stored within the database, as are all of the columns defined for the view, along with the data rows. Therefore, any changes to the raw data within the native tables will also be reflected in the data stored for the view. Keep in mind the performance issues with this. Every data change in the tables used in the views requires SQL Server to evaluate the effect the change has on the view. This requires more processing by SQL Server, causing a slowdown in performance. Temper this perceived gain of using an index with the downside of the extra processing required to keep the data up to date in two places for the table and two places for the index for those columns involved in the view.

Now that you are aware of the pros and cons of building indexes on views, and how they differ from indexes for tables, it is time to build an index on our view.

The aim of this index is to locate a record in the view quickly. We want to be able to find all the products for a customer based on his or her account number. Notice that we are not using `CustomerId` here. First of all, that column is not within the view, so it is unavailable for selection anyway, but we have to cater to when a customer phones up and supplies the account number. This customer will be unaware of his or her `ApressFinancial` internal `CustomerId`. Building the index is very quick and very simple, especially since you already know the basics from building indexes earlier in the book.

Try It Out: Indexing a View

1. The view we want to index is `vw_CustFinProducts`, as we know that was created with `SCHEMABINDING`. The unique clustered index will be on the `AccountNumber`, as we know that this will be unique. In a Query Editor query pane, enter the following code:

```
CREATE UNIQUE CLUSTERED INDEX ix_CustFinProds
ON CustomerDetails.vw_CustFinProducts (AccountNumber,ProductName)
```

2. Execute this code. When you do, you might get an error. The error I received was as follows:

```
Msg 1935, Level 16, State 1, Line 1
Cannot create index. Object 'vw_CustFinProducts' was created with the
following SET options off: 'ANSI_NULLS, QUOTED_IDENTIFIER'.
```

3. As was mentioned when discussing the options required to index a view, we didn't have these two options set to ON. We therefore have to re-create the view. From Object Explorer, right-click and select Script View As ➤ CREATE To ➤ New Query Editor Window, as you see in Figure 9-27.

Figure 9-27. *Scripting the view*

4. This brings up the code in a new Query Editor pane. Modify the two SET options and add in a DROP VIEW statement so that we can re-create the view. Executing the code should be successful.

```
USE [ApressFinancial]
GO
/****** Object:  View [CustomerDetails].[vw_CustFinProducts]
Script Date: 08/07/2008 12:31:54 ******/
SET ANSI_NULLS ON
GO
SET QUOTED_IDENTIFIER ON
GO
DROP VIEW  CustomerDetails.vw_CustFinProducts
GO
CREATE VIEW [CustomerDetails].[vw_CustFinProducts] WITH SCHEMABINDING
AS
SELECT c.CustomerFirstName + ' ' + c.CustomerLastName AS CustomerName,
c.AccountNumber, fp.ProductName, cp.AmountToCollect,
cp.Frequency, cp.LastCollected
FROM CustomerDetails.Customers c
JOIN CustomerDetails.CustomerProducts cp ON cp.CustomerId = c.CustomerId
JOIN CustomerDetails.FinancialProducts fp ON
  fp.ProductId = cp.FinancialProductId

GO
SET ANSI_NULLS OFF
GO
SET QUOTED_IDENTIFIER OFF
```

5. We can then move back to our pane with the CREATE INDEX statement. Executing that code should be successful now as well.

The index on a view has now been successfully created. As you can see, there are a number of restrictions, but not to the point that no index can exist. You just have to think about what you are doing, and if you have a query in your view that contains an item from the preceding list and you wish to create an index, you'll just have to find a way around it.

Summary

This chapter has given you the confidence, when building your own view, of knowing which options and features of views you wish to use. We have covered what a view is, how views can improve a database's security, how to encrypt your view, building a view using SQL Server Management Studio and a Query Editor pane, how to join two tables within a view, and indexing a view.

Creating a view when there is more than one table to retrieve data from on a regular basis is quite often a sensible solution, even more so when you wish to use views as a method of simplifying the database schema and abstracting the database data into a presentation layer for users.

Encrypting views may seem like a good idea to hide the schema of your database even further from potential users; however, do use encrypted views with caution, and always keep a backup of the source in a safe and secure environment. People have been known to keep a printout of the view just in case the source becomes corrupt. Use encrypted views sparsely, and only when really required.

Having seen three different methods to build a view, you should have found a method that suits you and your style of working. You may find that as time moves on, the tool used alters, as do the methods within that tool. Never discount any tool or option within SQL Server and banish it to the annals of history: always keep each option and tool in mind, for one day that area may be your savior. When starting out, switch between each method for building a view so that you are fully conversant with each method.

You will find that in most cases when building views, the SCHEMABINDING option will be a good option to have on a view, ensuring that a view that works today will always work. It would only be when someone deliberately removes your view from the system to complete table changes, and then doesn't correctly put it back, that you would find that a view has stopped working. Herein lies yet another scenario for keeping the code of encrypted views at hand: if you have encrypted views, along with SCHEMABINDING, and someone wishes to alter an underlying table, then you had better have the code available!

Finally, being aware of the differences between indexes on tables and indexes in views is crucial to a successful and well-performing view. If you are unsure, then try out the view with and then without an index within your development environment.

CHAPTER 10

■ ■ ■

Stored Procedures and Functions

Now that you know how to build queries of single executable lines of T-SQL code, it is time to look at how to place these into a **stored procedure** or a **function** within SQL Server, allowing them to be run as often as they are required.

Stored procedures and functions are two different types of objects that provide different, yet similar, functionality. You will see these differences within the examples, but the main point is that a stored procedure is a set of code that runs as its own unit of work, while a function, which also runs as its own unit of work, is contained within another unit of work. When building tables, you saw the system function GETDATE(). When I discuss functions later in this chapter, you will learn more about both the similarities and differences between these two types of objects.

While you may save queries on a disk drive somewhere, you have not stored them within SQL Server itself up to this point, nor have you saved them as multiple units of work. Often, however, you need to execute multiple queries in series from SQL Server. To do this, you employ stored procedures or functions. SQL Server assumes that a stored procedure or a function will be run more than once. Therefore, when it is executed for the first time, a query plan is created for it, detailing how best to execute the query. It is also possible, just like any other database object, to assign security to a stored procedure or a function, so that only specific users can run it, lending added security compared to a one-time-only query saved to a hard drive.

The aim of this chapter is to build a simple stored procedure that will insert a single record and then look at error handling and controlling the flow of execution within our procedure. You will then move on to building a user-defined function and invoking it. We'll look at some system functions in Chapter 11.

Therefore, this chapter will

- Describe what a stored procedure is.

- Explain the advantages of a stored procedure over a view.

- Cover the basic syntax for creating a stored procedure.

- Show how to set values within variables.

- Control the flow through a stored procedure.

- Look at the differences between a function and a stored procedure.

- Cover the basic syntax for creating a T-SQL user-defined function.

Finally, as this chapter completes your overview of objects within SQL Server, you will learn how you can create an alias, or a synonym, to give objects an alternative name. An alias provides its worth for client-based applications by protecting the client from any changes to the structure of the database, such as a change of the schema owner of an object.

What Is a Stored Procedure?

In the simplest terms, a stored procedure is a collection of compiled T-SQL commands that are directly accessible by SQL Server. The commands placed within a stored procedure are executed as one single unit, or **batch**, of work—the benefit of this is that network traffic is greatly reduced, as single SQL statements are not forced to travel over the network; hence, this reduces network congestion. In addition to SELECT, UPDATE, or DELETE statements, stored procedures are able to call other stored procedures, use statements that control the flow of execution, and perform aggregate functions or other calculations.

Any developer with access rights to create objects within SQL Server can build a stored procedure. There are also hundreds of system stored procedures, all of which start with a prefix of sp_, within SQL Server. Under no circumstances should you attempt to modify any system stored procedure that belongs to SQL Server, as this could corrupt not only your database, but also other databases, requiring you to perform a full restore.

There is little point in building a stored procedure just to run a set of T-SQL statements only once; conversely, a stored procedure is ideal for when you wish to run a set of T-SQL statements many times. The reasons for choosing a stored procedure are similar to those that would persuade you to choose a view rather than letting users access table data directly. Stored procedures also supply benefits; for example, SQL Server will always cache a stored procedure plan in memory, and it is likely to remain in cache and be reused, whereas ad hoc SQL plans created when running ad hoc T-SQL may or may not be stored in the procedure cache. The latter may lead to bloating of the procedure cache with lots of very similar plans for similar batches, as SQL Server won't match plans that use the same basic code but with different parameter values.

Stored procedures give your application a single proven interface for accessing or manipulating your data. This means that you keep data integrity, make the correct modifications or selections to the data, and ensure that users of the database do not need to know structures, layouts, relationships, or connected processes required to perform a specific function. We can also validate any data input and ensure that the data brought into the stored procedure is correct.

Just like a view and tables, we can grant very specific execute permission for users of stored procedures (the only permission available on a stored procedure is EXECUTE).

To prevent access to the source code, you can encrypt stored procedures, although this really ought to be used in only the most required cases. The code itself isn't actually encrypted; it is only obfuscated, which means it is possible to decrypt the code if required. Therefore, it isn't a total prevention of viewing the code, but it does stop stray eyes. It also limits what can be seen in a tool called SQL Server Profiler, which is used to profile performance of stored procedures, code, and so on, thus causing difficulty in checking what is happening if there is a problem. Therefore, to reiterate, you need to carefully justify any "encryption" you wish to do.

CREATE PROCEDURE Syntax

Begin a stored procedure with a CREATE PROCEDURE statement. The CREATE PROCEDURE syntax offers a great many flexible options and extends T-SQL with some additional commands. The syntax generally appears as follows:

```
CREATE PROCEDURE procedure_name
[ { @parameter_name} datatype [= default_value] [OUTPUT]]
[ { WITH [RECOMPILE | ENCRYPTION | RECOMPILE, ENCRYPTION } ]
AS
[BEGIN]
   statements
[END]
```

First of all, it is necessary to inform SQL Server which action you wish to perform. Obviously, we wish to create a stored procedure, so we need to supply a CREATE PROCEDURE statement.

The next part of the syntax is to give the procedure a name. It would be advisable, just as it is with any SQL Server object, to adhere to a naming standard. Everyone has their own standard within their installation, but if you prefix the name with sp_, a very common naming convention, then you will know what that object is. However, this is not something I recommend for two reasons. The first is that stored procedures prefixed by sp_ are seen as system stored procedures. The second is that you can hit some unnecessary compile locks due to system stored procedure lookups. Therefore, do avoid this naming convention.

Many people adopt a different naming convention whereby the prefix defines what the stored procedure will do; for example, an update would have a prefix of up, a deletion dt, and a selection sl. There are many different prefixes you could use, but once you have decided on your standard, you should stick with it.

Some procedures may require information to be provided in order for them to do their work; this is achieved by passing in a parameter. For example, passing in a customer number to a stored procedure would provide the necessary information to allow creation of a list of transactions for a statement. More than one parameter can be passed in: all you do is separate them with a comma.

Any parameter defined must be prefixed with an @ sign. Not all procedures will require parameters, so this is optional; however, if you do wish to pass in parameters to a stored procedure, name the parameters and follow them with the data type and, where required, the length of the data to pass in. For example, the following specifies a parameter of name L_Name, with varchar data type of length 50:

```
@L_Name varchar(50)
```

You can also specify a default value in the event that a user does not provide one at execution time. The value specified must be a constant value, like 'DEFAULT' or 24031964, or it can be NULL. It is not possible to define a variable as a default value, since the procedure cannot resolve this when the procedure is built. For example, if your application is commonly, but not exclusively, used by the marketing department, you could make the department variable optional by setting a default of 'marketing':

```
@department varchar(50) = 'marketing'
```

Thus, in this example, if you were from marketing, you would not need to provide the department input. If you were from information services, however, you could simply provide an input for department that would override the default.

It is also possible to return a value, a number of values, or even a table of data from a stored procedure using a parameter to pass the information out. The parameter would still be defined as if it was for input, with one exception and one extra option. First of all, the exception: it is not possible to define a default value for this parameter. If you try to do so, no errors will be generated, but the definition will be ignored. The extra syntax option that is required is to suffix the parameter with the keyword OUTPUT. This must follow the data type definition:

```
@calc_result varchar(50) OUTPUT
```

You are not required to place OUTPUT parameters after the input parameters; they can be intermixed. Conventionally, however, try to keep the OUTPUT parameters until last, as it will make the stored procedure easier to understand.

■**Tip** Output parameters can also be input parameters, and therefore can be used to pass a value in as well as retrieve a value out.

Before continuing, one last thing about parameters needs to be discussed, and it has to do with executing the procedure and working with the defined parameters. When it comes to executing a stored procedure that has input parameters, you have two ways to run it.

The first method is to name the stored procedure and then pass the input values for the parameters in the same order that they are defined. SQL Server will then take each comma-delimited value set and assign it to the defined variable. However, this does make an assumption that the order of the parameters does not change, and that any default value-defined parameters are also set with a value.

The second, and preferred, method of executing a stored procedure is to name the parameter, and follow this with the value to pass in. We are then ensuring that, at execution time, it doesn't matter what order the stored procedure has named the parameters, because SQL Server will be able to match the parameter defined with the parameter defined within the stored procedure. We then don't need to define a value for parameters that already have default values. Also, if the stored procedure needs to be expanded, for backward compatibility, any new parameters can be defined with default values, therefore removing the need to change every calling code. There will be examples of each of the two different methods of passing in values to parameters within this chapter.

Next come two options that define how the stored procedure is built. First of all, just as a reminder, a stored procedure, when first run without an existing plan in the procedure cache, is compiled into an execution plan, which is an internal data structure in SQL Server that describes how it should go about performing the operations requested within the stored procedures. SQL Server stores the compiled code for subsequent executions, which saves time and resources.

However, the RECOMPILE option on a stored procedure dictates to SQL Server that every time the stored procedure is run, the whole procedure is recompiled. Typically, when a parameter can greatly affect the number of rows returned, you may want to add the RECOMPILE option to a stored procedure to force the optimizer to produce the best plan every time (i.e., you want to avoid reuse of a plan that may not be very good for certain parameter values).

The second of the two options is the ENCRYPTION keyword. It is possible to encrypt—well, obfuscate at least—a stored procedure so that the contents of the stored procedure cannot be viewed easily. Keep in mind that ENCRYPTION does not secure the data, but rather protects the source code from inspection and modification. Both ENCRYPTION and RECOMPILE are preceded by the WITH keyword and can be employed together when separated by a comma:

```
CREATE PROCEDURE sp_do_nothing
    @nothing int
    WITH ENCRYPTION, RECOMPILE
AS
    SELECT something FROM nothing
```

The keyword AS defines the start of the T-SQL code, which will be the basis of the stored procedure. AS has no other function, but is mandatory within the CREATE PROCEDURE command defining the end of all variable definitions and procedure creation options. Once the keyword AS is defined, you can then start creating your T-SQL code.

It is then possible to surround your code with a BEGIN...END block. I tend to do this as a matter of course so that there is no doubt where the start and end of the procedure lie.

Returning a Set of Records

One method of achieving output from a stored procedure is to return a set of records, also known as a **recordset**. This recordset may contain zero, one, or many records as a single batch of output. This is achieved through the use of the SELECT statement within a stored procedure—what is selected is returned as the output of the stored procedure. Don't be fooled into thinking, though, that we can only return one recordset within a stored procedure, as this is not true: we can return as many recordsets as we wish.

In this chapter, you will see single recordsets of data returned and how these look within Query Editor. Returning single, or even multiple, recordsets should not really concern you at this stage. It's of more concern to developers in languages such as C#, VB .NET, and so on. Multiple recordsets will only concern you when we move on to more advanced stored procedures with multiple queries.

Creating a Stored Procedure: Management Studio

Now that you have seen some of the merits of a stored procedure over other methods of working with data, it is time to create the first stored procedure in this chapter. This stored procedure will be built within SQL Server Management Studio to insert a customer into the CustomerDetails. Customers table from the information passed to it. This is also the first part in our overall security solution. By using a stored procedure to enter the data into the underlying table, we will be in control of what data is entered, as the data can be validated and verified. You can also remove all access from the table and leave the stored procedure to serve as the only method of inserting data (you would also have stored procedures that update, delete, and retrieve data). We will look at this toward the end of the chapter.

Try It Out: Creating a Stored Procedure Using SQL Server Management Studio

1. Navigate to the ApressFinancial database, find the Programmability node, and right-click Stored Procedures. From the pop-up menu, select New Stored Procedure.

2. This opens a Query Editor pane with code from a basic stored procedure template—the template called Create Stored Procedure (New Menu) to be exact. You can either alter the procedure by changing the template options by clicking Ctrl+Shift+M, or just write the code from scratch. As we have chosen to create a stored procedure via the Object Explorer, we will use the template this time. Figure 10-1 shows the template options that can be changed.

Figure 10-1. *A stored procedure's blank template*

3. The first three options, shown in Figure 10-2, are not part of the stored procedure syntax; they are extra options used within the comments of the stored procedure. The first option is very useful because it will probably be a dbo account that adds the stored procedure to the database, and therefore it will be hard to track who the actual creator of the stored procedure was. It may be that only one account "releases" all the code to production for deployment. The second option, Create Date, is not quite as relevant, as this can be found by interrogating system views. The Description option is excellent and should form part of every stored procedure, as it will allow a short description of what the stored procedure is trying to achieve. Never go into too much detail in a description, because not everyone has good discipline in updating the comments when the stored procedure changes. However, a short "we are trying to achieve" set of text is perfect.

Parameter	Type	Value
Author		Robin Dewson
Create Date		24 March 2008
Description		is is to insert a customer

Figure 10-2. *First set of template options filled*

4. We can now move to the template options that form part of the CREATE PROCEDURE syntax. The first option is the name. I have called this apf_insCustomer to define that it's a stored procedure in the ApressFinancial database and that we are inserting a row in the CustomerDetails.Customers table. Then we can insert two parameters, as this is what the template is set up for. The first two parameters will be used to populate CustomerFirstName and CustomerLastName. We will look at the rest in a moment. The parameter values do not have to be the same name as the columns they will be working with, but it is best to have similar names. The data type and data length should be defined as the same type and length as the columns they will be used for. Failure to do this could lead to problems with data truncation if you make the parameter columns too long, for example. We also remove the values in the default options. Your template options should now look similar to what you see in Figure 10-3.

Figure 10-3. *The remaining parameters*

5. Click OK. The code will now look like the following:

```
-- ================================================
-- Template generated from Template Explorer using:
-- Create Procedure (New Menu).SQL
--
```

```
    -- Use the Specify Values for Template Parameters
    -- command (Ctrl-Shift-M) to fill in the parameter
    -- values below.
    --
    -- This block of comments will not be included in
    -- the definition of the procedure.
    -- =============================================
SET ANSI_NULLS ON
GO
SET QUOTED_IDENTIFIER ON
GO
    -- =============================================
    -- Author: Robin Dewson
    -- Create date: 24 Mar 2008
    -- Description: This is to insert a customer
    -- =============================================
CREATE PROCEDURE apf_InsertCustomer
    -- Add the parameters for the stored procedure here
    @FirstName varchar(50) = ,
    @LastName varchar(50) =
AS
BEGIN
    -- SET NOCOUNT ON added to prevent extra result sets from
    -- interfering with SELECT statements.
    SET NOCOUNT ON;

    -- Insert statements for procedure here
    SELECT @FirstName, @LastName
END
GO
```

6. We can now define the remaining parameters. There are one or two points to make before we progress. First of all, the parameters can be in any order, although it is best to try and group parameters together. The second point is that parameters like @CustTitle, @AddressId, @AccountNumber, and @AccountTypeId in this example are showing the numerical reference values that would come from values defined in a graphical front end. You may be wondering why the stored procedure is not generating these values from other information passed. For example, why is the stored procedure not producing the title ID from Mr., Miss, etc.? It is likely that the operator using the front end had a combo box with a list of possible values to choose from, with IDs corresponding to titles. In the case of the address, the ID would link back to an external address database, so rather than holding the whole address, we could receive just the ID selected when the operator used the address lookup. The code with the remaining parameters is shown here:

```
CREATE PROCEDURE CustomerDetails.apf_InsertCustomer
    -- Add the parameters for the function here
    @FirstName varchar(50) ,
    @LastName varchar(50),
    @CustTitle int,
    @CustInitials nvarchar(10),
    @AddressId int,
    @AccountNumber nvarchar(15),
    @AccountTypeId int
```

7. Moving on to the remaining section of the stored procedure, we will take the values of our parameters and use these as input to the relevant columns. The remaining code for the stored procedure is as follows:

```
AS
BEGIN
    -- SET NOCOUNT ON added to prevent extra result sets from
    -- interfering with SELECT statements.
    SET NOCOUNT ON;

    INSERT INTO CustomerDetails.Customers
    (CustomerTitleId,CustomerFirstName,CustomerOtherInitials,
    CustomerLastName,AddressId,AccountNumber,AccountType,
    ClearedBalance,UnclearedBalance)
    VALUES (@CustTitle,@FirstName,@CustInitials,@LastName,
    @AddressId,@AccountNumber,@AccountTypeId,0,0)

END
GO
```

8. When you execute the preceding code, providing you have made no typing mistakes, you should see the following output:

```
Command(s) completed successfully.
```

9. This will have added the stored procedure to the database. We can check this. Move back to Object Explorer, right-click Stored Procedures, and select Refresh. After the refresh, you should see the stored procedure in the Object Explorer, as shown in Figure 10-4.

Figure 10-4. *Object Explorer with the stored procedure listed*

10. We have completed our first developer-built stored procedure within the system. Inserting data using the stored procedure will now be demonstrated so we can see the procedure in action. To execute this stored procedure, we need to specify its name and pass the data in with parameters. There are two ways we can progress. The first method is to pass the data across in the same order as the parameters defined within the stored procedure as follows:

```
CustomerDetails.apf_InsertCustomer 'Henry','Williams',
1,NULL,431,'22067531',1
```

11. If you execute this, you should see the following output:

```
(1 row(s) affected)
```

12. However, there is a downside to this method: if someone alters the stored procedure and places a new parameter in the middle of the existing list or changes the order of the parameters, or perhaps you don't know the order of the parameters, then you are at risk for errors. The preferred method is to name the parameters and the values as shown in the next example. Notice as well that the order has changed.

```
CustomerDetails.apf_InsertCustomer @CustTitle=1,@FirstName='Julie',
@CustInitials='A',@LastName='Dewson',@AddressId=6643,
@AccountNumber='SS865',@AccountTypeId=6
```

13. Again, if you execute this, you should see the same results:

```
Command(s) completed successfully.)
```

You can check that the two customers have been entered if you wish. Let's take a look at two different methods for executing procedures next.

Different Methods of Executing

There are two different methods of executing a stored procedure. The first is to just call the stored procedure, as you saw in the preceding example. The second method is to use the EXEC(UTE) command. Both have the end result of invoking the stored procedure, but which is better for you to use depends on the particular situation.

No EXEC

It is possible to call a stored procedure without prefixing the stored procedure name with the EXEC(UTE) statement. However, the stored procedure call must be the first statement within a batch of statements if you wish to exclude this statement.

With EXEC

As we have just indicated, if the stored procedure call is the second or subsequent statement within a batch, then you must prefix the stored procedure with the EXEC(UTE) statement. On top of this, if you are calling a stored procedure within another stored procedure, then you will need to prefix the call with the EXEC(UTE) statement.

Using RETURN

One method of returning a value from a stored procedure to signify an error is to use the RETURN statement. This statement immediately stops a stored procedure and passes control back out of it. Therefore, any statements after the RETURN statement will not be executed.

It is not compulsory to have a RETURN statement within your code; it is only really necessary when you either wish to return an error code or exit from a stored procedure without running any further code from that point. A logical RETURN is performed at the end of a stored procedure, returning a value of 0.

By default, 0 is returned if no value is specified after the RETURN statement, which means that the stored procedure was successful. Any other integer value could mean that an unexpected result occurred and that you should check the return code, although it is possible to return the number of rows affected by the stored procedure, for example. Notice that the word "error" wasn't mentioned, as it may be valid for a nonzero return code to come out of a stored procedure.

In this example, we will create a stored procedure that will return two output parameters back to the calling procedure or code, indicating the cleared and uncleared balances of a specific customer.

We will also use the RETURN option to indicate whether the customer ID passed to the stored procedure finds no rows. Note that this is not an error, as the stored procedure code will be working as expected.

So you are probably wondering when to use output parameters and when to use RETURN. Output parameters are used to return information back to a calling set of code and can handle any data type. On the other hand, a RETURN can only return an integer numeric value and is used more often for indicating success or failure.

Try It Out: Using RETURN and Output Parameters

1. The Template Explorer contains a template set up for output parameters. Navigate to this template, shown in Figure 10-5, and double-click it.

Figure 10-5. *Template Explorer with the OUTPUT stored procedure*

2. This will open up a new Query Editor pane with the basics of the relevant stored procedure, which is shown, reformatted, in the following code block. Take a moment to peruse this code. First of all, the first batch within the template sets up checks to see whether the stored procedure already exists, and if it does, deletes the procedure through the DROP PROCEDURE command. After running DROP PROCEDURE, just like after dropping any object, all of the permissions associated with that object are lost when we re-create it as we discussed earlier.

```
-- =================================================
-- Create stored procedure with OUTPUT parameters
-- =================================================
-- Drop stored procedure if it already exists
IF EXISTS (
  SELECT *
    FROM INFORMATION_SCHEMA.ROUTINES
   WHERE SPECIFIC_SCHEMA = N'<Schema_Name, sysname, Schema_Name>'
     AND SPECIFIC_NAME = N'<Procedure_Name, sysname, Procedure_Name>'
)
   DROP PROCEDURE <Schema_Name, sysname, Schema_Name>.
   <Procedure_Name, sysname, Procedure_Name>
GO

CREATE PROCEDURE <Schema_Name, sysname, Schema_Name>.
<Procedure_Name, sysname, Procedure_Name>
    <@param1, sysname, @p1> <datatype_for_param1, , int> =
    <default_value_for_param1, , 0>,
    <@param2, sysname, @p2> <datatype_for_param2, , int>  OUTPUT
AS
    SELECT @p2 = @p2 + @p1
```

```
GO

-- =================================================
-- Example to execute the stored procedure
-- =================================================
DECLARE <@variable_for_output_parameter, sysname, @p2_output>
<datatype_for_output_parameter, , int>

EXECUTE <Schema_Name, sysname, Schema_Name>.
<Procedure_Name, sysname, Procedure_Name> <value_for_param1, , 1>,
<@variable_for_output_parameter, sysname, @p2_output> OUTPUT

SELECT <@variable_for_output_parameter, sysname, @p2_output>
GO
```

3. Now that we have seen the code, it is time to update the template parameters. Again, we find that the template is not ideal for our final solution, as we only have one input parameter and two output parameters. However, we have populated the template parameters we need. This stored procedure will belong to the CustomerDetails schema. We have one integer input parameter for the customer ID, followed by the first of our output parameters for cleared balances. Once you have entered these settings, as shown in Figure 10-6, click OK.

Figure 10-6. *Template values for the OUTPUT stored procedure*

4. Let's look at the code that was generated. The first section of code checks whether the stored procedure exists. If it does, then we delete it using the DROP PROCEDURE statement.

```
-- =================================================
-- Create stored procedure with OUTPUT parameters
-- =================================================
-- Drop stored procedure if it already exists
IF EXISTS (
  SELECT *
    FROM INFORMATION_SCHEMA.ROUTINES
   WHERE SPECIFIC_SCHEMA = N'CustomerDetails'
     AND SPECIFIC_NAME = N'apf_CustBalances'
)
    DROP PROCEDURE CustomerDetails.apf_CustBalances
GO
```

5. Move on to the second section, which creates the contents of the stored procedure; we'll go through each part of it in turn. This stored procedure takes three parameters: an input parameter of @CustId, and two output parameters that will be passed back to either another stored procedure or a program, perhaps written in C#, etc. Don't worry, it is possible to use Query Editor to see the value of the output parameter. When defining parameters in a stored procedure, there is no need to specify that a parameter is set for input, as this is the default; however, if we do need to define a parameter as an output parameter, we have to insert OUTPUT as a suffix to each parameter.

Tip If we define an OUTPUT parameter but do not define a value within the stored procedure, it will have a value of NULL.

```
CREATE PROCEDURE CustomerDetails.apf_CustBalances
    @CustId int,
    @ClearedBalance money OUTPUT, @UnclearedBalance money OUTPUT
AS
```

6. Take a look at the next section of code, which is very similar to what we have covered several times earlier in the book where we are assigning values to variables:

```
SELECT @ClearedBalance = ClearedBalance, @UnclearedBalance = UnclearedBalance
  FROM Customers
 WHERE CustomerId = @CustId
```

7. The final section of the stored procedure returns a value from a system global variable, @@ERROR. We'll look at this variable in the next chapter, but in essence, this variable returns a number if an error occurred. From this, the calling code can tell whether there have been problems and can then decide whether to ignore any values in the OUTPUT parameter.

```
    RETURN @@Error
GO
```

8. This completes the stored procedure definition. The template continues defining how to execute the stored procedure. The first part of this section defines the variables that hold the output values and the return value. We do not need to define a variable for the input value, although you could if it was required. Then we move to the EXECUTE section of code. When a value is returned from a stored procedure, it is set on the left-hand side of the stored procedure call and is not a parameter value. Then the stored procedure is defined with the three parameters. Note that each output parameter has to have the OUTPUT keyword after it. The final section of the code is a SELECT statement displaying the values returned and the output parameter.

```
-- ==============================================
-- Example to execute the stored procedure
-- ==============================================
DECLARE @ClearedBalance Money, @UnclearedBalance Money
DECLARE @RetVal int

EXECUTE @RetVal=CustomerDetails.apf_CustBalances 1,
@ClearedBalance OUTPUT,
@UnclearedBalance OUTPUT

SELECT @RetVal AS ReturnValue, @ClearedBalance AS ClearedBalance,
@UnclearedBalance AS UnclearedBalance
GO
```

9. Now that the template has been altered with the changes we need, execute the template by pressing Ctrl+E or F5 or clicking the execute button on the toolbar. This will create the stored procedure and run the examples at the end to demonstrate the procedure. Of course, we can run this section of code as many times as we want because the whole scenario, from dropping and losing the stored procedure through to re-creating the stored procedure, is all there, ready for us. The stored procedure will pass back its output parameter value to the @ClearedBalance and @UnclearedBalance variables defined within the execution batch and the return value to the @RetVal variable. From there, once the variables are set, the values can be printed out using a SELECT statement. This will produce the output shown in Figure 10-7 in the results pane.

	ReturnValue	ClearedBalance	UnclearedBalance
1	0	4311.22	0.00

Figure 10-7. *Results after running the OUTPUT stored procedure*

We have now built two very basic stored procedures in which we are performing an INSERT and a SELECT. Next we look at control of flow.

Controlling the Flow

When working on a stored procedure, there will be times when it is necessary to control the flow of information through it. The main control of flow is handled with an IF...ELSE statement. You can also control the flow with a WHILE...BREAK statement.

> ■**Note** The GOTO statement can also control the flow of a stored procedure. You can use this statement to jump to a label within a stored procedure, but this can be a dangerous practice and really is something that should be avoided. For example, it might be better to nest the stored procedure calls.

Controlling the flow through a stored procedure will probably be required when a procedure does anything more than working with one T-SQL statement. The flow will depend on your procedure taking an expression and making a true or false decision, and then taking two separate actions depending on the answer from the decision.

IF . . . ELSE

At times, a logical expression will need to be evaluated that results in either a true or false answer. This is where an IF...ELSE statement is needed. There are many ways of making a true or false condition, and most of the possibilities involve relational operators such as <, >, =, and NOT; however, these can be combined with string functions, other mathematical equations, comparisons between values in local variables, or even system-wide variables. It is also possible to place a SELECT statement within an IF...ELSE block, as long as a single value is returned.

A basic IF...ELSE would perhaps look like the following:

```
IF A=B
   Statement when True
ELSE
   Statement when False
```

IF...ELSE statements can also be nested and would look like the following; this example also shows you how to include a SELECT statement within an IF decision:

```
IF A=B
    IF (SELECT ClearedBalance FROM Customers WHERE CustomerId = 1) > $20000
        Statement2 when True
    ELSE
        Statement2 when False
ELSE
    Statement when False
```

As you can see, there is only one statement within each of the IF...ELSE blocks. If you wish to have more than one line of executable code after the IF or the ELSE, you must include another control-of-flow statement, the BEGIN...END block. Before we can try this out, let's take a look at how to code for multiple statements within an IF...ELSE block.

BEGIN . . . END

If you wish to execute more than one statement in the IF or ELSE code block, you need to batch the statements up. To batch statements together within an IF...ELSE, you must surround them with a BEGIN...END block. If you try to have more than one statement after the IF, the second and subsequent statements will run no matter what the setting of the IF statement is.

So if you have

```
DECLARE @VarTest
SET @VarTest = 2
IF @VarTest=1
SELECT 1
SELECT 2
```

then the SELECT 2 statement would run no matter what value you have for @VarTest. If you only want SELECT 2 to run when @VarTest is 1, then you would code the example, thus placing the code you want to run within the BEGIN...END block.

```
DECLARE @VarTest
SET @VarTest = 2
IF @VarTest=1
BEGIN
    SELECT 1
    SELECT 2
END
```

If you use an ELSE statement after a second or subsequent statement after an IF that has no BEGIN...END block, you would get an error message. Therefore, the only way around this is to use BEGIN...END.

WHILE . . . BREAK Statement

The WHILE...BREAK statement is a method of looping around the same section of code from zero to multiple times based on the answer from a Boolean test condition, or until explicitly informed to exit via the keyword BREAK.

The syntax for this command is as follows:

```
WHILE Boolean_expression
    { sql_statement | statement_block }
    [ BREAK ]
    { sql_statement | statement_block }
    [ CONTINUE ]
    { sql_statement | statement_block }
```

The code defined for the WHILE statement will execute while the Boolean expression returns a value of True. You can have other control-of-flow statements such as an IF...ELSE block within your WHILE block. This is where BREAK and CONTINUE could be used if required. You may wish to test a condition and, if it returns a particular result, BREAK the loop and exit the WHILE block. The other option that can be used is the CONTINUE statement. This moves processing straight to the WHILE statement again and will stop any execution of code that is defined after it. The best way to illustrate these concepts is to show a simple example of these three options in action.

Try It Out: WHILE...BREAK

1. The first option demonstrates how to build a WHILE loop and then test the value of a variable. If the test returns True, we will break out of the loop; if it returns False, we will continue processing. Within the example, there are two SELECT statements before and after an IF...ELSE statement. In this example, the first SELECT will show the values of the variables, but the IF test will either stop the loop via BREAK or will move the code back to the WHILE statement via the CONTINUE statement. Either of these actions will mean that the second SELECT will not execute.

   ```
   DECLARE @LoopCount int, @TestCount int
   SET @LoopCount = 0
   SET @TestCount = 0
   WHILE @LoopCount < 20
   BEGIN
       SET @LoopCount = @LoopCount + 1
       SET @TestCount = @TestCount + 1
       SELECT @LoopCount, @TestCount
       IF @TestCount > 10
          BREAK
       ELSE
          CONTINUE
       SELECT @LoopCount, @TestCount
   END
   ```

2. When the code is executed, we don't actually make it around the 20 loops due to the value of @TestCount causing the break. The output is shown in Figure 10-8.

	[No column name]	[No column name]
1	1	1

	[No column name]	[No column name]
1	2	2

	[No column name]	[No column name]
1	3	3

	[No column name]	[No column name]
1	4	4

	[No column name]	[No column name]
1	5	5

	[No column name]	[No column name]
1	6	6

	[No column name]	[No column name]
1	7	7

	[No column name]	[No column name]
1	8	8

	[No column name]	[No column name]
1	9	9

	[No column name]	[No column name]
1	10	10

	[No column name]	[No column name]
1	11	11

Figure 10-8. *WHILE with BREAK and CONTINUE*

3. If we change the code to remove the ELSE CONTINUE statement, the second SELECT statement will be executed. The two rows changed have been highlighted. We are not going to execute the two lines because they have been commented out by prefixing the code with two hyphens, --.

```
DECLARE @LoopCount int, @TestCount int
SET @LoopCount = 0
SET @TestCount = 0
WHILE @LoopCount < 20
BEGIN
    SET @LoopCount = @LoopCount + 1
    SET @TestCount = @TestCount + 1
    SELECT @LoopCount, @TestCount
    IF @TestCount > 10
        BREAK
---    ELSE
---        CONTINUE
    SELECT @LoopCount, @TestCount
END
```

A snapshot of some of the output from this is shown in Figure 10-9.

The third statement we'll look at in this section is the CASE statement. While not a control-of-flow statement for your stored procedure, it can control the output displayed based on decisions.

	(No column name)	(No column name)
1	1	1

	(No column name)	(No column name)
1	1	1

	(No column name)	(No column name)
1	2	2

	(No column name)	(No column name)
1	2	2

	(No column name)	(No column name)
1	3	3

	(No column name)	(No column name)
1	3	3

	(No column name)	(No column name)
1	4	4

	(No column name)	(No column name)
1	4	4

Figure 10-9. *WHILE with BREAK only*

CASE Statement

When a query has more than a plain true or false answer—in other words, when there are several potential answers—you should use the CASE statement.

A CASE statement forms a decision-making process within a SELECT or UPDATE statement. It is possible to set a value for a column within a recordset based on a CASE statement and the resultant value. Obviously, with this knowledge, a CASE statement cannot form part of a DELETE statement.

Several parts of a CASE statement can be placed within a stored procedure to control the statement executed depending on each scenario. Two different syntax structures exist for the CASE statement depending on how you want to test a condition or what you want to test. Let's take a look at all the parts to the first CASE statement syntax:

```
CASE expression
WHEN value_matched THEN
    statement
[[WHEN value_matched2 THEN]
    [Statement2]]
...
...
...
[[ELSE]
    [catch_all_code]
END
```

First of all, you need to define the expression that is to be tested. This could be the value of a variable, a column value from within the T-SQL statement, or any valid expression within SQL Server. This expression is then used to determine the values to be matched in each WHEN statement.

You can have as many WHEN statements as you wish within the CASE condition, and you do not need to cover every condition or possible value that could be placed within the condition. Once a condition is matched, then only the statements within the appropriate WHEN block will be executed. Of course, only the WHEN conditions that are defined will be tested. However, you can cover yourself for any value within the expression that has not been defined within a WHEN statement by using an

ELSE condition. This is used as a catchall statement. Any value not matched would drop into the ELSE condition, and from there you could deal with any scenario that you desire.

The second syntax is where you don't define the expression prior to testing it and each WHEN statement performs any test expression you desire.

```
CASE
    WHEN Boolean_expression THEN result_expression
    [ ...n ]
    [
    ELSE else_result_expression
    ]
END
```

As just indicated, CASE statements form part of a SELECT, UPDATE, or INSERT statement, therefore possibly working on multiple rows of data. As each row is retrieved from the table, the CASE statement kicks in, and instead of the column value being returned, it is the value from the decision-making process that is inserted instead. This happens after the data has been retrieved and just before the rows returned are displayed in the results pane. The actual value is returned initially from the table and is then validated through the CASE statement; once this is done, the value is discarded if no longer required.

Now that you are familiar with CASE statements, we can look at them in action.

Try It Out: Using the CASE Statement

1. Our first example will demonstrate the first CASE syntax, where we will take a column and test for a specific value. The results of this test will determine which action will be performed. We will prepopulate the TransactionDetails.TransactionTypes table first so that you can see how populating this table and the CASE statement work.

   ```
   INSERT INTO TransactionDetails.TransactionTypes
   (TransactionDescription,CreditType,AffectCashBalance)
   VALUES ('Deposit',1,1)
   INSERT INTO TransactionDetails.TransactionTypes
   (TransactionDescription,CreditType,AffectCashBalance)
   VALUES ('Withdrawal',0,1)
   INSERT INTO TransactionDetails.TransactionTypes
   (TransactionDescription,CreditType,AffectCashBalance)
   VALUES ('BoughtShares',1,0)
   SELECT TransactionDescription,
   CASE CreditType
   WHEN 0 THEN 'Debiting the account'
   WHEN 1 THEN 'Crediting the account'
   END
   FROM TransactionDetails.TransactionTypes
   ```

2. Execute this code, and you should see the output shown in Figure 10-10.

Figure 10-10. *Simple CASE statement output*

3. A customer can have a positive or negative `ClearedBalance`. The `CASE` statement that follows will demonstrate this by showing either `In Credit` or `Overdrawn`. In this case, we want to use the second `CASE` syntax. We cannot use the first syntax, as we have an operator included within the test and we are not looking for a specific value. The code is defined as follows:

```
SELECT CustomerId,
CASE
WHEN ClearedBalance < 0 THEN 'OverDrawn'
WHEN ClearedBalance > 0 THEN ' In Credit'
ELSE 'Flat'
END, ClearedBalance
FROM CustomerDetails.Customers
```

4. Execute the code. This produces output similar to what you see in Figure 10-11.

Figure 10-11. *Searched CASE statement output*

Bringing It All Together

Now that you have seen the control-of-flow statements, we can bring all of this together in our most complex set of code so far. The aim of this stored procedure is to take a "from" and "to" date, which can be over any period, and return the movement of a particular customer's transactions that have affected the cash balance. This mimics your bank statement when it says whether you have spent more than you have deposited.

This example includes one topic that is not covered until the next chapter: joining data from more than one table together. For the moment, just accept that when you see the statement JOIN, all it is doing is taking data from another table and allowing you to work with it.

So let's build that example.

Try It Out: Bringing It All Together

Note In this example, we are performing a loop around rows of data within a table. This example demonstrates some of the functionality just covered with decisions and control of flow. SQL Server works best with sets of data, rather than a row at a time. However, there will be times that row-by-row processing like this happens. In SQL Server 2008, you have the option to write .NET-based stored procedures, and this example would certainly be considered a candidate for this treatment. Our example works with one row at a time, where you would have a running total of a customer's balance so that you can calculate interest to charge or to pay.

1. First of all, let's create our stored procedure. We have our CREATE PROCEDURE statement that we enter in an empty Query Editor pane, and then we name the procedure with our three input parameters.

```
CREATE PROCEDURE CustomerDetails.apf_CustMovement @CustId bigint,
@FromDate datetime, @ToDate datetime
AS
BEGIN
```

2. We then need three internal variables. This stored procedure will return one row of transactions at a time while we are still in the date range. As we move through each row, we need to keep a running balance of the amounts for each transaction. We know that the data in the TransactionDetails.Transactions table has an ascending TransactionId as each transaction is entered, so the next transaction from the one returned must have a higher value. Therefore, we can store the transaction ID in a variable called @LastTran and use that in our filtering. Once the variables are declared, we then set them to an initial value. We use @StillCalc as a test for the WHILE loop. This could be any variable as we are using the CONTINUE and BREAK statements to determine when we should exit the loop.

```
DECLARE @RunningBal money, @StillCalc Bit, @LastTran bigint

SELECT @StillCalc = 1, @LastTran = 0, @RunningBal = 0
```

3. We tell the loop to continue until we get no rows back from our SELECT statement. Once we get no rows, we know that there are no more transactions in the date range.

```
WHILE @StillCalc = 1
BEGIN
```

4. Our more complex SELECT statement will return one row where the TransactionId is greater than the previous TransactionId returned; the transaction would affect the customer's cash balance; and the transaction is between the two dates passed in. If there is a transaction, then we add or subtract the value from the @RunningBal variable. We use a CASE statement to decide whether we need to make the value a negative value for adding to the variable.

```
SELECT TOP 1 @RunningBal = @RunningBal + CASE
            WHEN tt.CreditType = 1 THEN t.Amount
            ELSE t.Amount * -1 END,
            @LastTran = t.TransactionId
    FROM CustomerDetails.Customers c
    JOIN TransactionDetails.Transactions t ON t.CustomerId = c.CustomerId
    JOIN TransactionDetails.TransactionTypes tt ON
      tt.TransactionTypeId = t.TransactionType
```

```
        WHERE t.TransactionId > @LastTran
          AND tt.AffectCashBalance = 1
          AND DateEntered BETWEEN @FromDate AND @ToDate
        ORDER BY DateEntered
```

5. If we get a row returned, then we continue the loop. Once we get no rows returned, we know that there are no further transactions in the date range.

```
    IF @@ROWCOUNT > 0
      -- Perform some interest calculation here...
        CONTINUE
    ELSE
        BREAK
END

SELECT @RunningBal AS 'End Balance'
END
GO
```

6. We can now create the stored procedure and test our results. The example is going to check whether Vic McGlynn, customer ID 1, has had a positive or negative movement on her cash balance in the month of August 2008. The code to find this out follows. First of all, we insert some `TransactionDetails.Transactions` records to test it out. We also prefix the stored procedure with an `EXEC(UTE)` statement, as this is part of a batch of statements.

```
INSERT INTO TransactionDetails.Transactions
(CustomerId,TransactionType,DateEntered,Amount,RelatedProductId)
 VALUES (1,1,'1 Aug 2008',100.00,1),
 (1,1,'3 Aug 2008',75.67,1),
 (1,2,'5 Aug 2008',35.20,1),
 (1,2,'6 Aug 2008',20.00,1)
EXEC  CustomerDetails.apf_CustMovement 1,'1 Aug 2008','31 Aug 2008'
```

7. Execute the preceding code, which should return a value that we expect, as shown in Figure 10-12.

	End Balance
1	120.47

Figure 10-12. *Complex stored procedure output*

User-Defined Functions

As you have just seen, a stored procedure takes a set of data, completes the work as required, and then finishes. It is not possible to take a stored procedure and execute it within, for example, a SELECT statement. This is where **user-defined functions** (UDFs) come about. There are two methods of creating UDFs: through T-SQL or .NET. Both provide the same functionality, which takes a set of information and produces output that the query invoking the function can further use. UDFs are very similar to stored procedures, but it is their ability to be used within another query that provides their power. You have already seen a few system-defined functions within this book, including GETDATE(), which gets today's date and time and returns it within a query such as SELECT GETDATE().

■**Tip** If you want to learn more about .NET-based functions, take a look at *Pro SQL Server 2005 Assemblies* by Julian Skinner and Robin Dewson (Apress, 2005).

Scalar Functions

Functions come in two types: scalar and table-valued. The following shows the basic syntax to define a scalar function:

```
CREATE FUNCTION [ schema_name. ] function_name
( [ { @parameter_name _data_type [ = default ] [ READONLY ] } [ ,...n ]  ] )
RETURNS return_data_type
    [ WITH <function_option> [ ,...n ] ]
    [ AS ]
    BEGIN
                function_body
        RETURN scalar_expression
    END
```

Note that zero, one, or more parameters can be passed in to the function. Prefix each parameter in the definition with the local variable definition @ sign, and define the data type. Every parameter can be modified within the function as part of the function's execution, unless you place the keyword READONLY after the data type. Also, as with stored procedures, it is possible to call a function without specifying one or more of that function's parameters. However, you can only do that if the parameters that you omit have been defined to have default values. In that case, you can call the function with the keyword DEFAULT in the location that the parameter is expected. The use of default values is demonstrated within the example that follows.

A scalar function can only return a single value, and the RETURNS clause in the definition defines the type of data that will be returned. All data types, with the exception of the timestamp data type, can be returned.

The contents of a function are similar to a stored procedure, with the exceptions already discussed. You must place a RETURN statement when you want the function to complete and return control to the calling code.

Table-Valued Functions

The basic syntax for a table-valued function follows. Most of the syntax is similar; however, this time, you're returning a TABLE data type, and the data to return is defined in terms of a SELECT statement.

```
CREATE FUNCTION [ schema_name. ] function_name
( [ { @parameter_name parameter_datatype [ = default ] [ READONLY ] } [ ,...n ]   ]
RETURNS TABLE
    [ WITH <function_option> [ ,...n ] ]
    [ AS ]
    RETURN [ ( ] select_stmt [ ) ]
```

A table function is not built in this chapter, but will be completed in Chapter 12, as I want to show more advanced T-SQL with this functionality, and you need to read Chapter 11 before I can do that.

■**Note** It is also possible to define a stored procedure to receive a TABLE data type as an input-only parameter.

Considerations When Building Functions

Functions must be robust. If an error is generated within a function, whether it is from invalid data being passed in or from errors in the logic, then the function will stop executing at that point, and the T-SQL calling the function will cancel. A function must also not alter any external resource such as a table, and it must not execute a system function that alters resources, such as a function that sends an e-mail. Finally, you need to know whether a function can be used in computed columns.

Once a column is added to a table, there are five Boolean value-based properties that you can inspect, listed shortly, that are assigned to a function by SQL. The values of the properties can be checked by using the COLUMNPROPERTY function once the function has been added to a column. However, once a function has been built, you can check its suitability using the OBJECTPROPERTY function to check whether it is deterministic. You will see the OBJECTPROPERTY soon.

If you wish to use OBJECTPROPERTY or COLUMNPROPERTY, the function call is the same. The syntax is as follows:

```
SELECT COLUMNPROPERTY (OBJECT_ID('schema.table'),
'columnname', 'property')
SELECT OBJECTPROPERTY(OBJECT_ID('schema.object'), 'property')
```

Here are the five properties you can check against a computed column:

- IsDeterministic: If you call the function and it returns the same value every time, then you can define the function as being deterministic. GETDATE() is not deterministic, as it returns a different value each time.

- IsPrecise: A function returns this value to determine if it is precise or imprecise. For example, an exact number is precise, but a floating-point number is imprecise.

- IsSystemVerified: If SQL Server can determine the values of the first two properties, this will be set to true; otherwise, it will be set to false.

- SystemDataAccess: This is true if any system information is accessed.

- UserDataAccess: This is true if any user data from the local instance of SQL Server is used.

SQL Server defines whether a column is deterministic and whether the result from the function produces a precise value or an imprecise value. Also, unless you specify the PERSISTED keyword when defining a column, the values will not be stored in the table but rather will be recalculated each time the row is returned. There are, of course, valid scenarios for having the column computed each time, but you have to be aware that there will be a small performance overhead with this. By defining the column with the PERSISTED keyword, the value will be stored in the table and will only change when a value in one of the columns used to perform the calculation alters. So there is a trade-off with space and speed.

In the following exercise, you will build a scalar function to calculate an amount of interest either gained or lost based on an amount, an interest rate, and two dates. Once the function is built, you will then see a simple usage of the function and check its deterministic value. In Chapter 12, when your T-SQL knowledge is advanced, you will then use this function against the TransactionDetails.Transactions table to calculate interest for every transaction entered.

Try It Out: A Scalar Function to Calculate Interest

1. The first part of creating a function is to define its name, including the schema it will belong to, and then the parameter values that will be coming into it. This function will calculate the amount of interest from a defined rate, and will use two dates for the number of days the interest shall last. The first parameter, the interest rate, has a default value of 10, defining 10%.

```
CREATE FUNCTION TransactionDetails.fn_IntCalc
(@InterestRate numeric(6,3)=10,@Amount numeric(18,5),
 @FromDate Date, @ToDate Date)
```

2. Next, you need to define what data type is to be returned. In this instance, it is a numeric data type with up to five decimal places. This granularity may not be required for you, but it is defined here so that in an audit situation, accurate global summation of interest can be accrued (recall the example about interest earlier?).

```
RETURNS numeric(18,5)
```

3. In this example, EXECUTE AS specifies that the function will execute in the same security context as the calling code. This security context is determined by the AS CALLER clause. It is possible to alter the security context of EXECUTE AS to another account. Doing so is ideal when you want to ensure that no matter what the account is that is connected, the function can be called. Conversely, you can set up a function so that only specific accounts can execute the code.

```
WITH EXECUTE AS CALLER
```

4. Now that the preliminaries have been dealt with, we can move on to building the remainder of the function. A local variable that will hold the interest is defined using the same data type and size as the RETURNS definition. Then the variable is set using the calculation required to calculate the interest.

```
AS
BEGIN
    DECLARE @IntCalculated numeric(18,5)
    SELECT @IntCalculated = @Amount *
            ((@InterestRate/100.00) * (DATEDIFF(d,@FromDate, @ToDate) / 365.00))
```

5. Finally, the RETURN statement returns the calculated value, taking into account whether a NULL value is being returned.

```
    RETURN(ISNULL(@IntCalculated,0))
END
GO
```

6. You can now test the function by executing it against a set of values. The interest rate default value demonstrates how to specify default parameter values when invoking a function. The results are showing in Figure 10-13.

```
SELECT TransactionDetails.fn_IntCalc(DEFAULT,2000,'Mar 1 2008','Mar 10 2008')
```

Figure 10-13. *Inline function results for interest*

7. It is now possible to check if the function is deterministic using the OBJECTPROPERTY function. This returns a value of 0, or FALSE, because this function returns a different value each time. Therefore, this function could not be used as a computed column.

```
SELECT OBJECTPROPERTY(OBJECT_ID('TransactionDetails.fn_IntCalc'),
  'IsDeterministic');
GO
```

In Chapter 12, when you'll see more advanced T-SQL, this function will be updated to calculate interest for customer transactions. Also in Chapter 12, you will see how to build an inline table-valued function.

Summary

In this chapter, you have met stored procedures and functions, which are collections of T-SQL statements compiled and ready to be executed by SQL Server. You have learned the advantages of a stored procedure over an ad hoc query, encountered the basic CREATE PROCEDURE and CREATE FUNCTION syntaxes, and created some simple stored procedures and functions.

The basics of building a stored procedure are very simple and straightforward. Therefore, building a stored procedure within Query Editor may be as attractive as using a template. As stored procedures are sets of T-SQL statements combined together, you will tend to find that you build up your query, and then at the end surround it with a CREATE PROCEDURE statement.

You have seen both in-line and table T-SQL-based functions. To reiterate, it is possible to also have functions that are written using .NET code, which provides you with more possibilities regarding functionality and other processing abilities.

Probably the largest area of code creation outside of data manipulation and searching will be through control-of-flow statements. We will look at other areas, such as error handling, in Chapter 11, which aims to advance your T-SQL knowledge.

■ ■ ■

T-SQL Essentials

Now that you know how to build and work with SQL Server objects, and insert, update, and delete data as well as retrieve it, we can move on to more of the T-SQL essentials required to complete your programming knowledge.

Potentially the most important area covered by this chapter is error handling. After all, no matter how good your code is, if it cannot cope when an error occurs, then it will be hard to keep the code stable and reliable. There will always be times that the unexpected happens, either from strange input data to something happening in the server. However, this is not the only area of interest. You will be looking at joining tables together, performing aggregations of data, and grouping data together. Finally, there will be times that you wish to hold data either in a variable or within a table that you only want to exist for a short period. Quite a great deal to cover, but this chapter and the next will be the stepping stones that move you from a novice to a professional developer.

This chapter will therefore look at the following:

- Joining two or more tables to see more informational results
- Having a method of storing information on a temporary basis via variables
- How to hold rows of information in a nonpermanent table
- How to aggregate values
- Organizing output data into groups of relevant information
- Returning unique and distinct values
- Looking at and using system functions
- Error handling: how to create your own errors, trap errors, and make code secure

Using More Than One Table

Throughout this book, the SELECT and UPDATE statements have only dealt with and covered the use of one table. However, it is possible to have more than one table within our SELECT or UPDATE statement, but we must keep in mind that the more tables included in the query, the more detrimental the effect on the query's performance. When we include subsequent tables, there must be a link of some sort between the two tables, known as a **join**. A join will take place between at least one column in one table and a column from the joining table. The columns involved in the join do not have to be in any key within the tables involved in the join. However, this is quite uncommon, and if you do find you are joining tables, then there is a high chance that a relationship exists between them, which would mean you do require a primary key and a foreign key. This was covered in Chapter 3.

It is possible that one of the columns on one side of the join is actually a concatenation of two or more columns. As long as the end result is one column, this is acceptable. Also, the two columns that are being joined do not have to have the same name, as long as they both have similar data types. For example, you can join a char with a varchar. What is not acceptable is that one side of the JOIN names a column and on the other side is a variable or literal that is really a filter that would be found in a WHERE statement.

Joining two tables together can become quite complicated. The most basic join condition is a straight join between two tables, which is called an INNER JOIN. An INNER JOIN joins the two tables, and where there is a join of data using the columns from each of the two tables, then the data is returned. For example, if there is a share in the shares table that has no price and you are joining the two tables on the share ID, then you would only see output where there is a share with a share price. You will see this in action in this chapter.

It is possible to return all the rows from one table where there is no join. This is known as an OUTER JOIN. Depending on which table you want the rows always to be returned from, this will either be a LEFT OUTER JOIN or a RIGHT OUTER JOIN. Taking our shares example, we could use an OUTER JOIN so that even when there is no share price, we can still list the share. This example will also be demonstrated later in this chapter.

The final type of join is the scariest and most dangerous join. If you wish for every row in one table to be joined with every row in the joining table, then you would use a CROSS JOIN. So if you had 10 rows in one table and 12 rows in the other table, you would see returned 120 rows of data (10×12). As you can imagine, this type of join just needs two small tables to produce even a large amount of output.

Although not the most helpful of syntax demonstrated within the book, the syntax for joining two tables is as follows:

```
FROM tablea
 [FULL[INNER|OUTER|CROSS]] JOIN tableb
{ON tableb.column1 = tablea.column2 {AND|OR tableb.column...}}
```

The best way to look at the syntax is within a described example. We will use two tables to demonstrate the inner join in this example: ShareDetails.Shares and ShareDetails.SharePrices.

Joining two tables could not be simpler. All the columns in both tables are available to be returned through the query, so we can list the columns desired as normal. However, if there are two columns of the same name, they must be prefixed with the name, or the alias name, of the table from which the information is derived.

▓**Note** It is recommended that whenever a join does take place, whether the column name is unique or not, all columns be prefixed with the table or alias name. This saves time if the query is expanded to include other tables, but it also clarifies exactly where the information is coming from.

Try It Out: Joining Two Tables

1. The first join we will look at is the INNER JOIN. This is where we have two tables, and we want to list all the values where there is a join. In this case, we want to list all the shares where there is a share price, and we want to see every share price for that share. Notice that we don't need to define the word INNER. This is presumed if nothing else is specified. Also take note that, like columns, we have defined aliases for the table names. This makes prefixing columns easier. We are joining the two tables on ShareId, as this is the linking column between the two tables. Enter the following code:

```
SELECT s.ShareDesc,sp.Price,sp.PriceDate
  FROM ShareDetails.Shares s
  JOIN ShareDetails.SharePrices sp ON sp.ShareId = s.ShareId
```

2. Once you have executed the code, you should see the output that appears in Figure 11-1. There is no output for ShareIds 3, 4, and 5, as they have no share price.

	ShareDesc	Price	PriceDate
1	ACME'S HOMEBAKE COOKIES INC	2.34125	2008-08-01 16:10:00.000
2	ACME'S HOMEBAKE COOKIES INC	2.17000	2008-08-01 14:54:00.000
3	ACME'S HOMEBAKE COOKIES INC	2.21000	2008-08-01 11:22:00.000
4	ACME'S HOMEBAKE COOKIES INC	2.41750	2008-08-01 10:16:00.000
5	ACME'S HOMEBAKE COOKIES INC	2.21250	2008-08-01 10:12:00.000
6	ACME'S HOMEBAKE COOKIES INC	2.15500	2008-08-01 10:10:00.000
7	FAT-BELLY.COM	45.20000	2008-08-03 10:10:00.000
8	FAT-BELLY.COM	43.22000	2008-08-02 10:10:00.000
9	FAT-BELLY.COM	41.10000	2008-08-01 10:10:00.000

Figure 11-1. *First inner join*

3. We can take this a stage further and filter the rows to only list the share price row that matches the CurrentPrice in the ShareDetails.Shares table. This could be done by filtering the data on a WHERE statement, and from a performance perspective it would be better, as neither of these columns are within an index and there could be a large number of rows for ShareDetails.SharePrices for each share as time goes on; but for this example, it demonstrates how to add a second column for the join.

```
SELECT s.ShareDesc,sp.Price,sp.PriceDate
  FROM ShareDetails.Shares s
  JOIN ShareDetails.SharePrices sp ON sp.ShareId = s.ShareId
   AND sp.Price = s.CurrentPrice
```

4. Execute the preceding code, which returns two rows as shown in Figure 11-2. As you can see, an INNER JOIN is very straightforward.

	ShareDesc	Price	PriceDate
1	ACME'S HOMEBAKE COOKIES INC	2.34125	2008-08-01 16:10:00.000
2	FAT-BELLY.COM	45.20000	2008-08-03 10:10:00.000

Figure 11-2. *Inner join with multiple join columns*

5. The next join we look at is an OUTER JOIN—more specifically, a LEFT OUTER JOIN. In this instance, we want to return all the rows in the left table, whether there is any data in the right table or not. The left table in this case is the ShareDetails.Shares table, as it is the left named table of the two we are concerned with. Enter the following code:

```
SELECT s.ShareDesc,sp.Price,sp.PriceDate
  FROM ShareDetails.Shares s
  LEFT OUTER JOIN ShareDetails.SharePrices sp ON sp.ShareId = s.ShareId
```

6. Once you execute this code, you should see the missing shares from the previous example listed, as you see in Figure 11-3. Notice that where no data exists in the ShareDetails.SharePrices table, the values are displayed as NULL. OUTER JOINS are a good tool when checking other queries. For example, the results in Figure 11-3 demonstrate that quite rightly, the bottom three shares should have been missing in the first example, as they did not meet our criteria. This may not be so obvious when there are large volumes of data, though.

	ShareDesc	Price	PriceDate
1	ACME'S HOMEBAKE COOKIES INC	2.34125	2008-08-01 16:10:00.000
2	ACME'S HOMEBAKE COOKIES INC	2.17000	2008-08-01 14:54:00.000
3	ACME'S HOMEBAKE COOKIES INC	2.21000	2008-08-01 11:22:00.000
4	ACME'S HOMEBAKE COOKIES INC	2.41750	2008-08-01 10:16:00.000
5	ACME'S HOMEBAKE COOKIES INC	2.21250	2008-08-01 10:12:00.000
6	ACME'S HOMEBAKE COOKIES INC	2.15500	2008-08-01 10:10:00.000
7	FAT-BELLY.COM	45.20000	2008-08-03 10:10:00.000
8	FAT-BELLY.COM	43.22000	2008-08-02 10:10:00.000
9	FAT-BELLY.COM	41.10000	2008-08-01 10:10:00.000
10	NetRadio Inc	NULL	NULL
11	Texas Oil Industries	NULL	NULL
12	London Bridge Club	NULL	NULL

Figure 11-3. *Left outer join*

7. To get around this problem, we can add a WHERE statement that lists those shares that do not have an item in ShareDetails.SharePrices. This is one method of achieving our goal. We will look at the other later in the chapter when we examine EXISTS. We know that when there is a missing share price, Price and PriceDate will be NULL. It is also necessary to know that Price cannot have a NULL value inserted in any rows of data. If it could, then we would need to use another method, such as EXISTS.

```
SELECT s.ShareDesc,sp.Price,sp.PriceDate
  FROM ShareDetails.Shares s
  LEFT OUTER JOIN ShareDetails.SharePrices sp ON sp.ShareId = s.ShareId
WHERE sp.Price IS NULL
```

8. This time we will only have three rows returned, as you see in Figure 11-4.

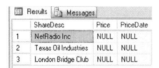

	ShareDesc	Price	PriceDate
1	NetRadio Inc	NULL	NULL
2	Texas Oil Industries	NULL	NULL
3	London Bridge Club	NULL	NULL

Figure 11-4. *Left outer join for no share prices*

9. The next example is a RIGHT OUTER JOIN. Here we expect the table on the RIGHT to return rows where there are no entries on the table in the left. In our example, such a scenario does not exist, as it would break referential integrity; however, we can swap the tables around, which shows the same results as our first LEFT OUTER JOIN example. Take note that you don't have to alter the column order after the ON, as it is the table definition that defines the left and right tables.

```
SELECT s.ShareDesc,sp.Price,sp.PriceDate
  FROM ShareDetails.SharePrices sp
  RIGHT OUTER JOIN ShareDetails.Shares s ON sp.ShareId = s.ShareId
```

10. Executing this code gives you the results shown in Figure 11-5.

Figure 11-5. *Right outer join*

11. If you want a `LEFT OUTER JOIN` and a `RIGHT OUTER JOIN` to be available at the same time, then you need to choose the `FULL OUTER JOIN`. This returns rows from both the left and right tables if there are no matching rows in the other table. So to clarify, if there is a row in the left table but no match in the right table, the row from the left table will be returned with `NULL` values in the columns from the right table, and vice versa. This time we are going to break referential integrity and insert a share price with no share. We will then delete the row.

```
INSERT INTO ShareDetails.SharePrices
(ShareId, Price, PriceDate)
VALUES (99999,12.34,'1 Aug 2008 10:10AM')

SELECT s.ShareDesc,sp.Price,sp.PriceDate
   FROM ShareDetails.SharePrices sp
   FULL OUTER JOIN ShareDetails.Shares s ON sp.ShareId = s.ShareId
```

12. Once the preceding code has been executed, you will see the results that appear in Figure 11-6. Notice that we have rows from the `ShareDetails.Shares` table when there is no share price, and vice versa.

Figure 11-6. *Full outer join*

13. The final demonstration is with a CROSS JOIN. This is a Cartesian join between our ShareDetails.Shares and ShareDetails.SharePrices tables. A CROSS JOIN cannot have any filtering on it; therefore, it cannot include a WHERE statement. As we are joining every row with every row, there is no need to provide an ON statement, because there is no specific row-on-row join.

```
SELECT s.ShareDesc,sp.Price,sp.PriceDate
  FROM ShareDetails.SharePrices sp
  CROSS JOIN ShareDetails.Shares s
```

14. The preceding code, when executed, generates a large amount of output. Figure 11-7 shows only a snippet of the output.

7	ACME'S HOMEBAKE COOKIES INC	45.20000	2008-08-03 10:10:00.000
8	ACME'S HOMEBAKE COOKIES INC	43.22000	2008-08-02 10:10:00.000
9	ACME'S HOMEBAKE COOKIES INC	41.10000	2008-08-01 10:10:00.000
10	ACME'S HOMEBAKE COOKIES INC	12.34000	2008-08-01 10:10:00.000
11	FAT-BELLY.COM	2.34125	2008-08-01 16:10:00.000
12	FAT-BELLY.COM	2.17000	2008-08-01 14:54:00.000

Figure 11-7. *Cross join*

Variables

There will be times when you'll need to hold a value or work with a value that does not come directly from a column. Or perhaps you'll need to retrieve a value from a single row of data and a single column that you want to use in a different part of a query. It is possible to do this via a variable.

A **variable** can be declared at any time within a set of T-SQL, whether it is ad hoc or a stored procedure or trigger. However, a variable has a finite lifetime.

To inform SQL Server that you wish to use a variable, use the following syntax:

```
DECLARE @variable_name datatype, @variable_name2 datatype
```

All variables have to be preceded with an @ sign, and as you can see from the syntax, more than one variable can be declared, although multiple variables should be separated by a comma and can be held on more than one line of code, just like all other T-SQL syntax. All variables can hold a NULL value, and there is not an option to say that the variable cannot hold a NULL value. By default, then, when a variable is declared, it will have an initial value of NULL. However, as part of the changes in SQL Server 2008, it is also possible to assign a value at the time of declaration. You'll see this in the first set of the following code. To assign a value to a variable, you can use a SET statement or a SELECT statement. It is standard to use SET to set a variable value when you are not working with any tables, and it is useful when you want to set the values of multiple variables at the same time. It is also useful when you want to check the system variables @@ERROR or @@ROWCOUNT following some other DML statements. You see these system variables later within this chapter. Let's take a look at some examples to see more of how to work with variables and their lifetime.

Try It Out: Declaring and Working with Variables

1. In this example, we define two variables; in the first, we are placing the current date and time using the system function GETDATE(), and in the second, we are setting the value of the variable @CurrPriceInCents to the value from a column within a table with a mathematical function tagged on. Once these two have been set using SET and SELECT, we then list them out, which can only be done via a SELECT statement.

```
DECLARE @MyDate datetime=GETDATE(), @CurrPriceInCents money
SELECT @CurrPriceInCents = CurrentPrice * 100
  FROM ShareDetails.Shares
 WHERE ShareId = 2
SELECT @MyDate,@CurrPriceInCents
```

2. Execute the code, and you will see something like the results shown in Figure 11-8. The first column shows your current data and time.

Figure 11-8. *Working with our first variable*

3. If we change the query, however, into two batches, the variables in the second batch will not exist, and when we try to execute all of the code at once, we get an error. Enter the code as it appears here; the only real change is the GO statement shown in bold:

```
DECLARE @MyDate datetime= GETDATE(), @CurrPriceInCents money
SELECT @CurrPriceInCents = CurrentPrice * 100
  FROM ShareDetails.Shares
 WHERE ShareId = 2
        GO
SELECT @MyDate,@CurrPriceInCents
```

4. The error returned when this code is executed is defined as the following results, where we are being informed that SQL Server doesn't know about the first variable in the last statement. This is because SQL Server is parsing the whole set of T-SQL before executing, rather than one batch at a time.

```
Msg 137, Level 15, State 2, Line 1
Must declare the scalar variable "@MyDate".
```

5. Remove the GO statement so we can see one more example of how variables work. We also need to remove the WHERE statement in the example so that we return all rows from the ShareDetails.Shares table. The value that will be assigned to the variable @CurrPriceInCents will be the last value returned from the query of data. The code we wish to execute is as follows. We have kept the two lines in the query, but they have now been prefixed with two dashes: --. This indicates to SQL Server that the lines of code have been commented out and should be ignored.

```
DECLARE @MyDate datetime= GETDATE(), @CurrPriceInCents money
SELECT @CurrPriceInCents = CurrentPrice * 100
  FROM ShareDetails.Shares
-- WHERE ShareId = 2
--GO
SELECT @MyDate,@CurrPriceInCents
```

6. If we look at the results that this produces, as shown in Figure 11-9, we can see that the value in the second column is from the last row in the ShareDetails.Shares table, which could also be found by performing SELECT * FROM ShareDetails.Shares.

Figure 11-9. *Variables and batches*

Temporary Tables

There are two types of temporary tables: local and global. These temporary tables are created in tempdb and not within the database you are connected to. They also have a finite lifetime. Unlike a variable, the time such a table can "survive" is different.

A local temporary table survives until the connection it was created within is dropped. This can happen when the stored procedure that created the temporary table completes, or when the Query Editor window is closed. A local temporary table is defined by prefixing the table name by a single hash mark: #. The scope of a local temporary table is the connection that created it only.

A global temporary table is defined by prefixing the table name by a double hash mark: ##. The scope of a global temporary table differs significantly. When a connection creates the table, it is then available to be used by any user and any connection, just like a permanent table. A global temporary table will only then be "deleted" when all connections to it have been closed.

In Chapter 8, when looking at the SELECT statement, you were introduced to SELECT...INTO, which allows a permanent table to be built from data from either another table or tables, or from a list of variables. We could make this table more transient by defining the INTO table to reside within the tempdb. However, it will still exist within tempdb until it is either dropped or SQL Server is stopped and restarted. This is slightly better, but not perfect for when you just want to build an interim table between two sets of T-SQL statements.

Requiring a temporary table could happen for a number of reasons. Building a single T-SQL statement returning information from a number of tables can get complex, and perhaps could even not be ideally optimized for returning the data quickly. Splitting the query into two may make the code easier to maintain and perform better. To give an example, as our customers "age," they will have more and more transactions against their account IDs. It may be that when working out any interest to accrue, the query will take a long time to run, as there are more and more transactions. It might be better to create a temporary table just of the transactions you are interested in, then pass this temporary table to code that then calculates the interest rather than trying to complete all the work in one pass of the data.

When it comes time to work with a temporary table, such a table can be built either by using the CREATE TABLE statement or by using the SELECT...INTO command. Let's take a look at temporary tables in action.

Try It Out: Temporary Tables

1. The first example will create a local temporary table based on the CREATE TABLE statement. We will then populate the table with some data and retrieve the data. We will then open up a different Query Editor pane and try to retrieve data from the table to show that it is local. Also of interest here is how we can use a SELECT statement in conjunction with an INSERT statement to add the values. Providing that the number of columns returned in the SELECT match either the number of columns within the table or the number of columns in the INSERT column list, using a SELECT statement is a great way of populating tables, especially temporary tables. First, create the temporary table. For the moment, just enter the code, don't execute it.

```
CREATE TABLE #SharesTmp
(ShareDesc varchar(50),
Price numeric(18,5),
PriceDate datetime)
```

2. Next, we want to populate the temporary table with information from the ShareDetails.Shares and the ShareDetails.SharePrices tables. Because we are populating every column within the table, we don't need to list the columns in the INSERT INTO table part of the query. Then we use the results from a SELECT statement to populate many rows in one set of T-SQL. You can execute the code now if you want, but when we get to the third part in a moment, run the SELECT * from the same Query Editor window.

```
INSERT INTO #SharesTmp
SELECT s.ShareDesc,sp.Price,sp.PriceDate
  FROM ShareDetails.Shares s
    JOIN ShareDetails.SharePrices sp ON sp.ShareId = s.ShareId
```

3. The final part is to prove that there is data in the table.

```
SELECT * FROM #SharesTmp
```

4. When the code is executed, you should see the output that appears in Figure 11-10.

	ShareDesc	Price	PriceDate
1	ACME'S HOMEBAKE COOKIES INC	2.34125	2008-08-01 16:10:00.000
2	ACME'S HOMEBAKE COOKIES INC	2.17000	2008-08-01 14:54:00.000
3	ACME'S HOMEBAKE COOKIES INC	2.21000	2008-08-01 11:22:00.000
4	ACME'S HOMEBAKE COOKIES INC	2.41750	2008-08-01 10:16:00.000
5	ACME'S HOMEBAKE COOKIES INC	2.21250	2008-08-01 10:12:00.000
6	ACME'S HOMEBAKE COOKIES INC	2.15500	2008-08-01 10:10:00.000
7	FAT-BELLY.COM	45.20000	2008-08-03 10:10:00.000
8	FAT-BELLY.COM	43.22000	2008-08-02 10:10:00.000
9	FAT-BELLY.COM	41.10000	2008-08-01 10:10:00.000

Figure 11-10. *Temporary table*

5. Open up a fresh Query Editor and then try to execute the following code:

```
SELECT * FROM #SharesTmp
```

6. Now instead of returning a set of results like those shown in Figure 11-10, you will get an error message.

```
Msg 208, Level 16, State 0, Line 1
Invalid object name '#SharesTmp'.
```

7. If we change the whole query to now work with a global temporary variable, you will see a different end result. To ensure we are starting afresh, clear all the Query Editors, or execute the following DROP TABLE command in the first Query Editor:

    ```
    DROP TABLE #SharesTmp
    ```

8. Enter the following code, taking note of the double hash marks, in one of the Query Editors:

    ```
    CREATE TABLE ##SharesTmp
    (ShareDesc varchar(50),
    Price numeric(18,5),
    PriceDate datetime)
    INSERT INTO ##SharesTmp
    SELECT s.ShareDesc,sp.Price,sp.PriceDate
      FROM ShareDetails.Shares s
      JOIN ShareDetails.SharePrices sp ON sp.ShareId = s.ShareId
    SELECT * FROM ##SharesTmp
    ```

9. When you execute the code, you should see the same results as you did with the first query (refer back to Figure 11-10).

10. Move to a new Query Editor, ensuring that you leave the previous Query Editor pane still open. Then enter the following SELECT statement:

    ```
    SELECT * FROM ##SharesTmp
    ```

11. When this is executed, you see the same results again, as shown originally in Figure 11-10.

It is not until the first Query Editor pane that defined the global table is closed or until a DROP TABLE ##SharesTmp is executed that the table will disappear.

Aggregations

An **aggregation** is where SQL Server performs a function on a set of data to return one aggregated value per grouping of data. This will vary from counting the number of rows returned from a SELECT statement through to figuring out maximum and minimum values. Combining some of these functions with the DISTINCT function, discussed later in the "Distinct Values" section, can provide some useful functionality. An example might be when you want to show the highest value for each distinct share to demonstrate when the share was worth the greatest amount.

Let's dive straight in by looking at different aggregation types and working through examples of each.

COUNT/COUNT_BIG

COUNT/COUNT_BIG is probably the most commonly used aggregation, and it finds out the number of rows returned from a query. You use this for checking the total number of rows in a table, or more likely the number of rows returned from a particular set of filtering criteria. Quite often this is used to cross-check the number of rows from a query in SQL Server with the number of rows an application is showing to a user.

The syntax is COUNT(*) or COUNT_BIG(*). There are no columns defined, as it is rows that are being counted.

Note The difference in these two functions is that COUNT returns an integer data type, and COUNT_BIG returns a bigint data type.

Try It Out: Counting Rows

1. This example will count the number of rows in the Shares table. We know that we have only inserted five rows, so we expect a returned value of 5 from the following code:

```
SELECT COUNT(*) AS 'Number of Rows'
FROM ShareDetails.Shares
```

2. Execute the code, and you will see the results shown in Figure 11-11.

Figure 11-11. *Using COUNT()*

3. Of course, we could add a filter such as the following, which counts the number of shares where the price is greater than $10:

```
SELECT COUNT(*) AS 'Number of Rows'
FROM ShareDetails.Shares
WHERE CurrentPrice > 10
```

4. Execute the code, and you will now see a count of 2, shown in Figure 11-12, as expected.

Figure 11-12. *COUNT with a filter*

SUM

If you have numeric values in a column, it is possible to aggregate them as a summation. The ideal scenario for this is to aggregate the number of transactions in a bank account to see how much the balance has changed by. This could be daily, weekly, monthly, or over any time period required. A negative amount would show that more has been taken out of the account than put in, for example.

The syntax can be shown as SUM(column1|@variable|Mathematical function). The summation does not have to be of a column, but could include a math function. One example would be to sum up the cost of purchasing shares, so you would multiply the number of shares bought by the cost paid.

Try It Out: Summing Values

1. We can do a simple SUM to add up the amount of money that has passed through the account as a withdrawal. The transaction type for this from the TransactionDetails.Transactions table is where the column TransactionType has a value of 1.

```
SELECT SUM(Amount) AS 'Amount Deposited'
  FROM TransactionDetails.Transactions
 WHERE CustomerId = 1
   AND TransactionType = 1
```

2. Executing this code adds up two rows we inserted for customer 1. The results are 100+75.67, as shown in Figure 11-13.

Figure 11-13. *SUMming values*

MAX/MIN

On a set of data, it is possible to get the minimum and maximum values of a column of data. This is useful if you want to see values such as the smallest share price or the greatest portfolio value, or in other scenarios outside of our example, as the maximum number of sales of each product in a period of time, or the minimum sold, so that you can see if some days are quieter than others.

Try It Out: MAX and MIN

1. In this example, we will see how to find the maximum and minimum values for a share with one statement. Enter the following code:

```
SELECT MAX(Price) MaxPrice,MIN(Price) MinPrice
FROM ShareDetails.SharePrices
WHERE ShareId = 1
```

2. Executing the code produces the results shown in Figure 11-14.

Figure 11-14. *Find the maximum and minimum.*

AVG

As you might expect, the AVG aggregation returns the average value from the rowset of a column of data. All of the values are summed up and then divided by the number of rows that formed the underlying result set.

Try It Out: Averaging It Out

1. Our last aggregation example will produce an average value for the share prices found for share ID 1. Enter the following code:

```
SELECT AVG(Price) AvgPrice
FROM ShareDetails.SharePrices
WHERE ShareId = 1
```

2. Once you have executed the code, you should see the results shown in Figure 11-15.

Figure 11-15. *Finding the average*

Now that we have taken a look at aggregations, we can move on to looking at grouping data. Aggregations, as you have seen, are useful but limited. In the next section, we can expand these aggregations so that they are used with groups of data.

Grouping Data

Using aggregations, as has just been demonstrated, works well when you just want a single row of results for a specific filtered item. If you wish to find the average price of several shares, you may be thinking you need to provide a SELECT AVG() for each share. This section will demonstrate that this is not the case. By using GROUP BY, you instruct SQL Server to group the data to return and provide a summary value for each grouping of data. To clarify, as you will see in the upcoming examples, we could remove the WHERE ShareId=1 statement, which would then allow us to group the results by each different ShareId. In Chapter 12, where you will look at more advanced T-SQL, you will see how it is possible to create more than one grouped set. For the moment, though, let's keep it straightforward.

The basic syntax for grouping is defined in the following code. It is possible to expand GROUP BY further to include rolling up or providing cubes of information, which, as part of grouping sets, you will see in Chapter 12.

```
GROUP BY [ALL] (column1[,column2,...])
```

The option ALL is a bit like an OUTER JOIN. If you have a WHERE statement as part of your SELECT statement, any grouping filtered out will still return a row in the results, but instead of aggregating the column, a value of NULL will be returned. I tend to use this as a checking mechanism. I can see the rows with values and the rows without values, and visually this will tell me that my filtering is correct.

When working with GROUP BY, the main point that you have to be aware of is that any column defined in the SELECT statement that does not form part of the aggregation *must* be contained within the GROUP BY clause and be in the same order as the SELECT statement. Failure to do this will mean that the query will give erroneous results, and in many cases, will use a lot of resources in giving these results.

Try It Out: GROUP BY

1. This first example will demonstrate how to find maximum and minimum values for every share that has a row in the ShareDetails.SharePrices table where the share ID < 9999. This means that the row we added earlier when looking at joins that has no Share record will be excluded. The code is as follows:

```
SELECT ShareId, MIN(Price) MinPrice, Max(Price) MaxPrice
  FROM ShareDetails.SharePrices
WHERE ShareId < 9999
GROUP BY ShareId
```

2. When the code is executed, you will see the two shares listed with their corresponding minimum and maximum values, as shown in Figure 11-16.

	ShareId	MinPrice	MaxPrice
1	1	2.15500	2.41750
2	2	41.10000	45.20000

Figure 11-16. *Max and min of a group*

3. If we wish to include any rows where there is a Price row, but the ShareId has a value of 9999 or greater, then we would use the ALL option with GROUP BY. In the following example, we are also linking into the ShareDetails.Shares table to retrieve the share description:

```
SELECT sp.ShareId, s.ShareDesc,MIN(Price) MinPrice, Max(Price) MaxPrice
  FROM ShareDetails.SharePrices sp
  LEFT JOIN ShareDetails.Shares s ON s.ShareId = sp.ShareId
WHERE sp.ShareId < 9999
GROUP BY ALL sp.ShareId, s.ShareDesc
```

4. When you execute the code, the Price row that is outside of the filtering returns a NULL value. The other rows return details as shown in Figure 11-17.

	ShareId	ShareDesc	MinPrice	MaxPrice
1	99999	NULL	NULL	NULL
2	1	ACME'S HOMEBAKE COOKIES INC	2.15500	2.41750
3	2	FAT-BELLY.COM	41.10000	45.20000

Figure 11-17. *A JOIN with a max and min group*

HAVING

When using the GROUP BY clause, it is possible to supplement your query with a HAVING clause. The HAVING clause is like a filter, but it works on aggregations of the data rather than the rows of data prior to the aggregation. Hence, it has to be included with a GROUP BY clause. It will also include the aggregation you wish to check. The code would therefore look as follows:

```
GROUP BY column1[,column2...]
HAVING [aggregation_condition]
```

The aggregation_condition would be where we place the aggregation and the test we wish to perform. For example, my bank charges me if I have more than 20 nonregular items pass through my account in a month. In this case, the query would group by customer ID, counting the number of nonregular transactions for each calendar month. If the count were less than or equal to 20 items, then you would like this list to not include the customer in question. To clarify this, the query code would look something like the following if we were running this in August 2008:

```
SELECT CustomerId,COUNT(*)
FROM CustomerBankTransactions
WHERE TransactionDate BETWEEN '1 Aug 2008 ' AND '31 Aug 2008 '
GROUP BY CustomerId
HAVING COUNT(*) > 20
```

Try It Out: HAVING

1. In the following example, we will use the MIN aggregate function to remove rows where the minimum share price is greater than $10. This query is taken from our GROUP BY ALL example shown earlier. Although we have kept the ALL option within the GROUP BY statement, it is ignored, as it is followed by the HAVING clause.

```
SELECT sp.ShareId, s.ShareDesc,MIN(Price) MinPrice, Max(Price) MaxPrice
  FROM ShareDetails.SharePrices sp
  LEFT JOIN ShareDetails.Shares s ON s.ShareId = sp.ShareId
 WHERE sp.ShareId < 9999
  GROUP BY ALL sp.ShareId, s.ShareDesc
HAVING MIN(Price) > 10
```

2. The results on the executed code will only return one value, as you see in Figure 11-18, not only ignoring ACME as its share price is below $10, but also the share 99999 that has a MinPrice value of NULL.

Figure 11-18. *When you wish to only have certain aggregated rows*

Even if we changed the HAVING to being less than $10, the share ID 99999 would still be ignored due to HAVING overriding the GROUP BY ALL. Not only that, NULL, as you know, is a "special" value and is neither less than nor greater than any value.

Distinct Values

With some of our tables in our examples, multiple entries will exist for the same value. To clarify, in the ShareDetails.SharePrices table, there are multiple entries for each share as each price is stored. There may be some shares with no price, of course. But what if you want to see a listing of shares that does have prices, but you only want to see each share listed once? This is a simple example, and we will see more complex examples later on when we look at using aggregations within SQL Server. That aside, the example that follows serves it purpose well.

The syntax is to place the keyword DISTINCT after the SELECT statement and before the list of columns. The following list of columns is then tested for all the rows returned, and for each set of unique distinct values, one row will be listed.

Try It Out: Distinct Values

1. We have to join the ShareDetails.Shares and ShareDetails.SharePrices tables again so that we know we are only returning rows that have a share price. We had that code in our JOIN section earlier in the chapter. It is replicated here, and you can execute it if you wish:

```
SELECT s.ShareDesc,sp.Price,sp.PriceDate
  FROM ShareDetails.Shares s
  JOIN ShareDetails.SharePrices sp ON sp.ShareId = s.ShareId
```

2. As you know, this returns multiple rows for each share. Placing DISTINCT at the start of the column list doesn't make any difference, because there are different prices and different price dates.

```
SELECT DISTINCT s.ShareDesc,sp.Price,sp.PriceDate
  FROM ShareDetails.Shares s
  JOIN ShareDetails.SharePrices sp ON sp.ShareId = s.ShareId
```

3. To get a list of shares that have a value, it is necessary to remove the last two columns and only list the ShareDesc column.

```
SELECT DISTINCT s.ShareDesc
  FROM ShareDetails.Shares s
  JOIN ShareDetails.SharePrices sp ON sp.ShareId = s.ShareId
```

4. When you execute this code, you will see the desired results, as shown in Figure 11-19.

Figure 11-19. *Finding unique values*

Functions

To bring more flexibility to your T-SQL code, you can use a number of functions with the data from variables and columns. This section does not include a comprehensive list, but it does contain the most commonly used functions and the functions you will come across early in your development career. They have been split into three categories: date and time, string, and system functions. There is a short explanation for each, with some code demonstrating each function in an example with results.

Date and Time

The first set of functions involve either working with a variable that holds a date and time value or using a system function to retrieve the current data and time.

DATEADD()

If you want to add or subtract an amount of time to a column or a variable, then display a new value in a rowset or set a variable with that new value, DATEADD() will do this. The syntax for DATEADD() is

```
DATEADD(datepart, number, date)
```

The datepart option applies to all of the date functions and details what you want to add from milliseconds to years. These are defined as reserved words and therefore are not surrounded by quotation marks. There are a number of possible values, as detailed in Table 11-1.

Table 11-1. *Potential Values for datepart*

datepart Definition	Meaning
isowk, isoww	ISOWeek is a numbering system used to give every week in the calendar a unique, ascending number. An ISO week starts on a Monday, and Week 1 is the week containing the first Thursday of that year. For example, in 2008, the first Thursday occurred on January 3, so Week 1 ran from December 31, 2007, through January 6, 2008.
tz	Timezone offset
ns	Nanosecond
mcs	Microsecond
ms	Millisecond
ss, s	Second
mi, n	Minute
hh	Hour
dw, w	Weekday
wk, ww	Week
dd, d	Day
dy, y	Day of year
mm, n	Month
qq, q	Quarter
yy, yyyy	Year

Taking the second option of the datepart function, to add the value, make the number positive, and to subtract a number, make it negative. Moving to the final option of the datepart function, this can be either a value, a variable, or a column date type holding the date and time you wish to change.

Try It Out: DATEADD()

1. We will set a local variable to a date and time. After that, we will add four hours to the value and display the results, as shown in Figure 11-20.

```
DECLARE @OldTime datetime
SET @OldTime = '24 March 2008 3:00 PM'
SELECT DATEADD(hh,4,@OldTime)
```

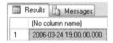

Figure 11-20. *Adding hours to a date*

2. Taking the reverse, we will take the same variable and remove six hours. The results should appear as shown in Figure 11-21.

```
DECLARE @OldTime datetime
SET @OldTime = '24 March 2008 3:00 PM'
SELECT DATEADD(hh,-6,@OldTime)
```

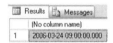

Figure 11-21. *Subtracting hours from a date*

DATEDIFF()

To find the difference between two dates, you would use the function DATEDIFF(). The syntax for this function is

```
DATEDIFF(datepart, startdate, enddate)
```

The first option contains the same options as for DATEADD(), and startdate and enddate are the two days you wish to compare. A negative number shows that the enddate is before the startdate.

Try It Out: DATEDIFF()

We will set two local variables to a date and time. After that, we find the difference in milliseconds.

```
DECLARE @FirstTime datetime, @SecondTime datetime
SET @FirstTime = '24 March 2008 3:00 PM'
SET @SecondTime = '24 March 2008 3:33PM'
SELECT DATEDIFF(ms,@FirstTime,@SecondTime)
```

Figure 11-22 shows the results after executing this code.

Figure 11-22. *The difference between two dates*

DATENAME()

Returning the name of the part of the date is great for using with things such as customer statements. Changing the number 6 to the word June makes for more pleasant reading.

The syntax is

```
DATENAME(datepart, datetoinspect)
```

We will also see this in action in DATEPART().

Try It Out: DATENAME()

In this example, we will set one date and time and then return the day of the week. We know this to be a Monday.

```
DECLARE @StatementDate datetime
SET @StatementDate = '24 March 2008 3:00 PM'
SELECT DATENAME(dw,@StatementDate)
```

Figure 11-23 shows the results after executing this code.

Figure 11-23. *The day name of a date*

DATEPART()

If you wish to achieve returning part of a date from a date variable, column, or value, you can use DATEPART() within a SELECT statement.

As you may be expecting by now, the syntax has datepart as the first option, and then the datetoinspect as the second option, which returns the numerical day of the week from the date inspected.

```
DATEPART(datepart, datetoinspect)
```

Try It Out: DATEPART()

1. We need to set only one local variable to a date and time. After that, we find the day of the month.

```
DECLARE @WhatsTheDay datetime
SET @WhatsTheDay = '24 March 2008 3:00 PM'
SELECT DATEPART(dd, @WhatsTheDay)
```

Figure 11-24 shows the results after executing this code.

Figure 11-24. *Finding part of a date*

2. To produce a more pleasing date and time for a statement, we can combine DATEPART() and DATENAME() to have a meaningful output. The function CAST(), which we will look at in detail shortly, is needed here, as it is a data type conversion function.

```
DECLARE @WhatsTheDay datetime
SET @WhatsTheDay = '24 March 2008 3:00 PM'
SELECT DATENAME(dw, @WhatsTheDay) + ', ' +
CAST(DATEPART(dd,@WhatsTheDay) AS varchar(2)) + ' ' +
DATENAME(mm,@WhatsTheDay) + ' ' +
CAST(DATEPART(yyyy,@WhatsTheDay) AS char(4))
```

3. When this is executed, it will produce the more meaningful date shown in Figure 11-25.

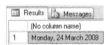

Figure 11-25. *Finding and concatenating to provide a useful date*

GETDATE()/SYSDATETIME()

GETDATE() is a great function for returning the exact date and time from the system. You have seen this in action when setting up a table with a default value, and at a couple of other points in the book. There are no parameters to the syntax. If you need greater accuracy to nanoseconds and further, then use SYSDATETIME().

String

This next section will look at some functions that can act on those data types that are character-based, such as varchar and char.

ASCII()

ASCII() converts a single character to the equivalent ASCII code.

Try It Out: ASCII()

1. This example will return the ASCII code of the first character within a string. If the string has more than one character, then only the first will be taken.

```
DECLARE @StringTest char(10)
SET @StringTest = ASCII('Robin     ')
SELECT @StringTest
```

2. Executing the code, you will see the ASCII value of the letter "R" returned, as shown in Figure 11-26.

Figure 11-26. *An ASCII value*

CHAR()

The reverse of ASCII() is the CHAR() function, which takes a numeric value and turns it into an alpha-numeric character.

Try It Out: CHAR()

1. In this example, we will define a local variable. Notice that the variable is a character-based data type. We then place the ASCII() value of "R" in to this variable. From there, we convert back to a CHAR(). There is an implicit conversion from a character to a numeric. If the conversion results in a value greater than 255—the last value for an ASCII character—then NULL is returned. Enter the following code:

```
DECLARE @StringTest char(10)
SET @StringTest = ASCII('Robin     ')
SELECT CHAR(@StringTest)
```

2. Executing the code, you will see an "R," as shown in Figure 11-27.

Figure 11-27. *Changing a number to a character*

3. The same result would be derived using a data type that is expected that is numeric-based.

```
DECLARE @StringTest int
SET @StringTest = ASCII('Robin     ')
SELECT CHAR(@StringTest)
```

LEFT()

When it is necessary to return the first *n* left characters from a string-based variable, you can achieve this through the use of LEFT(n), replacing n with the number of characters you wish to return.

Try It Out: LEFT()

1. In this example, we will take the first three characters from a local variable. Here we are taking the first three characters from Robin to return Rob:

```
DECLARE @StringTest char(10)
SET @StringTest = 'Robin     '
SELECT LEFT(@StringTest,3)
```

2. As expected, you should get the results shown in Figure 11-28 when you execute the code.

Figure 11-28. *The first LEFT characters*

LOWER()

To change alphabetic characters within a string, ensuring that all characters are in lowercase, you can use the LOWER() function.

Try It Out: LOWER()

1. Our LOWER() example will combine this function along with another string function, LEFT(). Like all our functions, they can be combined together to perform several functions all at once.

```
DECLARE @StringTest char(10)
SET @StringTest = 'Robin     '
SELECT LOWER(LEFT(@StringTest,3))
```

2. As you can see, this results in showing *rob* in lowercase, as shown in Figure 11-29.

Figure 11-29. *Changing letters to lowercase*

LTRIM()

There will be times that leading spaces will occur in a string and you'll want to remove them. LTRIM()
will trim these spaces on the left.

Try It Out: LTRIM()

1. To prove that leading spaces are removed by the LTRIM() function, we have to change the value within our local
   variable. On top of that, we have to put a string prefixing the variable to show that the variable has had the spaces
   removed.

```
DECLARE @StringTest char(10)
SET @StringTest = '    Robin'
SELECT 'Start-'+LTRIM(@StringTest),'Start-'+@StringTest
```

2. We produce two columns of output, as shown in Figure 11-30: the first with the variable trimmed and the second
   showing that the variable did have the leading spaces.

Figure 11-30. *Removing spaces from the left*

RIGHT()

The opposite of LEFT() is, of course, RIGHT(), and this function returns a set of characters from the
right-hand side.

Try It Out: RIGHT()

1. Keep the variable used in LTRIM(), as it will allow us to return bin, which are the three characters on the right-
   hand side of our variable.

```
DECLARE @StringTest char(10)
SET @StringTest = '    Robin'
SELECT RIGHT(@StringTest,3)
```

2. The results should appear as shown in Figure 11-31.

Figure 11-31. *Returning a number of characters starting from the right*

RTRIM()

When you have a CHAR() data type, no matter how many characters you enter, the variable will be filled on the right, known as right-padded, with spaces. To remove these, use RTRIM. This changes the data from a fixed-length CHAR() to a variable-length value.

Try It Out: RTRIM()

1. This example has no spaces after Robin, and we will prove the space padding with the first column returned from the following code. The second column has the spaces trimmed.

```
DECLARE @StringTest char(10)
SET @StringTest = 'Robin'
SELECT @StringTest+'-End',RTRIM(@StringTest)+'-End'
```

2. The results are as expected, as shown in Figure 11-32.

Figure 11-32. *Removing spaces from the right*

STR()

Some data types have implicit conversions. We will see later how to complete explicit conversions, but a simple conversion that will take any numeric value and convert it to a variable-length string is STR(), which we look at next.

Try It Out: STR()

1. Our first example demonstrates that we cannot add a number, 82, to a string.

```
SELECT 'A'+82
```

2. When the preceding code is executed, you will see the following error:

```
Msg 245, Level 16, State 1, Line 1
Conversion failed when converting a value of type varchar to type int.
```

3. Changing the example to include the STR() function will convert this numeric to a string of varying length such as varchar().

```
SELECT 'A'+STR(82)
```

4. Instead of an error, we now see the desired result, which appears in Figure 11-33. However, it isn't really desirable as there are spaces between the letter and the number. Leading zeros are translated to spaces.

Figure 11-33. *Changing a number to a string*

5. By including an LTRIM() function, we can remove those spaces.

```
SELECT 'A'+LTRIM(STR(82))
```

6. This code now produces the correct results, as you see in Figure 11-34.

Figure 11-34. *Changing a number to a string and removing leading spaces*

SUBSTRING()

As you have seen, you can take a number of characters from the left and from the right of a string. To retrieve a number of characters that do not start with the first or last character, you need to use the function SUBSTRING(). This has three parameters: the variable or column, which character to start the retrieval from, and the number of characters to return.

Try It Out: SUBSTRING()

1. Define the variable we wish to return a substring from. Once complete, we can then take the variable, inform SQL Server we wish to start the substring at character position 3, and return the remaining characters.

```
DECLARE @StringTest char(10)
SET @StringTest = 'Robin     '
SELECT SUBSTRING(@StringTest,3,LEN(@StringTest))
```

2. And we have the desired result, as shown in Figure 11-35.

Figure 11-35. *Returning part of a string from within a string*

UPPER()

The final example is the reverse of the LOWER() function and changes all characters to uppercase.

Try It Out: UPPER()

1. After the declared variable has been set, we then use the UPPER() function to change the value to uppercase.

```
DECLARE @StringTest char(10)
SET @StringTest = 'Robin     '
SELECT UPPER(@StringTest)
```

2. And as you can see from Figure 11-36, Robin becomes ROBIN.

Figure 11-36. *Changing the case of a string to uppercase*

System Functions

System functions are functions that provide extra functionality outside of the boundaries that can be defined as string, numeric, or date related. Three of these functions will be used extensively throughout our code, and therefore you should pay special attention to CASE, CAST, and ISNULL.

CASE WHEN. . .THEN. . .ELSE. . .END

The first function is when we wish to test a condition. WHEN that condition is true THEN we can do further processing, ELSE if it is false, then we can do something else. What happens in the WHEN section and the THEN section can range from another CASE statement to providing a value that sets a column or a variable.

The CASE WHEN statement can be used to return a value or, if on the right-hand side of an equality statement, to set a value. Both of these scenarios are covered in the following examples.

Try It Out: CASE

1. The example will use a CASE statement to add up customers' TransactionDetails.Transactions for the month of August. If the TransactionType is 0, then this is a Debit; if it is a 1, then it is a Credit. By using the SUM aggregation, we can add up the amounts. Combine this with a GROUP BY where the TransactionDetails.Transactions are split between Credit and Debit, and we get two rows in the results set: one for debits and one for credits.

```
SET QUOTED_IDENTIFIER OFF
SELECT CustomerId,
CASE WHEN CreditType = 0 THEN "Debits" ELSE "Credits" END
```

```
AS TranType,SUM(Amount)
  FROM TransactionDetails.Transactions t
  JOIN TransactionDetails.TransactionTypes tt ON
        tt.TransActionTypeId = t.TransactionType
WHERE t.DateEntered BETWEEN '1 Aug 2008' AND '31 Aug 2008'
GROUP BY CustomerId,CreditType
```

2. When the code is run, you should see the results shown in Figure 11-37.

	CustomerId	TranType	(No column name)
1	1	Debits	55.20000
2	1	Credits	175.67000

Figure 11-37. *Decisions within a string*

CAST()/CONVERT()

These are two functions used to convert from one data type to another. The main difference between them is that CAST() is ANSI SQL–92 compliant, but CONVERT() has more functionality.

The syntax for CAST() is

```
CAST(variable_or_column AS datatype)
```

This is opposed to the syntax for CONVERT(), which is

```
CONVERT(datatype,variable_or_column)
```

Not all data types can be converted between each other, such as converting a datetime to a text data type, and some conversions need neither a CAST() nor a CONVERT(). There is a grid in Books Online that provides the necessary information.

If you wish to CAST() from numeric to decimal or vice versa, then you need to use CAST(); otherwise, you will lose precision.

Try It Out: CAST()/CONVERT()

1. The first example will use CAST to move a number to a char(10).

```
DECLARE @Cast int
SET @Cast = 1234
SELECT CAST(@Cast as char(10)) + '-End'
```

2. Executing this code results in a left-filled character variable, as shown in Figure 11-38.

	(No column name)
1	1234 -End

Figure 11-38. *Changing the data type of a value*

3. The second example completes the same conversion, but this time we use the CONVERT() function.

```
DECLARE @Convert int
SET @Convert = 5678
SELECT CONVERT(char(10),@Convert) + '-End'
```

4. As you can see from Figure 11-39, the only change is the value output.

Figure 11-39. *Changing the data type of a value, using the non-ANSI standard*

ISDATE()

Although ISDATE() is a function that works with dates and times, this system function takes a value in a column or a variable and confirms whether it contains a valid date or time. The value returned is 0, or false, for an invalid date, or 1 for true if the date is okay. The formatting of the date for testing within the ISDATE() function has to be in the same regional format as you have set with SET DATEFORMAT or SET LANGUAGE. If you are testing in a European format but have your database set to US format, then you will get a false value returned.

Try It Out: ISDATE()

1. The first example demonstrates where a date is invalid. There are only 30 days in September.

```
DECLARE @IsDate char(15)
SET @IsDate = '31 Sep 2008'
SELECT ISDATE(@IsDate)
```

2. Execute the code, and you should get the results shown in Figure 11-40.

Figure 11-40. *Testing if a value is a date*

3. Our second example is a valid date.

```
DECLARE @IsDate char(15)
SET @IsDate = '30 Sep 2008'
SELECT ISDATE(@IsDate)
```

4. This time when you run the code, you see a value of 1, as shown in Figure 11-41, denoting a valid entry.

Figure 11-41. *Showing that a value is a date*

ISNULL()

Many times so far, you have seen NULL values within a column of returned data. As a value, NULL is very useful, as you have seen. However, you may wish to test whether a column contains a NULL or not. If there were a value, you would retain it, but if there were a NULL, you would convert it to a value. This function could be used to cover a NULL value in an aggregation, for example. The syntax is

```
ISNULL(value_to_test,new_value)
```

where the first parameter is the column or variable to test if there is a NULL value, and the second option defines what to change the value to if there is a NULL value. This change only occurs in the results and doesn't change the underlying data that the value came from.

Try It Out: ISNULL()

1. In this example, we define a char() variable of ten characters in length and then set the value explicitly to NULL. The example will also work without the second line of code, which is simply there for clarity. The third line tests the variable, and as it is NULL, it changes it to a date. Note, though, that a date is more than ten characters, so the value is truncated.

```
DECLARE @IsNull char(10)
SET @IsNull = NULL
SELECT ISNULL(@IsNull,GETDATE())
```

2. As expected, when you execute the code, you get the first ten characters of the relevant date, as shown in Figure 11-42.

Figure 11-42. *Changing the NULL to a value if the value is a NULL*

ISNUMERIC()

This final system function tests the value within a column or variable and ascertains whether it is numeric or not. The value returned is 0, or false, for an invalid number, or 1 for true if the test is okay and can convert to a numeric.

■**Note** Currency symbols such as £ and $ will also return 1 for a valid numeric value.

Try It Out: ISNUMERIC()

1. Our first example to demonstrate ISNUMERIC() defines a character variable and contains alphabetic values. This test fails, as shown in Figure 11-43.

```
DECLARE @IsNum char(10)
SET @IsNum = 'Robin        '
SELECT ISNUMERIC(@IsNum)
```

Figure 11-43. *Checking whether a value is a number and finding out it is not*

2. This second example places numbers and spaces into a char field. The ISNUMERIC() test ignores the spaces, provided that there are no further alphanumeric characters.

```
DECLARE @IsNum char(10)
SET @IsNum = '1234        '
SELECT ISNUMERIC(@IsNum)
```

Figure 11-44 shows the results of running this code.

Figure 11-44. *Finding out a value is numeric*

RAISERROR

Before we look at handling errors, you need to be aware of what an error is, how it is generated, the information it generates, and how to generate your own errors when something is wrong. The T-SQL command RAISERROR allows us as developers to have the ability to produce our own SQL Server error messages when running queries or stored procedures. We are not tied to just using error messages that come with SQL Server; we can set up our own messages and our own level of severity for those messages. It is also possible to determine whether the message is recorded in the Windows error log or not.

However, whether we wish to use our own error message or a system error message, we can still generate an error message from SQL Server as if SQL Server itself raised it. Enterprise environments typically experience the same errors on repeated occasions, since they employ SQL Server in very specific ways depending on their business model. With this in mind, attention to employing RAISERROR can have big benefits by providing more meaningful feedback as well as suggested solutions for users.

By using RAISERROR, the whole SQL Server system acts as if SQL Server raised the error, as you have seen within this book.

RAISERROR can be used in one of two ways; looking at the syntax will make this clear.

```
RAISERROR ({msg_id|msg_str} {,severity,state}
          [,argument [ ,...n ] ])
          [WITH option [ ,...n ]]
```

You can either use a specific msg_id or provide an actual output string, msg_str, either as a literal or a local variable defined as string-based, containing the error message that will be recorded. The msg_id references system and user-defined messages that already exist within the SQL Server error messages table.

When specifying a text message in the first parameter of the RAISERROR function instead of a message ID, you may find that this is easier to write than creating a new message:

```
RAISERROR('You made an error', 10, 1)
```

The next two parameters in the RAISERROR syntax are numerical and relate to how severe the error is and information about how the error was invoked. Severity levels range from 1 at the innocuous end to 25 at the fatal end. Severity levels of 2 to 14 are generally informational. Severity level 15 is for warnings, and levels 16 or higher represent errors. Severity levels from 20 to 25 are considered fatal, and require the WITH LOG option, which means that the error is logged in the Windows Application Event log and the SQL Error log and the connection terminated; quite simply, the stored procedure stops executing. The connection referred to here is the connection within Query Editor, or the connection made by an application using a data access method like ADO.NET. Only for a most extreme error would we set the severity to this level; in most cases, we would use a number between 1 and 18.

The last parameter within the function specifies state. Use a 1 here for most implementations, although the legitimate range is from 1 to 127. You may use this to indicate which error was thrown by providing a different state for each RAISERROR function in your stored procedure. SQL Server does not act on any legitimate state value, but the parameter is required.

A msg_str can define parameters within the text. By placing the value, either statically or via a variable, after the last parameter that you define, msg_str replaces the message parameter with that value. This is demonstrated in an upcoming example. If you do wish to add a parameter to a message string, you have to define a conversion specification. The format is

```
% [[flag] [width] [. precision] [{h | l}]] type
```

The options are as follows:

- flag: A code that determines justification and spacing of the value entered:
  - - (minus): Left-justify the value.
  - + (plus): The value shows a + or a - sign.
  - 0: Prefix the output with zeros.
  - #: Preface any nonzero with a 0, 0x, or 0X, depending on the formatting.
  - (blank): Prefix with blanks.
- width: The minimum width of the output.
- precision: The maximum number of characters used from the argument.

- h: Character types:

    - d or i: Signed integer.

    - o: Unsigned octal.

    - s: String.

    - u: Unsigned integer.

    - x or X: Unsigned hex.

To place a parameter within a message string where the parameter needs to be inserted, you would define this by a % sign followed by one of the following options: d or i for a signed integer, p for a pointer, s for a string, u for an unsigned integer, x or X for an unsigned hexadecimal, and o for an unsigned octal. Note that float, double, and single are not supported as parameter types for messages. You will see this in action in the upcoming examples.

Finally, there are three options that could be placed at the end of the RAISERROR message. These are the WITH options:

- LOG places the error message within the Windows error log.

- NOWAIT sends the error directly to the client.

- SETERROR resets the error number to 50000 within the message string only.

When using any of these last WITH options, do take the greatest of care, as their misuse can create more problems than they solve. For example, you may unnecessarily use LOG a great deal, filling up the Windows Application Event log and the SQL Error log, which leads to further problems.

There is a system stored procedure, sp_addmessage, that can create a new global error message that can be used by RAISERROR by defining the @msgnum. The syntax for adding a message is

```
sp_addmessage [@msgnum =]msg_id,
[@severity = ] severity , [ @msgtext = ] 'msg'
    [ , [ @lang = ] 'language' ]
    [ , [ @with_log = ] 'with_log' ]
    [ , [ @replace = ] 'replace' ]
```

The parameters into this system stored procedure are as follows:

- @msgnum: The number of the message is typically greater than 50000.

- @severity: Same as the preceding, in a range of 1 to 25.

- @lang: Use this if you need to define the language of the error message. Normally this is left empty.

- @with_log: Set to 'TRUE' if you wish to write a message to the Windows error log.

- @replace: Set to 'replace' if you are replacing an existing message and updating any of the preceding values with new settings.

▨Note Any message added will be specific for that database rather than the server.

It is time to move to an example that will set up an error message that will be used to say a customer is overdrawn.

Try It Out: RAISERROR

1. First of all, we want to add a new user-defined error message. To do this, we will use sp_addmessage. We can now add any new SQL Server message that we wish. Any user-defined error message must be greater than 50000, so the first error message would normally be 50001.

    ```
    sp_addmessage @msgnum=50001,@severity=1,
    @msgtext='Customer is overdrawn'
    ```

2. We can then perform a RAISERROR to see the message displayed. Notice that we have to define the severity again. This is mandatory, but would be better if it was optional, and then you could always default to the severity defined.

    ```
    RAISERROR (50001,1,1)
    ```

3. When this is executed, we will see the following output:

    ```
    Customer is overdrawn
    Msg 50001, Level 1, State 1
    ```

4. This is not the friendliest of messages, as it would be better to perhaps give out the customer number as well. We can do this via a parameter. In the code that follows, we replace the message just added and now include a parameter where we are formatting with flag 0, which means we are prefixing the output with zeros; then we include the number 10, which is the precision, so that means the number will be ten digits; and finally we indicate the message will be unsigned using the option u.

    ```
    sp_addmessage @msgnum =50001,@severity=1,
    @msgtext='Customer is overdrawn. CustomerId= %010u',@replace='replace'
    ```

5. We can then change the RAISERROR so that we add on another parameter. We are hard coding the customer number as customer number 243, but we could use a local variable.

    ```
    RAISERROR (50001,1,1,243)
    ```

6. Executing the code now produces output that is much better and more informative for debugging, if required.

    ```
    Customer is overdrawn. CustomerId= 0000000243
    Msg 50001, Level 1, State 1
    ```

Now that you know how you can raise your own errors if scenarios crop up that need them, we can take a look at how SQL Server can deal with errors. We do come back to RAISERROR when looking at these two options next.

Error Handling

When working with T-SQL, it is important to have some sort of error handling to cater to those times when something goes wrong. Errors can be of different varieties; for example, you might expect at least one row of data to be returned from a query, and then you receive no rows. However, what we are discussing here is when SQL Server informs us there is something more drastically wrong. We have seen some errors throughout the book, and even in this chapter. There are two methods of error catching we can employ in such cases. The first uses a system variable, @@ERROR.

@@ERROR

This is the most basic of error handling. It has served SQL Server developers well over the years, but it can be cumbersome. When an error occurs, such as you have seen as we have gone through the book creating and manipulating objects, a global variable, @@ERROR, would have been populated with the SQL Server error message number. Similarly, if you try to do something with a set of data that is invalid, such as dividing a number by zero or exceeding the number of digits allowed in a numeric data type, then SQL Server will populate this variable for you to inspect.

The downside is that the @@ERROR variable setting only lasts for the next statement following the line of code that has been executed; therefore, when you think there might be problems, you need to either pass the data to a local variable or inspect it straight away. The first example demonstrates this.

Try It Out: Using @@ERROR

1. This example tries to divide 100 by zero, which is an error. We then list out the error number, and then again list out the error number. Enter the following code and execute it:

```
SELECT 100/0
SELECT @@ERROR
SELECT @@ERROR
```

2. It is necessary in this instance to check both the Results and Messages tab. The first tab is the Messages tab, which shows you the error that encountered. As expected, we see the Divide by zero error encountered message.

```
Msg 8134, Level 16, State 1, Line 1
Divide by zero error encountered.

(1 row(s) affected)

(1 row(s) affected)
```

3. Moving to the Results tab, you should see three result sets, as shown in Figure 11-45. The first, showing no information, would be where SQL Server would have put the division results, had it succeeded. The second result set is the number from the first SELECT @@ERROR. Notice the number corresponds to the msg number found in the Messages tab. The third result set shows a value of 0. This is because the first SELECT @@ERROR worked successfully and therefore set the system variable to 0. This demonstrates the lifetime of the value within @@ERROR.

Figure 11-45. *Showing @@ERROR in multiple statements*

4. When we use the RAISERROR function, it also sets the @@ERROR variable, as we can see in the following code. However, the value will be set to 0 using our preceding example. This is because the severity level was below 11.

```
RAISERROR (50001,1,1,243)
SELECT @@ERROR
```

5. When the code is executed, you can see that @@ERROR is set to 0, as shown in Figure 11-46.

Figure 11-46. *When severity is too low to set @@ERROR*

6. By changing the severity to 11 or above, the @@ERROR setting will now be set to the message number within the RAISERROR.

```
RAISERROR (50001,11,1,243)
SELECT @@ERROR
```

7. The preceding code produces the same message as seen within our RAISERROR example, but as you can see in Figure 11-47, the error number setting now reflects that value placed in the msgnum parameter.

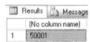

Figure 11-47. *With a higher severity, the message number is set.*

Although a useful tool, it would be better to use the next error-handling routine to be demonstrated, TRY...CATCH.

TRY. . .CATCH

It can be said that no matter what, any piece of code has the ability to fail and generate some sort of error. For the vast majority of this code, you will want to trap any error that occurs, check what the error is, and deal with it as best you can. As you saw previously, this could be done one statement at a time using @@ERROR to test for any error code. A new and improved functionality exists whereby a set of statements can try and execute, and if any statement has an error, it will be caught. This is known as a TRY...CATCH block.

Surrounding code with the ability to try and execute a slice of code and to catch any errors and try to deal with them has been around for quite a number of years in languages such as C++. Gladly, we now see this within SQL Server.

The syntax is pretty straightforward. There are two "blocks" of code. The first block, BEGIN TRY, is where there is one or more T-SQL statements that you wish to try and run. If any of statements have an error, then no further processing within that block will execute, and processing will switch to the second block, BEGIN CATCH.

```
BEGIN TRY
    { sql_statement | statement_block }
END TRY
BEGIN CATCH
    { sql_statement | statement_block }
END CATCH
```

When you generate your own error via a RAISERROR, then a bit of care has to be taken with the severity setting, as this determines how your code works within a TRY...CATCH scenario. If you raise an error with a severity level of 0 to 10, then although an error is generated and will be received by the calling program, whether that is Query Editor or a program such as C#, then processing will continue without moving to the CATCH block. This can be seen as a "warning" level. Changing the severity level to 11 or above will transfer the control to the CATCH block of code. Once within the CATCH block, you can raise a new error or raise the same error by using values stored within SQL Server system functions.

The system functions that can be used to find useful debugging information are detailed here:

- ERROR_LINE(): The line number that caused the error or performed the RAISERROR command. This is physical rather than relative (i.e., you don't have to remove blank lines within the T-SQL to get the correct line number, unlike some software that does require this).

- ERROR_MESSAGE(): The text message.

- ERROR_NUMBER(): The number associated with the message.

- ERROR_PROCEDURE(): If you are retrieving this within a stored procedure or trigger, the name of it will be contained here. If you are running ad hoc T-SQL code, then the value will be NULL.

- ERROR_SEVERITY(): The numeric severity value for the error.

- ERROR_STATE(): The numeric state value for the error.

TRY...CATCH blocks can be nested, and when an error occurs, the error will be passed to the relevant CATCH section. This would be done when you wanted an overall CATCH block for "general" statements, and then you could perform specific testing and have specific error handling where you really think an error might be generated.

Not all errors are caught within a TRY...CATCH block, unfortunately. These are compile errors or errors that occur when deferred name resolution takes place and the name created doesn't exist. To clarify these two points, when T-SQL code that is either ad hoc or within a stored procedure, SQL Server compiles the code, looking for syntax errors. However, not all code can be fully compiled and is not compiled until the statement is about to be executed. If there is an error, then this will terminate the batch immediately. The second is that if you have code that references a temporary table, for example, then the table won't exist at run time and column names won't be able to be checked. This is known as **deferred name resolution**, and if you try to use a column that doesn't exist, then this will also generate an error, terminating the batch.

There is a great deal more to TRY...CATCH blocks in areas that are quite advanced. So now that you know the basics, let's look at some examples demonstrating what we have just discussed.

Try It Out: TRY. . .CATCH

1. Our first example is a straight error where we have defined an integer local variable. Within our error-handling block, after outputting a statement to demonstrate that we are within that block, we try to set a string to the variable. This is a standard error and immediately moves the execution to the CATCH block; the last SELECT is not executed.

```
DECLARE @Probs int
BEGIN TRY
   SELECT 'This will work'
   SELECT @Probs='Not Right'
   SELECT 10+5,
    'This will also work, however the error means it will not run'
END TRY
BEGIN CATCH
   SELECT 'An error has occurred at line ' +
      LTRIM(STR(ERROR_LINE())) +
      ' with error ' + LTRIM(STR(ERROR_NUMBER())) + ' ' + ERROR_MESSAGE()
END CATCH
```

2. When we run the code, we will see the first statement and then the SELECT statement that executes when the error is caught. We use the system functions to display relevant information, which appears in Figure 11-48.

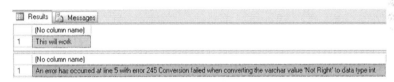

Figure 11-48. *An error is caught.*

3. Our second example demonstrates nesting TRY...CATCH blocks and how execution can continue within the outer block when an error arises within the second block. We keep the same error and see the error message, The second catch block. But once this is executed, processing continues to And then this will now work.

```
DECLARE @Probs int
BEGIN TRY
   SELECT 'This will work'
   BEGIN TRY
     SELECT @Probs='Not Right'
      SELECT 10+5,
     'This will also work, however the error means it will not run'
   END TRY
   BEGIN CATCH
      SELECT 'The second catch block'
   END CATCH
   SELECT 'And then this will now work'
END TRY
BEGIN CATCH
   SELECT 'An error has occurred at line ' +
      LTRIM(STR(ERROR_LINE())) +
      ' with error ' + LTRIM(STR(ERROR_NUMBER())) + ' ' + ERROR_MESSAGE()
END CATCH
```

4. As expected, we see three lines of output, as shown in Figure 11-49. The code in the outer CATCH block doesn't run, as the error is catered to within the inner block.

Figure 11-49. *An error is caught in a nested batch.*

5. This time, we see how our T-SQL code can be successfully precompiled and execution started. Then when we try to display results from a temporary table that doesn't exist, the CATCH block does not fire, as execution terminates immediately.

```
DECLARE @Probs int
BEGIN TRY
    SELECT 'This will work'
    BEGIN TRY
        SELECT * FROM #Temp
    END TRY
    BEGIN CATCH
        SELECT 'The second catch block'
    END CATCH
    SELECT 'And then this will now work'
END TRY
BEGIN CATCH
    SELECT 'An error has occurred at line ' +
        LTRIM(STR(ERROR_LINE())) +
        ' with error ' + LTRIM(STR(ERROR_NUMBER())) + ' ' + ERROR_MESSAGE()
END CATCH
```

6. When the code is run in the Messages tab, we see the following output, detailing one row has been returned, which comes from the first SELECT statement. We then see the SQL Server error. Looking at Figure 11-50, you also see just the first SELECT statement output.

```
(1 row(s) affected)
Msg 208, Level 16, State 0, Line 5
Invalid object name '#Temp'.
```

Figure 11-50. *What happens when SQL Server terminates execution*

7. The final example demonstrates how to reraise the same error that caused the CATCH block to fire. Recall with RAISERROR it is only possible to list a number or a local variable. Unfortunately, it is not possible to call the relevant function directly or via a SELECT statement. It is necessary to load the values into local variables.

```
DECLARE @Probs int
SELECT 'This will work'
BEGIN TRY
    SELECT @Probs='Not Right'
    SELECT 10+5,
    'This will also work, however the error means it will not run'
END TRY
BEGIN CATCH
    DECLARE @ErrMsg NVARCHAR(4000)
    DECLARE @ErrSeverity INT
    DECLARE @ErrState INT
    SELECT 'Blimey! An error'

    SELECT
        @ErrMsg = ERROR_MESSAGE(),
        @ErrSeverity = ERROR_SEVERITY(),
        @ErrState = ERROR_STATE();

    RAISERROR (@ErrMsg,@ErrSeverity,@ErrState)
END CATCH
```

Summary

The text for this chapter is not the most fluid, but the information contained will be very useful as you start using SQL Server. Each section we have covered contains a great deal of useful and pertinent information, and rereading the chapter and maybe even trying out different ideas based on the basics demonstrated will give you a stronger understanding of what is happening. The main areas of focus were error handling and joining tables to return results. Take time to fully understand what is happening and how you can use these two features.

■ ■ ■

Advanced T-SQL

By now, you really are becoming proficient in SQL Server 2008 and writing code to work with the data and the objects within the database. Already you have seen some T-SQL code and encountered some scenarios that have advanced your skills as a T-SQL developer. We can now look at more advanced areas of T-SQL programming to round off your knowledge and really get you going with queries that do more than the basics.

This chapter will look at the occasions when you need a query within a query, known as a subquery. This is ideal for producing a list of values to search for, or for producing a value from another table to set a column or a variable with. It is also possible to create a transient table of data to use within a query, known as a common table expression. We'll look at both subqueries and common table expressions within the chapter.

From there, we'll explore how to take a set of data and pivot the results, just as you can do within Excel. We'll also take a look at different types of ranking functions, where we can take our set of data and attach rankings to rows or groups of rows of data.

We will move away from our ApressFinancial example on occasion to the AdventureWorks sample that was mentioned in Chapter 1 as part of the samples database. This will allow us to have more data to work through the examples. It is not necessary to fully appreciate this database for the examples, as it is the code that is the important point. However, the text will give an overview of the tables involved as appropriate.

Subqueries

A **subquery** is a query on the data that is found within another query statement. There will only be one row of data returned and usually only one column of data as well. It can be used to check or set a value of a variable or column, or used to test whether a row of data exists in a WHERE statement.

To expand on this, there may be times when you wish to set a column value based on data from another query. One example we have is the ShareDetails.Shares table. If we had a column defined for MaximumSharePrice that held the highest value the share price had gone for that year, rather than doing a test every time the share price moved, we could use the MAX function to get the highest share price, put that value into a variable, and then set the column via that variable. The code would be similar to that defined here:

```
ALTER TABLE ShareDetails.Shares
ADD MaximumSharePrice money
DECLARE @MaxPrice money
SELECT @MaxPrice = MAX(Price)
    FROM ShareDetails.SharePrices
  WHERE ShareId = 1
SELECT @MaxPrice
UPDATE ShareDetails.Shares
SET MaximumSharePrice = @MaxPrice
WHERE ShareId = 1
```

In the preceding code, if we wished to work with more than one share, we would need to implement a loop and process each share one at a time. However, we could also perform a subquery, which implements the same functionality as shown in the code that follows. The subquery still finds the maximum price and sets the column. Notice that this time we can update all shares with one statement. The subquery joins with the main query via a WHERE statement so that as each share is dealt with, the subquery can take that ShareId and still get the maximum value. If you want to run the following code, then you still need the ALTER TABLE statement used previously, even if you did not run the preceding code.

▓**Note** We call this type of subquery a **correlated subquery**.

```
SELECT ShareId,MaximumSharePrice
FROM ShareDetails.Shares
UPDATE ShareDetails.Shares
SET MaximumSharePrice = (SELECT MAX(SharePrice)
                                        FROM ShareDetails.SharePrices sp
                         WHERE sp.ShareId = s.ShareId)
FROM ShareDetails.Shares s
SELECT ShareId,MaximumSharePrice
FROM ShareDetails.Shares
```

We also came across a subquery way back in Chapter 7 when we were testing whether a backup had successfully completed or not. The code is replicated here, with the subquery section highlighted in bold. In this instance, instead of setting a value in a column, we are looking for a value to be used as part of a filtering criteria. Recall from Chapter 7 that we know the last backup will have the greatest backup_set_id. We use the subquery to find this value (as there is no system function or variable that can return this at the time of creating the backup). Once we have this value, we can use it to reinterrogate the same table, filtering out everything but the last row for the backup just created.

▓**Note** Don't forget that for the FROM DISK option, you will have a different file name than the one in the following code.

```
DECLARE @BackupSet AS INT
SELECT @BackupSet = position
  FROM msdb..backupset
```

```
WHERE database_name='ApressFinancial'
  AND backup_set_id=
                        (SELECT MAX(backup_set_id)
                        FROM msdb..backupset s
                        WHERE database_name='ApressFinancial')
IF @BackupSet IS NULL
BEGIN
    RAISERROR('Verify failed. Backup information for database
        ''ApressFinancial'' not found.', 16, 1)
END
RESTORE VERIFYONLY
FROM DISK = 'C:\Program Files\Microsoft SQL Server\MSSQL.10.MSSQLSERVER\MSSQL\Backup\
ApressFinancial\ApressFinancial_backup_200808061136.bak'
WITH FILE = @BackupSet,
NOUNLOAD,
NOREWIND
```

In both of these cases, we are returning a single value within the subquery, but this need not always be the case. You can also return more than one value. One value must be returned when you are trying to set a value. This is because you are using an equals (=) sign. It is possible in a WHERE statement to look for a number of values using the IN statement.

IN

If you wish to look for a number of values in your WHERE statement, such as a list of values from the ShareDetails.Shares table where the ShareId is 1, 3, or 5, then you can use an IN statement. The code to complete this example would be

```
SELECT *
  FROM ShareDetails.Shares
 WHERE ShareId IN (1,3,5)
```

Using a subquery, it would be possible to replace these numbers with the results from the subquery. The preceding query could also be written using the code that follows. The example shown here is deliberately obtuse to show how it is possible to combine a subquery and an aggregation to produce the list of ShareIds that form the IN:

```
SELECT *
  FROM ShareDetails.Shares
 WHERE ShareId IN (SELECT ShareId
                     FROM ShareDetails.Shares
                    WHERE CurrentPrice > (SELECT MIN(CurrentPrice)
                                            FROM ShareDetails.Shares)
                      AND CurrentPrice < (SELECT MAX(CurrentPrice)
                                            FROM ShareDetails.Shares))
```

Both of these examples replace what would require a number of OR statements within the WHERE filter such as you see in this code:

```
SELECT *
  FROM ShareDetails.Shares
 WHERE ShareId = 1
   OR ShareId = 3
   OR ShareId = 5
```

These are just three different ways a subquery can work. The fourth way involves using a subquery to check whether a row of data exists or not, which we'll look at next.

EXISTS

EXISTS is a statement that is very similar to IN, in that it tests a column value against a subset of data from a subquery. The difference is that EXISTS uses a join to join values from a column to a column within the subquery as opposed to IN, which compares against a comma-delimited set of values and requires no join.

Over time, our ShareDetails.Shares and ShareDetails.SharePrice tables will grow to quite a large size. If we wanted to shrink them, we could use cascading deletes so that when we delete from the ShareDetails.Shares table, we would also delete all the SharePrice records. But how would we know which shares to delete? One way would be to see what shares are still held within our TransactionDetails.Transactions table. We would do this via EXISTS, but instead of looking for ShareIds that exist, we would use NOT EXISTS.

At present, we have no shares listed within the TransactionDetails.Transactions table, so we would see all of the ShareDetails.Shares listed. We can make life easier with EXISTS by giving tables an alias, but we also have to use the WHERE statement to make the join between the tables. However, we aren't really joining the tables as such; a better way of looking at it is to say we are filtering rows from the subquery table.

The final point to note is that you can return whatever you wish after the SELECT statement in the subquery, but it should only be one column or a value, and it is easiest to use an asterisk in conjunction with an EXISTS statement. If you do set a column or value, then the value returned cannot be used anywhere within the main query and is discarded, so there is nothing to gain by returning a value from a column.

■**Note** When using EXISTS, it is most common in SQL Server to use * rather than a constant like 1, as it simply returns a true or false setting.

The following code shows EXISTS in action prefixed with a NOT:

```
SELECT *
  FROM ShareDetails.Shares s
 WHERE NOT EXISTS (SELECT *
                     FROM TransactionDetails.Transactions t
                    WHERE t.RelatedShareId = s.ShareId)
```

■**Note** Both EXISTS and IN can be prefixed with NOT.

Tidying Up the Loose End

We have a loose end from a previous chapter that we need to tidy up. In Chapter 10, you built a scalar function to calculate interest between two dates using a rate. It was called the TransactionDetails. fn_IntCalc customer. When I demonstrated this, you had to pass in the specific information; however, by using a subquery, it is possible to use this function to calculate interest for customers based on their transactions. Doing this involves calling the function with the "from date" and the "to date" of the relevant transactions. Let's try out the scalar function now. Then I'll explain in detail just what is going on.

Try It Out: Using a Scalar Function with Subqueries

1. The first part of the query is straightforward and similar to what was demonstrated initially. Here you are returning some data from the `TransactionDetails.Transactions` table:

```
SELECT t1.TransactionId, t1.DateEntered,t1.Amount,
```

2. The second part of the query is where it is necessary to compute the "to date" for calculating the interest, as `DateEntered` will be used as the "from date." To do this, it is necessary to find the next transaction in the `TransactionDetails.Transactions` table. To do that, you need to find the minimum `DateEntered`—using the minimum function—where that minimum `DateEntered` is greater than that for the transaction you are on in the main query. However, you also need to ensure you are doing this for the same customer as the `SELECT` used previously. You need to make a join from the main table to the subquery joining on the customer ID. Without this, you could be selecting any minimum date entered from any customer.

```
SELECT MIN(DateEntered)
  FROM TransactionDetails.Transactions t2
        WHERE t2.CustomerId = t1.CustomerId
           AND t2.DateEntered> t1.DateEntered) as 'To Date',
```

3. Finally, you can put the same query into the call to the interest calculation function. The final part is where you are just looking for the transactions for customer ID 1.

```
    TransactionDetails.fn_IntCalc(10,t1.Amount,t1.DateEntered,
(SELECT MIN(DateEntered)
        FROM TransactionDetails.Transactions t2
        WHERE t2.CustomerId = t1.CustomerId
          AND t2.DateEntered> t1.DateEntered)) AS 'Interest Earned'
  FROM TransactionDetails.Transactions t1
 WHERE CustomerId = 1
```

4. Once you have the code together, you can then execute the query, which should produce output as seen in Figure 12-1.

	TransactionId	DateEntered	Amount	To Date	Interest Earned
1	1	2008-08-01 00:00:00.000	100.00000	2008-08-03 00:00:00.000	0.05479
2	2	2008-08-03 00:00:00.000	75.67000	2008-08-05 00:00:00.000	0.04146
3	3	2008-08-05 00:00:00.000	35.20000	2008-08-06 00:00:00.000	0.00964
4	4	2008-08-06 00:00:00.000	20.00000	NULL	0.00000
5	5	2007-10-11 09:08:33.373	100.00000	2007-10-13 09:16:41.827	0.05479
6	7	2007-10-13 09:16:41.827	200.00000	2008-08-01 00:00:00.000	16.05478

Figure 12-1. *Using a subquery to call a function*

The APPLY Operator

It is possible to return a table as the data type from a function. The table data type can hold multiple columns and multiple rows of data as you would expect, and this is one of the main ways it differs from other data types, such as varchar, int, and so on. Returning a table of data from a function allows the code invoking the function the flexibility to work with returned data as if the table permanently existed or was built as a temporary table.

To supply extensibility to this type of function, SQL Server provides you with an operator called APPLY, which works with a table-valued function and joins data from the calling table(s) to the data returned from the function. The function will sit on the right-hand side of the query expression, and through the use of APPLY, can return data as if you had a RIGHT OUTER JOIN or a LEFT OUTER JOIN on a "permanent" table. Before you see an example, you need to be aware that there are two types of APPLY: a CROSS APPLY and an OUTER APPLY:

- CROSS APPLY: Returns only the rows that are contained within the outer table where the row produces a result set from the table-valued function.

- OUTER APPLY: Returns the rows from the outer table and the table-valued function whether a join exists or not. This is similar to an OUTER JOIN, which you saw in Chapter 11. If no row exists in the table-valued function, then you will see a NULL value in the columns from that function.

CROSS APPLY

In our example, we will build a table-valued function that accepts a CustomerId as an input parameter and returns a table of TransactionDetails.Transactions rows.

Try It Out: Table Function and CROSS APPLY

1. Similar to Chapter 10, you will create a function with input and output parameters, followed by a query detailing the data to return. The difference is that a table will be returned. Therefore, you need to name the table using a local variable followed by the TABLE clause. You then need to define the table layout for every column and data type.

```
CREATE FUNCTION TransactionDetails.ReturnTransactions
(@CustId bigint) RETURNS @Trans TABLE
(TransactionId bigint,
CustomerId bigint,
TransactionDescription nvarchar(30),
DateEntered datetime,
Amount money)
AS
BEGIN
 INSERT INTO @Trans
 SELECT TransactionId, CustomerId, TransactionDescription,
         DateEntered, Amount
   FROM TransactionDetails.Transactions t
   JOIN TransactionDetails.TransactionTypes tt ON
          tt.TransactionTypeId = t.TransactionType
  WHERE CustomerId = @CustId
    RETURN
END
GO
```

2. Now that we have the table-valued function built, we can call it and use CROSS APPLY to return only the Customer rows where there is a customer number within the table from the table-valued function. The following code demonstrates this:

```
SELECT c.CustomerFirstName, CustomerLastName,
Trans.TransactionId,TransactionDescription,
DateEntered,Amount
FROM CustomerDetails.Customers AS c
  CROSS APPLY
  TransactionDetails.ReturnTransactions(c.CustomerId)
  AS Trans
```

3. The results from the preceding code are shown in Figure 12-2, where you can see that only rows from the CustomerDetails.Customers table are displayed where there is a corresponding row in the TransactionDetails.Transactions table.

	CustomerFirstName	CustomerLastName	TransactionId	TransactionDescription	DateEntered	Amount
1	Robin	McGlynn	1	Deposit	2008-08-01 00:00:00.000	100.00
2	Robin	McGlynn	2	Deposit	2008-08-03 00:00:00.000	75.67
3	Robin	McGlynn	3	Withdrawal	2008-08-05 00:00:00.000	35.20
4	Robin	McGlynn	4	Withdrawal	2008-08-06 00:00:00.000	20.00
5	Robin	McGlynn	5	Withdrawal	2007-10-11 09:08:33.373	100.00
6	Robin	McGlynn	7	BoughtShares	2007-10-13 09:16:41.827	200.00
7	Jack	Mason	NULL	NULL	NULL	NULL
8	Bernie	McGee	NULL	NULL	NULL	NULL
9	Julie	Dewson	NULL	NULL	NULL	NULL
10	Kirsty	Hull	NULL	NULL	NULL	NULL
11	Henry	Williams	NULL	NULL	NULL	NULL
12	Julie	Dewson	NULL	NULL	NULL	NULL

Figure 12-2. *CROSS APPLY from a table-valued function*

OUTER APPLY

As mentioned previously, OUTER APPLY is very much like a RIGHT OUTER JOIN on a table, but you need to use OUTER APPLY when working with a table-valued function.

For our example, we can still use the function we built for the CROSS APPLY. With the code that follows, we are expecting those customers that have no rows returned from the table-valued function to be listed with NULL values:

```
SELECT c.CustomerFirstName, CustomerLastName,
Trans.TransactionId,TransactionDescription,
DateEntered,Amount
FROM CustomerDetails.Customers AS c
  OUTER APPLY
  TransactionDetails.ReturnTransactions(c.CustomerId)
  AS Trans
```

When this is executed, you will see the output shown in Figure 12-3.

Figure 12-3. *OUTER APPLY from a table-valued function*

Common Table Expressions

In Chapter 11, we had a look at temporary tables by defining a table in code prefixing the name with a hash mark (#). Temporary tables allow you to split a complex query or a query that, if built as one unit, would run slowly due to the complexity of the joins SQL Server would have to do. Therefore, creating a set of subdata in the first query would aid the performance of the query in the second. Another scenario where you may use temporary tables is when you wish to create some sort of grouping of information and then use that grouping for further analysis. As an example, you might create a temporary table that contains a sum of each day's transactions within a bank account. The second part of the query takes the temporary table and uses it to calculate the daily interest accrued.

A **common table expression** (CTE) is a bit like a temporary table. It's transient, lasting only as long as the query requires it. Temporary tables are available for use during the lifetime of the session of the query running the code or until they are explicitly dropped. The creation and use of temporary tables is a two- or three-part process: table creation, population, and use. A CTE is built in the same code line as the SELECT, INSERT, UPDATE, or DELETE statements that use it.

The best way to understand a CTE is to demonstrate an example with some code. Within the AdventureWorks database, there are a number of products held in the Production.Product table. For this example, let's say you want to know the maximum list price of stock you're holding over all the product categories. Using a temporary table, this would be a two-part process, as follows:

```
USE AdventureWorks
GO
SELECT p.ProductSubcategoryID, s.Name,SUM(ListPrice) AS ListPrice
  INTO #Temp1
  FROM Production.Product p
  JOIN Production.ProductSubcategory s ON s.ProductSubcategoryID =
    p.ProductSubcategoryID
 WHERE p.ProductSubcategoryID IS NOT NULL
 GROUP BY p.ProductSubcategoryID, s.Name

SELECT ProductSubcategoryID,Name,MAX(ListPrice)
  FROM #Temp1
  GROUP BY ProductSubcategoryID, Name
HAVING MAX(ListPrice) = (SELECT MAX(ListPrice) FROM #Temp1)

DROP TABLE #Temp1
```

However, with CTEs, this becomes a bit simpler and more efficient. In the preceding code snippet, we've created a temporary table. This table has no index on it, and therefore SQL Server will complete a table scan operation on it when executing the second part. In contrast, the upcoming code snippet uses the raw AdventureWorks tables. There is no creation of a temporary table, which would have used up processing time, and also existing indexes could be used in building up the query as well rather than a table scan.

The CTE is built up using the WITH statement, which defines the name of the CTE you'll be returning—in this case, ProdList—and the columns contained within it. The columns returned within the CTE will take the data types placed into it from the SELECT statement within the brackets. Of course, the number of columns within the CTE has to be the same as the table defined within the brackets. This table is built up, returned, and passed immediately into the following SELECT statement outside of the WITH block where the rows of data can then be processed as required. Therefore, the rows returned between the brackets could be seen as a temporary table that is used by the statement outside of the brackets.

```
WITH ProdList (ProductSubcategoryID,Name,ListPrice) AS
(
SELECT p.ProductSubcategoryID, s.Name,SUM(ListPrice) AS ListPrice
  FROM Production.Product p
  JOIN Production.ProductSubcategory s ON s.ProductSubcategoryID =
    p.ProductSubcategoryID
  WHERE p.ProductSubcategoryID IS NOT NULL
  GROUP BY p.ProductSubcategoryID, s.Name
)
SELECT ProductSubcategoryID,Name,MAX(ListPrice)
  FROM ProdList
  GROUP BY ProductSubcategoryID, Name
  HAVING MAX(ListPrice) = (SELECT MAX(ListPrice) FROM ProdList)
```

When the code is executed, the results should resemble the output shown in Figure 12-4.

Figure 12-4. *CTE output*

Recursive CTE

A **recursive CTE** is where an initial CTE is built and then the results from that are called recursively in a UNION statement, returning subsets of data until all the data is returned. This gives you the ability to create data in a hierarchical fashion, as we will see in our next example.

The basis of building a recursive CTE is to build your initial query just as you saw earlier, but then append to that a UNION ALL statement with a join on the cte_name. This works so that in the "normal" CTE, data is created and built with the cte_name, which can then be referenced within the CTE from the UNION ALL. The syntax that you can see here demonstrates how this looks in its simplest form:

```
WITH cte_name ( column_name [,...n] )
AS
(
CTE_query_definition
UNION ALL
CTE_query_definition with a join on cte_name
)
```

As with all UNION statements, the number of columns must be the same in all queries that make up the recursive CTE. The data types must also match up.

▓**Caution** Care *must* be taken when creating a recursive CTE. It is possible to create a recursive CTE that goes into an infinite loop. While testing the recursive CTE, you can use the MAXRECURSION option, as you will see in our next example.

The following example demonstrates a recursive query that will list every employee, their job title, and the name of their manager. We have our anchor CTE, which returns the CEO of Adventure-Works. The CEO doesn't have a "boss," but we still need to return data as if he had, of the same data type as well. To resolve this dilemma, the example returns spaces that are converted to the correct data type and length. Once we have that anchor, we can then recursively call the second query, which will continue to return data, moving down the hierarchy as more data is added in until no more levels exist. So on the anchor, the EmployeeReportingStructure CTE will have the level 0, or CEO data, within it. The recursive query will then add to the CTE the level 1 employees, which then allows the recursive query to work with that data to populate level 2, and so on. From this, you should see how it is possible to create an infinite loop. To stop this from happening, as mentioned, we can put on the SELECT query that invokes the CTE and returns the data. This is an option to define how many invocations of the recursive query are made. In our example, we set the invocation maximum count to four via OPTION (MAXRECURSION 4).

```
USE AdventureWorks;
GO
WITH EmployeeReportingStructure
(ManagerID, EmployeeID, EmployeeLevel, Level,
ManagerContactId,ManagerTitle,ManagerFirst,ManagerLast,
EmployeeTitle,EmployeeFirst,EmployeeLast)
AS
(
-- Anchor member definition
    SELECT e.ManagerID, e.EmployeeID, e.Title as EmployeeLevel,
        0 AS Level,
        e.ContactId as ManagerContactId,
        CAST(' ' as nvarchar(8)) as ManagerTitle,
        CAST(' ' as nvarchar(50)) as ManagerFirst,
        CAST(' ' as nvarchar(50)) as ManagerLast,
        c.Title as EmployeeTitle,c.FirstName as EmployeeFirst,
        c.LastName as EmployeeLast
    FROM HumanResources.Employee AS e
    INNER JOIN Person.Contact c ON c.ContactId = e.ContactId
    WHERE ManagerID IS NULL
    UNION ALL
-- Recursive member definition
    SELECT e.ManagerID, e.EmployeeID, e.Title as EmployeeLevel, Level + 1,
        e.ContactId as ManagerContactId,
        m.Title as ManagerTitle,m.FirstName as ManagerFirst,
        m.LastName as ManagerLast,
        c.Title as EmployeeTitle,c.FirstName as EmployeeFirst,
        c.LastName as EmployeeLast
    FROM HumanResources.Employee AS e
    INNER JOIN Person.Contact c ON c.ContactId = e.ContactId
    INNER JOIN EmployeeReportingStructure  AS d
        ON d.EmployeeID = e.ManagerID
    INNER JOIN Person.Contact m ON m.ContactId = d.ManagerContactId
)
```

```
-- Statement that executes the CTE
SELECT ManagerID, EmployeeID,
ISNULL(ManagerTitle+' ','')+ManagerFirst+' '+ManagerLast as Manager,
EmployeeLevel,
ISNULL(EmployeeTitle+' ','')+EmployeeFirst+' '+EmployeeLast as Employee,
Level
FROM EmployeeReportingStructure
ORDER BY Level,EmployeeLast,EmployeeFirst
OPTION (MAXRECURSION 4)
```

CTEs are used not only as standalone expressions, but also within other functions, such as pivoting data, which you will see in action next.

Pivoting Data

If you have ever used Excel, then you have probably had to pivot results of the data so that rows of information are pivoted into columns of information. It is now possible to perform this kind of operation within SQL Server 2008 via a PIVOT statement. Pivoted data can also be changed back using the UNPIVOT statement, where columns of data can be changed into rows of data. In this section, you will see both these statements in action. We will be using the AdventureWorks example in this section. The table involved in this example is the SalesOrderDetail table belonging to the Sales schema. This holds details of products ordered, the quantity requested, the price they are at, and the discount on the order received.

PIVOT

Before we see PIVOT in action, we need to look at the information that we will pivot. The following code lists three products, and for each product, we will sum up the amount sold, taking the discount into account:

```
USE AdventureWorks
GO
SELECT productID,UnitPriceDiscount,SUM(linetotal)
  FROM Sales.SalesOrderDetail
  WHERE productID IN (776,711,747)
  GROUP BY productID,UnitPriceDiscount
  ORDER BY productID,UnitPriceDiscount
```

This produces one line of output for each product/discount combination, as you can see in the following results:

711	0.00	143788.908000
711	0.02	11421.237324
711	0.05	4384.931245
711	0.10	2679.760530
711	0.15	3131.779950
747	0.00	501788.197700
776	0.00	1198796.448000
776	0.02	23020.131792
776	0.35	32906.152500

By using PIVOT, we can alter this data so that we can create columns for each of the products. Each row is defined for the discount, giving a cross-reference of products to discount.

```
SELECT pt.Discount,ISNULL([711],0.00) As Product711,
    ISNULL([747],0.00) As Product747,ISNULL([776],0.00) As Product776
FROM
(SELECT sod.LineTotal, sod.ProductID, sod.UnitPriceDiscount as Discount
    FROM Sales.SalesOrderDetail sod) so
PIVOT
(
SUM(so.LineTotal)
FOR so.ProductID IN ([776], [711], [747])
) AS pt
ORDER BY pt.Discount
```

Before we execute this code, let's take a look at what is happening. First of all, you need to create a subquery that contains the columns of data that the PIVOT operator can use for its aggregation (it will also be used later for displaying in the output). No filtering has been completed at this point—any columns not used in the aggregation will be ignored. The code generates a table-valued expression with an alias of so. From this table, you then instruct SQL Server to PIVOT the columns while completing an aggregation on a specific column—in our case, a SUM of the LineTotal column from the table value expression. It is also at this point you define the columns to create via the FOR statement—in our case, a column for each product of the three products. This is the equivalent to using GROUP BY for the aggregation, and it's also the equivalent of filtering data from the so table value expression. However, within the so table value expression, there's also a third column, UnitPriceDiscount. Without this, the output from the PIVOT would produce one row with three columns—one for each product. So this table value expression with the PIVOT produces a temporary result set, which we name pt. We can then use this temporary result set to produce our output.

When you run the code, you should see output similar to what is shown in Figure 12-5.

	Discount	Product711	Product747	Product776
1	0.00	143788.908000	501788.197700	1198796.448000
2	0.02	11421.237324	0.000000	23020.131792
3	0.05	4384.931245	0.000000	0.000000
4	0.10	2679.760530	0.000000	0.000000
5	0.15	3131.779950	0.000000	0.000000
6	0.20	0.000000	0.000000	0.000000
7	0.30	0.000000	0.000000	0.000000
8	0.35	0.000000	0.000000	32906.152500
9	0.40	0.000000	0.000000	0.000000

Figure 12-5. *Pivot data results*

UNPIVOT

The reverse of PIVOT is, of course, UNPIVOT, which will unpivot data by placing column data into rows. You can prove this by unpivoting the data just pivoted using the preceding query. The code that follows will rebuild the pivot and place the data into a temporary table. From that temporary table, you can unpivot the data.

▓**Note** UNPIVOT is not the exact reverse of PIVOT. PIVOT performs an aggregation and hence merges possible multiple rows into a single row in the output. UNPIVOT does not reproduce the original table-valued expression result because rows have been merged. Besides, NULL values in the input of UNPIVOT disappear in the output, whereas there may have been original NULL values in the input before the PIVOT operation.

```
USE AdventureWorks
go
SELECT pt.Discount,ISNULL([711],0.00) As Product711,
    ISNULL([747],0.00) As Product747,ISNULL([776],0.00) As Product776
INTO #Temp1
FROM
(SELECT sod.LineTotal, sod.ProductID, sod.UnitPriceDiscount as Discount
  FROM Sales.SalesOrderDetail sod) so
PIVOT
(
SUM(so.LineTotal)
FOR so.ProductID IN ([776], [711], [747])
) AS pt
ORDER BY pt.Discount
```

UNPIVOT has similarities to PIVOT in that you build a CTE—in this case, calling it up1—which you then use as the basis of unpivoting. Once the CTE is defined, you then use UNPIVOT with the column definitions of the columns to create, DiscountAppl and ProductID. Using IN defines the rows that will be produced back from the UNPIVOT.

```
SELECT ProductID,Discount, DiscountAppl
  FROM (SELECT Discount, product711, Product747, Product776
        FROM #Temp1) up1
UNPIVOT ( DiscountAppl FOR ProductID
    IN (Product711, Product747, Product776)) As upv2
WHERE DiscountAppl <> 0
ORDER BY ProductID
```

When the preceding code is executed, the data is unpivoted, as shown in Figure 12-6.

	ProductID	Discount	DiscountAppl
1	product711	0.00	143788.908000
2	product711	0.02	11421.237324
3	product711	0.05	4384.931245
4	product711	0.10	2679.760530
5	product711	0.15	3131.779950
6	Product747	0.00	501788.197700
7	Product776	0.00	1198796.448000
8	Product776	0.02	23020.131792
9	Product776	0.35	32906.152500

Figure 12-6. *Unpivoted data results*

Now that we have pivoted data, we can take a look at how we can rank output.

Ranking Functions

With SQL Server 2008, it's possible to rank rows of data in your T-SQL code. **Ranking functions** give you the ability to rank each row of data to provide a method of organizing the output in an ascending sequence. You can give each row a unique number or each group of similar rows the same number. You may be wondering what is wrong with other methods of ranking data, which might include IDENTITY columns. These types of columns do provide unique numbers, but gaps can form. You are also tied in to each row having its own number when you may wish to group rows together.

So then, why not use GROUP BY? Well, yes, you can use GROUP BY, but what if the grouping was over more than one column? In this case, processing the data further would require knowledge about those columns. Ranking functions make it possible to provide a value that allows data to be ranked in the order required, and then that value can be used for splitting the data into further groupings.

There are four ranking functions, which I'll discuss in detail in upcoming sections:

- ROW_NUMBER: Allows you to provide sequential integer values to the result rows of a query.

- RANK: Provides an ascending, nonunique ranking number to a set of rows, giving the same number to a row of the same value as another. Numbers are skipped for the number of rows that have the same value.

- DENSE_RANK: Similar to RANK, but each row number returned will be one greater than the previous setting, no matter how many rows are the same.

- NTILE: Takes the rows from the query and places them into an equal (or as close to equal as possible) number of specified numbered groups, where NTILE returns the group number the row belongs to.

▓**Note** These ranking functions can only be used with the SELECT and ORDER BY statements. Sadly, they can't be used directly in a WHERE or GROUP BY clause, but you can use them in a CTE or derived table.

The following code demonstrates a CTE with the ranking function ROW_NUMBER():

```
WITH OrderedOrders AS
(SELECT SalesOrderID, OrderDate,
ROW_NUMBER() OVER (order by OrderDate)as RowNumber
FROM Sales.SalesOrderHeader )
SELECT *
FROM OrderedOrders
WHERE RowNumber between 50 and 60;
```

The syntax for ranking functions is shown as follows:

```
<function_name>() OVER([PARTITION BY <partition_by_list>]
ORDER BY <order_by_list>)
```

Taking each option as it comes, you can see how this can be placed within a SELECT statement, for example:

- function_name: Can be one of ROW_NUMBER, RANK, DENSE_RANK, and NTILE

- OVER: Defines the details of how the ranking should order or split the data

- PARTITION BY: Details which data the column should use as the basis of the splits

- ORDER BY: Details the ordering of the data

ROW_NUMBER

Our first ranking function, ROW_NUMBER, allows your code to guarantee an ascending sequence of numbers to give each row a unique number. Until now, it has not been possible to guarantee sequencing of numbers, although an IDENTITY-based column could potentially give a sequence, providing all INSERTs succeeded and no DELETEs took place.

This function is ideal for giving your output a reference point—for example, "Please take a look at row 10 and you'll see . . ." Another use for this function is to break the data into exact chunks for scrolling purposes in GUI systems. For example, if five rows of data are returned, row 1 could be displayed, and then Next would allow the application to move to row 2 easily rather than using some other method.

The following is an example that shows how the ROW_NUMBER() function can provide an ascending number for each row returned when inspecting the Employee view. This is a view in AdventureWorks that shows details of employees who work within the AdventureWorks company. The ROW_NUMBER() function is nondeterministic, and since the ORDER BY within the OVER function doesn't produce a unique sequence of data (because there might be several people with the same last name, for example), then you would need to find some other way to achieve uniqueness, if getting the same order with each execution were mandatory.

```
USE AdventureWorks
GO
SELECT ROW_NUMBER() OVER(ORDER BY LastName) AS RowNum,
    FirstName + ' ' + LastName
  FROM HumanResources.vEmployee
  WHERE JobTitle = 'Production Technician - WC60'
  ORDER BY LastName
```

When we execute the code, we see the names in last name order, as shown in Figure 12-7.

	RowNum	[No column name]
1	1	Kim Abercrombie
2	2	Jay Adams
3	3	Nancy Anderson
4	4	Bryan Baker
5	5	Ed Dudenhoefer
6	6	Maciej Dusza
7	7	Charles Fitzgerald
8	8	Guy Gilbert
9	9	Brandon Heidepriem
10	10	Karan Khanna
11	11	Eugene Kogan
12	12	James Kramer
13	13	Rebecca Laszlo

Figure 12-7. *Rows with row numbering*

It's also possible to reset the sequence to give a unique ascending number within a section, or partition of data, using the PARTITION BY option. This would be ideal if, for example, in the same marathon you had different races, such as male, female, disabled male, disabled female, over 60s, and so on. Using the category the runner is in as the basis of the partition, no matter in which order the runners cross the line, we would still have the right numbering for each category.

The following example will reset the sequential number at each change of first letter in the last name of the employees:

```
USE AdventureWorks
GO
SELECT ROW_NUMBER()
  OVER(PARTITION BY SUBSTRING(LastName,1,1)
  ORDER BY LastName) AS RowNum, FirstName + ' ' + LastName
  FROM HumanResources.vEmployee
 WHERE JobTitle = 'Production Technician - WC60'
 ORDER BY LastName
```

When we execute the code, as the first letter of the last name alters, we see the RowNum column, which contains the value for ROW_NUMBER() alter, as shown in Figure 12-8.

RowNum	(No column name)
1	Kim Abercrombie
2	Jay Adams
3	Nancy Anderson
1	Bryan Baker
1	Ed Dudenhoefer
2	Maciej Dusza
1	Charles Fitzgerald
1	Guy Gilbert
1	Brandon Heidepriem
1	Karan Khanna
2	Eugene Kogan
3	James Kramer
1	Rebecca Laszlo

Figure 12-8. *Rows with row numbering resetting on change of last name, first letter*

RANK

If a row of data is returned that contains the same values as another row as defined in the ORDER BY clause of your statement, the keyword RANK will give these rows the same numerical value. An internal count is kept so that on a change of value, you will see a jump in the value. For example, say you watch a sport like golf, and in a golf tournament you're following Tiger Woods, who wins the tournament on a score of 4 under par; but Colin Montgomery, Arnold Palmer, and Lee Westwood are joint second on 3 under par. Finally, Michelle Wie finishes her round on 2 under par. Tiger would have the value 1; Colin, Arnold, and Lee would have the value 2; and Michelle would have the value 5. This is exactly what RANK does. This function would also be useful in applications that wanted to return different rankings of data but only show the data from one rank at any one time on each page.

The example to demonstrate RANK uses the vEmployeeDepartment view, in which there are more rows with the same value than in vEmployee. Here the ROW_NUMBER() function is used as it was in the previous example, enabling a cross-check where the RANK function skips to the right number. When you run the query, you'll find that there are five rows with a Department called Document Control. RANK will assign these rows the number 1. When the Department changes to Engineering, RANK will change to the value 6.

```
USE AdventureWorks
GO
SELECT ROW_NUMBER() OVER(ORDER BY Department) AS RowNum,
       RANK() OVER(ORDER BY Department) AS Ranking,
       FirstName + ' ' + LastName AS Employee, Department
  FROM HumanResources.vEmployeeDepartment
 ORDER BY RowNum
```

The results are shown in Figure 12-9, where you can see in the Ranking column that the values remain static when the values are the same, and then skip to the correct number on a change of value.

Figure 12-9. *Ranking and row numbering*

DENSE_RANK

DENSE_RANK gives each group the next number in the sequence and does not jump forward if there is more than one item in a group. In our golf example from the previous section, for example, Michelle Wie would have a value of 3 instead of a value of 5 because her score is the third highest. The following code demonstrates DENSE_RANK:

```
USE AdventureWorks
GO
SELECT ROW_NUMBER() OVER(ORDER BY Department) AS RowNum,
       DENSE_RANK() OVER(ORDER BY Department) AS Ranking,
       CONVERT(varchar(25),FirstName + ' ' + LastName), Department
  FROM HumanResources.vEmployeeDepartment
 ORDER BY RowNum
```

The results can be seen in Figure 12-10. Notice that this time, on change of Department, the Ranking becomes 2 when Document Control becomes Engineering, instead of moving to 6.

Figure 12-10. *Dense ranking and row numbering*

NTILE

Batching output into manageable groups has always been tricky. For example, if you have a batch of work that needs cross-checking among a number of people, then GROUP BY has to be used, though this wouldn't give an even split. NTILE is used to give the split a more even, although approximated, grouping. The value in parentheses after NTILE defines the number of groups to produce, so NTILE(25) would produce 25 groups of as close a split as possible of even numbers.

```
USE AdventureWorks
GO
SELECT NTILE(10) OVER(ORDER BY Department) AS NTile,
        FirstName + ' ' + LastName, Department
  FROM HumanResources.vEmployeeDepartment
```

This produces 10 groups of 29 rows each. In Figure 12-11, you will see where the first batch ends and the second batch commences.

	NTile	(No column name)	Department
1	1	Tengiz Kharatishvili	Document Control
2	1	Zainal Arifin	Document Control
3	1	Sean Chai	Document Control
4	1	Karen Berge	Document Control
5	1	Chris Norred	Document Control
6	1	Michael Sullivan	Engineering
7	1	Sharon Salavaria	Engineering
8	1	Roberto Tamburello	Engineering
9	1	Gail Erickson	Engineering
10	1	Jossef Goldberg	Engineering
11	1	Terri Duffy	Engineering
12	1	Laura Norman	Executive
13	1	Ken Sánchez	Executive
14	1	Christian Kleinerman	Facilities and Maintenance

Figure 12-11. *Batching output into groups of data*

PowerShell Within SQL Server

When you installed SQL Server 2008 in Chapter 1, you installed three components for PowerShell: Windows PowerShell version 1.0, SQL Server 2008 PowerShell DLL files called **snap-ins**, and a utility used to run the snap-ins. The utility, sqlps, is a command-prompt–based utility that you invoke from the PowerShell option, which you have seen already in several screenshots within the book.

So how does this utility fit in with SQL Server? Two different programming methods are already available: T-SQL, which you have been learning within this book, and .NET-based objects, which I have mentioned a couple of times. .NET-based objects allow you to extend SQL Server using .NET technology. PowerShell sits between these two technologies. It provides you with more logical expressions than T-SQL, but you don't have to learn .NET as well, and you don't have to deal with the security implications of deploying a .NET assembly onto a server. For example, not many ISPs allow you to deploy a .NET-based assembly onto a shared server.

PowerShell is also a scripting language, so for those of you who have used Visual Basic for Applications (VBA) within Excel or other products, you can use VBA to produce more feature-rich applications. In fact, by using VBA within Excel, many large financial organizations run major applications because of the richness that VBA can provide. Although you can't expect PowerShell to have a similar level of functional richness as VBA, PowerShell does provide the ability to produce feature-rich tools that allow you to administer servers and improve the functionality within SQL Server agent-based jobs, similar to the maintenance plan you saw in Chapter 7.

PowerShell uses SQL Server 2008 client connectivity to attach to a database. When installing SQL Server in Chapter 1, client connectivity was one of the options available that you selected to install. The client connectivity components allow PowerShell to connect to a SQL Server installation from SQL Server 2000 onward, so you can leverage the functionality within PowerShell throughout your organization. However, SQL Server 2005 does require Service Pack 2, and SQL Server 2000 requires Service Pack 4.

The aim of this section is to introduce you to PowerShell, demonstrate how to find the commands available within PowerShell, and show you how to invoke SQL commands. PowerShell will become a major part of SQL Server, and this section will give you a flavor of what could be possible. You will see how to instantiate PowerShell from SQL Server Management Studio (SMSS). You could also use a command prompt and enter the command for powershell.exe, but you would need to load the snap-ins manually. One example where you might use the command prompt method would be for client rollouts, where the rollout requires PowerShell to run without manual intervention. Finally, you'll see how it's possible to use PowerShell in SQL Server Agent jobs. You saw a SQL Server Agent job in Chapter 7 when you built a maintenance plan.

Try It Out: PowerShell Within SSMS

1. Locate the `CustomerDetails.Customers` table within the Tables node, right-click, and select Start Power-Shell, as shown in Figure 12-12.

Figure 12-12. *Starting PowerShell from SSMS*

2. This invokes the `sqlps` utility with the default path set to the `CustomerDetails.Customers` table, as shown in Figure 12-13.

Figure 12-13. *PowerShell ready for instructions*

3. You can get a list of the possible commands within this utility by using the `get-help` command. For those of you who have used Unix, `get-help` is similar to the `man` command. It is possible to expand on `get-help` and send the output to a text file, where you can then see the list of commands. By using the redirect option, `>`, you can redirect the output to a text file. Enter the following code and press Enter, which places all the commands to a text file in your My Documents folder:

```
get-help * > c:\users\rdewson\documents\powershell\powershell.txt
```

4. Although this produces a nice list that you can use as a reference, it still doesn't tell you much about each command. It is possible to get more details by using the `-detailed` switch within `get-help`. In the next example, you will see detailed information about the cmdlet `get-date`. The output will also be redirected to a text file, as it is much easier to read than a scrolling screen. Enter the following code and press Enter. Once run, you can open the text file and read the contents.

■**Note** The first set of items in the powershell.txt file is in the category type of Alias. This is where commands have been given a short-named alias. For example, the cmdlet `get-member` has an alias of `gm`, meaning you could use either `get-member` or `gm` to perform the same action.

```
get-help -detailed get-date > c:\users\rdewson\documents\powershell\get-date.txt
```

5. When you open up the file generated in the previous step and inspect the contents, you will notice that the `get-date` cmdlet can take a number of different options and parameters. For example, the following code retrieves only the time:

```
get-date -DisplayHint time
```

6. At this point, you can navigate around the help system, but this isn't very helpful for working with SQL Server. Let's move on to the next step, which will demonstrate how to run a basic T-SQL-based query. This is where you will use the `invoke-sqlcmd` cmdlet. In this example, you will invoke a simple query. In Figure 12-14, you can see the cmdlet that uses the `-query` parameter followed by a string of the T-SQL query to run, and then the query with the results below this.

Figure 12-14. *Using the SELECT command within sqlps*

7. It is possible to run queries against other servers or even instances by suffixing the query with the -serverinstance parameter followed by a string of the server\instance. So if you were on a different server, you could have invoked the previous query with the following code. Notice that the instance is not defined, because this is using the default instance:

```
invoke-sqlcmd -query
"SELECT CustomerFirstName + ' ' + CustomerLastName
FROM CustomerDetails.Customers" -serverinstance "FAT-BELLY"
```

8. However, what if you want to run a number of commands or you wish to run a command repetitively? It is possible to create a file that you can use as an input option with one or more SQL Server commands. The suffix of the file can be anything, although it is usual to give the file a .sql suffix. Create a file called invoke-cmd-ex.sql with the following code within it:

```
SELECT CustomerFirstName + ' ' + CustomerLastName
FROM CustomerDetails.Customers

SELECT 'Query2'

SELECT CustomerFirstName + ' ' + CustomerLastName
FROM CustomerDetails.Customers
WHERE customerid > 1

DECLARE @return_value int,
        @ClearedBalance money,
        @UnclearedBalance money

EXEC @return_value = [CustomerDetails].[apf_CustBalances]
        @CustId = 1,
        @ClearedBalance = @ClearedBalance OUTPUT,
        @UnclearedBalance = @UnclearedBalance OUTPUT
SELECT @ClearedBalance
```

9. You can use the following code to invoke the file you have just saved within the sqlps command prompt utility. This code also sends the output to a file within the same folder as the input.

```
invoke-sqlcmd -inputfile "c:\users\rdewson\documents\powershell\
invoke-cmd-ex.sql" | out-file -filepath c:\users\rdewson\documents\
powershell\multipleoutput.txt"
```

10. If you do use multiple outputs, then the column headings must be the same from each output. If the first column is called "Name" in one output and "Product" in the second output, then the output from the second file will not be generated. The following code, which is very similar to the previous example but gives the columns names, produces only one set of output:

```
SELECT CustomerFirstName + ' ' + CustomerLastName AS 'Name'
FROM CustomerDetails.Customers

SELECT 'Query2'

SELECT CustomerFirstName + ' ' + CustomerLastName AS 'AnotherName'
FROM CustomerDetails.Customers
WHERE customerid > 1

DECLARE @return_value int,
        @ClearedBalance money,
        @UnclearedBalance money

EXEC @return_value = [CustomerDetails].[apf_CustBalances]
        @CustId = 1,
        @ClearedBalance = @ClearedBalance OUTPUT,
        @UnclearedBalance = @UnclearedBalance OUTPUT
SELECT @ClearedBalance
```

It is more common to use PowerShell for database administration tasks that invoke T-SQL, such as setting up reindexing jobs that supplement commands already available to SQL Server Agent processes or existing T-SQL commands. When a snapshot of a production database is taken every night and copied to a nonproduction box for batch-reporting purposes, you could build a PowerShell script that ensures that no connections to the snapshot database occur when reloading the nonproduction server and then performs the reload, producing an error if connections occur.

Summary

We are coming toward the end of the book, and you are well primed with T-SQL knowledge of what you can achieve within stored procedures and functions. In Chapter 13, we'll take a look at triggers, and all you have learned with programming T-SQL can also be applied there as well.

Subqueries are one of the most commonly used areas of T-SQL, but common table expressions are also useful, so knowing these areas well will enable you to move forward at a rapid pace. Combine this knowledge with the functionality covered in Chapter 11, especially when working with JOINs, and you should start to see how powerful T-SQL can be at working with time-based data.

You have also been introduced to PowerShell within SQL Server 2008. PowerShell has become quite a powerful addition to Windows, and I have no doubt it will become just as powerful for administrator functions and especially SQL Server Agent jobs.

One last piece of advice: if a query starts becoming very complex, you may find that it starts performing badly. We don't look at performance of queries within this book, although we have discussed indexes and how they can help your query perform better. Always take a step back and think, "Would this work better as two queries, where the first query creates a subset of data?" Writing the most complex of queries that process all the data in one pass of the data may not always be the best answer.

CHAPTER 13

■ ■ ■

Triggers

Although you have become quite proficient in using SQL Server 2008, you really ought to know about one last aspect of it. Triggers are that one last step, and this chapter is the missing link in the foundation of your knowledge and skill set.

There will be times when a modification to data somewhere within your database will require an automatic action on data elsewhere, either in your database, another database, or elsewhere within SQL Server; a trigger is the object that will do this for you. When a modification to your data occurs, SQL Server will fire a trigger, which is a specialized stored procedure that will run, performing the actions that you desire. Triggers are similar to constraints but more powerful, and they require more system overhead, which can lead to a reduction in performance. Triggers are most commonly used to perform business rules validation, carry out cascading data modifications (changes on one table causing changes to be made on other tables), keep track of changes for each record (audit trail), or do any other processing that you require when data on a specific table is modified. You actually have come across triggers when looking at Declarative Management Framework earlier in the book in Chapter 3. These specialized system triggers are built to ensure the system's integrity. You will see how these work by building your own DDL trigger later in this chapter.

The aim of this chapter is as follows:

- Describe what a trigger is.

- Detail potential problems surrounding triggers.

- Show the `CREATE TRIGGER` T-SQL syntax.

- Discuss when to use a constraint and when to use a trigger.

- Show the system tables and functions specific to triggers.

- Demonstrate the creation of a trigger through a template and straight T-SQL commands.

- Talk about image data types and the problems that surround updating these columns and firing a trigger.

First of all, let's see just what constitutes a trigger.

What Is a Trigger?

A **trigger** is a specialized stored procedure that can execute either on a data modification, known as a Data Modification Language (DML) trigger, or on a data model action, such as `CREATE TABLE`, known as a Data Definition Language (DDL) trigger. DML triggers are pieces of code attached to a specific table that are set to automatically run in response to an `INSERT`, `DELETE`, or `UPDATE` command. However, a DDL trigger is attached to an action that occurs either within a database or within a server. The first part of the chapter will look at DML triggers, followed by an investigation of DDL triggers.

▨**Note** Unlike stored procedures, you cannot manually make a trigger run, you cannot use parameters with triggers, and you cannot use return values with triggers.

The DML Trigger

Triggers have many uses. Perhaps the most common for a DML trigger is to enforce a business rule. For example, when a customer places an order, check that he has sufficient funds or that you have enough stock; if any of these checks fail, you can complete further actions or return error messages and roll back the update.

DML triggers can be used as a form of extra validation—for example, to perform complex checks on data that a constraint could not achieve. Keep in mind that using constraints instead of triggers gives you better performance, but triggers are the better choice when dealing with complex data validation. Another use for a DML trigger is to make changes in another table based on what is about to happen within the original triggered table. For example, when you add an order, you would create a DML trigger that would reduce the number of that item in stock. Finally, DML triggers can be used to create an automated audit trail that generates a change history for each record. Since the Sarbanes-Oxley Act (SOX) of 2002, DML triggers for the purpose of logging changes over time are created more and more often.

We can create separate triggers for any table action except SELECT, or triggers that will fire on any combination of table actions. Obviously, as no table modifications occur on a SELECT statement, it is impossible to create such a trigger. There are three main types of triggers:

- INSERT trigger
- DELETE trigger
- UPDATE trigger

You can also have a combination of the three types of triggers.

Triggers can update tables within other databases if desired, and it is also possible for triggers to span servers as well, so don't think the scope of triggers is limited to the current database.

It is possible for a trigger to fire a data modification, which in turn will execute another trigger, which is known as a **nested trigger**. For example, imagine you have Table A, which has a trigger on it to fire a modification within Table B, which in turn has a trigger on it that fires a modification within Table C. If a modification is made to Table A, then Table A's trigger will fire, modifying the data in Table B, which will fire the trigger in Table B, thus modifying data in Table C. This nesting of triggers can go up to 32 triggers deep before you reach the limit set within SQL Server; however, if you start getting close to that sort of level, you either have a very complex system, or perhaps you have been overly zealous with your creation of triggers!

It is possible to switch off any nesting of triggers so that when one trigger fires, no other trigger can fire; however, this is not usually the norm. Be aware that your performance will suffer greatly when you start using nested triggers; use them only when necessary.

▨**Note** There is one statement that will stop a DELETE trigger from firing. If you issue a TRUNCATE TABLE T-SQL command, it is as if the table has been wiped without any logging. This also means that a DELETE trigger will not fire, as it is not a deletion per se that is happening.

As with stored procedures, do take care when building triggers: you don't want to create a potentially endless loop in which a trigger causes an update, which fires a trigger already fired earlier within the loop, thereby repeating the process.

CREATE TRIGGER Syntax for DML Triggers

The creation of a trigger through T-SQL code can be quite complex if you use the full trigger syntax. However, the reduced version that I cover here is much more manageable and easier to demonstrate. When building a trigger, it can be created for a single action or for multiple actions. To expand on this, a trigger can be for insertion of a record only, or it can cover inserting and updating the record.

■**Note** Although this chapter will demonstrate DML triggers on tables, a trigger can also be placed on a view as well, so that when data is modified through a view, it too can fire a trigger if required.

Here is the syntax for creating a basic trigger:

```
CREATE TRIGGER [schema_name.]trigger_name
ON {table|view}
[WITH ENCRYPTION]
{
{{FOR {AFTER|INSTEAD OF} {[INSERT] [,] [UPDATE] [,] [DELETE]}
AS
[{IF [UPDATE (column)
[{AND|OR} UPDATE (column)]] ]
COLUMNS_UPDATE()]
sql_statements}}
```

Let's explore the options in this syntax more closely:

- CREATE TRIGGER schema_name.trigger_name: First of all, as ever, you need to inform SQL Server what you are attempting to do, and in this instance, you wish to create a trigger. The name for the trigger must also follow the SQL Server standards for naming objects within a database, and a trigger should also belong to a schema just like other objects. In this chapter, you name the triggers starting with tg to indicate the object is a trigger, followed by the type of trigger (ins for insert, del for delete, and upd for update), and then the name of the root table the trigger will be associated with.

- ON {table|view}: It is then necessary to give the name of the single table or view that the trigger relates to, which is named after the ON keyword. Each trigger is attached to one table only.

- [WITH ENCRYPTION]: As with views and stored procedures, you can encrypt the trigger using the WITH ENCRYPTION options so that the code cannot be viewed by prying eyes.

- {FOR|AFTER|INSTEAD OF}:

  - The FOR|AFTER trigger will run the code within the trigger after the underlying data is modified. Therefore, if you have any constraints on the table for cascading changes, then the table and these cascades will complete before the trigger fires. You either specify FOR or AFTER.

  - INSTEAD OF: The most complex of the three options to understand as a trigger defined with this option will run the T-SQL within the trigger rather than allow the data modification to run. This includes any cascading. To clarify, if you have an INSTEAD OF trigger that will execute on a data INSERT, then the insertion will not take place.

- {[INSERT] [,] [UPDATE] [,] [DELETE]}: This section of the syntax determines on what action(s) the trigger will execute. This can be an INSERT, an UPDATE, or a DELETE T-SQL command. As mentioned earlier, the trigger can fire on one, two, or three of these commands, depending on what you wish the trigger to do. Therefore, at this point, you need to mention which combination of commands, separated by a comma, you wish to work with.

- AS: The keyword AS defines that the trigger code has commenced, just as the AS keyword defined the start of a stored procedure. After all, a trigger is just a specialized stored procedure.

- [{IF UPDATE (column) [{AND|OR} UPDATE (column)]]: This option can be used within a trigger that is not available within a stored procedure, and that is the test to check whether a specific column has been modified or not. This happens through the use of the UPDATE() keyword. By placing the name of the column to test in between the parentheses, a logical TRUE or FALSE will be returned depending on whether the column has been updated or not. The deletion of a record will not set the UPDATE test to TRUE or FALSE, as you are removing an item and not updating it. An INSERT or an UPDATE record manipulation will set the UPDATE test to the necessary value.

- COLUMNS_UPDATE(): This has functionality similar to UPDATE(), but instead of testing a specific named column, it tests multiple columns in one test.

- sql_statements: At this point, you code the trigger just like any other stored procedure.

The main thought that you must keep in mind when building a trigger is that a trigger fires after each record is flagged to be modified, but before the modification is actually placed into the table. Therefore, if you have a statement that updates many rows, the trigger will fire after each record is flagged, not when all the records have been dealt with.

Note Keep in mind, the FOR trigger executes before the underlying data is modified; therefore, a trigger can issue a ROLLBACK for that particular action if so desired.

Now that you know how to create a trigger, we'll look at which situations they best apply to, as opposed to constraints.

Why Not Use a Constraint?

There is nothing stopping you from using a constraint to enforce a business rule, and in fact, constraints should be used to enforce data integrity. Constraints also give you better performance than triggers. However, they are limited in what they can achieve and what information is available to them to complete their job.

Triggers are more commonly used for validation of business rules, or for more complex data validation, which may or may not then go on to complete further updates of data elsewhere within SQL Server.

A constraint is only able to validate data that is within the table the constraint is being built for or a specified value entered at design time. This is in contrast to a trigger, which can span databases, or even servers, and check against any data set at design time or built from data collected from other actions against any table. This can happen if the necessary access rights are given to all objects involved.

However, constraints are the objects to use to ensure that data forming a key is correct, or when referential integrity needs to be enforced through a foreign key constraint.

At times a fine line will exist between building a constraint and a trigger, when the trigger is meant to perform a very simple validation task. In this case, if the decision deals with any form of data integrity, then use a constraint, which will give you better performance than using a trigger.

If the object to be built is for business rules and may require complex validation, needs to handle multiple databases or servers, or requires advanced error handling, then build a trigger. For example, a trigger must be used if you need a change on one table to result in an action (update, delete, etc.) on a table that is located in another database. You might have this situation if you keep an audit trail (change history) database separate from your production database. It is doubtful that you would want to use a trigger if you are doing something simple like verifying that a date field only contains values within a certain range.

Deleted and Inserted Logical Tables

When a table is modified, whether this is by an insertion, modification, or removal, an exact record of the row of data is held in two system logical tables called DELETED and INSERTED. When a record is inserted into a table within a database, a full copy of the insertion of the record is placed into the INSERTED table. Every item of information placed into each column for the insertion is then available for checking. If a deletion is performed, a record of the row of data is placed in the DELETED table. Finally, when an update occurs on a row of data, a record of the row before the modification is placed in the DELETED table, and then a copy of the row of data after the modification is placed in the INSERTED table.

The INSERTED and DELETED tables will hold one record from each table for each modification. Therefore, if you perform an UPDATE that updates 100 rows, the DELETED logical table is populated with the 100 rows prior to the UPDATE. The modification then takes place, and the INSERTED table is populated with 100 rows. Finally, the trigger will fire. Once the trigger has completed, the data for that table is removed from the relevant logical tables.

These tables are held within the tempdb temporary database, and therefore triggers will affect the performance of the tempdb and will be affected by any other process utilizing tempdb. However, it is not possible to complete any further processing on these tables, such as creating an index, as they are held in a version store, and the data can only be interrogated via a SELECT statement and cannot be modified. You can only access these tables within a trigger to find out which records have been inserted, updated, or deleted.

Note There are two version stores within each instance of SQL Server. This is an advanced topic, and we don't cover it, but in essence, one version store holds versions of each row of data where you have online index build operations on them, and the other index store is for rows of data where you don't have online index build operations. These exist to reduce the amount of I/O on the transaction log.

To check what columns have been modified, it would be possible to compare each and every column value between the two tables to see what information had been altered. Luckily, as was discussed when we examined the syntax, there is a function, UPDATE(), that can test whether a column has been modified.

Now that you are fully up to date as to what a DML trigger is and how it works, it is time to create and test the first trigger within the database.

Creating a DML FOR Trigger

The first trigger we will be looking at is a DML trigger to work with a customer record when a transaction occurs. The following example will demonstrate how to create a trigger on a data insertion, but also what happens to that INSERT when there is a problem in the trigger itself. As we are near the end of the book, our T-SQL within the trigger will be more advanced than some of the code so far.

Try It Out: Creating a Trigger in Query Editor

The purpose of our example is to change a customer's account balance when a financial transaction occurs as defined by an INSERT in the TransactionDetails.Transactions table. We want to change the balance AFTER the row has been inserted into the TransactionDetails.Transactions table. This is so we do not change the customer's account balance if later in the INSERT of the row a problem occurs and the INSERT does not complete.

1. Ensure that Query Editor is running and that you are logged in with an ID that can insert objects into the database. First of all, it is necessary to give the trigger a meaningful name. Then you define the table that the trigger will be attached to, which in this case is the TransactionDetails.Transactions table. The final part of the start of the trigger will then define the type of trigger and on what actions the trigger will execute. This will be a FOR AFTER trigger on an INSERT on the TransactionDetails.Transactions table. The first part of the code looks as follows:

```
USE ApressFinancial
GO
CREATE TRIGGER TransactionDetails.trgInsTransactions
ON TransactionDetails.Transactions
AFTER INSERT
AS
```

2. It is now time to enter the remainder of the code for the trigger. We need to retrieve the Amount and TransactionType from the INSERTED table to be able to use these in the update of the CustomerDetails. Customers table. We can JOIN from the INSERTED table to the TransactionDetails.TransactionTypes table to find out whether we are dealing with a credit or a debit transaction. If it is a debit, then through the use of a subquery and a CASE statement we can alter the Amount by multiplying it by -1 so that we are reducing a customer's balance. Notice the subquery includes a WHERE statement so that if we are entering a transaction type that does not affect the cash balance, such as recording a share movement, then the ClearedBalance will not be altered. The final action is to update the customer's balance, which we will do via an UPDATE statement. There is a great deal to take in, so take time over the code. Also, the two examples of running this trigger should clear up any queries you will have.

■**Note** This trigger does have a deliberate bug, which is included so that you can see a little later in this section what happens when a trigger has a bug.

```
UPDATE CustomerDetails.Customers
   SET ClearedBalance = ClearedBalance +
      (SELECT CASE WHEN CreditType = 0
                   THEN i.Amount * -1
                   ELSE i.Amount
                   END
         FROM INSERTED i
         JOIN TransactionDetails.TransactionTypes tt
           ON tt.TransactionTypeId = i.TransactionType
        WHERE AffectCashBalance = 1)
   FROM CustomerDetails.Customers c
   JOIN INSERTED i ON i.CustomerId = c.CustomerId
```

3. Execute the code to create the trigger in the database. We can test the trigger now by inserting a cash withdrawal or deposit relating to the two transaction types we currently have. We will list the customer balance before executing the `INSERT` into the `TransactionDetails.Transactions` table, and then we will add the row and look at the balance again to show that it has changed. Enter the following code, which inserts a withdrawal of $200 from CustomerId 1's account:

```
SELECT ClearedBalance
  FROM CustomerDetails.Customers
 WHERE customerId=1

INSERT INTO TransactionDetails.Transactions (CustomerId,TransactionType,
Amount,RelatedProductId, DateEntered)
VALUES (1,2,200,1,GETDATE())

SELECT ClearedBalance
  FROM CustomerDetails.Customers
 WHERE customerId=1
```

4. Execute the code. As you see in Figure 13-1, the results should show that the balance has dropped by $200 as expected. You could also double-check that the transaction exists in the `TransactionDetails.Transactions` table.

Figure 13-1. *Balance reduction after trigger action*

5. Our next test simulates a noncash transaction that has been recorded. For example, if you bought some shares, there would be the cash transaction removing the funds from your bank account, `TransactionType=2`, and then a second row entered on `TransactionType=3`, which is the equities product showing the addition of shares. This is a simple accounting procedure of one debit and one credit. Enter the following code:

```
SELECT ClearedBalance
  FROM CustomerDetails.Customers
 WHERE customerId=1

INSERT INTO TransactionDetails.Transactions (CustomerId,TransactionType,
Amount,RelatedProductId, DateEntered)
VALUES (1,3,200,1,GETDATE())

SELECT ClearedBalance
  FROM CustomerDetails.Customers
 WHERE customerId=1
```

6. Now execute the code. Instead of seeing two rows where the balance hasn't altered, we see the following error message and on the Results tab only one set of output, as shown in Figure 13-2. The trigger has a bug in that the subquery will return a `NULL` value where the transaction type does not affect a cash balance, and it has not accounted for that scenario. There are two reasons for showing you an error: the first is to demonstrate how to alter a trigger; the second, more importantly, is to determine whether the `INSERT` statement succeeded or failed.

```
(1 row(s) affected)
Msg 515, Level 16, State 2, Procedure trgInsTransactions, Line 6
Cannot insert the value NULL into column 'ClearedBalance', table
'ApressFinancial.CustomerDetails.Customers'; column does not allow nulls.
UPDATE fails.
The statement has been terminated.
```

Figure 13-2. *Balance not updated*

7. To reiterate, the INSERT statement is correct and would normally work. However, as the trigger has a bug, the transaction did not insert the data and was rolled back. You can see this by inspecting the TransactionDetails. Transactions table with the following code and the results shown in Figure 13-3:

```
SELECT *
  FROM TransactionDetails.Transactions
 WHERE CustomerId=1
```

	TransactionId	CustomerId	TransactionType	DateEntered	Amount	ReferenceDetails	Notes	RelatedShareId	RelatedProductId
1	1	1	1	2008-08-01 00:00:00.000	100.00000	NULL	NULL	NULL	1
2	2	1	1	2008-08-03 00:00:00.000	75.67000	NULL	NULL	NULL	1
3	3	1	2	2008-08-05 00:00:00.000	35.20000	NULL	NULL	NULL	1
4	4	1	2	2008-08-06 00:00:00.000	20.00000	NULL	NULL	NULL	1
5	5	1	2	2007-10-13 09:08:33.373	200.00000	NULL	NULL	NULL	1

Figure 13-3. *Transaction table listing*

8. We can change a trigger using the ALTER TRIGGER command. The changes to the code occur in the subquery: we surround the single column we will have returned with an ISNULL() test. If the result is NULL, then we transpose this with the value of 0 as the cash balance is not to alter. The code we need to change is in **BOLD**.

```
ALTER TRIGGER TransactionDetails.trgInsTransactions
ON TransactionDetails.Transactions
AFTER INSERT
AS
UPDATE CustomerDetails.Customers
   SET ClearedBalance = ClearedBalance +
      ISNULL((SELECT CASE WHEN CreditType = 0
                  THEN i.Amount * -1
                  ELSE i.Amount
                  END
         FROM INSERTED i
         JOIN TransactionDetails.TransactionTypes tt
           ON tt.TransactionTypeId = i.TransactionType
        WHERE AffectCashBalance = 1),0)
   FROM CustomerDetails.Customers c
   JOIN INSERTED i ON i.CustomerId = c.CustomerId
```

9. Once the changes have been completed, you can then execute the code to alter the trigger. You can now rerun our test, which will add a row to the TransactionDetails.Transactions table without altering the balance. If you like, you can also list the TransactionDetails.Transactions table to prove that the INSERT succeeded this time, as Figure 13-4 demonstrates.

```
SELECT ClearedBalance
  FROM CustomerDetails.Customers
 WHERE customerId=1
```

```
INSERT INTO TransactionDetails.Transactions (CustomerId,TransactionType,
Amount,RelatedProductId, DateEntered)
VALUES (1,3,200,1,GETDATE())
```

```
SELECT ClearedBalance
  FROM CustomerDetails.Customers
 WHERE customerId=1
```

Figure 13-4. *Transactions table with no balance change*

Checking Specific Columns

It is possible to check whether a specific column or set of columns have been updated via the UPDATE() or COLUMNS_UPDATED() functions available within a trigger. This can reduce the amount of processing within the trigger and therefore speed up your batch and transactions. Checking columns and only performing specific T-SQL code if a column is altered will reduce trigger overheads. As you will see, only when an amount or type of transaction has altered do you really need to perform an UPDATE on the CustomerDetails.Customers table.

The first statement we will look at is UPDATE().

Using UPDATE()

The UPDATE() function is a very simple yet powerful tool to a developer who is building a trigger. It is possible to check against a specific column, or a list of columns, to see whether a value has been inserted or updated within that column. It is not possible to check whether a value has been deleted for a column, because, quite simply, you cannot delete columns; you can only delete whole rows of data. If you wish to check more than one column at the same time, place the columns one after another with either an AND or an OR depending on what you wish to happen. Each individual UPDATE() will return TRUE if a value has been updated. If there are a number of columns, each column will have to be defined separately—for example:

```
IF UPDATE(column1) [AND|OR UPDATE(column2)]
```

You can use this function to deal with updates to the TransactionDetails.Transactions table. For example, there will be times that a transaction record has been incorrectly inserted. The trigger we created previously would have to be modified to deal with an UPDATE to alter the CustomerDetails. Customers ClearedBalance. The UPDATE would remove the value within the DELETED table and then apply the value within the INSERTED table. However, what if the alteration has nothing to do with any transaction that would alter the cash balance? For example, we were changing the date entered. By simply checking each column as necessary, it is possible to see whether an update is required to the CustomerDetails.Customers table. The two columns that would interest us are Amount and TransactionType.

Try It Out: UPDATE() Function

1. Within Query Editor, let's alter our trigger to deal with an UPDATE first of all before moving to the UPDATE() function. The first part of the alteration is to tag an UPDATE to the AFTER statement.

```
ALTER TRIGGER TransactionDetails.trgInsTransactions
ON TransactionDetails.Transactions
AFTER INSERT,UPDATE
AS
```

2. Then we need to deal with the undoing of the amount in the DELETED table row from the CustomerDetails. Customers table. The actions on the ClearedBalance need to be the opposite of the addition.

```
UPDATE CustomerDetails.Customers
   SET ClearedBalance = ClearedBalance -
      ISNULL((SELECT CASE WHEN CreditType = 0
                    THEN d.Amount * -1
                    ELSE d.Amount
                    END
         FROM DELETED d
         JOIN TransactionDetails.TransactionTypes tt
           ON tt.TransactionTypeId = d.TransactionType
         WHERE AffectCashBalance = 1),0)
   FROM CustomerDetails.Customers c
   JOIN DELETED d ON d.CustomerId = c.CustomerId
```

3. The remainder of the trigger is the same. Once you have added in the following code, execute it so that the trigger is altered:

```
UPDATE CustomerDetails.Customers
   SET ClearedBalance = ClearedBalance +
      ISNULL((SELECT CASE WHEN CreditType = 0
                    THEN i.Amount * -1
                    ELSE i.Amount
                    END
         FROM INSERTED i
         JOIN TransactionDetails.TransactionTypes tt
           ON tt.TransactionTypeId = i.TransactionType
         WHERE AffectCashBalance = 1),0)
   FROM CustomerDetails.Customers c
   JOIN INSERTED i ON i.CustomerId = c.CustomerId
```

4. We can test that the trigger works by reducing the amount of a withdrawal—in this case, `TransactionId` number 5—which currently sits at a value of $200. The following code will list the transactions for `CustomerId=1` and the current cleared balance. We then alter the amount of withdrawal from $200 down to $100. The final actions will list the tables to prove the update to the `TransactionDetails.Transactions` and `CustomerDetails.Customers` tables has succeeded.

```
SELECT *
  FROM TransactionDetails.Transactions
 WHERE CustomerId = 1
SELECT ClearedBalance
  FROM CustomerDetails.Customers
 WHERE CustomerId = 1
UPDATE TransactionDetails.Transactions
   SET Amount = 100
 WHERE TransactionId = 5
SELECT *
  FROM TransactionDetails.Transactions
 WHERE CustomerId = 1
SELECT ClearedBalance
  FROM CustomerDetails.Customers
 WHERE CustomerId = 1
```

5. Once you execute the code, the transactions amount and cleared balances are altered, as shown in Figure 13-5. So now we know the trigger has worked and will do these actions no matter what happens to the transaction table.

	TransactionId	CustomerId	TransactionType	DateEntered	Amount
1	1	1	1	2008-08-01 00:00:00.000	100.00000
2	2	1	1	2008-08-03 00:00:00.000	75.67000
3	3	1	2	2008-08-05 00:00:00.000	35.20000
4	4	1	2	2008-08-06 00:00:00.000	20.00000
5	5	1	2	2007-10-13 09:08:33.373	200.00000
6	7	1	3	2007-10-13 09:16:41.827	200.00000

	ClearedBalance
1	4111.22

	TransactionId	CustomerId	TransactionType	DateEntered	Amount
1	1	1	1	2008-08-01 00:00:00.000	100.00000
2	2	1	1	2008-08-03 00:00:00.000	75.67000
3	3	1	2	2008-08-05 00:00:00.000	35.20000
4	4	1	2	2008-08-06 00:00:00.000	20.00000
5	5	1	2	2007-10-13 09:08:33.373	100.00000
6	7	1	3	2007-10-13 09:16:41.827	200.00000

	ClearedBalance
1	4211.22

Figure 13-5. *Transactions and balances*

6. We are now going to alter the trigger to test the `Amount` and `TransactionType` columns. If there is an update, we will complete the actions described previously; if not, then we will skip this processing. We will prove which path the trigger takes by using the system function `RAISERROR`, which you saw in the discussion of error handling in Chapter 11. Each section of the `IF` statement will have an appropriate `RAISERROR`.

7. We will now alter the trigger to only update the `CustomerDetails.Customers` table if `Amount` or `TransactionType` is altered. If we execute this code, we will have a `RAISERROR` saying this is what we have done. Similarly, if we don't update the table, we will have an appropriate but different `RAISERROR`. The trigger is defined in the following code with the alterations shown in **BOLD**. Once you have made the same changes, execute the code to alter the trigger.

```
ALTER TRIGGER TransactionDetails.trgInsTransactions
ON TransactionDetails.Transactions
AFTER INSERT,UPDATE
AS
IF UPDATE(Amount) OR Update(TransactionType)
BEGIN
UPDATE CustomerDetails.Customers
   SET ClearedBalance = ClearedBalance -
      ISNULL((SELECT CASE WHEN CreditType = 0
                     THEN d.Amount * -1
                     ELSE d.Amount
                     END
         FROM DELETED d
         JOIN TransactionDetails.TransactionTypes tt
           ON tt.TransactionTypeId = d.TransactionType
         WHERE AffectCashBalance = 1),0)
   FROM CustomerDetails.Customers c
   JOIN DELETED d ON d.CustomerId = c.CustomerId

UPDATE CustomerDetails.Customers
   SET ClearedBalance = ClearedBalance +
      ISNULL((SELECT CASE WHEN CreditType = 0
                     THEN i.Amount * -1
                     ELSE i.Amount
                     END
         FROM INSERTED i
         JOIN TransactionDetails.TransactionTypes tt
           ON tt.TransactionTypeId = i.TransactionType
         WHERE AffectCashBalance = 1),0)
   FROM CustomerDetails.Customers c
   JOIN INSERTED i ON i.CustomerId = c.CustomerId
RAISERROR ('We have completed an update',10,1)
END
ELSE
RAISERROR ('Updates have been skipped',10,1)
```

8. We can now test out the example, which will not update the `Amount` or `TransactionType` but will alter the `DateEntered`.

```
SELECT *
  FROM TransactionDetails.Transactions
 WHERE TransactionId=5
SELECT ClearedBalance
  FROM CustomerDetails.Customers
 WHERE CustomerId = 1
UPDATE TransactionDetails.Transactions
   SET DateEntered = DATEADD(dd,-1,DateEntered)
 WHERE TransactionId = 5
```

```
SELECT *
  FROM TransactionDetails.Transactions
 WHERE TransactionId=5
SELECT ClearedBalance
  FROM CustomerDetails.Customers
 WHERE CustomerId = 1
```

9. Once you have run this code, you will see the Results tab showing the DateEntered being altered but the
   ClearedBalance not, as Figure 13-6 illustrates. However, at this point, we don't know if this is because we
   have removed and then readded the amount, giving a null effect.

Figure 13-6. *Details where updates have been skipped*

10. Moving to the Messages tab, we can see the RAISERROR that occurred when we skipped updating the
    CustomerDetails.Customers table. There are also fewer "row(s) affected" messages.

```
(1 row(s) affected)
(1 row(s) affected)
Updates have been skipped
(1 row(s) affected)
(1 row(s) affected)
(1 row(s) affected)
```

This brings us to the end of looking at the UPDATE() function. Let's move on to COLUMNS_UPDATED().

Using COLUMNS_UPDATED()

Instead of working with a named single column, the COLUMNS_UPDATED() function can work with
multiple columns. It does this through the use of bit flags rather than naming columns. There are
eight bits in a byte, and a bit can be either off (a value of 0) or on (a value of 1).

COLUMNS_UPDATED() checks the bits of a single byte, which is provided by SQL Server, to see
whether a column has been updated. It can do this by correlating a bit with a column in the underlying table. So to clarify, the TransactionDetails.Transactions table has nine columns. The first
column, TransactionId, would relate to the first bit within the byte. The Amount column is the fifth
column and therefore would relate to the fifth bit within the byte. If the first bit is on (a value of 1),
the TransactionId column has been updated. Similarly, if the fourth bit is on, the Amount column has
been updated.

■**Note** Confusingly, when talking about bits, the first bit is known as bit 0, the second bit is known as bit 1, and the byte is made up of bits 0 through 7. Therefore, the TransactionId column is bit 0, and the Amount column is bit 4. We will use this convention from this point onward.

The bit flag settings are based on the column order of the table definition. To test for a bit value, you use the ampersand (&) operator to test a specific bit or multiple set of bits. Before we discuss how this works, inspect Table 13-1. A bit value increases by the power of 2 as you progress down the bit settings, as you can see.

Table 13-1. *Bit Settings and the Equivalent Decimal Value*

Bit	Value
0	1
1	2
2	4
3	8
4	16
5	32
6	64
7	128

■**Note** Another point about bits is that they work from right to left. For example, 00000010 shows bit 1 is set and therefore a value of 2.

Now if bits 2 and 4 are switched on within a byte—in other words, if they have a setting of true (00010100)—then the value is 4 + 16, which equates to 20. Therefore, to test whether the third and fifth columns of our table have *both* been altered, we would use the following syntax:

```
IF COLUMNS_UPDATE() & 20 = 20
```

This is a great deal to take in and understand, so I have included the following code to help you to understand this further. Here we have a byte data type variable. We then set the variable to a value; in this case, we believe that bits 0 and 1 will be set. By using the & operator, we can check this. To reiterate, slightly confusingly, it's not the bit position we have to test, but the corresponding bit value, so bit 0 has a value of 1.

```
DECLARE @BitTest varbinary
SET @BitTest = 3
SELECT @BitTest & 1,@BitTest & 2,@BitTest & 4,@BitTest & 8,@BitTest & 16
```

As a byte contains eight bits, COLUMNS_UPDATED() can only test the first eight columns on this basis. Obviously, tables will contain more than eight columns, as you have seen with the TransactionDetails.Transaction table we have just been using.

Once a table has more than eight columns, things change. Instead of being able to test COLUMNS_ UPDATED() & 20 > 0 to check whether columns 3 or 5 have updated, it is necessary to SUBSTRING() the value first. Therefore, to test columns 3 or 5, the code needs to read as follows:

```
IF (SUBSTRING(COLUMNS_UPDATED(),1,1) & 20) > 0
```

However, even this is not the correct solution, although we are almost there. It is necessary to substring the COLUMNS_UPDATED() into eight-bit chunks for each set of eight columns. However, we need to involve the power() function to get the correct value to test for. The syntax for the power() section of the test is as follows:

```
power(2,(column_to_test - 1))
```

Therefore, if you wish to test whether column 9 has been updated, the statement would be as follows, where we take the second set of eight columns using the SUBSTRING character 2, and then test the first column of the second set of eight—in other words, column 8 + 1 = 9.

```
IF (SUBSTRING(COLUMNS_UPDATED(),2,1)=power(2,(1-1)))
```

The following tests columns 1, 4, and 10 to see whether any of them has changed:

```
IF (SUBSTRING(COLUMNS_UPDATED(),1,1)=power(2,(1-1))
OR SUBSTRING(COLUMNS_UPDATED(),1,1)=power(2,(4-1))
OR SUBSTRING(COLUMNS_UPDATED(),2,1)=power(2,(2-1)))
```

We can use this function to deal with updates to the TransactionDetails.Transactions table. For example, there will be times that a transaction record has been incorrectly inserted. The trigger we created previously would have to be modified to deal with an UPDATE that alters the customer's ClearedBalance. The UPDATE would remove the value within the DELETED table and then apply the value within the INSERTED table. However, what if the alteration has nothing to do with any transaction that would alter the cash balance? For example, say we were changing the date entered. By simply checking each column as necessary, it is possible to see whether an update is required to the CustomerDetails.Customers table. The two columns that would interest us are Amount and TransactionType.

Try It Out: COLUMNS_UPDATED()

The example in this section will take the same example as UPDATE() and convert it to use COLUMNS_UPDATED(). It is a two-line change. The following test will see whether either the TransactionType *or* the Amount has altered by checking the two column settings using the power() function. Alter the trigger and follow the previous example to ensure you get the same results.

```
ALTER TRIGGER TransactionDetails.trgInsTransactions
ON TransactionDetails.Transactions
AFTER UPDATE,INSERT
AS
    IF (SUBSTRING(COLUMNS_UPDATED(),1,1) = power(2,(3-1))
    OR SUBSTRING(COLUMNS_UPDATED(),1,1) = power(2,(5-1)))
BEGIN
UPDATE CustomerDetails.Customers
   SET ClearedBalance = ClearedBalance -
      ISNULL((SELECT CASE WHEN CreditType = 0
                  THEN d.Amount * -1
                  ELSE d.Amount
                  END
```

```
                FROM DELETED d
                JOIN TransactionDetails.TransactionTypes tt
                   ON tt.TransactionTypeId = d.TransactionType
                WHERE AffectCashBalance = 1),0)
        FROM CustomerDetails.Customers c
        JOIN DELETED d ON d.CustomerId = c.CustomerId

    UPDATE CustomerDetails.Customers
        SET ClearedBalance = ClearedBalance +
            ISNULL((SELECT CASE WHEN CreditType = 0
                        THEN i.Amount * -1
                        ELSE i.Amount
                        END
                FROM INSERTED i
                JOIN TransactionDetails.TransactionTypes tt
                   ON tt.TransactionTypeId = i.TransactionType
                WHERE AffectCashBalance = 1),0)
        FROM CustomerDetails.Customers c
        JOIN INSERTED i ON i.CustomerId = c.CustomerId
    RAISERROR ('We have completed an update ',10,1)
    END
    ELSE
    RAISERROR ('Updates have been skipped',10,1)
```

Now that we have covered DML triggers, we can take a look at DDL triggers.

DDL Triggers

Checking whether an action has happened on an object within SQL Server either on a database or within the server is not code that you will write every day. As more and more audit requirements are enforced on companies to ensure that their data is safe and has not been amended, auditors are now also turning their attention to areas that may cause that data to be altered. A DDL trigger is like a data trigger, as it can execute on the creation, deletion, or modification of rows within system tables rather than on user tables. So how does this help you?

I am sure we can all recall specific stories involving major institutions having a program running that removed funds or stock. My favorite is one in which a developer wrote a program that calculated interest on clients' accounts. Obviously, there needed to be roundings, so the bank always rounded down to the nearest cent. However, all the "down roundings" added up each month to a fairly substantial amount of money. Of course, auditors saw that the data updates were correct, as the amount on the transaction table matched the amount in the client's account. The interest calculation stored procedure also passed QA at the time. However, once it was live, the developer altered the stored procedure so that all the down roundings were added up in a local variable, and at the end of the process, the amount was added to a "hidden" account. It was a simple stored procedure that never went wrong, and of course it was obfuscated, so nobody by chance could see what the developer had done. They could, of course, see the code as it is only obfuscated, but as it never went wrong, they had no need to. If the stored procedure needed an update, it was the "old" correct code that went live, and the developer simply waited until the time was right and reapplied his code. Auditors could not figure out why at a global level thousands of dollars could not be accounted for over time. Of course, eventually they did, but if they had a DDL trigger so that they received an e-mail or some other notification whenever a stored procedure was released, they could have immediately seen two releases of the stored procedure and asked "Why?" within minutes. Our example will demonstrate this in action.

You have also seen some system DDL triggers as I mentioned at the start of the chapter with the Declarative Management Framework. They are a great deal more complex than the trigger that will be demonstrated and also interact with Management Studio to show what is happening, but in essence they are the same.

First of all, let's look at database scoped events, then toward the end of the section, you will pull the information together in a working example.

DDL_DATABASE_LEVEL_EVENTS

This section presents a listing of all the events that can force a DDL trigger to execute. Similar to DML triggers that can execute on one or more actions, a DDL trigger can also be linked to one or more actions. However, a DDL trigger is not linked to a specific table or type of action. Therefore, one trigger could execute on any number of unrelated transactions. For example, the same trigger could fire on a stored procedure being created, a user login being dropped, and a table being altered. I doubt if you will create many, if any, triggers like this, but it is possible.

There are two ways that you can create a trap for events that fire. It is possible to either trap these events individually (or as a comma-separated list) or as a catchall. You will see how to do this once we have looked at what events are available.

Database-Scoped Events

Table 13-2 lists all the DDL database actions that can be trapped. This is quite a comprehensive list and covers every database event there is. Many of the actions you will recognize from previous chapters, although the commands have spaces between words rather than underscores.

Table 13-2. *Possible Database Scoped Events to Listen For*

CREATE_TABLE	ALTER_TABLE	DROP_TABLE
CREATE_VIEW	ALTER_VIEW	DROP_VIEW
CREATE_SYNONYM	DROP_SYNONYM	CREATE_FUNCTION
ALTER_FUNCTION	DROP_FUNCTION	CREATE_PROCEDURE
ALTER_PROCEDURE	DROP_PROCEDURE	CREATE_TRIGGER
ALTER_TRIGGER	DROP_TRIGGER	CREATE_EVENT_NOTIFICATION
DROP_EVENT_NOTIFICATION	CREATE_INDEX	ALTER_INDEX
DROP_INDEX	CREATE_STATISTICS	UPDATE_STATISTICS
DROP_STATISTICS	CREATE_ASSEMBLY	ALTER_ASSEMBLY
DROP_ASSEMBLY	CREATE_TYPE	DROP_TYPE
CREATE_USER	ALTER_USER	DROP_USER
CREATE_ROLE	ALTER_ROLE	DROP_ROLE
CREATE_APPLICATION_ROLE	ALTER_APPLICATION_ROLE	DROP_APPLICATION_ROLE
CREATE_SCHEMA	ALTER_SCHEMA	DROP_SCHEMA
CREATE_MESSAGE_TYPE	ALTER_MESSAGE_TYPE	DROP_MESSAGE_TYPE

Table 13-2. *Possible Database Scoped Events to Listen For (Continued)*

CREATE_CONTRACT	ALTER_CONTRACT	DROP_CONTRACT
CREATE_QUEUE	ALTER_QUEUE	DROP_QUEUE
CREATE_SERVICE	ALTER_SERVICE	DROP_SERVICE
CREATE_ROUTE	ALTER_ROUTE	DROP_ROUTE
CREATE_REMOTE_ SERVICE_BINDING	ALTER_REMOTE_ SERVICE_BINDING	DROP_REMOTE_SERVICE_BINDING
GRANT_DATABASE	DENY_DATABASE	REVOKE_DATABASE
CREATE_SECEXPR	DROP_SECEXPR	CREATE_XML_SCHEMA
ALTER_XML_SCHEMA	DROP_XML_SCHEMA	CREATE_PARTITION_FUNCTION
ALTER_PARTITION_FUNCTION	DROP_PARTITION_FUNCTION	CREATE_PARTITION_SCHEME
ALTER_PARTITION_SCHEME	DROP_PARTITION_SCHEME	

DDL Statements with Server Scope

Database-level events are not the only events that can be trapped within a trigger; server events can also be caught.

Table 13-3 shows the DDL statements that have the scope of the whole server. Many of these you may not come across for a while, if at all, so we will concentrate on database-scoped events.

Table 13-3. *DDL Server Scoped Statements You Can Listen For*

CREATE_LOGIN	ALTER_LOGIN	DROP_LOGIN
CREATE_HTTP_ENDPOINT	DROP_HTTP_ENDPOINT	GRANT_SERVER_ACCESS
DENY_SERVER_ACCESS	REVOKE_SERVER_ACCESS	CREATE_CERT
ALTER_CERT	DROP_CERT	

A DDL trigger can also accept every event that occurs within the database and, within the T-SQL code, decide what to do with each event, from ignoring upward. However, catching every event results in an overhead on every action.

▨**Note** It is not possible to have a trigger that fires on both server and database events; it's one or the other.

The syntax for a DDL trigger is very similar to that for a DML trigger:

```
CREATE TRIGGER trigger_name
ON {ALL SERVER|DATABASE}
[WITH ENCRYPTION]
{
{{FOR |AFTER } {event_type,...}
AS
sql_statements}}
```

The main options that are different are as follows:

- ALL SERVER|DATABASE: The trigger fires either for the server or the database you are attached to when creating the trigger.

- Event_type: This is a comma-separated list from either the database or server list of DDL actions that can be trapped.

▓**Note** You can also catch events that can be grouped together. For example, all table and view events can be defined with a group, or this group can be refined down to just table events or view events. The only grouping we will look at is how to catch every database-level event.

Dropping a DDL Trigger

Removing a DDL trigger from the system is not like removing other objects where you simply say DROP object_type object_name. With a DDL trigger, you have to suffix this with the scope of the trigger:

```
DROP TRIGGER trigger_name ON {DATABASE|ALL SERVER}
```

EVENTDATA()

As an event fires, although there are no INSERTED and DELETED tables to inspect what has changed, you can use a function called EVENTDATA(). This function returns an XML data type containing information about the event that fired the trigger. The basic syntax of the XML data is as follows, although the contents of the function will be altered depending on what event fired:

```
<SQLInstance>
    <PostTime>date-time</PostTime>
    <SPID>spid</SPID>
    <ComputerName>name</ComputerName>
</SQLInstance>
```

I won't detail what each event will return in XML format; otherwise, we will be here for many pages. However, in one of the examples that follow, we will create a trigger that will fire on every database event, trap the event data, and display the details.

Database-level events have the following base syntax, different from the previously shown base syntax:

```
<SQLInstance>
    <PostTime>date-time</PostTime>
    <SPID>spid</SPID>
    <ComputerName>name</ComputerName>
    <DatabaseName>name</DatabaseName>
    <UserName>name</UserName>
    <LoginName>name</LoginName>
</SQLInstance>
```

The XML elements can be described as follows:

- PostTime: The date and time of the event firing
- SPID: The SQL Server process ID that was assigned to the code that caused the trigger to fire
- ComputerName: The name of the computer that caused the event to fire
- DatabaseName: The name of the database that caused the event to fire
- UserName: The name of the user who caused the event to fire
- LoginName: The login name of the user who caused the event to fire

It's time to see a DDL trigger in action.

Try It Out: DDL Trigger

1. This first example will create a trigger that will execute when a stored procedure is created, altered, or dropped. When it finds this action, it will check the time of day, and if the time is during the working day, then the action will be disallowed and be rolled back. On top of this, we will raise an error listing the stored procedure. This will allow you to see how to retrieve information from the EVENTDATA() function. The final action is to roll back the changes if an action is happening during the working day and send an e-mail.

```
CREATE TRIGGER trgSprocs
ON DATABASE
FOR CREATE_PROCEDURE, ALTER_PROCEDURE, DROP_PROCEDURE
AS
IF DATEPART(hh,GETDATE()) > 9 AND DATEPART(hh,GETDATE()) < 17
BEGIN
    DECLARE @Message nvarchar(max)
    SELECT @Message =
      'Completing work during core hours. Trying to release - '
      + EVENTDATA().value
        ('(/EVENT_INSTANCE/TSQLCommand/CommandText)[1]','nvarchar(max)')
    RAISERROR (@Message, 16, 1)
    ROLLBACK
EXEC msdb.dbo.sp_send_dbmail
    @profile_name = 'SQL Server Database Mail Profile',
    @recipients = 'robin@fat-belly.com',
    @body = 'A stored procedure change',
    @subject = 'A stored procedure change has been initiated and rolled back
during core hours'

END
```

2. We can now test the trigger. Depending on what time of day you run the code, the following will either succeed or fail:

```
CREATE PROCEDURE Test1
AS
SELECT 'Hello all'
```

3. Try running the preceding code between 9 a.m. and 5 p.m. so that it is possible to see the creation fail. Running the code in the afternoon provided me with the following error:

```
Msg 50000, Level 16, State 1, Procedure trgSprocs, Line 11
Completing work during core hours.
Trying to release - CREATE PROCEDURE Test1
AS
SELECT 'Hello all'
Mail queued.
Msg 3609, Level 16, State 2, Procedure Test1, Line 3
The transaction ended in the trigger. The batch has been aborted.
```

4. It is necessary to drop the preceding trigger so we can move on, unless of course you are now outside of the prohibited hours and you wish the trigger to remain.

```
DROP TRIGGER trgSprocs ON DATABASE
```

5. We can create our second DDL trigger. This time we will not look for any specific event but wish this trigger to execute on any action that occurs at the database. This will allow us to see the XML data generated on any event we want to.

```
CREATE TRIGGER trgDBDump
ON DATABASE
FOR DDL_DATABASE_LEVEL_EVENTS
AS
    SELECT EVENTDATA()
```

6. This trigger can be tested by successfully creating the stored procedure we couldn't create in our first example.

```
CREATE PROCEDURE Test1
AS
SELECT 'Hello all'
```

7. Check the results window. You should see results that you have not seen before. What is returned is XML data, and the results window displays the data as shown in Figure 13-7.

Figure 13-7. *Event data XML*

8. If you click the row, a new Query Editor pane opens after a few moments, and the XML data is transposed into an XML document layout. Each of the nodes can be inspected just like the CommandText node was earlier.

```
<EVENT_INSTANCE>
  <EventType>CREATE_PROCEDURE</EventType>
  <PostTime>2007-10-13T11:53:48.703</PostTime>
  <SPID>54</SPID>
  <ServerName>FAT-BELLY</ServerName>
  <LoginName>FAT-BELLY\rdewson</LoginName>
  <UserName>dbo</UserName>
  <DatabaseName>ApressFinancial</DatabaseName>
  <SchemaName>dbo</SchemaName>
  <ObjectName>Test1</ObjectName>
  <ObjectType>PROCEDURE</ObjectType>
```

```
<TSQLCommand>
  <SetOptions ANSI_NULLS="ON" ANSI_NULL_DEFAULT="ON"
ANSI_PADDING="ON" QUOTED_IDENTIFIER="ON"
ENCRYPTED="FALSE" />
  <CommandText>
CREATE PROCEDURE Test1
AS
SELECT 'Hello all'
</CommandText>
  </TSQLCommand>
</EVENT_INSTANCE>
```

Summary

DML triggers should be seen as specialized and specific stored procedures set up to help your system with maintaining data integrity, cascading updates throughout a system, or enforcing business rules. If you take out the fact that there are two system tables, INSERTED and DELETED, and that you can check what columns have been modified, then the whole essence of a trigger is that it is a stored procedure that runs automatically when a set data-modification condition arises on a specific table.

DDL triggers will be built mainly for security or reporting of system changes to compliance departments and the like. With the EventData() XML information available to a trigger, a great deal of useful information can be inspected and used further.

Coding a trigger is just like coding a stored procedure with the full control of flow, error handling, and processing that is available to you within a stored procedure object.

The aim of this chapter was to demonstrate how a trigger is fired and how to use the information that is available to you within the system to update subsequent tables or to stop processing and roll back the changes.

The DML triggers built within this chapter have demonstrated how to use the virtual tables, as well as how to determine whether a column has been modified. The DDL triggers built have demonstrated how you can trap events and determine what has been changed within either a database or a server.

■■■

SQL Server 2008 Reporting Services

As a beginner learning how to use SQL Server 2008, the final piece of the jigsaw puzzle is discovering how to retrieve data from a database and place it on a report. Various reporting tools inhabit the marketplace. Some, such as the Business Objects stable of products, are very powerful, but they're generic tools that cater to many different data sources. Microsoft has produced its own reporting tool, Reporting Services, which is becoming more and more powerful with each version. The aim of this chapter is to introduce you to Reporting Services so you can see some of what is achievable.

Building a report is a straightforward process of creating a connection, defining the data to return, and then placing the data along with either other in-built functions or functions that you build yourself. Once you build the report, you can deploy it to a reporting web server where users throughout your organization can access it. It is possible for your user base to then export reports in formats such as PDF or Excel, e-mail reports, and embed reports in applications.

Reporting Services is not just for SQL Server–based data. It can also retrieve data from a myriad of data repositories to enhance and expand your SQL Server reports. Don't get confused and believe that Reporting Services is like Business Objects Crystal Reports in the sense that it has the same amount of functionality. Reporting Services is improving and expanding its functionality, but Crystal Reports allows connection to a greater set of data sources and can also produce more powerful graphs in its reports. SQL Server Reporting Services is designed and streamlined for SQL Server.

This chapter will show you how to use Reporting Services to build a simple report, deploy it, and then view the results in a web browser. If, at the end of the exercises, you think this is something that you will use, then I recommend you read *Pro SQL Server 2008 Reporting Services* by Rodney Landrum, Shawn McGehee, and Walter J. Voytek II (Apress, 2008), as it does require a whole book to learn how to use this tool well.

In this chapter, I will cover the following:

- Understanding the Reporting Services architecture
- Configuring Reporting Services
- Building a report to return data

Let's dive straight in and look at the architecture.

Reporting Services Architecture

When you installed SQL Server 2008 way back in Chapter 1, one of the options was to include Reporting Services. At the time, you completed a default Native installation, which built two databases and created the necessary setup required to be able to build reports on your desktop. I also mentioned that if you were in a larger organization, it was possible to set up using SharePoint as the report repository.

If you had chosen the SharePoint Integrated mode, then your Reporting Services would have been deployed onto a SharePoint web server farm. The deployment would have placed components on the farm to allow interaction with SharePoint. SharePoint is a good technology to have within a large organization for many reasons, not the least of which is that it's a managed central resource point with features for archiving data, tracking changes, and showing the history of any changes made. You can protect data so that no changes can be made. This allows auditors to know that no information within a report has been altered either accidentally or maliciously.

In comparison to Integrated mode, Native mode is deployed as a standalone set of components on your machine. Interaction with SQL Server, the designer, and the report viewer all occurs locally, except when you're connecting to data remotely.

If you take a look at Figure 14-1, which is taken from Books Online, you can see how Reporting Services is built. The architecture will still work if you take the Report Server components and place them on a SharePoint web server.

Figure 14-1. *Reporting Services architecture*

I won't delve any more into the specific architecture, but it's useful to know a little about the data layer level, which contains two SQL Server databases and a lot of options for data sources.

SQL Server 2008 Reporting Services uses two SQL Server databases (ReportServer and ReportServerTempDB) to store the information used by Reporting Services. The ReportServer database stores static metadata such as report definitions, data sources, users, roles, subscriptions, and schedule definitions. The ReportServerTempDB database stores temporary objects such as work tables or session data.

The report data sources can come from SQL Server, Analysis Services, Excel, Access, Oracle, flat files, or any OLE DB or Open Database Connectivity (ODBC) data sources. Using data-processing extensions, you can add new sources of data.

Now that you have some understanding of Reporting Services, let's start configuring this service using the configuration tool.

Configuring Reporting Services

It is necessary to use the Reporting Services Configuration tool to set up SQL Server Reporting Services for the server. You may find that this has been completed already on server instances that you're connecting to. However, for new installations, the service needs to have certain properties defined before you can build and display reports.

Try It Out: Configuring Reporting Services

1. Start up the Configuration tool by navigating to Start ➤ All Programs ➤ Microsoft SQL Server 2008 ➤ Configuration Tools ➤ Reporting Services Configuration Tools ➤ Reporting Services Configuration Manager. This displays a connection dialog, as shown in Figure 14-2. The server is the computer that you're currently running Reporting Services on, but you can find any other SQL Server instance using the Server Name and Report Server Instance properties. Once you're happy, select Connect.

Figure 14-2. *Connecting to a Report Server instance*

2. You should now be in the Reporting Services Configuration Manager screen where you can define many attributes of the Report Server setup. Figure 14-3 shows where you set up the server and start and stop the service. Ensure that the service is started.

Figure 14-3. *Report Server running status and details*

3. The first option in the service definition is the service account that Reporting Services will use within Windows to execute. Figure 14-4 shows that in this setup, Reporting Services is using a network account. You would use this account when you have SQL Server on one server but your IIS installation defined on another server within the network. You would also use this setup when the service needs to access resources over the network. However, to make the configuration secure, you should either use an existing Windows account with the least amount of authority to do what is required or create a Windows account specifically for Reporting Services.

Figure 14-4. *Defining the service account*

4. Figure 14-5 shows the configuration details used to access the Report Server. The virtual directory that Reporting Services will use to connect to and then display the content is defined in the virtual directory option. This can be an existing directory if you wish to keep the reports for all your SQL Server instances in one place. However, it's more likely that it will be a different virtual directory for each instance. You can administer each virtual directory so that just like SQL Server, if one instance crashes, it won't affect any other. If one virtual directory has problems, it shouldn't affect any other reporting virtual directory. If you see the warning triangle, as shown in Figure 14-5, then click Apply to create your virtual directory. If there is no warning triangle, then the virtual directory should already exist. Once the virtual directory has been created, you can access it via the Web service URL toward the bottom of the figure. However, let's complete the installation first.

Figure 14-5. *Creating the IIS folder and the URL for the Reporting Services pages*

5. After clicking Apply, you should see the directory built as shown in Figure 14-6.

Figure 14-6. *Folder created and URL defined*

6. Let's move on to the next option, Database. If you click Change Database, you should see the screen shown in Figure 14-7. Here you can create a new database for this Report Server instance or select an existing Report Server database to use. If you have several SQL Server instances on one server and it is appropriate to have just one Report Server instance (for example, in small organizational servers), then using an existing Report Server database is probably the correct option. You would also use an existing Report Server if you did not have many reports to produce or if the reports weren't intensive. There is not much point in having a Report Server for each instance if each Report Server only has a handful of reports. This example creates a new Report Server database.

Figure 14-7. *Creating the Report Server databases for your server*

7. Most of the options and settings for creating a database should be self-explanatory, as most were covered in Chapter 1 when you built your SQL Server installation. After clicking Next in the screen shown in Figure 14-7, you should come across the details for the server and the connection, as shown in Figure 14-8. The server is the SQL Server installation you wish to use, and the authentication type is either Windows or SQL Server, as seen in Chapter 1. Once you're satisfied with the details and have tested the connection, click Next.

8. If this database is linked directly and solely to a SQL Server database, that means you're working with an installation of one SQL Server to one Report Server. Therefore, a naming standard reflecting this might be useful. Figure 14-9 shows the Report Server database with a meaningful name, `ApressFinancialReports`.

Figure 14-8. *Building the connection with relevant credentials*

Figure 14-9. *Naming the Reporting Services database*

9. Figure 14-10 shows the final screen for the setup. This is where you define the login credentials between the Report Server service and the Report Server database. Although Reporting Services is web-based in its deployment, it doesn't use an ASP.NET authentication. This means that you have to create a separate connection for the Report Server to use. In Figure 14-10, the connection to the database uses the same credentials as Windows uses when starting the Report Server service. Once you're done, click Next. This brings up a summary; click Finish to build the database.

Figure 14-10. *Defining the credentials for Reporting Services to connect to the database*

10. Once you build the database, you will be brought back to the Reporting Services Configuration Manager, as shown in Figure 14-11. Here you define the configuration details that a report builder will use to access the reports. This should not be confused with the URL shown at the bottom of Figure 14-5, which is the URL users will access to see the reports. Click Apply to build the virtual directory and define the URL that you will use to design the reports.

I won't cover the remaining settings, because they're not required to build your first reports. Now that you have Reporting Services set up, it's time to move on to that first report.

Figure 14-11. *The Report Manager URL*

Building Your First Report Using Report Designer

In this section, you will call the Report Designer within Business Intelligence Development Studio to produce a simple report containing the list of transactions from the TransactionDetails.Transactions table. It will join the CustomerDetails.Customers table and also use some of the built-in reporting functions to produce the date, time, page numbers, and so on.

Try It Out: Using the Report Wizard

1. From the Start menu, select Programs ➤ Microsoft SQL Server 2008 ➤ SQL Server Business Intelligence Development Studio. Then select File➤ New ➤ Project.

2. You're presented with a Visual Studio–based dialog that displays a list of different projects that Business Intelligence Development Studio supports, as shown in Figure 14-12. There are three different report-based projects; you'll be working with the Report Server Project Wizard, which takes you through building a simple report step by step. It works in a similar fashion to wizards for other competitive reporting products. Give your project a meaningful name, and place the project in a logical location. Once you're happy, click OK.

Figure 14-12. *Selecting the relevant Business Intelligence project*

3. After the welcome screen from the wizard, you need to define the connection details. Give the new data source a name, ensure that Microsoft SQL Server is selected, and click Edit to build the connection details. You're presented with a connection dialog, as shown in Figure 14-13. You need to populate the server name with the server you want your report to connect to and retrieve the data from. Next, define the authentication to use, then set the database that this connection will use. If you have data coming from multiple servers or if you require multiple connections to the same server because of user credential restrictions on databases, then you can set up multiple data connections within the designer. You will see where this is possible in a few moments. Once you're happy, click OK.

Figure 14-13. *Report connection details*

4. This now brings you back to your data source dialog, as shown in Figure 14-14. Click Next.

Figure 14-14. *A complete data source connection*

5. You're now presented with the Query Designer, where you can enter T-SQL to build your set of data with, as shown in Figure 14-15. This designer works in a similar fashion to the View Designer you have seen already. The following T-SQL, which forms the query, can be seen in the figure as well.

```
SELECT c.CustomerFirstName + ' ' + c.CustomerLastName as 'Name',
    t.DateEntered, tt.TransactionDescription,t.Amount
FROM CustomerDetails.Customers c
JOIN TransactionDetails.Transactions t ON
    t.CustomerId = c.CustomerId
JOIN TransactionDetails.TransactionTypes tt ON
    tt.TransactionTypeId = t.TransactionType
```

Figure 14-15. *The Query Builder ready for the query definition*

6. Once you click OK, the next dialog asks you to define whether you want to build a tabular or matrix report. Select Tabular and click OK.

7. The final thing you need to define within this wizard is how to lay out the report. This is a simplistic approach for designing a report, but it is effective. As shown in Figure 14-16, work from the top down. Define which columns you want at the top of each page, then create a page break. The second area allows you to define how data is grouped on the page; this is where you can create a page break. The bottom option allows you to define the fields that are displayed for each row of data returned. You can either click Next to see a summary screen, or click Finish to define the report.

Figure 14-16. *Detailing the fields and how they are used in the report*

8. You're now able to see the report solution in the Report Designer. On the left-hand side of the screen shown in Figure 14-17, you can see the database connection you made a few steps earlier at the bottom of the list. On the right are details about the Report Definition Language (.rdl) file and a properties dialog similar to the properties dialog you saw in Chapter 5 when you were building tables. In the middle is the result of the details placed in the table layout designer shown in Figure 14-16. You can move these fields around, and you can even place aggregations or special fields on the report, such as a page number or the date the report was produced. You can find these options under the Built-in Fields option on the left.

9. Let's go back to the DataSet definition, because from this part of the designer it is possible to access a different set of dialogs for defining the data set. Highlight DataSet1 or the name you called it, right-click, and select Dataset Properties. The first option, Query, is just the same query you had earlier. However, if the query has a parameter that is passed to it and defined in using an @ prefixed variable, as demonstrated in the following code snippet, then you can define the parameter and a value in the second option, as shown in Figure 14-18. A similar screen is also displayed if you're running the report interactively.

```
WHERE c.CustomerId = @CustId
```

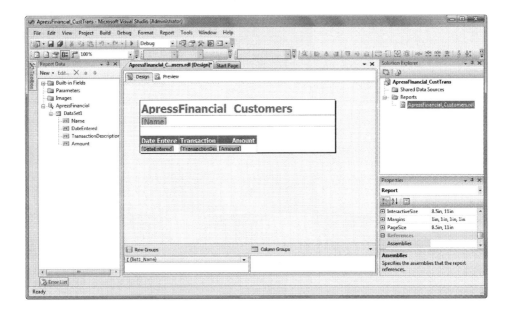

Figure 14-17. *The Query Builder ready for the query definition*

Figure 14-18. *A defined parameter with a default value*

10. The third option in the properties dialog is the Fields option, as seen in Figure 14-19. Any parameter returned from a stored procedure or any column defined in a query can be given a more user-friendly name by altering the details in the left-hand column. The left-hand column shows the value displayed in the report, and the right-hand column shows the name of the field that sources the data.

Figure 14-19. *Demonstrating the ability to alter the field names in the report*

11. The penultimate option deals with how to define the returned data. For example, you can define the collation and determine whether columns should be a fixed width or stretch to the largest size for the data. Figure 14-20 shows the six possible options.

12. The last part of defining the data set concerns filtering the data. This is useful if you have a stored procedure that returns data that requires further filtering. As you can see in Figure 14-21, we have nothing to define. Once you're done, click OK.

13. Now click OK or Cancel.

There is much more to learn concerning reports, including deploying them to a Report Server. However, because of the many things you need to consider, I fully recommend you read *Pro SQL Server 2008 Reporting Services* by Rodney Landrum, Shawn McGehee, and Walter J. Voytek II (Apress, 2008).

Figure 14-20. *The ability to change some reporting options*

Figure 14-21. *The ability to define a filter for the data*

Summary

This brings us to the end of *Beginning SQL Server 2008 for Developers*. Throughout the book, you've followed an example that has demonstrated how to report data. You have seen an overview of how to build a simple report, preview the results, and then deploy a report that's ready for users.

At this point, you should be relatively proficient in SQL Server 2008, although there is a great deal still to learn. However, the aim of this book was to take you right from the beginning and make you proficient enough to be able to complete development tasks within SQL Server. The next move for you would be to read *Accelerated SQL Server 2008* by Rob Walters, Michael Coles, Robin Dewson, Donald Farmer, Fabio Claudio Ferracchiati, and Robert Rae (Apress, 2008) and *Pro SQL Server 2005 Assemblies* by Robin Dewson and Julian Skinner (Apress, 2005).

Good luck!

Index

You Need the Companion eBook

5550472R0

Made in the USA
Lexington, KY
21 May 2010